Using Korean

This is a guide to Korean language usage for students who have already acquired the basics of the language. Unlike a conventional grammar, it highlights those areas of vocabulary and grammar which cause the most difficulty to English speakers. Clear, readable and easy to consult, it is essential for all those who wish to take their Korean beyond the beginner's level.

- ideal for those who wish to extend their knowledge of Korean and organize accumulated bits of information into a comprehensive picture
- designed to promote the fluency and accuracy vital to effective communication
- focuses on the appropriateness of different language styles
- provides excellent coverage of proverbs, idioms, and sound symbolism
- offers up-to-date guidance on points of grammar and vocabulary
- tailored to the needs of the English-speaking user

MIHO CHOO is Adjunct Associate Professor in the Department of Linguistics at the University of Hawaii at Manoa.

HYE-YOUNG KWAK is based in the Department of Linguistics at the University of Hawaii at Manoa.

Other titles in this series

Using Korean

A guide to contemporary usage

MIHO CHOO

with

HYE-YOUNG KWAK

CAMBRIDGE UNIVERSITY PRESS
Cambridge, New York, Melbourne, Madrid, Cape Town, Singapore, São Paulo, Delhi

Cambridge University Press
The Edinburgh Building, Cambridge CB2 8RU, UK

Published in the United States of America by Cambridge University Press, New York

www.cambridge.org
Information on this title: www.cambridge.org/9780521667883

First published 2008

Printed in the United Kingdom at the University Press, Cambridge

A catalogue record for this publication is available from the British Library

ISBN 978-0-521-66788-3 paperback

Contents

Acknowledgements

Writing this book has been a huge challenge, and it would have been impossible without one very special person – William O'Grady. We are deeply indebted to him for his endless enthusiasm for the project, not to mention his enormous help from beginning to end with matters of content, translation, editing, and even formatting.

We are also grateful to the anonymous reviewers from Cambridge University Press for their valuable comments and advice, to Albert Rue Burch for his careful reading of various parts of our book, to Hae-Young Kim for sharing her lecture notes with us, and to Boonho Choo, Eun Young Kwak, Yong Won Kwak, Hyang Suk Song, and Jin Sun Choe for their assistance with the selection of Korean examples. Sang-gu Kang and Kyu-seek Hwang deserve our thanks for helping with the translation of the Korean examples into English.

Finally, we gratefully acknowledge the patience and support of the editorial and production team at Cambridge University Press, especially Helen Barton, Rosina Di Marzo, Sheila Sadler, Kate Brett, Sarah Parker, and Peter Ducker.

Style and usage

1 Sentence endings

Like English, Korean has different styles of speaking and writing that reflect the genre, the setting, and the audience. A chat in a gym with a friend employs quite different words and constructions than a news report to a national TV audience. This chapter focuses on the use of sentence-final verb endings, whose selection is sensitive to whether the genre is written or spoken, to whether the setting is formal or informal, and to how close the speaker feels to the hearer. (The verb form is also affected by the relationship between the speaker and the referent of the subject of the sentence, as we will see in the next chapter.)

1.1 Statements and questions

Style in Korean can be marked by sentence endings. There are two major types of formal endings (존댓말) and two types of casual endings (반말). Whereas 존댓말 signals general courtesy and the more formal use of language, 반말 connotes intimacy and informality. The two tables below illustrate these contrasts for the basic (present tense) forms of two action verbs, two descriptive verbs, and the copula verb.

Statements (with a non-honorific subject):

존댓말 (Formal)		반말 (Casual)	
합니다 style	해요 style	해 style	한다/하다 style
줍니다; 받습니다	줘요; 받아요	줘; 받아	준다; 받는다
큽니다; 작습니다	커요; 작아요	커; 작아	크다; 작다
학생입니다	학생이에요	학생이야	학생이다

NOTE: The 한다 style is also used for neutral/impersonal writing (see **1.5**).

Questions (with a non-honorific subject):

존댓말 (Formal)		반말 (Casual)	
합니까 style	해요 style	해 style	하니 (하냐) style
줍니까; 받습니까	줘요; 받아요	줘; 받아	주니; 받니 (주냐; 받냐)
큽니다; 작습니다	커요; 작아요	커; 작아	크니; 작으니 (크냐; 작으냐)
학생입니까	학생이에요	학생이야	학생이니 (학생이냐)

NOTE: -느냐 instead of -냐 is also possible with action verbs (주느냐, 받느냐), but it is rarely used these days.

1.1.1 Distance versus politeness

It is often asserted that 존댓말 is necessarily 'polite' and that 반말 is 'non-polite' or even 'impolite,' but this is not right – no one style is polite (or not polite) in all situations. A formal style can in fact be considered impolite and distant if used with a close friend. The casual styles are by nature friendly and affectionate, but if they are used to the wrong person or in the wrong situation, they can be impolite. Ultimately, politeness lies in behaving in a considerate manner toward others. Each of the four styles is 'polite' as long as it is properly used.

Use of the formal 합니다/합니까 and 해요 styles indicates a psychological distance between the speaker and the hearer. For that reason, these styles are used between people whose relationship is socially constrained in some way. They may have just been introduced, they may not know each other well, or they may be participating in a public meeting. Perhaps they have a very different social status, or perhaps their friendship developed after college. It's even possible that they are simply old. A 60-year-old son could say 어머님, 어디 가세요? to his 85-year-old mother, whereas a young child would usually say 엄마, 어디 가?

Some Korean textbooks equate formal styles with speech to people of higher social standing or greater age, and casual styles with speech to someone who is younger or of lower social status. But this is misleading. Which style, for example, should students use to a younger waitress? The answer is that a formal 존댓말 style should be employed – unless the waitress is a close friend with whom they feel comfortable enough to use a casual 반말 style.

You should of course use 존댓말 when speaking to a social superior, but even the other person's lower social rank or younger age does not warrant use of 반말. Regardless of age or status, you should not use 반말 to a stranger (unless he or she is a pre-adolescent child). This is why the only permissible first-time greeting is the highly formal 처음 뵙겠습니다 'How do you do?' The point is also made clear by the expression 언제 봤다고 반말이야! ('When did he ever see me – what justifies his using 반말 to me!').

This doesn't mean that you should stick with 존댓말 no matter who you are speaking to. 존댓말 may be less likely than 반말 to get you into trouble, but it is not appropriate between close friends, especially for young people like high-school or college students.

Closeness, as well as respect, is highly valued in Korean culture. Use of the formal style can hurt the feelings of those who wish to be addressed in a more friendly way. A friendship may be damaged by use of 존댓말, and a couple in a romantic relationship who normally use an intimate casual style with each other will suddenly switch to a formal style after they fight, to demonstrate the distance they feel from each other.

1.1.2 Formal versus casual – some general guidelines

Here are some general guidelines that will help you decide whether a formal style is called for. As you can see, both the speaker–hearer relationship and the setting in which the speech act takes place are relevant to the choice of style.

- A formal style is necessary for addressing strangers or casual acquaintances, regardless of their age or social status (unless they are pre-adolescent children). The use of 반말 is automatic among close friends from childhood up to college (as long as they are in a similar age group), but it takes time and mutual agreement before it is used in a relationship that develops after college. The question 말 놓을까요/틀까요? 'Shall we switch to a casual style?' might be asked before the transition to 반말.

- Use of a formal ending is required when the other person has a higher social status, so you should always use a formal ending to your boss or professor, for example.

- If you are the boss or professor, you have a choice between a formal and a casual style, unless the other person is older than you (in which case 존댓말 has to be used). In most cases, the choice depends on the setting, your personality (whether you like to be formal or casual), the age of your students or social subordinates (the older they are, the more appropriate a formal ending), and the familiarity you feel with them. It is common for a boss or senior person to mix occasional 반말 with 존댓말 when his feelings are not clear-cut (e.g., he doesn't feel comfortable using just 반말, but 존댓말 only is too formal). When addressed in 존댓말 by a teacher or boss in a one-on-one situation, a younger person may feel uncomfortable, in which case (s)he may ask, 말씀 낮추세요/ 놓으세요 'Please speak to me in a casual style.'

- Younger speakers are often encouraged to use 반말 when speaking with parents and older relatives in close-knit families, and even with older but extremely close friends. There is perhaps more 반말 in the speech of a husband to his wife than vice versa among older couples, but mutual 반말 is common these days in the younger generation between romantic partners or husband and wife.

- A formal style is called for in public settings such as meetings, interviews, conferences, and so on.

One factor that supersedes all others in the choice of style is the setting. Even two people who are in a romantic relationship and who normally use 반말 to each other must switch to 존댓말 if they are in a formal meeting with other people. Professors who are close friends and who chat with each other in 반말 while drinking 소주 at a 포장마차, will switch to 존댓말 if they are at a formal faculty meeting. And even elementary school students who use nothing but 반말 to each other will switch to 존댓말 during formal classroom meetings (called 'Home Room' in Korea).

1.1.3 합니다/합니까 *style versus* 해요 *style*

The 합니다/합니까 style is usually mixed with the 해요 style even in formal situations, except in the case of news broadcasts, ceremonies, job interviews, public lectures and announcements, and so on, where the 합니다/합니까 style is used almost exclusively. In general, the more formal the situation is, the more the 합니다/합니까 style will be favored over the 해요 style. (Men tend to use the 합니다/합니까 style more than women do.)

   In comparison to the 합니다/합니까 style, the more widely used 해요 style sounds soft and gentle. Most TV talk shows are conducted in the 해요 style, occasionally mixed with the 합니다/합니까 style, and it is employed in daily conversations with adult acquaintances or strangers. It is also used with close friends if the friendship developed after college or in adulthood, and with elder family members if 'respect' is more valued than 'closeness.'

   In addition to its use with verbs, -요 (-이요 after a consonant) can also be added to just about any word or phrase that stands alone as a separate utterance (책이요, 학교에서요, 그럼요, 건강하시구요). Its effect in such cases is to convert an otherwise casual-sounding utterance into a formal style. Even 아닙니다요 is possible, but it should be avoided in formal situations since this pattern is used to casually emphasize the point of view of the speaker or to make a correction.

1.1.4 해 *style versus* 한다/하니 *style*

The 해 and 한다/하니 styles are often mixed in speech to children and in conversations among children, adolescents, college students, or very close adult friends of similar age. The 해 style is derivable from the 해요 style by simply dropping -요. (The only exception here involves -이다. We say 책이야 and 얼마야 even though their 해요 style versions are 책이에요 and 얼마예요, respectively.)

- The 해 style sounds more gentle and intimate, compared to the 한다/하니 style.

- 하니 style questions are rarely acceptable with older siblings, parents, and senior friends, even in situations that favor use of 반말. Questions in such situations are better formulated with the 해 style ending – hence 뭐 해? rather than 뭐 하니?

- Perhaps because it is somewhat blunt-sounding, the 하냐 form is employed more commonly by males. (For a different use of 하냐 in indirect quotes, see **22.1**.)

- The 한다 style is also used, often with a dramatic tone, to express an exclamatory statement that is not intended for anyone in particular (너무 안됐다. 'That is too bad, I'm sorry to hear that.').

- As we will see in **22.1**, the 한다 style is also used in the expression of reports and quotes.

1.2 What about commands?

Commands are often made in a more deferential style than statements or questions, with more use of formal endings and of the -시 suffix (see *2.1.2*).

존댓말 (Formal)		반말 (Casual)	
하시오 style	*해요* style	*해* style	*해라* style
믿으시오	믿어요	믿어	믿어라
믿으십시오	믿으세요		

NOTE: Most descriptive verbs cannot be used as commands (exceptions include 겸손해라 'be modest' and 건강하세요 'be healthy'). When they have the 해라 ending, descriptive verbs usually take on an exclamatory meaning (어휴, 기막혀라! 'How ridiculous!' or 아이고 추워라! 'How cold!').

- The -(으)시오 ending is mostly restricted to written signs and instructions in contemporary Korean.

  미시오/당기시오.   *Push/Pull.*

  잔디밭에 들어가지 마시오.   *Keep off the grass.*

- The -(으)십시오 ending is used regardless of the addressee's age or status to convey high formality and deference (e.g., in a formal setting, or in the speech of salespeople and others serving the public). Due to its high formality and somewhat impersonal flavor, it is more often used in business letters or informational documents than in speaking.

  정문을 이용하십시오.   *Use the front door, please.*

  영수증을 보관하십시오.   *Please keep the receipt.*

- The -(으)세요 ending is preferred for a formal but personal command.

  이쪽으로 오세요.   *Come this way, please.*

  잠시만 기다리세요.   *Just a moment, please.*

  불고기 2 인분 주세요.   *Two orders of pulgogi, please.*

- The -어요 ending is used with adult acquaintances or adulthood friends who are not older than the speaker.

이쪽으로 와요.	*Come this way, please.*
잠시만 기다려요.	*Just a moment, please.*

- The 해 style sounds more gentle and intimate, compared to the 해라 style. The 해라 style is rarely acceptable with older siblings, parents, and senior friends, even in situations that favor use of 반말. Commands in such situations are better formulated in the 해 style – hence 전화해 may be okay while 전화해라 is not.

1.3 What about proposals?

The following table illustrates the four major styles for proposals.

존댓말 (Formal)		반말 (Casual)	
합시다 style	*해요* style	*해* style	*하자* style
믿읍시다	믿어요	믿어	믿자

NOTE₁: There are no proposal forms for most descriptive verbs in Korean (exceptions include 솔직하자 'Let's be frank' and 건강합시다 'Let's be healthy').
NOTE₂: 믿자꾸나 instead of 믿자 may be used by an older person to a much younger person.

- The 합시다 style does not sound as formal as other formal statement or question styles when there is a particular intended audience. Even though it is employed among people who are on 존댓말 terms, it is not particularly recommended for use with someone who you have just met. It sounds rather blunt to say 식사하러 갑시다 'Let's go eat' or 핸드아웃 좀 같이 봅시다 'Let's share the handout' to someone who you are unfamiliar with even if that person is your age. The 합시다 style is mostly used among adults of similar age and status who are familiar with each other, especially males.

- The 합시다 style sounds highly formal when the proposal is addressed to a general audience, as in advertisements or in the speech of leaders.

건강은 건강할 때 지킵시다.	*Let's protect our health while we are healthy.*
불우이웃을 도웁시다.	*Let's help our less fortunate neighbors.*
자연을 보호합시다.	*Let's preserve nature.*

- The -요 ending is softer than the -시다 ending and may be used for gentle suggestions like 같이 가요 or 같이 가세요 to someone you don't know well (use the latter if the person is older or superior).

- The 하자 style is slightly more casual than the 해 style but is far more frequently used, perhaps because the 해 style can be misinterpreted as a command.

1.4 Speech samples

The following speech samples illustrate how different sentence endings are used, depending on the situational context.

News broadcast: only 합니다 style

공무원이 사실상 오늘부터 주5일 근무제에 들어갔습니다. 근로자 300명 이상 사업장도 다음 주부터 주5일 근무에 합류하게 돼 본격적인 주말 연휴시대가 시작됩니다. 김기철 기자가 보도합니다.

Today was effectively the first day for public servants to start the five-day work week schedule. Work places with over 300 employees will join the system from next week, so the real era of long weekends is about to begin. Ki-chul Kim reporting.

Weather Forecast: only 합니다 style

각 지역의 내일 날씨입니다. 중부지방 낮 기온은 서울 28도 등으로 오늘보다 낮겠습니다. 남부지방의 낮 기온은 오늘보다 6도 이상 낮겠습니다. 전국적으로 흐린 가운데 비가 오겠고 비의 양은 전국이 5에서 30mm 가량으로 많지는 않겠습니다. 서해와 남해 해상에서는 2에서 4m로 점차 높은 파도가 일겠습니다.

Here is tomorrow's weather forecast for each area. The day-time temperatures in the central region will be lower than today, with 28(C) degrees in Seoul, and so on. The southern region's day-time temperature will be more than 6 degrees lower than today. The entire nation will be cloudy and rainy, but there will be only a little precipitation, ranging from 5 to 30 mm. Waves in western and southern waters will gradually increase in size, ranging from 2 to 4 meters.

Job interview: mostly 합니다 style by interviewee; 합니다/해요 style by interviewer

A: 서하늘씨, 우리 회사에 지원하게 된 동기를 말씀해 주시겠습니까?

B: 제가 이번에 미래 회사에 지원하게 된 동기는 이동통신 분야에 원래 관심이 많았고 또 제 전공을 살리고 싶어서입니다.

A: 이쪽 분야에서 일해 본 경험이 있나요?

B: 지난 일년간 동양 회사에서 인턴십을 통해 경험을 쌓았습니다.

> *A: Ms. Ha-nul Seo, would you tell us your motivation for applying to our company?*
> *B: I decided to apply to the Mirae Company because I have always been very interested in wireless communication, and I also wanted to make use of my university major.*
> *A: Do you have work experience in this field?*
> *B: Over the past year, I built up my experience through an internship at the Dong Yang company.*

With a stranger: 합니다/해요 style

> A: 저, 죄송하지만 말씀 좀 여쭙겠습니다. 경복궁을 가려고 하는데 길 좀 가르쳐 주시겠어요?
> B: 저기 사거리에서 우회전해서 한 100 미터 정도 걸어가시면 돼요.
> A: 네, 감사합니다.
>
> *A: Excuse me, but may I ask you a question? I am trying to go to Kyŏngbok Kung. Can you help me with directions?*
> *B: If you make a right turn at the intersection over there and walk about 100 meters, it's right there.*
> *A: Oh okay, thank you.*

NOTE: 뭐 좀 물어볼게요 'Let me ask you a question' is more appropriate than 말씀 좀 여쭙겠습니다 when speaking to a younger person.

With a travel agent: mostly 합니다 style by agent; 합니다/해요 style by customer

> A: 네, 스마일 여행사입니다.
> B: 안녕하세요. 저, 제주도 가는 여행 상품을 좀 알아보려고 하는데요. 2 박 3 일로 가는 상품은 한 사람당 얼마예요?
> A: 숙식비 포함해서 일인당 40 만원입니다.
> B: 7 월달에 가려고 하는데, 언제 언제 출발하죠?
> A: 매주 월요일과 목요일에 출발합니다.
> B: 네, 알았습니다. 그럼 좀 생각해 보고 다시 전화 드릴게요.
> A: 네, 그러세요. 감사합니다.
>
> *A: Hello, this is Smile Travel.*
> *B: Hi. Well, I'm trying to get some information on travel packages for Cheju Island. How much is it per person for a two-night, three-day package?*
> *A: It is ₩400,000 per person, including hotel and meals.*
> *B: I'm planning a trip this July. Which days do you have flights?*
> *A: There are flights every Monday and Thursday.*
> *B: I see. Let me think about it some more and call you back.*
> *A: Sure, no problem. Thank you.*

Between close friends: casual style

> A: 너, 이번 일요일 동창 모임에 가니?
> B: 응, 갈거야. 이번엔 그동안 안 나왔던 친구들이 많이 나온다고 하더라.
> 만나서 같이 가자.
> A: 그럴까? 그래. 그럼 6 시에 대학로역 앞에서 보자.
> *A: Are you going to the class reunion this Sunday?*
> *B: Yes, I am. I heard that many of our friends will be there who we haven't seen for*
> *a long time. Let's meet and go together.*
> *A: Shall we? Alright. Then I'll see you at Taehangno station at 6 o'clock.*

1.5 When it comes to writing

Of the four major types of endings we have discussed so far, the 합니다, 해요,
and 해 styles are used primarily in the spoken language, while the 한다 style is
common both in casual speech and in impersonal writing for an unspecified
audience.

The following table presents a comparison between the casual 한다/하니/
해라/하자 speech styles and the impersonal endings used in writing. As you can
see, there are differences in the forms for questions and commands.

	Casual (spoken) 한다/하니(하냐)/해라/하자 style		Impersonal (written) 한다/하는가/하라/하자 style	
Statement	본다 좋다	찾는다 책이다	Same as to the left	
Question	보니/보(느)냐 좋으니/좋으냐	찾니/찾(느)냐 뭐니/뭐냐	보는가 좋은가	찾는가 무엇인가
Command	봐라	찾아라	보라	찾으라
Proposal	보자	찾자	Same as to the left	

- The 한다 style is used for statements in all scientific and impersonal writing,
  including newspapers, articles, journals, magazines, books, and so forth.
- -는가 is used for action verbs and -(은)가 is used for descriptive verbs for
  questions in questionnaires or exams.

  한글은 언제 만들어졌는가?　　*When was hangŭl invented?*
  속담과 격언은 어떻게 다른가?　*How are proverbs different from adages?*
  중력이란 무엇인가?　　　　　*What is gravity?*

  NOTE: -(은)가 for descriptive verbs can be used for musing (just like the -나 ending;
  see **1.7**) – 행복한가 'I wonder whether he's happy,' 학생인가 'I wonder whether
  he's a student.'

- The 하라 style is used for commands in written instructions, as in exams. (An exception here is 주라, which can be used in casual speech to mean 'give it to me.')

  다음 물음에 답하라.   *Answer the following questions.*

  빈칸에 알맞은 단어를 쓰라.   *Fill in the blanks with appropriate words.*

  NOTE: The written style ending is -(으)라 while the casual speech ending is -아/어라.

- In impersonal writing of certain types (such as headlines, announcements, and want ads), the sentence often ends in a noun rather than a verb.

  4 월 이후 입주가능   *Move-in possible after April.*

  미 대통령 내주 방한   *Visit of the U.S. president to Korea next week.*

  유경험자 환영   *People with experience welcome.*

  나이 제한 없음   *No age restrictions.*

  사진 동봉할 것   *Photo to be enclosed.*

  It is also common in headlines for sentences to be cut short, making it sometimes look as if they end in the casual speech 해 style.

  올 들어 가장 추워   *Coldest day so far this year*

  입시경쟁 갈수록 심해   *Entrance exam getting more competitive*

  내일부터 추워질 듯   *It may get cold from tomorrow.*

- None of the impersonal written styles employ the subject honorific -시 or any other honorific expressions (see **2.6**).

Matters are somewhat different in the case of letter writing, where any of the four spoken styles can be used. Business letters are always written in the formal style (합니다, 합니까, 하십시오), while personal letters may employ a formal or a casual style depending on the relationship between the parties.

  The 하시오 style in commands appears in written signs or exam instructions.

  속도를 줄이시오.   *Reduce speed.*

  다음 질문에 답하시오.   *Answer the following questions.*

The primarily spoken 합니다 and 해요 styles are often used in advertisements, informational documents, and children's stories in order to give a spoken flavor and a feeling of more personal involvement with the reader.

1.6 Writing samples

Newspaper article: 한다 style for non-specified audience

> 노무현 대통령은 12 일 오후 (이하 한국시간) 그리스, 루마니아, 핀란드 등 유럽
> 3 개국 순방을 마치고 미국 워싱턴으로 향한다.
> *After visiting three European countries, Greece, Romania, and Finland, President
> Roh Moo-hyun is leaving for Washington D.C. in the United States in the afternoon
> of the 12th (Korean standard time).*

Advertisement: shortened expressions and 합니다 style

> 젊음을 돌려 드립니다. *We restore your youth for you.*
>   주름살 감소   *Wrinkles reduction*
>   체지방 감소   *Fat reduction*
>   갱년기 증상 개선   *Alleviation of menopausal symptoms*
>
> 사원모집 *Company recruiting employees*
>   교차로와 함께 성장할 참신한 인재를 모집합니다.
>   *Kyoch'aro is hiring new and fresh talent to grow with the company.*

Recipe: 한다 style (expressed as statements rather than commands)

> 잡채요리법:
> 1. 소고기는 가늘게 채 썰고 표고 버섯은 물에 불린 후 채 썰어 준비된 양념장에
>   재워 둔다. (양념장 재료: 간장, 마늘, 후추, 참기름, 설탕)
> 2. 당면과 시금치는 끓는 물에 살짝 데쳐 둔다.
> 3. 당근과 양파는 채 썰어 놓는다.
> 4. 후라이팬에 식용유를 두르고 준비된 당근, 양파, 소고기, 버섯 순으로 볶아
>   낸다.
> 5. 볶은 재료를 준비해 둔 당면, 시금치와 함께 담아 간을 맞추고, 깨소금, 설탕,
>   참기름을 더 넣고 버무린다.
> *Chapch'ae Recipe:*
> 1. *Cut beef into thin slices and shred pyogo mushrooms after soaking in water.
>   Marinate the beef and mushrooms in the prepared sauce. (sauce ingredients:
>   soy sauce, garlic, black pepper, sesame oil, and sugar)*
> 2. *Parboil vermicelli and spinach lightly in boiling water.*
> 3. *Shred a carrot and an onion.*
> 4. *Pour cooking oil into a frying pan and stir-fry the carrot, onion, beef, and
>   mushroom in that order.*
> 5. *Combine the stir-fried items with the prepared vermicelli and spinach, and mix
>   well, adding soy sauce, sesame seeds, sugar, and sesame oil.*

Personal letter to a social superior: mixture of 합니다 and 해요 styles

오 선생님께,

　선생님, 안녕하세요. 잘 지내시죠? 저도 잘 있습니다. 한국어 강의하고 논문 자료 수집하면서 바쁘게 지내요. 남편과 아이들도 잘 있구요.

　그런데 선생님, 한가지 부탁드릴 게 있습니다. 다름이 아니라 제일대학 한국어 강사 자리에 지원해 보려고 하는데 선생님께서 추천서 좀 써 주실 수 있나 해서요. 바쁘신 거 알면서도 이렇게 또 부탁을 드리게 됐습니다. 참고하시라고 제 이력서와 그쪽 학교 자리에 대한 정보를 같이 넣었습니다. 선생님 편지 받으시면 잘 받으셨는지 저한테 이메일이나 전화로 알려 주실 수 있을까요?

　선생님 연구와 집필에 많은 성과가 있기 바랍니다. 건강하시구요. 그럼, 안녕히 계세요.

김영란 드림

Professor Oh,

Hi Professor Oh, how are you? I hope you are doing well. I am doing fine myself. I've been busy teaching Korean and collecting data for my thesis. My husband and children are all fine, too.

By the way, I have a favor to ask of you. I am trying to apply for a Korean teaching position at Jeil University and am wondering whether you would be able to write a letter of recommendation for me. Even though I know that you are busy, I have ended up having to ask you for a favor again. For your reference, I have enclosed my résumé and the job info. Would you let me know by e-mail or phone when you receive this letter?

I hope you make lots of progress in your research and writing. Please take care. Good-bye.

Sincerely,
Young-nan Kim

Personal letter to a niece: mixture of casual styles

사랑하는 조카 성아에게,

　그동안 잘 지냈겠지? 논문도 잘 돼 가고? 이모도 새로 시작한 일하랴 한국어 책 쓰는 거 마무리하랴 바쁘게 지내고 있단다. 이모부도 물론 잘 있고.

　그런데 성아야, 한가지 부탁할 게 있어. 딴 게 아니라 이모 책 쓰는데 필요한 자료 중에서 여기서 구할 수 없는 게 하나 있는데 네가 그 곳에서 한 권 사서 부쳐 줄 수 있을까 해서. 너 요즘 무지 바쁜 거 아는데 이렇게 또 부탁을 하게 돼서 미안하다. (이모로부터 거한 크리스마스 선물을 기대해도 좋음!) 책 제목하고 저자, 출판사등은 네 답장 받는대로 알려줄게.

　그럼 건강하게 잘 지내기 바란다. 엄마 아빠한테 안부 전하구. 안녕.

이모가

My dear niece Sung-ah,

I trust that you've been doing well. Your thesis is going well too, I hope. I've been busy with my new job and also trying to finish up writing the book on Korean. Your uncle is doing fine, too.

By the way, I have a favor to ask of you, Sung-ah. Among the materials that I need for my book-writing, there's one book that is not available here. So, I'm wondering whether you can buy a copy there and mail it to me. Sorry that I have to ask you again like this because I know how terribly busy you are. (You can expect a huge Christmas present from me!) I'll let you know the book title, the author, and the publisher, as soon as I receive your response.

Take care then. And say hello to your parents for me. Bye.

Your aunt

1.7   A few minor styles

An important minor style is exemplified by 하네 (for a statement), 하나 (for a question), 하게 (for a command), and 하세 (for a proposal). Authoritarian-sounding and old-fashioned, these forms are now used only among (mostly male) adults of equal social status or by a senior addressing a grown-up junior. Typical cases include parents-in-law speaking to sons-in-law or older professors speaking to college students.

할말이 좀 있네.	*I have something to say to you.*
자네 언제 졸업하나?	*When are you graduating?*
자네 퇴근후에 좀 들르게.	*Drop by after you get off work.*
한 잔 하고 가세.	*Let's have a drink before going home.*

The -네 and -나 endings have taken on special meanings in contemporary Korean: -네 is used to express moderate exclamation/surprise, and -나 is used to express wonderment.

금방 있었는데 없어졌네.	*It was just here, but it has disappeared.*
밤에 비가 왔나?	*I wonder whether it rained overnight.*
감기가 오나? 머리가 아프네.	*I wonder whether I'm coming down with a cold. I'm getting a headache.*

A few other minor styles, although still used by older people, are uncommon in contemporary Korean. The styles exemplified by 갔소 and 했소 are archaic and old-fashioned when it comes to letter writing, and they sound authoritarian when used in spoken sentences such as 당장 어떻게 안 되겠소? 'Can't it be somehow taken care of right away?' The -수 variant of this style (갔수, 했수) is used quite casually among older women or to older mothers by their grown-up children.

The -리다 ending is employed among very old folks in place of -을게요.

내가 내일 가리다.	*I will go tomorrow.*
이따가 잠깐 들르리다.	*I will stop by later for a minute.*

NOTE: The spoken form of 들르다 is 들리다; see **8.3**.

The -(으)마 ending has the same meaning as -리다, but is casually used by adults to a much younger person to whom they are close.

내가 하나 사서 보내마.	*I'll buy one and send it to you.*
아기는 내가 업으마.	*Let me piggyback the baby.*

The -거라 ending for commands (-너라 if the verb is 오다), as in 가거라, 보거라, and 오너라, sounds somewhat archaic but may be used by older adults to a much younger person (e.g., a grandparent to a grandchild). It is otherwise heard mostly in historical dramas.

Finally, the following styles (-나이다/나이까, -느니라, -시옵소서) are archaic and are reserved for historical dramas, poems/proverbs, and prayers.

손님이 찾아오셨(사옵)나이다.	*A guest is here to see you.*
마님, 부르셨나이까?	*Ma'am, did you call me?*
한 우물을 파야 하느니라.	*You must dig just one well. (Focus your efforts.)*
부디 굽어살피시옵소서.	*May God help us.*

2 Honorifics

As explained in the previous chapter, the styles associated with sentence endings signal formality or psychological distance between the speaker and the hearer. Coexisting and interacting with these contrasts is a system of distinctions relating to the status of the person being TALKED ABOUT, particularly the referent of the sentence's subject and occasionally the direct object.

2.1 Subject honorification: the suffix -시

The suffix -시 (으시 after a consonant), is attached to the verbal root to show deference toward the referent of the subject. (When -시 combines with 어 in the 해요 style, they become 세; when it occurs with -었, contraction yields -셨.)

할머니께서 좀 편찮으신 거 같으세요.
My grandmother seems to be a little sick.

사장님께서 한국으로 출장가셨습니다.
The boss went on a business trip to Korea.

Use of -시 is mainly sensitive to considerations of age and social standing, although the setting and the genre have some role to play as well. (A somewhat parallel phenomenon involving the use of the special subject marker -께서 is discussed in **2.4**.)

2.1.1   -시 *in statements and questions – general guidelines*

In general, -시 is used to indicate respect toward the referent of the subject when that person is older and/or has a higher occupational or social status. However, several subtleties and special considerations must be taken into account.

- Usually, -시 is called for if you or the hearer has a personal relationship to the referent of the subject (a grandparent, a teacher, a boss, etc.).
- Use of -시 is unnecessary for other people, even those who are older or have a higher social status (including colleagues, neighbors, and even the president of the country) – unless the person is within hearing range or the setting is formal.
- When the speaker and the hearer have different relationships to the referent of the subject, there is no single rule as to whose viewpoint should be adopted.

For example, when speaking about a close friend to the friend's student, one may choose to use or not use -시:

이 교수가/교수님이 오늘 못 온다네요/오신다네요.

I heard that Professor Lee cannot come today.

It is perhaps more common and appropriate for speakers to take the hearer's position and to use -시 where the hearer would be required to use it. However, speaking from the hearer's position is not always more appropriate. If, for example, the referent of the subject is the speaker's professor but the hearer's student/daughter, the speaker should retain his/her own perspective and use -시.

- You may not have to use -시 when talking to your parents (especially your mother) about themselves. (The use of -시 in this case usually indicates conservatism.)

엄마, 어디 가(요)?   *Mom, where are you going?*

However, when you are speaking to someone outside your immediate family, you should use -시 if the subject refers to your parents.

엄마 어디 가셨는데요.   *My mom went somewhere.*

- Romantic partners and extremely close friends generally do not use -시 for each other, regardless of age.

- When age conflicts with social standing or occupational position, mutual use of -시 is expected. So, a social superior uses -시 for an older subordinate when the subject refers to him/her, and a social subordinate uses it for a younger superior under those same circumstances. The more formal and hierarchical the work environment is, the more obligatory is use of -시 for a superior despite age differences.

- -시 is not used in news broadcasts or in written material such as newspapers, magazines, books, and so on that are intended for a general audience (see **2.6** and **9.1**).

한국을 방문하고 있는 클린턴 대통령은 암스트롱에게 전화를 걸어 승리를 축하한다고 전했다. (동양일보)

President Clinton, who was visiting Korea, called Armstrong and congratulated him on his victory. (Tong'yang Daily Press)

- In formulaic greetings such as 안녕하십니까 or 안녕하세요, -시 is used regardless of the age and social standing of the subject when a formal ending is called for.

- -시 should also be used in cases where the referent of the subject is closely connected to a person who is worthy of honorification. (How close is close? One's age or health is undoubtedly close to the person, but what about one's car, clothes, house, or book? When in doubt, use -시 if the hearer is the person in question or someone related to him/her.)

할머니께서 감기가 드셨어요.	*My grandmother has a cold.*
장모님이 연세가 많으세요?	*Is your mother-in-law old?*
손님, 신장이 어떻게 되세요?.	*Ma'am/Sir, what is your height?*
아버님께서 부도가 나셨거든요.	*My father had his company pay cheque bounce.*
교수님, 사무실이 넓으시네요.	*Professor, your office is big.*
사장님, 모자가 잘 어울리십니다.	*Boss, your hat looks good on you.*
사모님, 따님이 미인이세요.	*Ma'am, your daughter is a beauty.*

- These days, almost anything can trigger honorification in the speech of some people, especially service industry workers, provided it refers to something that is associated in some way with a guest or client. Some of the following examples involve over-honorification and may sound strange, but they are all actual quotes.

전화 오셨습니다. (by a hotel front desk clerk)
  Here is a phone call for you.

보험료가 비싸시다구요? (in an advertisement)
  You think the insurance premium is expensive?

복사기 잉크가 떨어지셨다구요? (in an advertisement)
  So your copy machine cartridge ran out of ink?

저기 보이시는 저 건물입니다. (by a security guard)
  It's that building that you see [that is seen] *over there.*

꼬들꼬들 볶음밥이 되실 수 있으시죠. (in a TV cooking show)
  It can turn into very dry fried rice.

- People who are normally on 반말 terms may use -시 for each other to produce special effects such as amusement or sarcasm. For instance, mothers often say to their child in an amusingly affectionate way, 우리 아기가 또 배가 고프시구나! 'My baby is hungry again!'

2.1.2　The subject honorific -시 and hearer-related sentence endings

The following tables offer an integrated picture of the relationship between the subject-related honorific suffix -시 and hearer-related sentence endings.

Statements (with an honorific subject): in basic (present) tense

존댓말　(Formal)		반말　(Casual)	
합니다 style	*해요* style	*해* style	*한다/하다* style
믿으십니다	믿으세요	믿으셔	믿으신다
친절하십니다	친절하세요	친절하셔	친절하시다
선생님이십니다	선생님이세요	선생님이셔	선생님이시다

NOTE: -(으)셔요 is old fashioned compared to -(으)세요.

Questions (with an honorific subject): in basic (present) tense

존댓말　(Formal)		반말　(Casual)	
합니까 style	*해요* style	*해* style	*하니 (하냐)* style
믿으십니까	믿으세요	믿으셔	믿으시니
친절하십니까	친절하세요	친절하셔	친절하시니
선생님이십니까	선생님이세요	선생님이셔	선생님이시니

NOTE: -(으)시니 alternates with -(으)시냐 (믿으시냐, 친절하시냐, 선생님이시냐).

In choosing the right style and verb form, a speaker must take into account his/her relationship both to the referent of the subject and to the hearer. For instance, if you ask a stranger whether (s)he is Professor Kim, you must use 김교수님이십니까?/김교수님이세요? – with both a formal sentence ending (for the stranger who is the hearer) and the honorific suffix -시 (since that person is also the referent of the subject). On the other hand, if you are asking your younger sister whether someone is Professor Kim, you will say 김선생님이셔?/김선생님이시니? – with a casual sentence ending (for your sister), but the honorific suffix -시 (for the professor).

If you are speaking about your younger sister to a close friend, you will say 내 동생이야, with neither a formal ending nor the honorific suffix -시. On the other hand, if you are talking to your professor, you will use 제 동생이에요, with a formal ending (for your professor, who is the hearer). But you will not use -시, since the referent of the subject is your younger sister. (See *3.2.1* for 내 vs. 제.)

One should be especially careful when the hearer and the referent of the subject are identical and happen to be someone with whom one has to be formal. For example, when you say to your teacher, 'You go first' or 'You look tired,' the teacher is both the hearer and the referent of the subject. Therefore, the sentence has to have both a formal ending AND -시 – you must say 먼저 가십시오/가세요 and 피곤해 보이십니다/보이세요.

2.1.3 -시 *in commands and proposals*

Additional guidelines apply in the case of commands and proposals.

Commands:

존댓말 (Formal)		반말 (Casual)	
하시오 style	*해요* style	*해* style	*해라* style
믿으시오	믿어요	믿어	믿어라
믿으십시오	믿으세요		

* Courtesy calls for the use of -시 in commands even when the referent of the subject is not normally honorific. The so-called honorific -시 is used as a marker of deference to help soften the command and make it more acceptable to the hearer.

* Formal situations (classroom instructions, conferences, and formal meetings) tend to require more use of -시 in commands. For example, in speaking to much younger students, most teachers will say:

수업시간에 잡담하지 마세요.
  Do not have private conversations during class.

다음 주까지 교과서를 준비하세요.
  Please have your textbooks ready by next week.

In questions and statements, though, they would not use -시:

숙제 해 왔어요?   *Have you brought your homework?*

기말시험에 결석하면 안 됩니다.   *You must not miss your final exam.*

Similar practices are found in the speech of a boss to his workers or a senior person to his junior.

* The more formal the situation is, the more -시 is used, especially when the subject refers to a large group of people.

앉아 계실 때는 안전벨트를 매십시오. *Please wear a seatbelt while seated.*

화재발생시에는 계단을 이용하십시오. *Please use stairs when there's a fire.*

* Psychological distance also plays a role. -시 is more likely to be used when one doesn't know the hearer, regardless of his/her age. For instance, (잠시만) 기다리세요 is used instead of 기다려요 to a stranger on the phone. And a

fifty-year-old customer who is speaking to a much younger waitress should say:

고기 좀 바싹 구워 주세요.   *Please make my meat well done.*

계산서 좀 갖다 주세요.   *Bring me the bill please.*

- The use of -시 and formal endings in all sentence types is perhaps most common among salespeople, who tend to employ these forms with all customers, regardless of age.

- In general, the deferential use of -시 in commands takes place in circumstances that are similar to those associated with the use of the formal 합니다 and 해요 styles in that the relevant factors involve formality and psychological distance. Those who are on 반말 terms do not have to worry about using -시 in their commands to each other, so you will never need to say 가시라 or 가셔 to a close friend unless it is for amusement or dramatic effect.

Proposals:

존댓말 (Formal)		반말 (Casual)	
합시다 style	*해요* style	*해* style	*하자* style
앉읍시다	앉아요	앉아	앉자
앉으십시다	앉으세요		

- In proposals, where the subject refers jointly to the speaker and the hearer, use of -시 has lost much of its honorific impact – especially in the -(으)십시다 ending. For some reason, -시 does not have the same effect here that it has in command forms such as 드십시오 and 같이 드세요, where it increases the level of formality and deference.

- The -(으)십시다 ending (드십시다, 앉으십시다), with the honorific -시, is used only by quite old, mostly male speakers.

- The -(으)세요 form is softer than the -(으)십시다 form and may be used for gentle proposals (저하고 같이 가세요. 'Let's go together.'). Where additional deference is called for, the proposal is usually made indirectly, by changing it into a question or suggestion (see **6.1**).

2.1.4   *Special subject-honorific verbs*

In the case of certain basic actions and relations, subject honorification must be expressed by the use of a special honorific verb. (The suffix -시 is an inherent part of these special verbs.)

Plain form	Honorific counterpart
먹다	드시다, 잡수시다
밥먹다	식사 하시다, 진지 잡수시다
마시다	드시다, 하시다
배고프다	시장하시다
있다	계시다 'stay; be' or 있으시다 'have' (see 2.1.5)
자다	주무시다
죽다	돌아가시다
아프다	편찮으시다 (entire body), 아프시다 (specific area)

영수야, 저녁 먹어라. 배 고프지?
  Youngsu, have dinner. You're hungry, aren't you?

할머니, 진지 잡수세요. 시장하시지요?
  Grandma, have dinner. You're hungry, aren't you?.

아빠, 안녕히 주무셨어요? 아침식사 하셨어요?
  Good morning, Dad. Have you eaten breakfast?

저는 커피부터 마실래요. 아빠도 커피 한 잔 드실/하실 거죠?
  I'm going to have coffee first. You'll have a cup of coffee too, Dad, right?

할머니 돌아가시던 날 어항에 물고기도 한 마리 죽었다.
  The day when Grandma died, one fish in the fish tank died too.

할아버지가 요즘 좀 편찮으세요. 무릎이 많이 아프시대요.
  My grandpa is not feeling well these days. His knee hurts a lot, he says.

- The verbs 드시다 and 식사하시다 are sufficiently respectful for most purposes in contemporary Korean, but some senior adults may prefer to hear 잡수시다 and 진지 잡수시다.

- 돌아가시다 is frequently glossed in English as 'pass away,' but this is misleading. While 돌아가시다 is both euphemistic and respectful, English 'pass away' is simply euphemistic, which is why it can be used even for a child (as can 목숨을 잃다 and 사망하다). In contrast, 돌아가시다 can be used in personal conversations only for an older or socially superior person (see **9.1**).

2.1.5   Tricky subjects

It is not always straightforward to identify the subject of a Korean sentence, and it is important to look beyond the subject particle -이/가 (see **19.1**). The verb 있다/없다, for instance, can be ambiguous.

Verb	있다 (neg: 없다)	있다 (neg: 없다)
Meaning	'have'	'stay; be'
Honorific form	있으시다 (없으시다)	계시다 (안 계시다)

When 있다/없다 means 'have/not have,' as in 이모가 없어요 'I don't have an aunt,' 'I' is the understood subject. So even though 이모 takes the particle -가, it is not the subject of the sentence and there is no honorific suffix on the verb. (For the same reason, -가 cannot be replaced by -께서 in this context.) On the other hand, if the understood subject refers to your teacher and you want to say '(My teacher) doesn't have an aunt,' 이모가 없으세요 is right because your teacher deserves the suffix -시.

Here are some additional examples containing an honorific subject and 있다 with the sense of 'have.'

사장님, 오늘 10 시에 회의 있으십니다.
Sir, you have a meeting at 10 o'clock today.

교수님, 지금 잠깐 시간 있으세요?
Professor, do you have a minute?

의견이 있으신 분은 발표해 주시기 바랍니다.
Please speak out if you have an opinion.

슬하에 자녀가 세 분 있으십니다.
They have three children.

When 있다 is used to mean 'stay' or 'be' rather than 'have,' the noun marked by -이/가 is the subject. So, 할머니가 집에 안 계세요 means 'Grandmother is not home,' and the special honorific verb is called for. (할머니가 안 계세요 'Grandmother is not home' or 'Grandmother doesn't exist' is an indirect way of indicating that one's grandmother has passed away.)

Psychological verbs such as 좋다, 싫다, and so on also call for caution. In the examples below, the understood subject (marked in bold-face in English) corresponds to the person/thing experiencing the state described by the sentence (coldness, enjoyment, need, and so forth). Only when that person is older and/or has higher social status is -시 used.

선생님, 밖에 안 추워요?   *Teacher, isn't **it** cold outside?*
선생님, 안 추우세요?   *Teacher, aren't **you** cold?*

저는 할아버지가 좋아요.	*I like my grandfather.*
아빠도 할아버지가 좋으세요?	*Do **you** also like grandpa, Dad?*
할아버지, 이 영화 재미있어요?	*Grandpa, is **this** movie fun?*
할아버지, 이 영화 재미있으세요?	*Grandpa, do **you** find this movie fun?*
저는 선생님이 필요해요.	*I need a teacher.*
선생님께서 책이 필요하시대요.	***The teacher** needs the book, I heard.*
할머니가 보고 싶어요.	*I miss Grandma.*
할머니가 저를 보고 싶어하세요.	***Grandma** misses me.*

2.1.6 *Complex verbs and* -시

When -시 is called for in expressions that consist of two verbs, it shows up sometimes on both verbs, sometimes just on the first verb, and sometimes just on the second verb. (The first column is for plain forms and the second one is for honorific forms.)

- -시 appears on both verbs:

할 수 있어요?	하실 수 있으세요?	*Can you do it?*
가 본 적이 있다.	가 보신 적이 있으시다.	*She has been there.*
오다 만났어.	오시다 만나셨어.	*He met them on his way here.*
피곤한 거 같아요.	피곤하신 거 같으세요.	*I think she's tired.*
쉬고 싶어요?	쉬시고 싶으세요?	*Would you like to rest?*
(집을) 팔게 됐어.	(집을) 파시게 되셨어.	*It turns out that he has to sell his house.*

- -시 appears on the first verb only:

갈 거예요?	가실 거예요?	*Are you going to go?*
바빠 가지고...	바쁘셔 가지고...	*Because she's busy...*
피곤한가 봐.	피곤하신가 봐.	*Looks like he's tired.*
책 읽나 보다.	책 읽으시나 보다.	*Seems like she's reading.*
떠나고 말았어.	떠나시고 말았어.	*He ended up leaving.*
걸어야 돼요.	걸으셔야 돼요.	*You must walk.*
안 와도 됩니다.	안 오셔도 됩니다.	*You don't have to come.*

- -시 appears on the second verb only:

들어 와요.	들어 오세요.	*Please come in.*
앉아 있어요.	앉아 계세요.	*Please be seated.*
젊어 보인다.	젊어 보이신다.	*He looks young.*
해 줘요.	해 주세요.	*Please do it for me.*
해 봐요.	해 보세요.	*Please give it a try.*
해 놓아요/둬요.	해 놓으세요/두세요.	*Please do it (for later use).*
해 치워요.	해 치우세요.	*Just do it and get it over with.*
잊어 버려요.	잊어 버리세요.	*Forget about it.*

If the verb has a special honorific counterpart (see *2.1.4*), that form must be used regardless of the verb's position. So the honorific form of 먹어 봐요 is 드셔 보세요 even though the -시 normally appears only on the second verb in -어/아 보다 patterns (해 보세요, 신어 보세요).

NOTE: Hereafter, the linking syllable -어/아 will be abbreviated as simply -어.

Matters are a bit different in quoted clauses. There, -시 appears either on the verb quoted or on the quoting verb, depending on the referent of the subject for each verb. For instance, 오래 (which is a reduced form of 오라고 해) can have -시 right after 오 or after 라.

할머니, 오빠가 오시래요 (< 오시라고 해요).
  Grandma, brother is asking you to come

오빠, 할머니가 오라셔 (< 오라고 하셔).
  Brother, grandma is asking you to come.

2.2   Object honorification

A small number of verbs are replaced by other verbs to indicate special respect for the referent of the direct or indirect object. These verbs are often called 'humble' verbs because object honorification is achieved by lowering the speaker/subject.

Plain form	Honorific counterpart
보다	뵙다
묻다/물어보다	여쭙다/여쭤보다
데리고 (가다)	모시고 (가다)
달라(고)	주십사(고)
(해)주다	(해)드리다
알리다 전하다	알려 드리다 전해 드리다
말하다 전화하다 축하하다 부탁하다 연락하다 약속하다	말씀드리다 전화드리다 축하드리다 부탁드리다 연락드리다 약속드리다

NOTE₁: 뵙다 is used for deliberate seeing only, not for seeing someone accidentally (from afar).

NOTE₂: When 하다 carries the meaning of 'convey,' it can be replaced by 드리다.

The following dialogue between an author (작가) and a publisher (출판인) illustrates the use of 주다 when the indirect object (or recipient) refers to oneself and 드리다 when it refers to another person.

A: 원고 마감일을 좀 연기해 주셨으면 하는데요.
B: 자꾸 연기해 달라 그러시면 곤란한데요. 다음 달까지는 출판에
   들어가야 하거든요.
A: 일주일만 좀 더 주실 수 없을까요?
B: 그럼 이번 한 번만 봐 드릴테니까 다음부터는 꼭 기한을 지켜 주셔야
   됩니다.
A: 고맙습니다. 약속드리겠습니다.

A: I am hoping that you'll give me an extension for the manuscript deadline.
B: It is difficult for me if you keep asking for an extension. The manuscript
   has to go into production by next month, you know.
A: Could you please give me just one more week?
B: Well, I'll give you a break just this time, but you must meet the deadline
   from next time.
A: Thank you. I promise.

When the referent of the subject and the referent of the direct or indirect object both call for special respect, an object-honorific verb carrying the -시 suffix is used (e.g., 할아버지가 책을 선생님께 드리셨어요).

Here are more examples of object honorific verbs. Notice that 보다 is replaced by 뵙다 when the direct object refers to a stranger or the speaker's teacher, and that 축하하다 is replaced by 축하드리다 when the indirect object refers to a friend's father, and so on.

처음 뵙겠습니다. 말씀 많이 들었습니다.
How do you do? I have heard a lot about you.

친구를 먼저 보고 나중에 선생님을 뵐거야.
I am going to meet my friend first and see my teacher later.

동생에게 용돈을 주고 할아버지께 선물을 드렸다.
I gave my brother pocket money and my grandfather a gift.

죄송하지만, 말씀 좀 여쭤 봐도 되겠습니까? (to a stranger)
Excuse me, but may I ask you something?

미안하지만, 말 좀 물어 봐도 될까요? (to a much younger stranger)
Excuse me, but can I ask you something?

학교 친구 한명 데리고 교수님도 모시고 온답니다.
She said that she would bring one of her classmates and also her teacher.

여동생에게 먼저 인사하고 시어머님 되실 분께도 인사를 드렸다.
I said hello to his younger sister first and greeted my future mother-in-law too.

나한테 도와 달라고 하지 말고 부장님께 도와 주십사고 부탁 드려.
Don't ask me for help; ask the supervisor to give you some help.

지은아 축하한다. 지은이 아버님도 축하드려요.
Congratulations, Ji-eun. Congratulations too to Ji-eun's father.

- In general, a person who merits -시 when (s)he is referent of the subject (that is, someone who is older and/or socially superior – a professor, boss, older neighbor, grandparent, parent-in-law, etc.) also deserves the object honorific verb when (s)he is referent of the direct or indirect object.

- On formal occasions (meeting someone for the first time, speaking at a professional meeting or ceremony, and in public announcements), the use of object-honorific verbs is expected as a courtesy, even when the referent of the object is younger or socially inferior – 안내 말씀 드리겠습니다 'May I have your attention?' (in public announcements), 잘 부탁드립니다 (see below), and so on.

> 잘 부탁드립니다 'I hope we have a good relationship; I am counting on you' is a request for cooperation or for a favor. It can be used at the end of a self-introduction to express the hope that the new relationship will go well or when you are asking for a favor. (In writing or formal speech, you can begin with 아무쪼록.)

2.3 Honorific nouns

A few special nouns, such as 말씀 for 말 and 진지 for 밥, are used to denote things associated with an esteemed person.

Plain noun	Honorific counterpart
자식; 아이(들)	자제분; 자녀
이름	성함; 존함
집	댁
병	병환

NOTE: 댁 cannot refer to one's own home, so it cannot be used to refer to your parents' or grandparents' residence if you live with them.

저희 집은 서울인데 선생님 댁은 어디세요?
   My place is in Seoul; where is your place?

어제는 친정집에 갔었고 시댁에는 다음 주에 가려고요.
   I went to my parents' house yesterday and intend to go to my husband's parents' house next week.

할아버지 말씀하시는 동안 아무 말 말고 잠자코 있도록 해.
   While Grandpa is speaking, make sure you don't say anything and stay quiet.

제 이름은 김기자인데 그쪽 성함은 어떻게 되세요?
   My name is Kija Kim; may I have your name?

저는 아이가 둘입니다. 자제분이 몇이세요?
   I have two children. How many do you have?

강아지가 병이 들었어. 근데 요즘 할아버지 병환은 좀 어떠시니?
   The puppy got sick. By the way, how is your grandfather's sickness these days?

아버님 존함이 어떻게 되세요?
   What is your father's name, may I ask?

NOTE: To give parents' or grandparents' names respectfully, -자 is attached after each syllable: 박자 교자 인자이십니다 'His name is Kyo-in Pak.'

Special care must be exercised in the use of nouns referring to age. Because 연세 is often treated as the honorific counterpart of 나이 and 생신 as the honorific counterpart of 생일, students often ask their teacher's 연세 or 생신, which makes the teacher feel very old! For this reason, age-related honorifics are usually reserved for those who can safely be considered old.

However, even this does not ensure that a person will be happy to be asked about his or her 나이 or 생일. We therefore usually resort to various indirect and euphemistic ways of asking about age, saying 몇 년생이세요? 'What was your birth year?' or 몇 학번이세요? or 학번이 어떻게 되세요? 'What was your college-entrance year?' In addition, we often turn to a formal equivalent (usually found in written documents) and ask 생년월일이 어떻게 되세요? 'In what year, month, date were you born?' Since it is very important in Korean language and culture to find out how old the other person is, there is no shortage of indirect ways of finding out someone's age.

2.4 Honorific particles

Two particles have honorific counterparts. Under the appropriate circumstances, -이/가 on a subject is replaced by -께서, while the indirect object markers -한테 and -에게 give way to -께.

The use of the honorific subject marker -께서 is on the decline, and is optional nowadays for many people. Its use is highly honorific, making it appropriate in formal settings, but it is generally not impolite to use -이/가 in most situations. However, some people use -께서 for honorific subjects on all occasions.

Use of -께 is likewise on the decline, as many people find that -한테 generally sounds fine, regardless of who the indirect object refers to. However, the honorific -께 must always be employed in personal letters (김교수님께 'Dear Professor Kim') if the recipient is someone who merits deference.

2.5 Use of honorifics in several basic expressions

	Formal	Semi-formal	Casual
Good-bye	안녕히 가세요/계세요.	잘 가요/있어요.	잘 가(라)/있어(라). 안녕.
Good night	안녕히 주무세요.	잘 자요.	잘 자(라).
Have you eaten?	진지 잡수셨어요? 식사하셨어요?	식사했어요? 밥 먹었어요?	밥 먹었어? 밥 먹었니?
How many of you are there?	몇 분이세요?	몇 명이에요?	몇 명이야? 몇 명이니?
What is your name?	성함이 어떻게 되세요?	이름이 어떻게 돼요? 이름이 뭐예요?	이름이 뭐야? 이름이 뭐니?
Eat; help yourself.	잡수세요. 드세요.	들어요. 먹어요.	먹어(라).

The expressions in the first column (with -시) are reserved for a formal setting and/or for individuals such as your friend's parents, strangers, your teacher, or your boss. Those in the middle column can be used for someone who you don't know well but is younger than you are. And the ones in the last column are for very close friends or children.

2.6 Non-use of honorific expressions in impersonal language

Honorific expressions are not employed in news broadcasts or in impersonal writing (as in newspapers and magazines). Because communication of this sort is intended for a non-specific general audience, there is no place for honorific suffixes (-시, -님), for honorific nouns (말씀, 연세, etc.), for honorific particles (-께, -께서), or for object-honorific verbs (드리다, 모시고, etc.), all of which are used to express PERSONAL respect. The following excerpt from a news report illustrates this point.

노무현 대통령은 김대중 전 대통령에게 위로의 말을 전했습니다.
President Roh conveyed his sympathetic words to the ex-president Kim.

Certain vocabulary items that are used in personal settings are also avoided in impersonal language. For instance, 선생 or 선생님 is replaced by 교사 or 교원 to refer to school teachers below the college level (교원대학교 'University of Teacher Education,' 교사 연수 'teacher training,' 교사 자격증 'teacher's certificate'). Similarly, 집 or 댁 is replaced by 자택, ...을 데리고/모시고 (가다) is replaced by ...을 동반하고 (가다), and so on (see **9.1**).

3 Address terms and pronouns

As with verb forms, the choice of address terms and pronouns is conditioned by the speaker's relationship with the person to whom (s)he is speaking or referring, as well as by the situation. These are highly important matters in Korean society: the wrong choice may negatively affect one's career as well as personal relationships.

3.1 Address terms (호칭)

Koreans typically address each other by name (with an appropriate suffix) or by title (also with an appropriate suffix; see *10.4.4*). The choice of address term is determined by the gender of the person being addressed, his or her relationship to the speaker, and his or her (apparent) age relative to the speaker. In general, address terms tend to be words with elevated or affectionate connotations. Thus 기사님 'technician' is preferred to the plainer and more literal 운전사 아저씨 for driver, and 언니 'older sister' is more welcome than the literal 올케 for an older sister-in-law.

3.1.1 Addressing an unfamiliar person or a stranger

The most appropriate way to get the attention of someone who you do not know personally (a waitress in a restaurant, or a stranger on the street) is to use any of the following hedging expressions:

저기요 (and 여기요, if it's a restaurant)
저...
저 실례지만...
저 죄송하지만...
여보세요 (when you have to shout to be heard)

When a specific address term is called for, one of the following is generally appropriate.

Person being addressed	Address term
Child	꼬마야, 애(야)
Student (younger looking)	학생

Unmarried female (younger looking)	학생, 아가씨, 언니
Unmarried male (younger looking)	학생, 총각, 젊은이
Older (married) adult [informal]	아줌마/아주머니, 언니, 아저씨
Older or socially superior adult	선생님 (for any profession) 사장님 (usually for business people) 사모님 (married female)
Very old person	할아버지/할머니 할아버님/할머님 [formal]
Technician, including cab/bus driver	기사님, 기사 아저씨 (male)
Customer	**(full name +) 손님** (김혜선) 손님 **(full name +) 고객님** (김혜선) 고객님 **full name + 님/씨** 김혜선 님/씨

NOTE: Depending on the situation, the term 아가씨 can be offensive because of its strong association these days with bar hostesses, low-level clerks, etc. On the other hand, many older married females will be happy to be called 아가씨 instead of 아줌마! Perhaps for this reason, some people, regardless of gender, like to use 언니 (literally a female's older sister) to address almost any female.

3.1.2 Addressing a non-family member who you already know

A variety of family terms are used for non-family members to show closeness.

Person being addressed	Address term
Close friends of similar age or younger and children	**first name + 아/야** 성철아, 성아야 **full name** 진성철, 진성아 **야, 애** **야 임마/자식아** [familiar/casual] **이봐, 이 사람아** (among older people)
Close friends who are somewhat older	**(first name +) 형/누나** (연규)형 'male's older brother/sister' **(first name +) 오빠/언니** (성아)언니 'female's older brother/sister' **(first name +) 선배** 'one's senior at school'
Boyfriend/girlfriend	**자기, 자기야** **first name + 아/야** 지선아, 연지야 **first name + 씨** [formal] 연규씨

Table continued on the next page

Friend's family	**friend's first name + family term** 영숙이 어머니/어머님, 오빠, etc. NOTE: -이 in 영숙이 is a particle (*19.2.2*).
Familiar (married) adult, such as neighbor	**아줌마/아주머니, 아저씨** **할아버지/할아버님; 할머니/할머님** **영감님** (among very old males)
Close male adult friend of similar age or younger	**last name + 형** 김형
Friend of similar age or younger with whom friendship developed after college	**full name + 씨** 김선아씨 **first name + 씨** 선아씨 NOTE: See *10.4.4* for discussion of *-씨*.
Familiar but much younger person by a senior person (e.g., professor to a student)	**name + 군** (male) 김군, 김민호군, 민호군 **name + 양** (female) 김양, 김미아양, 미아양 **name** (진)용주
Older or superior at workplace	**(last name) title + 님** (장) 사장님, (곽) 박사님 **(full name) title + 님** (오강일) 교수님 **선배님** 'one's senior at school'
Equal at workplace	**full name + 씨** 정미아씨
Close friend of same age or younger at workplace	**last name + title** 김과장, 김교수, 김박사, 닥터김 **foreign first name + title** 로스선생
Inferior at workplace	**미스/ 미스터 + last name**
Titleless job holder such as janitor	**(last name + 씨 +) 아저씨/아줌마** (김씨) 아저씨, (박씨) 아줌마

NOTE[1]: 형 may be used by female students for male seniors because 오빠 is often used to refer to a boyfriend who happens to be older.

NOTE[2]: Calling teachers by their first name or by using 미스 or 미스터 is not appropriate. The common ways of addressing teachers in English (including 미스 김 or 미스터 김) are not appropriate in Korean.

3.1.3 Addressing a family member

The full range of address terms for members of the extended family can be
daunting, but the following should suffice in most modern families.

Family member	Address term
Grandma/grandmother	할머니/할머님
Grandpa/grandfather	할아버지/할아버님
Mom/mother	엄마/어머니, 어머님
Mother-in-law	어머니, 어머님 (husband's mother) 어머님, 장모님 (wife's mother)
Dad/father	아빠/아버지, 아버님
Father-in-law	아버님 (husband's father) 아버님, 장인어른 (wife's father)
One's own children	**first name** + 아/야
Daughter-in-law	(새)아가, 어멈아, 에미야
Son-in-law	**last name** + 서방 박서방 **child's name** + 아범 용주아범
Aunt	이모, 이모님 (mother's sister) 고모, 고모님 (father's sister)
Aunt's husband	이모부, 이모부님 (mother's sister's husband) 고모부, 고모부님 (father's sister's husband)

Uncle	(외)삼촌 (mother's brother)
	삼촌 (father's brother)
	큰아버지, 큰아버님, 백부님
	   (father's older, married brother)
	작은아버지, 작은아버님, 숙부님
	   (father's younger, married brother)

Uncle's wife	외숙모 (mother's brother's wife)
	큰엄마, 큰어머니, 큰어머님, 백모님
	   (father's older-brother's wife)
	작은엄마, 작은어머니, 작은어머님, 숙모님
	   (father's younger-brother's wife)

Sibling	언니 (female's older sister) 오빠, 오라버니 (female's older brother) 형, 형님 (male's older brother) 누나, 누님, 누이 (male's older sister) (NOTE: 오라버니 & 누이 are old-fashioned.)

Table continued on the next page

Brother's wife (by female)	올케 올케 언니, (새)언니 (older-brother's wife)
Brother's wife (by male)	형수님 (older-brother's wife) 제수씨, 계수씨 (younger-brother's wife)
Sister's husband (by female)	형부 (older-sister's husband) 제부 (younger-sister's husband)
Sister's husband (by male)	자형, 매형 (older-sister's husband) 매제 (younger-sister's husband)
Spouse	여보 (traditional) 자기야 (romantic) **first name** + 아/야 (usually by a young couple) **child's name** + 아빠/엄마
Wife's sister	처형 (wife's older sister) 처제 (wife's younger sister)
Wife's brother-in-law	형님 (wife's older-sister's husband) 동서 (wife's younger-sister's husband)
Wife's brother	처남, 형님 (wife's older brother) 처남 (wife's younger brother)
Husband's sister	형님 (husband's older sister) 아가씨 (husband's younger sister)
Husband's brother	아주버님 (husband's older brother) 도련님 (husband's younger, single brother) 서방님 (husband's younger, married brother)
Husband's sister-in-law	형님 (husband's older-brother's wife) 동서 (husband's younger-brother's wife)

NOTE₁: Terms with -님 are formal and used by older people in general and for in-laws.

NOTE₂: The adjectives 큰 and 작은 (or the first name followed by an address term) are often used to distinguish among older and younger multiple siblings, aunts, sisters-in-law, and so forth (큰형, 작은형, 윤호오빠, 철호오빠, 큰고모, 작은고모, and so on).

Address terms for family members can be confusing even to native speakers, as people have less contact with members of their extended family these days than in the past. In addition, Koreans often replace the original address terms with the address terms that reflect their children's point of view. For instance, instead of calling one's husband's sister 아가씨 or 형님, 고모 'aunt' is often employed. A wife may even call her husband 아빠 'Dad,' using exactly the same term she employs for her own father.

Most address terms can also be used to refer to people who are being spoken about, even when they are not present.

우리 이모가 이번 겨울에 하와이에 놀러 오래요.
My aunt is telling me to come visit her in Hawaii this winter.

An exception in this regard is 여보, which is exclusively used to address one's spouse, not to talk about him/her. Reference to one's spouse, or to someone else's spouse, calls for use of the following terms, which are presented in approximate decreasing order of formality.

- One's wife: 제 처, 집사람, 안사람, 안식구, 이 사람, 와이프, 마누라
- Someone else's wife: 사모님, 부인, 와이프
- One's husband: 제 남편, 우리 남편, 이 사람, 신랑
- Someone else's husband: 부군, 바깥어른, 낭군, 아저씨, 남편, 신랑

Another difference involves the terms used by a wife for her husband's mother and father. Whereas a wife uses 어머니/어머님 and 아버님 as address terms, she normally adds the prefix 시- (시어머니/시어머님, 시아버님) when talking about (rather than to) her parents-in-law to people outside the family.

3.2 Pronouns and related words

Personal pronouns (the equivalent of English *I*, *you*, *he*, *she*, etc.) are best avoided in Korean. There's no need, for instance, to repeat 나는 or 저는 in sentence after sentence – the topic is assumed to be the same until there is an indication that it has changed.

안녕하십니까? 저는 텍사스대학교 학생입니다. 이름은 박성수입니다.
한국에서 왔습니다. 지금은 학교 기숙사에 살고 있습니다.

Hello, I am a student at the University of Texas. My name is Seongsoo Park.
I am from Korea. I am currently living in the school dorm.

If it is necessary to refer back to someone who was mentioned in a preceding sentence, the appropriate noun is usually repeated.

내가 혜수씨를 처음 만난 건 92 년 하와이에서였다. 그때 혜수씨는
영어교육학과 박사과정에 신입생이었다. 혜수씨하고 나는 처음부터
서로를 아주 편하게 느꼈던 것 같다. 그때 혜수씨는...

It was in Hawaii in 1992 when I first met Hyesoo. At that time, she was a new Ph.D. student in the Department of English as a Second Language. I think that Hyesoo and I felt comfortable with each other from the beginning. She...

This notwithstanding, there are a number of words in Korean that appear to do the work of pronouns under certain specific conditions.

3.2.1 First person pronouns and their equivalents

- 나/우리: used to refer to oneself/oneselves when speaking with close friends, children, one's students, siblings, parents (in a liberal family), and possibly even grandparents. Also used in writing for a non-specified audience.

- 저/저희: as humble counterparts of 나/우리, 저/저희 are used with teachers and bosses, with acquaintances or strangers who are not younger, as well as in formal meetings.

  NOTE: 나 + 가 → 내가; 저 + 가 → 제가; 나의/저의 can contract to 내/제.

> **Difference between 나 and 저**
>
> With 반말 endings, only 나 is appropriate (나는 안 갈래). But in the 해요 style, either 나 or 저 is used. If the hearer is clearly younger, 나 is appropriate even in 존댓말. For instance, a professor will use the -요 ending to a student but never 저, unless the student is older (내가 책을 빌려 줄게요). The more formal 합니다 style, however, calls for only 저 (제가 하겠습니다).

- 이쪽, 여기: can be used to refer to 'I/me' or 'we/us,' in addition to its basic meaning of 'this side' or 'here.'

  이쪽은 그쪽이 뭘 하든지 신경 안 써요.
  I don't care what you do.

  여기는 괜찮으니까 거기나 챙기세요.
  We're okay here, so you just worry about your stuff.

3.2.2 Second person pronouns and their equivalents

Extreme care is required in the use of second person pronouns (the equivalent of 'you'). In general, including for parents, teachers, or strangers, kinship terms or titles (아버지, 선생님, etc.), not pronouns, are called for. A second person pronoun (너 or 당신) should not be used except for the limited cases listed below.

- 너/너희: used for children or extremely close friends/siblings of a similar age or younger.

  네가 알아서 해.　　　　　　　　*You just take care of it.*
  너희들끼리 먼저 가라.　　　　　*You guys go first.*

  NOTE: 너 + 가 → 네가; for the spoken forms 니가 and 니들끼리, see **8.3**.

- 당신: extremely restricted (as in the first five examples below), although its use seems to be on the rise. (See *3.2.4* for the reflexive pronoun use of 당신.)

Traditionally used between husband and wife:

당신하고 결혼한 지 벌써 십년이 넘었어.

 It's already been over ten years since I married you.

In traditional song lyrics and in poems:

당신은 누구시길래 이렇게 내 마음 깊은 거기에 찾아와 ...

 I wonder who you are, to come so deeply into my heart...

For a non-specified audience in advertisements or questionnaires:

당신의 우리말 실력은 어느 정도입니까?

 How well do you know your native language?

As a sign of disrespect when arguing or fighting:

당신이 뭔데, 누구더러 당신이래?

 Who do you think you are to call me 'tangsin'?

As a semi-formal pronoun for someone with equal or lower status (uncommon):

당신을 사귄지 1 년이나 됐는데 아직도 당신이 어떤 사람인지 모르겠어요.

 It's been a year since we started dating, but I still can't figure you out.

The following words help fill the function of a second person pronoun under the right circumstances.

- 그쪽, 거기: frequently used with people of a similar age or younger. These forms are especially useful when one doesn't know the other person's name or doesn't feel comfortable using it.

그쪽이 먼저 끊으세요.	*You hang up first.*
그쪽이 내가 누구를 만나든 무슨 상관이에요?	*Why do you care who I go out with?*
거기도 먹지.	*Why don't you also eat?*

- 자기: used between romantic partners and between close (female) friends. (See *3.1.3 & 3.2.4* for other uses of 자기.)

자기 오늘 늦어요?	*Are you going to be late today?*

- 그대: used in song lyrics and in poems.

낙엽 떨어진 그 길을 정답게 걸었던 그대 그리고 나

 you and I, who used to walk in love along the road covered with fallen leaves

- 귀하: originally used on an envelope for an honorific recipient (승계호 교수님 귀하 'TO: Dr. Kyeho Seung'), but nowadays often used in automated calling instructions.

귀하의 비밀번호를 눌러 주십시오.

 Please press your PIN number.

귀하의 잔액은 5 불입니다.

 Your balance is five dollars.

- 본인: means 'person-in-question' or 'self.' It can therefore be anyone (me, you, he, her), but is often used to cleverly avoid the use of 'you.'

  본인이 직접 오라는데요.
  > *They say that you (the person-in-question) should come yourself.*

- 댁: used among older people to refer to an adult stranger.

  댁은 누구신지요?   *May I ask who you are?*

- 어르신: used for a very old person in a respectful way.

- 자네: used by a superior to a much younger adult or to an adolescent of lower status (like a student), or by a parent-in-law to a son-in-law.

- 제군 [formal]: used by a superior to subordinates or followers

  오늘 제군들에게 매우 쓸쓸한 소식 하나를 전해야겠다.
  > *I have to give you guys a piece of sad news today.*

- 여러분 [formal]: used toward a group of people

  신사숙녀 여러분   *Ladies and gentlemen...*
  친애하는 국민 여러분   *My dear fellow Koreans*
  여러분의 경험을 발표해 보세요.   *Try and talk about your own experiences.*

3.2.3 *Third person pronouns and their equivalents*

Korean does not have a well-established category of true third-person pronouns such as English *he* and *she*. When it is necessary to refer back to a previously mentioned person, several possibilities are available.

   One is to simply leave the person unmentioned, especially when he or she has been the topic of the conversation.

   A: 할아버지 오셨어요.   *Grandpa came.*
   B: 언제 오셨어요?   *When did he come?*
   A: 그저께요.   *The day before yesterday.*
   B: 어디 사시는데요?   *Where does he live?*
   A: 서울에요.   *In Seoul.*

A second option is to employ titles or kinship terms, which can be repeated as many times as needed.

   A: 할아버지 오셨어요.
   B: 할아버지가 언제 오셨어요?
   A: 그저께요.
   B: 할아버지가 어디 사시는데요?
   A: 서울에요.

Yet another possibility is to use a compound consisting of 이/그/저 plus a general noun.

이: is used to point out someone/something close to the speaker.

그: is used for someone/something either away from the speaker and close to the hearer or familiar to both the speaker and the hearer.

저: is used for someone/something away from both the speaker and the hearer but visible to both.

- (이/그/저) 기지배, 놈, 자식, 녀석: may be used affectionately or neutrally to refer to younger siblings or close friends, or by parents to refer to their own children.

이 기지배가 왜 이렇게 안 오지?   *I wonder why this girl is still not coming.*

그 녀석 참 귀엽게 생겼네.   *The kid looks very cute.*

It otherwise is used angrily to mean something like 'punk' or 'bastard.'

별 웃기는 자식 다 보겠네.
   What a ridiculous punk.

이놈의 세상이 어떻게 되려고...
   What's going to happen to this damned world...

- (이/그/저) 애, 애(네)들: used to refer to a child, a close friend, or a sibling of similar age or younger. (애 < 아이, 애 < 이 애, 쟤 < 저 애, 걔 < 그 애)

애 (<이 애) 는 제 친구고 쟤는 걔 동생이에요.
   This one is my friend and that one is that friend's younger brother.

그럼 쟤네들은 누구야? 걔네들은 애하고 같은 반 학생들이래요.
   Who are those kids then? They are the classmates of this guy, I heard.

- (이/그/저) 것/거: may be used to refer to one's own child or someone extremely close. (이게 < 이것이, 그게 < 그것이)

이게 어디가 아픈 모양이다.   *Seems like he's sick.*

그게 또 말썽을 부렸구나.   *Oh, that kid caused trouble again.*

- (이/그/저) 사람: may be used to refer to one's husband or wife or to any stranger in a neutral manner.

이 사람은 김치찌개만 있으면 돼요.
   Kimchitchigye is all he (my husband) needs.

걸어 가는데 그 사람이 갑자기 말을 걸어 왔어요.
   I was walking and he started talking to me all of a sudden.

- **(이/그/저) 여자, 남자**: used to refer to a stranger in a neutral manner; if used for an older or unfamiliar person to his or her face, this expression can be extremely insulting.

  어제 그 남자 누구니?   *Who was that guy yesterday?*

  A: 이 여자가 왜 이래, 정말?   *What's wrong with this woman, really?*

  B: 이 여자라니?   *Are you calling me 'this woman'?*

- **(이/그/저) 분**: used to refer to a stranger in a formal and respectful way.

  어제 그 분이 누구세요?   *Who was that person yesterday?*

  이 분은 제 고등학교   *This is my former high school teacher.*
     은사님이십니다.

- **(이/그/저) 이**: may be used to refer to one's husband or wife (usually among older couples).

Thanks to the influence of English, the following forms are employed in literary writing and song lyrics.

- **그, 그(들)**: used as a third person equivalent of '(s)he' and 'they' only in rather formal speech or writing (as well as in translations of pronouns in Western languages). In its literal use, it has the meaning of 'that' and is impersonal.

- **그녀**: used in writing by authors for 'she.'

- **그님**: used in song lyrics or in poems.

The following items can also be used as pronoun substitutes.

- **사람**: '(s)he [the person]'

  사람이 참 착한 거 같아요.   *She seems really nice.*

- **사람들**: 'they'

  사람들이 그러는데 그 음식점이 장사가 안 돼서 문을 닫았대.
     They say that the restaurant closed because its business wasn't good.

- **누가, 누군가가**: 'someone'

  누가 그러는데, 이 동네는 밤에 다녀도 안전하대요.
     Someone says that this neighborhood is safe to go around in even at night.

- **김모씨**: 'one Mr. Kim' (usually used in news report)

  경찰은 수표 위조범 김모씨 등 일당 4명을 검거했습니다.
     The police arrested a gang of four people including a Kim so-and-so for forgery of checks.

3.2.4 Reflexive pronouns

The following expressions are used as reflexive pronouns (roughly equivalent to 'myself,' 'himself,' 'oneself,' and so on).

- 저/지 [spoken/colloquial]: (See **8.3** for the 저/지 alternation.)

  내 동생은 저만 알어, 제(<저의) 생각만 하는 거 있지.
  My younger brother is self-centered. He only cares about himself.

  이 세상에서 지가 제일 잘난 줄 안다니까.
  He thinks he's the best in the world, you know.

- 자기: used for reference to a third party.

  혜수는 자기가 직접 가겠다고 말했다.
  Hyesu said that she would go herself.

  자기 일은 자기가 알아서 해야지.
  One should take care of one's own work.

  그 여자는 자기를 미인이라고 생각한다.
  She considers herself beautiful.

- 자신: can be used in combination with a personal pronoun/noun, or by itself for emphasis.

  그 여자는 (자기)자신을 미인이라고 생각한다.
  She considers herself beautiful.

  자신만 생각하지 말아요.
  Don't just think about yourself.

- 자체: used in an emphatic manner for any person or thing.

  건물 자체는 튼튼한 거 같습니다.
  The building itself seems solid.

- 당신: can be used for an honored third person referent.

  (할아버지) 당신이 손수 끓여서 드셨다.
  Grandfather cooked it himself and ate it.

  NOTE: 당신 is not used that often except for grandparents.

3.2.5   Indefinite pronouns

Korean has a series of words that can be used as either interrogative pronouns (question words) or indefinite pronouns.

Word	As question word	As indefinite pronoun
누구/누가	who	someone
뭐	what	something
어디	where	somewhere
어떻게	how	somehow
어느	which	some/certain
어떤	which/what type of	some/certain
몇	what/how many	several

어디 가세요?	*Where are you going?* or *Are you going somewhere?*
뭐 먹을까 ?	*What shall we eat?* or *Shall we eat something?*
누가 왔어?	*Who came?* or *Did someone come?*

When used with the special particles -(이)나, -도, -든(지), or -라도, indefinite pronouns as well as 아무 and 얼마 can take on interpretations equivalent to English *everyone, anything, nothing,* etc.

- Everyone, anyone

누구나 할 수 있는 일은 아니다.	*It's not something that everyone can do.*
아무나 할 수 있는 일은 아니다.	*It's not something that anyone can do.*
관심있는 사람은 **누구든지** 오세요.	*Anyone who is interested is welcome.*

- Everything, anything

그 사람 일이라면 **뭐든지** 다 알아.	*I know everything about him.*
아무거나 괜찮아.	*Anything will do.*

- Everywhere, anywhere

  휴가철에는 **어디나** 붐빈다.
  　It's crowded everywhere during vacation season.

  어디든지/아무 데라도 가고 싶어요.
  　I want to go just about anywhere.

  그런 사람은 **어디서든지** 환영을 받을 겁니다.
  　That kind of person will be welcome anywhere.

- Always, every time

언제나 환하게 웃으세요.	*Always have a bright smile.*
책만 보면 **언제나** 졸음이 온다.	*I get drowsy every time I read.*

- Any time

  언제든지/언제라도 전화 하세요.   *Call me any time.*

  아무 때나 들르세요.   *Drop by any time.*

- Every way, any way

  아무래도 괜찮아요.   *Any way is fine with me.*

- No matter what

  무슨 일이 있어도 절대 포기하지 마세요.

      Don't give up no matter what happens.

  어떻게(해서)든(지) 이 어려운 상황을 잘 이겨내 봅시다.

      Let's try to overcome this difficult situation no matter what it takes.

- As much as one likes

  부페니까 얼마든지 드세요.   *It's a buffet, so eat as much as you like.*

The following forms must be used in combination with a negated verb.

- No one, anyone

  아무도 장담 못한다.   *No one can guarantee it.*

  아무한테서도 연락이 없어요.   *There's no word from anyone.*

- Nothing, anything

  어느 것도 싼 게 없네요.   *Nothing is cheap.*

  아무 것도 안 샀다.   *I didn't buy anything.*

- Nowhere, anywhere

  아무 데도 안 갔다.   *I didn't go anywhere.*

  아무 데나 앉지 말고 여기 앉아.   *Don't sit just anywhere; sit here.*

- Not many, not much

  날짜가 얼마 안 남았다.   *There aren't many days left.*

  값이 얼마 안 돼요.   *It's not very expensive.*

4 Language for daily situations

Like every language, Korean has a large number of formulaic and fixed expressions for use in common everyday situations. This chapter focuses on frequent expressions of this type that you should find particularly useful.

4.1 Greetings

- Greeting someone who you have not seen in a very long time

  A: 오래간만입니다. 그동안 안녕하셨어요?
  B: 정말 오랜만이네요. 이게 얼마만이에요? 별일 없으시죠?
  A: 네, 별일 없어요. 다 잘 지내요. 근데, 요즘 어떠세요?
  B: 그럭저럭, 늘 그렇죠, 뭐.

    A: It's been a long time. How have you been?
    B: It's really been a long time. How long has it been? Is everything okay with you?
    A: Yes, everything's fine. We're doing well. How about you?
    B: It's alright, the same as always, I guess.

  A: 야, 오랜만이다. 그동안 어떻게 지냈어? 여자친구랑은 잘 돼가니?
  B: 잘 돼가긴. 벌써 깨진 지가 언젠데. 너는 요즘 어때?

    A: Wow, long time no see. How have you been? Is everything going well with your girlfriend?
    B: Going well, what are you talking about? We broke up a long time ago. How are YOU doing?

- Upon entering unfamiliar places

실례합니다. 실례하겠습니다.	*Excuse me.*
실례좀 해도 되겠습니까?	*Excuse me. Can I come in?*
저, 계십니까? 아무도 안 계세요?	*Hello, are you there? Is no one inside?*

- Upon returning to your home

학교/회사 다녀왔습니다.	*I'm home (from school/work).*
저 왔어요.	*I'm home. (or I'm here.)*

- Welcoming someone

어서 오세요.　　(in general)

오셨어요?　　(to a familiar person)

이제 오세요?　　(to someone you are expecting)

4.2 Leave-taking

- Upon leaving for school or work

A: 아빠 회사 갔다 올게.　　*Bye, Daddy is going to the office to work.*

B: 아빠, 안녕히 다녀오세요.　　*Bye, Daddy, have a good day.*

A: 학교 다녀오겠습니다.　　*Bye, I'm going to school.*

B: 그래, 잘 다녀와/갔다 와.　　*Okay, bye, have a good day.*

- Saying good-bye

A: 오늘 즐거웠습니다. 저 그럼... (가보겠습니다).

B: 조심해 가세요, 내일 회사에서 뵈어요.

A: 네, 들어가세요.

　A: I had fun today. Well, then...(I'll get going).
　B: Goodbye. I'll see you tomorrow in the office.
　A: Okay. Bye.

A: 시간이 벌써 이렇게 됐네요. 저 먼저 실례해야겠습니다.

　말씀들 나누세요.

B: 벌써 일어나시려고요? 좀 더 있다 가시지.

A: 집에 일이 좀 있어서요. 죄송합니다.

B: 그럼 살펴 가세요. 안 나갈게요.

　A: Wow, it's already this late. I think I'll have to be excused first.
　　Enjoy your chatting.
　B: You are going to leave this early? Why don't you stay a bit longer?
　A: I have something to take care of at home. I'm sorry.
　B: Alright, then, goodbye. Let me just see you off here.

A: 장인어른, 말씀 도중에 죄송한데요, 저 그만 가 봐야겠습니다.

B: 그래, 김서방, 그럼 가 봐. 운전 조심하고.

　A: Father-in-law, I'm sorry to interrupt but I think I'll have to get going.
　B: Okay, my son-in-law, go ahead and leave. Be careful with driving.

A: 연규야, 나 간다.   *Yeon-gyu, I'll be going.*

B: 응, 가. 또 보자. 연락할게.   *Okay, bye. See you again. I'll be in touch.*

- Talking to people who are sick

폭 쉬어.   *Get plenty of rest.*

몸조리 잘 하세요.   *Take good care of your health.*

빨리 낫기/나으시기 바래요.   *I hope you'll recover soon.*

속히 쾌유하시기 바랍니다.   *I wish you a speedy recovery.* [formal/written]

4.3　Expressing and responding to gratitude

- In formal speech or writing

대단히 감사합니다.   *Thank you very much.*

다시 한 번 감사드립니다.   *Thank you again.*

진심으로 감사드립니다.   *Thank you from the bottom of my heart.*

깊이 감사드리는 바입니다.   *I'd like to express my deep gratitude.*

- Expressing overwhelming gratitude

A: 너무너무 고맙습니다. 뭐라고 감사의 말씀을 드려야 할지
　　모르겠습니다. 이 신세를 어떻게 갚아야 할지 모르겠네요.

B: 별말씀을요.

　　A: Thank you so much. I don't know how I can thank you enough. I owe you
　　　so much that I don't know how I will ever repay you.
　　B: Don't mention it.

A: 그런데, 보수가 너무 적어서...

B: 별말씀을요. 이렇게 기회를 주신 것만 해도 황송하죠. 선생님하고
　　같이 일하게 된 것만 해도 감지덕지로 생각합니다.

　　A: But the compensation is so little…
　　B: Not at all. I'm grateful even just for the fact that you gave me this
　　　opportunity. I'm very thankful just to be able to work with you, sir.

- Gift giving and taking

A: 보내주신 선물 잘 받았어요. 잘 쓸게요.

B: 마음에 드셨으면 좋겠네요.

　　A: Thank you for the gift you sent me. I'll make good use of it.
　　B: I hope you like it.

A: 선물 감사합니다. 예쁘게 입을게요.

B: 마음에 들지 모르겠다.

A: 마음에 쏙 들어요. 고마워요.

B: 고맙긴.

> A: Thank you for the gift. I'll enjoy wearing it.
> B: I don't know whether you like it.
> A: I love it. Thank you.
> B: You're welcome.

A: 그냥 오셔도 되는데 뭘 이런 걸 갖고 오셨어요? 비쌀텐데,
　너무 과용하신 거 아니에요?

B: 별거 아니에요. 약소해요.

> A: You didn't have to do this; why did you bring this? It must be expensive,
>   I hope you didn't spend too much.
> B: It's nothing much. It's something small.

A: 이거 받아도 되는 건지 모르겠네요.

B: 뭘요. 부담갖지 말고 받으세요.

> A: I wonder whether I should accept this.
> B: It's nothing. Don't worry, just take it.

- After being treated to a meal

A: 잘 먹었습니다. 그런데, 미안해서 어쩌지요? 번번이 이렇게 신세를...

B: 아니에요. 신세는요?

> A: Thank you for the meal. But I feel bad. I keep imposing on you...
> B: Not at all. Imposing, what are you talking about?

A: 오늘 신세 많이 졌습니다. 폐만 끼치고 가네요.

B: 별말씀을요. 종종 놀러 오세요.

> A: Thank you for your hospitality; I owe you. I guess I was a bother.
> B: Don't mention it. Please come over often.

A: 고마워. 근데 출혈이 너무 큰 거 아니니?

B: 고맙긴. 그 정도야, 약소하지.

> A: Thanks. I hope you didn't go over your budget.
> B: No problem. That's nothing much.

- Routine thanking (e.g., at a store)

'네' is most appropriate in response to a ritualistic expressions of thanks, between a store clerk (점원) and a customer (손님), for instance.

A: 커피 여기 있습니다. 감사합니다.   *Here's your coffee. Thanks.*
B: 네.   *Sure.*
A: 안녕히 가세요. 또 오세요.   *Bye. Come again.*

NOTE: 천만에요 is a literal translation of English 'You're welcome,' and is used mainly by Koreans living in English-speaking countries. It is rarely used in this way in Korea.

- Responding to compliments

A: 정말 잘 하시네요.   *You're so good at it.*
B: 잘 하긴요. 별로예요.   *I'm not really good. I'm just okay.*

A: 이 과장 훌륭했어. 정말 대단한 능력이야.
B: 아이 뭘요. 과찬이십니다.

   A: Mr. Lee, you've done a fantastic job. Your abilities are truly amazing.
   B: Not at all. You're too kind.

4.4 Apologies and regrets

- Serious and formal apologies

대단히 죄송합니다.   *I'm truly sorry.*
드릴 말씀이 없습니다.   *I'm so sorry that I don't know what to say.*
사죄드립니다.   *I apologize. (I beg your forgiveness.)*
심려를 끼쳐드려 송구스럽습니다.   *I'm terribly sorry that I caused you concern.*
면목이 없습니다.   *I'm so sorry that I cannot face you.*

- A: 죄송합니다. 제 잘못입니다. 다시는 그런 일이 없도록 하겠습니다.
  B: 아니에요. 괜찮아요. 신경 쓰지 마세요.

   A: I'm sorry. It's my fault. I will make sure it won't happen again.
   B: No, it's okay. No need to worry.

  A: 엄마, 잘못했어요. 다시는 안 그럴 게요.
  B: 이번 한 번만 용서해 줄테니까 다음부터는 조심해야 된다.

   A: Mom, I'm sorry. I'll never do that again.
   B: I'll forgive you just this once so you must be careful from next time.

  A: 죄송합니다. 사과드립니다.
  B: 사과는요? 아무 일도 아닌 걸 갖고. 걱정 마세요.

   A: I'm very sorry. Please accept my apology.
   B: Apology, for what? Over nothing. Don't worry.

A: 미안하게 됐습니다.

B: 미안하다니요? 제가 오히려 더 미안하죠.

   A: I'm so sorry.
   B: Not at all. It's actually me who should be sorry.

A: 어제는 미안했어요. 사과할게요.

B: 무슨 말씀을요? 미안할 것도 많네요. 사실 미안한 건 나지요.

   A: I'm sorry about yesterday. I apologize.
   B: What are you talking about? There was nothing to be sorry for.
     Actually, I'm the one who should be sorry.

A: 쏘리!	*Sorry.*
B: 미안하다면 다야?	*Do you think sorry is enough?*
A: 사정이 있었어.	*I had some unavoidable circumstances.*
한 번만 봐 주라.	*Cut me some slack, please.*
B: 됐어, 뭐 그럴 수도 있지.	*Alright. It could happen, I guess.*

NOTE: 쏘리, borrowed from English, is the lightest apology and can be used only to someone with whom one is on 반말 terms.

- Expressing regret in a formal setting

  이번 사건에 대해 유감스럽게 생각합니다.
     We are truly sorry about the recent incident.

  양국 간에 불미스러운 일이 생긴 것을 유감으로 생각하는 바입니다.
     We regret that an unfortunate incident has occurred between the two countries.

4.5 'Excuse me but...'

> **The difference between 죄송(/미안)합니다 and 실례합니다**
>
> The literal translation of these two expressions can be misleading because either can correspond to English 'excuse me.' In such cases, 죄송합니다 offers a thankful way to start asking for a favor; it is not really an apology. In contrast, 실례합니다 is restricted to the following three cases: (1) asking a personal question, (2) calling for attention when entering someone else's place, or (3) addressing a stranger – all of which involve making an unwarranted imposition. In its third use, 실례합니다 can be replaced by 죄송합니다 if it is to ask for a favor, such as directions. (미안합니다 instead of 죄송합니다 is used to a person you don't know well, but is younger than you are.)

실례지만 결혼하셨어요?
   Excuse me, but are you married?

저 실례합니다, 안에 누구 계세요?
   Excuse me, is someone in?

실례지만/죄송하지만 전철역으로 가는 길 좀 가르쳐 주시겠습니까?
   Excuse me, but could you tell me how I can get to the subway station?

실례합니다/죄송합니다, 여기 자리 있나요?
   Excuse me, is this seat taken?

죄송하지만 제 가방 좀 잠깐 봐 주시겠어요?
   Excuse me, but could you watch my bag for a minute?

미안하지만 내일 모임장소가 어딘지 좀 알아봐 줄래요?
   I'm sorry, but can you find out for me where our meeting place is tomorrow?

4.6 Expressing condolences and encouragement

- Expressing condolences in formal speech or writing

애도의 뜻을 표합니다.	*Please accept my sincere condolences.*
삼가 조의를 표합니다.	*I express my deepest condolences.*
삼가 고인의 명복을 빕니다.	*I pray that his soul will be blessed.*

- Expressing condolences in person

얼마나 상심이 크세요. 뭐라고 위로의 말씀을 드려야 할지…
   You must be very sad. I can't find the words to console you…

충격이 크셨지요. 많이 힘드시죠?
   You must have been very shocked. It must be very hard on you.

제가 도움이 될 일 있으면 언제든지 말씀해 주세요
   Please let me know anytime if there is any way I can be of help.

NOTE: A sympathetic look or silence might be all you can offer under some
circumstances. In any event, 죄송(/미안)합니다 is to be avoided as it is not
equivalent to English 'sorry' in this situation. 죄송(/미안)합니다 can be used only
to apologize or to thank for a favor, not to express condolences.

- Encouragement

A: 새로 시작하는 사업이 잘 돼야 할텐데, 걱정이에요.
B: 너무 걱정하지 마세요. 잘 되실 거예요.
   A: I'm worried about the new business that we are undertaking. It's got to work out.
   B: Don't worry too much. It'll be fine.

A: 이번에 중간 고사를 완전히 죽 쒔어.
B: 괜찮아. 다음에 기말고사를 더 잘 보면 되지. 힘내.
   A: I completely messed up on the mid-term exam this time.
   B: That's okay. You can make up for it on the final exam. Cheer up.

A: 직장도 잘리고 여자친구한테도 차이고 요즘 같아선 정말
   살맛이 안 난다.
B: 용기를 내세요. 쨍하고 해뜰 날 반드시 올 거예요.

A: *I got laid off from work and got dumped by my girlfriend. If it's like this every day, I really have no desire to live.*
B: *Cheer up. After it rains, the sun will surely come out.*

4.7 Extending an invitation or making an offer

* Treating someone to a meal
  A: 교수님, 식사대접을 한 번 하고 싶은데 시간 괜찮으세요?
  B: 시간은 괜찮은데 학생이 무슨 돈이 있다고?
  > A: *Professor, I'd like to invite you to a meal. Would you have time for it?*
  > B: *My time is okay, but how can a student have the money?*

  A: 시간들 괜찮으시면 이번 금요일 저녁에 제가 한턱 내겠습니다.
  B: 야, 우리 과장님 최고다! 감사합니다.
  > A: *If you are available this Friday evening, I'll treat you to a nice dinner.*
  > B: *Wow, what a great manager! Thank you.*

  A: 오늘 저녁은 내가 쏠게. 뭐 먹고 싶은 거 있으면 말해.
  B: 저녁을 쏜다고? 흠...갑자기 랍스터가 땡기는데.
  > A: *Tonight's dinner is on me. Let me know if there's anything you want to eat.*
  > B: *You're paying? Hmm... suddenly I'm hungry for lobster.*

* At a person's house
  A: 차린 건 없지만 많이 드세요. 입맛에 맞으실지 모르겠네요.
  B: 맛있어 보이는데요. 잘 먹겠습니다.
  > A: *There's not much, but help yourself. I hope the food will be to your taste.*
  > B: *Everything looks delicious. Thank you, I'll enjoy it.*

4.8 Telephone expressions

* Asking who is calling
  실례지만 어디세요/ 누구세요?   *May I ask who's calling?*
  어디라고/누구시라고 전해 드릴까요? *Who may I tell him is calling?*
* Transferring a phone call
  전화 바꿔 드리겠습니다.   *I will put him on the phone.*
  전화 돌려/연결해 드리겠습니다.   *I will put you through (to the number).*
  잠시만 기다리세요.
  (잠시만 is formal-sounding compared to 잠깐만.)
* Answering a phone call which has been transferred to you
  전화 바꿨습니다.

- Taking/leaving messages

  메시지 전해 드릴까요? or 전할 말씀 있으세요?
  May I take a message? or *Would you like to leave a message?*

  그냥 전화 왔었다고 전해 주세요.
  Just tell him that I called.

  나중에 다시 걸겠다고 전해 주십시오.
  Please tell her that I will call again later.

  들어오면 저한테 전화 좀 해 달라고 전해 주시겠어요?
  Would you tell him to call me when he gets back?

- Saying 'bye'

  들어가세요. or 안녕히 계세요.
  들어가. or 안녕.
  끊어요.
  끊어. or 끊을게.

- Automated calling instructions

  카드의 비밀번호와 우물 '정'자 키를 눌러 주시기 바랍니다.
  Press your PIN number followed by the pound sign (key).

  NOTE: The pound sign resembles the Chinese character 井 ('정').

  통화를 원하시는 전화번호를 눌러 주십시오.
  Enter the phone number that you wish to call.

  국제통화를 원하시면 국가번호, 지역번호, 상대방 전화순으로
  입력하십시오.
  If you want to make an international call, enter the country code, then the area code, followed by the phone number you wish to call.

  통화 가능 시간은 한시간 십분입니다.
  You have 1 hour and 10 minutes of calling time.

  지금 거신 번호는 없는 번호이니 확인 후 다시 걸어 주시기 바랍니다.
  The number you dialed is not in service. Please check the number and dial again.

  지금은 전화를 받을 수 없어 소리샘으로 연결됩니다.
  The person at this number is not available, so you will be connected to the answering machine.

4.9 Congratulations and good wishes

- In formal speech or writing

희망찬 새해를 맞아 뜻하시는 일 모두 이루시기 바랍니다.
I hope all your wishes for the New Year will come true.

근심없고 평화로운 한 해가 되기를 기원합니다.
I wish you a happy New Year, free of worries and filled with peace.

좋은 일 많이 생기는 새해 맞이하기 바랍니다.
I wish you a happy New Year with lots of good news.

즐거운 성탄절이 되기를…
Wishing you a Merry Christmas…

결혼을 진심으로 축하합니다. 행복하세요!
Congratulations on your wedding. May your marriage be full of happiness!

아기의 탄생을 축하드립니다.
Congratulations on the birth of your new baby.

득남을/득녀를 축하드립니다.
Congratulations on your new baby boy/girl.

- Either in cards or in person

졸업을 축하합니다.   *Congratulations on your graduation.*

합격을 축하해요.   *Congratulations on passing the exam.*

건강하세요.   *Take care.*

크리스마스/추석 잘 보내세요.   *Have a good Christmas/Ch'usŏk.*

새해 복 많이 받으세요/받으십시오.   *Happy New Year.*

5 Conversational bridges

Conversations don't consist just of complete sentences. Speakers need ways to link their utterances, to indicate surprise, to get people's attention, and so forth. The appropriate use of these 'bridges' makes for more authentic and natural-sounding speech and contributes to smoother communication.

5.1 Fillers

Fillers provide a way to hesitate without 'losing the floor' during a conversation. They give speakers a chance to clear their throat, to politely get people's attention when beginning an utterance, or to think of the right word.

- 그러니까, 그러니깐 'so; let's see'

  내일 퀴즈 보는 날인데...그러니까, 결석을 하겠다 이 말인가?
    Tomorrow is our quiz day...so, are you saying that you will be absent from class?

  영주가 지난 주에 교통 사고를 당했어. 그러니깐 비가 많이 온
  수요일이었나 봐.
    Youngjoo got into a car accident last week. Let's see, I think it was Wednesday, when it rained a lot.

- 그럼 'well; then'

  그럼 또 연락하자.　　　　　　　*Well, let's get in touch again.*

  그럼 먼저 가 보겠습니다.　　　　*Well, excuse me, I will get going first.*

- (그) 왜...지(요)/잖아(요) 'you know,...'

  사진 이메일로 보내줄까? 아니면..그 왜... 요즘 유행하는 거 있지?
  블로그인가 뭔가 하는 거. 거기다 올릴까?
    Shall I send you photos by e-mail? Or you know, the thing that is popular these days? Blog or something. Shall I upload the photos there?

- 그래 'so...' (to introduce a question)

  그래, 요즘 어떻게 지내?　　　　*So, how are you doing these days?*

  그래, 언제 떠날 생각이야?　　　*So, when are you going to leave?*

- 글쎄(요) 'well; let's see'

  A: 이번에 새로 오신 과장님은 어떠세요?

  B: 글쎄요, 사람을 굉장히 편하게 대해 주시는 분 같아요.

    A: What's your new section chief like?
    B: Well, it seems like he makes people very comfortable.

- 뭐 'well; you know'

  A: 차 있는데 중고차를 또 샀어?

  B: 뭐, 내가 쓰려고 산 것이 아니라 동생 주려고.

    A: You bought a used car again even though you already have a car?
    B: Well, it was not for me to use but to give to my younger sister.

  A: 요새 자꾸 살이 쪄서 고민이에요.

  B: 날씬하신데요, 뭐.

    A: It bothers me that I keep gaining weight these days.
    B: You're slender, I think.

- 뭐예요/뭐야 'you know'

  가족여행을 간다 간다 하면서 한번도 못 갔지 뭐예요.

    We've been planning on our family trip, saying 'we're going, we're going,'
    but haven't made it even once, you know.

  친구 생일을 깜빡했지 뭐야.

    My friend's birthday slipped my mind, you know.

- 뭐라 그럴까(요) 'How shall I put it?'

  영화가 제작비는 많이 들여서 볼거리는 많지만, 뭐라 그럴까, 내용은 없다고나 할까…

    The movie offers a lot to see, thanks to the high production cost, but how shall I put it, shall I say that it lacks substance…

- 그게 뭐더라, 그게 뭐지(요) 'What do you call it?'

  A: 우리 이번에 피서 가서 뭐 할까?

  B: 하이킹도 하고 또 그게 뭐지, 바다 속에 들어가서 물고기 구경하는 거. 스노클링인가?

    A: What shall we do when we go on summer vacation this time?
    B: Let's do hiking and also what do you call it when we go into the ocean and watch the fish. Is it snorkeling?

- 어…, 에…, 음 'uh…'

  부탁이 있는데요, 어…, 돈 좀 빌려 줄 수 있어요?

    I have a favor to ask of you, uh…can you lend me some money?

- 어디 'well; now; let me see'

  어디 한 번 먹어 볼까?   *Well, shall I try it (the food)?*

  어디 누가 더 잘 하나 보자.   *Now, let's see who's doing it better.*

- 자 'well; here; here you are'

  자 이제 시작할까요?   *Well, shall we begin?*

  자 식기 전에 듭시다.   *Here, let's eat before it gets cold.*

- 저... 'well; excuse me'

  저 혹시 진호 아버님 아니세요?

    Excuse me, are you Jinho's father by any chance?

- 있지(요), 있잖아(요) 'well; excuse me'

  언니, 있지, 언니가 새로 산 옷 내일 좀 빌려 줄래?

    Sis, well, can I borrow your new clothes tomorrow?

  형, 있잖아요, 지난 번 형이 부탁한 일 다 못 끝냈는데, 시간 좀 더 줄 수 있어요?

    Brother, well, I haven't finished the work that you asked me to do.
    Can you give me some more time?

- 저기(요), 저기 있잖아(요) 'well; excuse me'

  저기 있잖아요, 내일 바쁘지 않으면 차 한 잔 하실래요?

    Well, if you're not busy tomorrow, would you like to have a cup of tea with me?

  저기...혹시 한국분이세요?

    Excuse me, are you Korean by any chance?

- 저기 말이에요/말이야 'you see, you know,...'

  엄마, 저기 말이에요, 제가 용돈이 다 떨어져 가거든요.

    Mom, you know, I'm running out of spending money.

5.2 Transition expressions

The following expressions are used in speaking or writing, particularly when there is a need to indicate a 'logical' relation between one sentence and another, to change the subject, or to mark a contrast.

- According to rumor

  소문에 의하면 이 작품은 한국영화 사상 최고의 코미디영화라고 한다.

    According to rumor, this movie is the best comedy in Korean movie history.

- Against one's will

  생일 모임을 조촐하게 가지려고 했는데 **본의 아니게** 규모가 커졌어요.

    I was planning on a small birthday party, but against my will it became large.

- As I said

앞서 **말씀드렸듯이**, 양국 정상 회담이 내일 열릴 예정입니다.
  As I said earlier, bilateral summit talks are scheduled for tomorrow.

아까 **말했다시피**, 나는 이번 투표에 참여하지 않을거야.
  As I said earlier, I'm not going to participate in the voting process this time.

- As you know; as is known

아시다시피 공부만 잘 한다고 성공하는 건 아니잖아요?
  As you know, doing well in school does not guarantee success.

주지하는 바와 같이 베토벤 교향곡 5 번은 '운명'이라는 명칭으로
널리 알려져 있다. [written/formal]
  As is generally known, Beethoven's symphony no. 5 is named 'Fate.'

- As you mentioned

그 친구를 어제 우연히 만났어. **네 말마따나** 성격이 아주 호탕하더라.
  *I met that friend yesterday by chance. As you mentioned, he is very manly
  and big-hearted.*

- At any rate; anyway; no matter what

시험에 합격했으면 좋았을 텐데. **어쨌든**, 결과를 알게 돼서 속이 시원해.
  *It would have been nice if I passed the test. At any rate, knowing the result makes
  me feel less burdened.*

그 친구는 **좌우간** 못하는 게 없어요.
  No matter what, there's nothing that person cannot do.

되든 안되든 **아무튼** 해 보자.
  Whether it works or not, let's try it, anyway.

열심히 훈련해서 뭐 해? **어차피** 경기에 나갈 선수들은 정해져 있는데.
  *What's the point of training hard? The competing players have already been
  designated anyway.*

- By the way

혜수가 이번 여름에 결혼했어? **그건 그렇고**, 너는 이번 여름에 뭐 했어?
  Hyesu got married this summer? By the way, what did you do this summer?

- Consequently

그 공장은 오랫동안 사용되지 않았다. **따라서/그 결과** 지금은 그 내부가
거의 다 파손되었다. [written/formal]
  *That factory was not used for a long time. Consequently, the interior is now
  almost entirely dilapidated.*

- For example

견과류라함은, **예컨대**, 밤, 은행, 호두, 잣 등을 말한다. [written/formal]
  *The so-called 'nut class' includes, for example, chestnuts, gingko nuts,
  walnuts, pine nuts, etc.*

운동을 좀 해 보세요. **예를 들어(서)** 조깅이나 수영같은 거요.
Try some exercise. Like jogging or swimming, for example.

- Frankly speaking

솔직히 말씀드리자면, 제가 좀 서운했었어요.
Frankly speaking, I was a little disappointed.

(툭) 까 놓고 말해서, 너는 너무 남에 대한 배려가 없어, 자식아.
Frankly speaking, you're really not considerate of others, dude. [familiar/casual]

- Furthermore

미스터 박은 이 프로젝트를 하기에는 너무 경험이 없고 **더욱이/ 더구나/ 더군다나** 추진력도 없습니다.
Mr. Park is too inexperienced and furthermore not very motivated for this project.

그 호텔은 서비스도 좋지 않고 **게다가** 청결하지도 않아요.
That hotel has bad service, and furthermore is not clean.

- In contrast

최신형 국산 디지털 카메라는 4 GB 메모리를 인식할 수 있습니다.
반면(에) 외국 제품들은 이러한 메모리에 대한 대처가 뒤떨어집니다.
The latest Korean-made digital camera can take a 4 GB memory card. In contrast, foreign products are behind in dealing with memory.

- Indeed; really

이번 사고는 **참으로/실로** 개탄스러운 일이 아닐 수 없습니다.
This accident is indeed deplorable. [written/formal]

그 사람은 **정말** 인간성이 좋아.
That person has a really good personality.

흉작 탓에 과일 값이 **그야말로** 금값이에요.
Because of a bad harvest, the price of fruit is really like the price of gold.

- In fact

무뚝뚝해 보이지만 **실은/사실** 아주 자상한 사람이야.
He appears to be brusque, but in fact, he's a very thoughtful person.

먼저 3 승을 거둔 우리팀은 **사실상** 본선 진출이 확정됐습니다.
Being the first team to have three wins, our team has in fact been guaranteed to advance to the championship game.

이 케이크, 고마워요. **안 그래도/그렇지 않아도** 단 게 먹고 싶었는데.
Thanks for this cake. In fact, I wanted to eat something sweet.

- In my opinion

제 생각에는 이번 상반기에 물가가 상승할 것 같습니다
In my opinion, it seems like prices will increase in the first half of the year.

내가 보기엔 집 값이 특히 많이 오를 것 같아.
In my opinion, it seems that especially home prices will increase a lot.

- In short

한마디로 말해서 건강 유지에는 스트레스 관리가 가장 중요하다.
In short, managing stress is the most important thing for your health.

대통령이 바뀐 후에도 큰 변화는 일어나지 않았다. 요는/요컨대 대통령
한 사람이 바꿀 수 있는 부분이 그렇게 많지는 않다는 것이다.
*There weren't any major changes after the change in presidents. In short,
this means that there isn't much that a president can change. [written/formal]*

- In some respects

독신으로 사는 것이 때론 외롭고 힘들지만, 어떤 면에서는/어떻게 보면
좋은 점도 많이 있어요.
*Living as a single person is sometimes lonely and tough; however, in some respects
there are many advantages as well.*

- In spite of that; even so; nevertheless

올해 우리 회사의 판매량은 감소했습니다. 그럼에도 불구하고, 타
회사와의 경쟁에 있어 여전히 우위를 차지하고 있습니다. [written/formal]
*This year, our company's sales decreased. In spite of that, in terms of
competition with other companies, we still have the upper hand.*

그 사람이 너한테 무례하게 행동하긴 했지. 그래도/그렇다 하더라도/
그렇다손 치더라도, 네가 좀 넓은 마음으로 이해해라.
*I understand that person was indeed rude to you. Even so, try to be
understanding and open-minded.*

네가 바쁜 건 아는데, (아무리) 그래도 그렇지 어떻게 엄마 생신을
잊을 수가 있니?
I know you're busy, but nevertheless how can you forget your mother's birthday?

- In the end; finally

지난 2 년간 다양한 홍보활동을 통해 이 제품에 대한 인지도를 높여
나갔습니다. 결과적으로 올해 매출은 2 억달러나 되었습니다.
*For the last two years, various public relations efforts raised the popularity
of the product. In the end, we had 200 million dollars in sales this year.*

후반 2 분을 남기고 우리 팀은 총공격을 펼쳤습니다. 결국/ 마침내
종료 직전 극적인 동점골이 터졌습니다.
*With 2 minutes left in the second half, our team made an offensive strike. Finally,
right before the end of the game, the tying goal was scored.*

- In other words; that is to say; so-called

그 친구는 아주 박식해. **이를테면/말하자면** 걸어다니는 백과사전이야.

  That person is very knowledgeable. In other words, he is a walking encyclopedia.

누군가에게 큰 역할이 주어진다는 것은, **곧/즉** 해야할 일이 많아진다는
의미이기도 하다. [written/formal]

  *The fact that someone is given a lot of responsibilities means (is to say) that there
  will also be an increased workload for him/her.*

박모씨는 가짜 명품, **이른바/소위** '짝퉁' 제품을 판 혐의로 구속
되었습니다. (이른바: [written/formal])

  Mr. Park was arrested for selling imitation name brands, the so-called, 'tchakt'ung.'

- No wonder; as expected; sure enough

아침에 그렇게 게으름 피우더니 **아니나 다를까**, 지각 했지. 뻔해.

  *After being that lazy in the morning, no wonder you were late. It was
  totally predictable.*

대한민국 축구 선수들 **역시** 막강한데요.

  South Korean soccer players are strong, just as expected.

우리가 반드시 승리할 줄 알았어, **그럼 그렇지**.

  I knew we were sure to win, and sure enough...

- Now that I think of it

A: 사과를 하루에 한 개씩 먹는 것이 몸에 좋대요.
B: **그러고 보니까** 내가 오늘 사과를 안 먹었네!

  A: They say that eating an apple once a day is good for your health.
  B: Now that I think of it, I didn't eat an apple today!

- On the one hand...on the other hand

오랫동안 준비해 오던 박사학위 논문을 끝마치게 돼서 **한편(으로는)**
굉장히 기쁘지만 **또 한편(으로는)** 많이 아쉽습니다.

  *On the one hand, I'm happy now that the dissertation I've been working on for a
  long time is finished; but on the other hand, I feel that I could have done better.*

- Otherwise

양측이 우호적으로 협상을 벌인다면 문제를 조속히 해결할 수 있다.
그렇지 않으면, 이 분쟁은 장기간 지속될 것이다.

  *If the two parties jointly engage in friendly negotiations, then problems can be
  quickly solved. Otherwise, the dispute will continue for a long time.*

- Rather; on the contrary

모자를 쓰는 것 자체가 탈모를 유발하지는 않는다. **오히려** 여름에는
모자가 강렬한 자외선으로부터 머리를 보호해 준다.

Wearing hats in and of itself does not cause hair loss. On the contrary,
in the summer, hats protect the head from UV rays.

칭찬은커녕 **도리어** 야단만 맞았어요.

Rather than praise, I just received punishment.

- Speaking of which

  A: 요즘 회사 사정이 많이 안 좋아지고 있다지?

  B: **말이 나왔으니까 말인데**, 잘하면 무더기로 명퇴를 당할지도 모른대.

    A: I hear that our company situation is getting very bad these days, is that right?
    B: Speaking of which, I heard that if we are unlucky, we may be faced with a call
       for massive 'voluntary' retirements.

- That's why; so

  A: 배가 고파서 이것저것 막 먹었더니 배가 아프네.

  B: **그러게** 내가 뭐라 그랬어? 조금만 먹으라고 했잖아.

    A: I was hungry, so I ate anything I could get my hands on
       and now my stomach hurts.
    B: So what did I say? I told you to just eat a little.

- Therefore

  어제 또 늦게 잤구나. **그러니까** 늘 아침에 일찍 못 일어나지.

    I bet you went to bed late again last night. That's why you can never
    get up early in the morning.

  그 당시 나는 성격이 매우 외향적이었다. **그래서** 내 주변에는 늘 많은
  친구들이 있었다.

    At that time, my personality was very outgoing. Therefore, I always had many
    friends around me.

  인간은 말을 할 수 있다. **그러므로/고로** 동물과 구별된다. [written/formal]

    Humans can speak. Therefore, they can be distinguished from animals.

- Too; also

  형이 공부를 잘 하더니 동생도 **역시** 잘 한다.

    The older brother did well in school, and the younger brother is doing well too.

  태풍으로 뱃길이 모두 끊기고 국내선 여객기 운항 **또한** 중단됐습니다.
  [written/formal]

    A typhoon caused sea routes to be closed and also domestic flights to be cancelled.

- Perhaps; maybe; in all likelihood

  아마 네가 이 프로젝트를 맡았어도 잘 했을 거야.

    Perhaps, if you had taken on this project, you would have done just as well.

  어쩌면 이번 겨울에 한국에 출장 갈지 모릅니다.

    I may go to Korea on a business trip this winter.

이 시력교정수술이 **혹시** 부작용을 낳을지는 좀 더 지켜 볼 일입니다.
It remains to be seen whether there will be side effects from the LASIK surgery.

모르면 몰라도 그 친구는 적어도 남을 속이지는 않을 거야.
In all likelihood, that person will not deceive other people at least.

5.3 Interjections

Interjections are typical of the spoken language, and are most common in more casual speech. As in English, their appropriateness varies with the speaker's personality and with the setting.

- Go! (when cheering someone or a team)

    우리 팀, **화이팅**!   *Go team, go!*

    힘내자, **아자아자 화이팅**!   *Cheer up, let's fight!*

- Cheers! (when making a toast)

    건배   *Bottoms up.*

    원샷 <one shot>   *Bottoms up.*

    위하여   *Cheers; To (our health, etc.)*

- Hurrah

    (우)와 /만세, 우리가 이겼다!   *Hurrah, we've won!*

- Go to hell

    염병할, 얼어 죽을, 빌어 먹을

- No way

    설마, 그럴리가.   *No way, it cannot be true.*

- Oh; oh by the way

    아, 알았다.   *Oh, I see.*

    참, 오늘 모임이 몇 시지요?   *Oh, what time is our meeting today?*

- Oh dear; oh boy; oh no

    아참/아차, 깜박 잊고 지갑을 안 갖고 나왔네.
    Oh dear, I forgot to bring my purse.

    이런, 가스불을 끄고 나온다는 게.
    Oh no, I should have turned off the gas before coming out.

    어휴, 답답해. 수십번 설명을 해도 이해를 못하니.
    Oh boy, how frustrating. You just don't get it no matter how many times I explain.

    어이 정말, 약속을 해 놓고 안 나타나면 어떡해!
    Oh boy, how can he not show up after having made an appointment!

저런, 어린 것이 일 하면서 공부하느라 얼마나 힘들까?
Oh dear, how tough it must be for a little child to study while working.

어떡해, 저렇게 어린 나이에 부모님이 돌아가셔서...
Oh no, to lose parents at such a young age...

어머(나), 불쌍해라. [feminine]
Oh no, how sad, I feel so sorry for them.

에그, 딱하기도 하지.
Oh no, how sad, I feel so sorry for them.

- Oh fuck; damn it

제기랄, 불법 주차 딱지를 또 받았네.
Oh fuck, I got another parking ticket.

젠장, 오늘은 왜 이렇게 되는 일이 없지?
Damn it, how come nothing's going well today?

- Oh my (goodness); oh my god

아이고, 이게 누구야? 어서 오세요.
Oh my goodness, who is this? Welcome.

어머(나), 반가워라. 이게 웬일이야? [feminine]
Oh my goodness, I'm so glad to see you. What brought you here?

아니, 또 늦었어?
Oh my god, you're late again?

어? 대문이 열려 있네! 나갈 때 분명히 잠갔는데.
Oh my god, the door is open! I swear I locked it when I went out.

- Jesus Christ

(원) 세상에, 이런 해괴한 일을 봤나.
Jesus Christ, I've never seen such a weird thing.

(하느님) 맙소사, 새치가 이렇게 많이 나다니...
Oh lord, so much gray hair...

내 원 참 기가 막혀, 자기가 잘못해 놓고 누구한테 큰 소리야?
Jesus Christ, how can he be yelling at me when he is the one at fault?

- Oops

아이고, 미안해요. 새로 산 가방에 커피를 쏟아서...
Oops, I'm so sorry. I poured coffee on your new purse...

엄마(야)! 넘어질 뻔했네. [feminine]
Oops, I almost tripped.

- Ouch

아야! 밥에 돌이 있네.   *Ouch! There's a rock in the rice.*

아이쿠, 아퍼!   *Ouch, it hurts!*

- Ta-dah

  짠! 찾았다.   *Ta-dah! I found it.*

  짠, 기대하시라.   *Ta-dah, guess what you are going to see.*

- What a bastard/bitch

  망할 놈/년, 미친 놈/년, 못된 놈/년

- What the heck; I don't care

  될 대로 되라지, **까짓것.**   *Que sera sera, what the heck.*

  에라, 모르겠다. 내일 하지 뭐.   *What the heck, I don't care. I will do it*
  tomorrow, I guess.

- Whew; phew

  아휴, 이제 살았다!   *Whew, I survived!*

  휴우, 십 년 감수했네.   *Phew, I got so scared that I lost 10 years*
  of my life.

- Wow, yeah

  야 신난다, 드디어 방학이다!   *Wow, exciting, it's a vacation at last!*

  와, 번지점프 정말 재미있다.   *Wow, isn't the bungee jump fun?*

  어쩜, 너무 멋있다!   *Wow, how cool! [feminine]*

  아싸, 또 이겼네.   *Yeah, I won again.*

- Yikes

  으, 징그러.   *Yikes, it's gross.*

Here are some additional examples expressing emotion or a strong reaction.

흥, 지가 잘났으면 얼마나 잘났어?
  Give me a break – who does he think he is?

체/치/피, 웃기고 있어 정말.
  Shhhh – give me a break.

애걔, 겨우 천원을 주세요?
  So little – are you giving me just ₩1,000?

아쭈, 겁도 없이 나한테 대들어 보겠다는 거야?
  How dare you – are you starting a fight with me?

얼씨구, 놀고 있네.
  Look at you – how ridiculous!

에이, 이런 대우를 받느니 차라리 그만두는 게 낫겠다.
  Gee – it would be better to quit than be treated like this.

6 Softening strategies

A vital feature of courteous communication in Korean is the avoidance of directness, especially with respect to commands, requests, and queries.

6.1 Use of questions in place of commands and proposals

Commands and proposals tend to be softened especially when the speaker is not close to the addressee, unless the action being requested is for the benefit of that person (잘 자요, 안녕히 가세요, etc.). This is very commonly achieved by expressing requests as questions.

Command forms:
소금 좀 주라/줘/줘요/주세요. (See **1.5** about 주라.)
  Please pass the salt.

Question forms:
소금 좀 줄래?/줄래요?/주실래요?/주시겠어요?
  Could you pass the salt?

The contrasts among the various sentence endings in these examples, and even the presence of the honorific suffix -시, don't have much to do with softening. Rather, the softening effect is associated with the use of the question.

A word of caution is in order here. The English patterns ('Would/Could you...?') typically used to translate Korean formal endings and honorific verb forms are misleading. Whereas these patterns can be used in English to anyone, including close friends or even children, the Korean formal endings and honorific verb forms are inappropriate for close friends or children. For example, you never say 소금 좀 주시겠어요? to a five-year-old child, even though you could say 'Could you pass me the salt?' in this situation in English. It is always appropriate to be courteous and polite no matter who you are speaking to, be it a child or a close friend, but it is not appropriate to be formal and deferential to such a person.

Proposal forms such as 믿으십시다, with both the formal 합시다 style and honorific -시, are not used, except by quite old, mostly male speakers. Where additional deference is called for, the proposal is usually made indirectly, by changing it into a suggestion or a question.

같이 갑시다.	*Let's go together.*	(most direct)
같이 가세요.	*Let's go together.*	
같이 가시죠.	*Why don't we go together?*	↓
같이 가실까요?	*Shall we go together?*	
같이 가시겠어요?	*Would you like to go together?*	(least direct)

6.2 Softening with the help of special verbs

6.2.1 The verb: 주다

Commands are often turned into requests with the help of 주다, which is used to indicate that compliance with the request would be of benefit to the speaker. Turning a command into a request for a favor has a dramatic softening effect.

The following examples illustrate how different sentence endings, in combination with the verb 주다, vary in terms of directness (and, therefore, courtesy). They are presented in descending order of directness, from most direct to least direct (softest).

조용히 하십시오.	*Keep quiet.*
좀 조용히 해 주십시오.	*Please keep quiet.*
좀 조용히 해 주시기 바랍니다.	*We'd like it if you would keep quiet.*
좀 조용히 해 주시겠습니까?	*Would you please keep quiet for us?*
좀 조용히 해 주실 수 있을까요?	*Would it be possible for you to keep quiet for us?*
빨리 오세요.	*Come right away.*
빨리 와 주세요.	*Please come right away.*
빨리 좀 와 주시기 바래요.	*We'd like you to come right away.*
빨리 좀 와 주시겠어요?	*Would you please come right away?*
빨리 좀 와 주실 수 있을까요?	*Would it be possible for you to come right away?*
사전 좀 빌립시다.	*Let me borrow your book.*
사전 좀 빌려 주세요.	*Please let me borrow your book.*
사전 좀 빌려 주시겠어요?	*Would you please let me borrow your book?*
사전 좀 빌릴 수 있을까요?	*Would it be possible to borrow your book?*

To further soften your request, you can start with 죄송하지만 'excuse me' (see **4.5**).

6.2.2   The verb: 보다

The auxiliary verb 보다 is widely used to soften the speaker's assertion by making it less direct and by reducing his/her commitment to the statement.

저는 가 보겠습니다.	*I'll get going.*
한번 해 보겠습니다.	*I'll give it a try.*
제가 알아보겠습니다.	*I'll try to find out about it.*

Use of 보다 turns a command into a suggestion such as 'Why don't you...(for your own sake)?'

Command:	이제 그만 가.	*Go now.*
Suggestion:	이제 그만 가 봐.	*Why don't you go now?*

Thanks to the use of 보다, commands become milder and less direct, creating the impression that the speaker is leaving some room for the other person to make a choice by saying 'Try it (if you'd like).'

이 거 하나 드셔 보세요.	*Try (to eat) this.*
이 영양크림 좀 발라 보세요.	*Try this nourishing cream.*

6.2.3   The verb: 되다

The -게 되다 pattern indicates that something happens in a way that is out of one's control. It can be used to avoid indicating direct involvement by the speaker in an event or a decision, thereby reducing his/her responsibility for it.

실례인 줄 알면서도 이렇게 늦게 전화드리게 됐습니다.
  Even though I know it's a breach of etiquette, I've ended up phoning you this late.

본의 아니게 약속을 어기게 돼서 죄송합니다.
  I'm sorry I ended up having to break my promise even though I didn't mean to.

한꺼번에 추천서를 3 통씩이나 부탁드리게 됐어요.
  It has turned out that I have to ask for as many as three recommendation letters.

어떻게 하다 보니까 그렇게 됐어요.
  One thing led to another and it just turned out that way.

여자 친구하고 헤어지게 됐어.
  It turns out that I'll be breaking up with my girlfriend.

오래 된 옷은 안 입게 된다.
  I tend not to wear old clothes.

자꾸 밤에 늦게 자게 된다.
  I keep ending up going to bed late at night.

The -게 되다 pattern can also be used to imply that because events have transpired beyond the control of the speaker, (s)he cannot take credit for them. By not bragging, the speaker softens his/her statement.

다음 학기에 전액 장학금을 타게 됐다.
It turns out that I'll be receiving a full scholarship next semester.

저 이번에 승진하게 됐습니다.
It turns out that I'll be getting promoted this time.

6.2.4   The verb: 하다

The verb 하다 provides a useful strategy for expressing a thought less directly, thereby softening the statement. As the following examples illustrate, expressions with 하다 are often more appropriate than their counterparts, especially in a formal situation.

어떤 걸로 하시겠어요?	*What would you like to have?*
뭐 드시겠어요?	*What would you like to eat?*
이 배 한 상자에 어떻게 해요?	*How much does a box of pears go for?*
이 배 한 상자에 얼마예요?	*How much is a box of these pears?*
나쁜 습관은 좀 고치도록 해.	*Make sure to correct your bad habits.*
나쁜 습관은 좀 고쳐.	*Correct your bad habits.*
너무 늦지 않도록 하세요.	*Make sure not to be too late.*
너무 늦지 마세요.	*Don't be too late.*

6.2.5   The verb: 그렇다

The expression 그렇다 proves especially useful when trying to avoid saying something unpleasant or something that one doesn't feel comfortable going into detail about. It therefore provides an efficient hedging device.

A: 이 옷 어때요?
B: 그 옷은 좀 그렇다. 색깔이 좀 그렇지 않니?
A: What do you think of these clothes?
B: Those clothes are a bit...not quite. Isn't the color a little off?

A: 이런 말씀 드리기 좀 그렇지만, 내일부터 못 나올 것 같습니다.
B: 아니, 이렇게 갑작스럽게 그만두면 어떻게 해요?
A: It's a bit hard for me to say this, but I won't be able to come, starting tomorrow.
B: What, how can you quit suddenly like this?

A: 무슨 일 있어요? 기분이 안 좋아 보여요.
B: 오늘 집안 분위기가 좀 그래서 나도 기분이 좀 그러네요.
A: Are you alright? You don't seem to be in a good mood.
B: I feel a little down because the atmosphere at home is kind of bad.

A: 무슨 안 좋은 일 있었어요?   *A: Has anything bad happened?*
B: 그럴 일이 좀 있었어요.   *B: There was something.*

A: 지금 전화 받으시기 괜찮으세요?

B: 지금은 좀 그런데요.

A: 그럼 나중에 전화 주시겠어요?

B: 네, 그럴게요. 죄송합니다.

   A: Are you able to talk on the phone right now?
   B: It's a bit difficult right now.
   A: Would you call me back later then?
   B: Sure, I'll do that. I'm sorry.

6.3 Softening with the help of special endings

The following endings offer a way to soften an assertion and/or close a sentence in a non-abrupt manner.

6.3.1 -데(요): *non-abrupt ending*

-데(요), which is derived from the connective 그런데 'but then/and then,' is in general used to imply that the speaker has something to add or that (s)he expects the listener to respond. It provides a nice way to avoid ending the dialogue too abruptly, and makes statements sound less direct and more polite than they would be with just -요.

A: 선생님 지금 댁에 계신지요?

B: 안 계시는데요. (실례지만 누구세요?)   (vs. 안 계세요.)
   A: Is the teacher home?
   B: He's not home. (But may I ask who's calling?)

A: 제가 뭐 도와 드릴 일 있나요?

B: 없는데요. (신경써 주셔서 감사합니다.)   (vs. 없어요.)
   A: Is there anything I can help with?
   B: No. (But thank you for your concern).

6.3.2 -지(요): *gentle questions and suggestions*

Questions with the -지(요) ending, as in 누구시죠?, are gentler than ones with the 해(요) style ending, as in 누구세요? (지요 is often reduced to 죠.)

지금 몇 시나 됐죠?	*What time is it now?*
여기가 어디죠?	*Where are we?*
다 합해서 얼마죠?	*How much is it in total?*

A direct proposal (앉읍시다) or command (앉으세요) turns into a soft suggestion with the -지(요)/죠 ending.

이쪽으로 앉으시지요.   *Why don't you sit over here?*

더운데 선풍기 좀 틀죠.   *It's hot; why don't we turn on the fan?*

6.3.3 -구(요): *gentle questions and commands*

-구(요) is associated with a softer variety of commands and questions. It is usually intermixed with the regular 해(요) style ending when there are multiple questions/commands.

그동안 잘 지냈어요? 논문은 잘 돼가구요?
  How have you been? And how is your dissertation going?

이거 무슨 나물이에요? 값은 얼마구요?
  What kind of vegetable is this? And how much is it?

5박 6일 패키지로 예약해 주세요. 호텔은 바닷가 근처로 잡아
주시구요.
  Please reserve a 5-night, 6-day package for me. And get a hotel near the beach.

그럼 건강하게 잘 지내세요. 한국 나오시면 연락 주시구요.
  Take care and goodbye. And let me know if you are coming to Korea.

6.3.4 -나요, -은가요: *gentle questions*

-나요 (for action verbs and past tense) and -은가요/ㄴ가요 (for present tense descriptive verbs) form gentle questions for which an answer is not strongly demanded.

진선이 지금 집에 있나요? 보통 몇 시쯤 들어오나요?
  Is Jin-sun home right now? Around what time does she usually come home?

김선생님 지금 댁에 계신가요? 보통 몇 시쯤 들어오시나요?
  Is Mr. Kim home right now? Around what time does he usually come home?

  NOTE: For some reason, 계시다 (the honorific counterpart of 있다) takes
    -ㄴ가요 more frequently than -나요.

국이 너무 싱거운가요? 소금이 좀 덜 들어갔나요?
  Is the soup too bland? Did it not have enough salt?

목 마르니? 찌개가 너무 짰나?
  Are you thirsty? I wonder whether the stew was too salty.

6.4 Other softening strategies

6.4.1 어떻게

Questions with 어떻게 are considered gentler than those with 왜. So 어떻게 오셨습니까? 'What brings you here?' is preferred to 왜 오셨습니까? 'Why are you here?'

The 어떻게 돼요/되세요? pattern offers a polite indirect way of asking for information in general.

전화번호가 어떻게 돼요?   (vs. 전화번호가 뭐예요?)
What is your phone number?

연세가 어떻게 되세요?   (vs. 연세가 몇이세요?)
How old are you?

가격이 어떻게 돼요?   (vs. 값이 얼마예요?)
What's the price?

사이즈가 어떻게 돼요?   (vs. 사이즈가 얼마예요/몇이에요?)
What's the size?

생일이 어떻게 돼요?   (vs. 생일이 언제예요?)
When is your birthday?

6.4.2 좀

Questions or commands are often softened by the use of an imploring 좀 'please!,' which literally means 'a little bit.'

좀 어떠세요?   *So, how are you feeling?*
어떻게 좀 안 될까요?   *Is there any way to make it work?*
방 청소 좀 해라. 빨리 좀 해!   *Please clean up the room. Quickly, please.*
제발 까불지 좀 마.   *Please calm down and behave.*
귀찮게 좀 하지 마라.   *Leave me alone, please.*

6.4.3 -고 해서

This is a useful hedging device when one doesn't want to pinpoint a specific reason or enumerate all the reasons for one's action. It is less direct than -어서.

A: 안녕하세요? 웬일이세요?

B: 드릴 말씀도 있고 해서 찾아 왔어요. (vs. 드릴 말씀이 있어서...)
A: How are you? What brought you here?
B: I have something to tell you and so forth, so I came to see you.

A: 아니, 그냥 와도 되는데 무슨 선물을 이렇게 많이 사 왔어요?

B: 그전에 신세진 것도 있고 해서요.   (vs. 신세진 것이 있어서요.)

> A: *Oh no, you didn't have to do this. What did you bring all these presents for?*
> B: *Because there's something I owe you from the past and stuff like that.*

A: 또 이사가시려구요?

B: 예, 교통도 좀 불편하고 해서 학교 근처로 가려구요.

> A: *You are going to move again?*
> B: *Yes, the commute is inconvenient and so on, so I am going to move near school.*

6.4.4 -는/은 편이다

This expression of approximation 'kind of...' is useful in toning down a statement when pointing out characteristics that are negative. It diminishes the negative impact of the statement.

공부를 못하는 편이야.   (vs. 공부를 못해.)

> *She's sort of not good academically.*

성격이 까다로운 편이다.   (vs. 성격이 까다롭다.)

> *He's kind of finicky.*

In general, -편이다 is a convenient way of making one's statement less assertive and less commital by not being specific.

A: 며느리가 자주 찾아 와요?   *Does your daughter-in-law come to see you often?*

B: 자주 오는 편이에요.   *She kind of does. (She tends to.)*

A: 지도 교수가 친절하니?   *Is your academic supervisor nice?*

B: 응, 그런 편이야.   *Yes, she is, kind of.*

6.4.5 -거 같다, -을까 하다/싶다

These are useful when it comes to softening the speaker's assertion.

음식이 맛이 좀 간 거 같다.

> *I think that the food has gone bad.*

두 사람이 승진하기 위해 서로 경쟁하는 거 같아요.

> *I think that those two are competing to get promoted.*

경기가 무승부로 끝날 거 같은데요.

> *I think that the game will end in a tie.*

제 생각엔 결혼을 졸업 후로 미루는 게 좋지 않을까 하는데요.

> *In my opinion, it might be better to postpone the wedding until after graduation.*

사업자금 좀 대 주실 수 있을까 해서 왔습니다.

> *I came wondering whether you can help me with my business start-up fund.*

그 장관이 내일 사임의사를 표명하지 않을까 싶습니다.

> *I think that the Cabinet minister may express his intention to resign tomorrow.*

7 Local dialects

Throughout this book, we focus on Standard Korean (표준말), which is spoken by educated people in the Seoul area. However, a familiarity with non-standard dialects (사투리) is also useful because they are often encountered when traveling and in movies and TV dramas. This section offers a brief summary of the distinctive features of various of these dialects. Aside from the fact that the *Kyŏngsang* dialect and the *Hamgyŏng* dialect have tones – unlike all other varieties of Korean – the differences involve mainly verb endings and the way certain words are pronounced. (In the examples of dialectal speech that follow, the standard Korean equivalents are provided in the right-hand column.)

7.1 *Ch'ungch'ŏng* dialect (충청도 사투리)

뭐여?	뭐야?	
성, 그게 아니여.	형, 그게 아니야. *(Brother, that's not it.)*	
안녕하세유?	안녕하세요?	
알것슈?	알겠어요?	*(Do you get it?)*
진지 드셨슈?	진지 드셨어요?	*(Have you eaten?)*
아니유, 안 먹었시유.	아니오, 안 먹었어요.	*(No, I haven't eaten.)*
어쩔 수 없어서 그랬나 벼.	...그랬나 봐.	*(Maybe she did it because she couldn't help it.)*

7.2 *Chŏlla* dialect (전라도 사투리)

뭣 땀세?	무엇때문에?	*(Because of what?)*
그란디	그런데	
그랑께 or 긍께	그러니까	
거시기	그것, 저기/거기	
정말로 부탁한당께.	정말 부탁한다.	*(I'm really counting on you.)*
방갑당께요. 오매 반가운 거.	반가워요. 정말 반갑다.	*(So glad to see you.)*
안녕하신구라?	안녕하세요?	
잘 계신당가요?	잘 계신가요?	*(Is he doing well?)*

그간에 잘 있었당가?	그동안 잘 있었니?	*(How have you been?)*
얼마만여이!	얼마만이야!	*(Long time, no see!)*
고맙구만이라이.	고마워요.	
미안하구만이라이.	미안해요.	
징하게 날씨가 좋아부러.	정말 날씨가 좋다.	*(The weather is so good.)*
여그 오시능마요.	여기 오시는구만요.	*(Here he comes.)*
워디 가셨습디여?	어디 가셨었어요?	*(Where have you been?)*

7.3 *Kyŏngsang* dialect (경상도 사투리)

반갑심니데이. or 반갑심더.	반갑습니다.	*(Nice meeting you.)*
고맙심니데이. or 고맙심더.	고맙습니다.	
욕봤심니데이. or 욕봤심더.	욕봤습니다, meaning 수고했습니다.	
오랜만임더.	오랜만입니다.	*(It's been a long time.)*
아임니더. or 아니라예.	아닙니다. 아니에요.	*(No, it's not; Not at all.)*
샘님 질문 있심더.	선생님 질문 있습니다.	
샘예 질문 있어예.	선생님 질문 있어요.	
수고 많네예.	수고 많네요.	*(You're working hard.)*
잘하시네예.	잘하시네요.	*(You're doing a good job.)*
그런데예.	그런데요.	
미안해예.	미안해요.	
어서 오이소.	어서 오세요.	*(Welcome.)*
퍼떡 오시이소.	빨리/얼른 오세요.	*(Come quickly.)*
안녕히 가이소.	안녕히 가세요.	
어디 가노?	어디 가냐?	*(Where are you going?)*
어디 갔더노?	어디 갔었니?	*(Where have you been?)*
와 그라노?	왜 그러니?	*(Why...?)*
뭐라카노?	뭐라고 하니?	*(What is she saying?)*
잘 가레이. or 잘 가그레이.	잘 가라.	*(Bye.)*
미안하데이. or 미안테이.	미안하다.	

7.4 *Cheju* dialect (제주도 사투리)

하르방/할망	할아버지/할머니
아방/어멍	아버지/어머니
혼저 옵서예.	어서 오십시오.
어드러 감수광?	어디 가세요?
고맙쑤다.	고맙습니다.
미안허우다.	미안합니다.
이거 얼마꽈?	이거 얼마입니까?

7.5 *Hamgyŏng* dialect (함경도 사투리)

아주바이	아저씨
무시기	무엇
날래 가지비.	빨리 가지.
하꼬마/함매?	합니다/합니까?
했소꼬마/했슴매?	했습니다/했습니까?
하겠소꼬마/하겠슴매?	하겠습니다/하겠습니까?

7.6 *P'yŏng'an* dialect (평안도 사투리)

덩거당	정거장	*(train station)*
과자가 보수라뎌.	과자가 부스러져.	*(The cookies are crumbling.)*
그 노래 드더 봔?	그 노래 들어 봤니?	*(Have you heard the song?)*
아무도 없었수다.	아무도 없었습니다.	*(There was no one.)*
그 사람 어드매 간?	그 사람 어디 갔니?	*(Where is he gone?)*

8 Written versus spoken language

Except for informal personal letters, written language differs from colloquial speech in many ways. (Many features of written language are also employed in formal speech.) Wherever possible throughout this book, we provide information about whether particular expressions are more appropriate for formal writing/ speech or colloquial speech. The following is a summary of recurring features of written/formal language. (Throughout this chapter, spoken counterparts are provided in square brackets.)

8.1 Grammatical differences

8.1.1 Sentence endings (see 1.5)

- Different sentence endings are used for formal writing.

폭죽행사가 열린다.	[...열립니다.]	*Fireworks will take place.*
들어가지 마시오.	[...마세요.]	*Do not enter.*
하늘을 보라.	[...봐라.]	*Look at the sky.*
통일은 가능한가?	[...가능합니까?]	*Is unification possible?*

- Sentences often end in a noun or are shortened in headlines or announcements.

정숙	[떠들지 마세요.]	*Keep quiet.*
접근금지	[접근하지 마세요.]	*Keep out.*
늦으면 절대 안 됨	[...안 됩니다.]	*No tardiness allowed.*
쉽지 않을 듯	[...않을 듯하다.]	*Looks like it won't be easy.*
항상 건강하길.	[...건강하길 바란다.]	*Take care.*

8.1.2 Particles (see ch. 19)

- Different particles are used for formal writing/speech.

전문가에게 문의하시오.	[전문가한테 문의하세요.]
	Consult an expert.
작가에게 원고를 보내라고 하십시오.	[작가보고/더러 원고를 보내라고 하세요.]
	Tell the author to send the manuscript.

낯선 사람과 대화할 때   [모르는 사람이랑 얘기할 때]
                              when talking with a stranger
10 월 9 일에 도착했다.   [10 월 9 일날 도착했다.]
                              They arrived on October 9th.

- Particles tend to be retained in formal writing/speech.

회사가 파산했다고 한다.   [회사 파산했댄다.]
                              I hear that the company went bankrupt.

학생들이 박물관으로 견학을 갔다. [학생들 박물관 견학 갔다.]
                              The students went to the museum.

8.1.3   Others

- No honorific expressions are used in impersonal writing/speech (see **2.6**).

서울 시장은 격노한 시민들에게 사죄의 뜻을 밝혔다.
The mayor of Seoul expressed his intention of apologizing to the infuriated citizens.

- Different types of pronouns are used in formal writing/speech (see **3.2**).

그는 누구인가?   [그 남자/여자/분/사람은 누구입니까?]

- Different quoting verb forms are used in formal writing/speech (see *22.1.2*).

위험하다고 한다.   [위험하다 그런다. or 위험하댄다.]
                            It's said to be dangerous.

방문한다고 밝혔다.   [방문한다 그랬어요. or 방문한댔어요.]
                            He announced that he would visit.

8.2 Vocabulary differences (see **9.1**)

Vocabulary tends to be more technical-sounding in formal writing/speech.

신장과 체중   [키하고 몸무게]   *height and weight*
신속한 회복을 바랍니다.   [빨리 낫기를 바랍니다.] *I wish you a speedy recovery.*
경찰에 검거되었다.   [경찰에 잡혔다.]   *He got arrested by the police.*
협상이 결렬되었다.   [협상이 깨졌다.]   *The negotiations fell through.*
바퀴가 파열되었다.   [타이어가 터졌다   *We got a flat tire.*
                             /빵꾸났다.]
화재가 발생했다.   [불이 났다.]   *A fire broke out.*
무척 많다.   [무지/되게/엄청 많다.] *There's a lot.*
대단히 감사합니다.   [정말 고맙습니다.]   *Thank you very much.*

8.3 Spelling/pronunciation differences

8.3.1 Contraction

Contraction in general is not allowed in highly formal writing. The spellings in square brackets below reflect what is said. (Some formal speech such as news broadcasts tend to use an extremely careful style of speech that is as faithful as possible to the written form of the language.) These spellings may or may not be permitted in writing, depending on the degree of formality. The more formal the writing, the less contraction is allowed. The following groups of examples are presented in approximate descending order of tolerability in writing with (a) being the most tolerable and (c) being the least. (A small glossary containing some of the less familiar items is provided at the end of the section.)

(a)	그러면	[그럼]	아니오	[아뇨]
	얼마지요	[얼마죠]	되었습니다	[됐습니다]
	보았어요	[봤어요]	나의/저의	[내/제]
	무엇	[뭐]	무엇이	[뭐가]
	무엇을	[뭘]	한 눈 파는 사이	[...새]
(b)	-것	[-거]	이것	[이거]
	이것이	[이게]	이것은	[이건]
	이것을	[이걸]	어느 것인가	[어느 건가]
	이야기	[애기]	이 아이	[애]
	그 아이	[걔]	저 아이	[쟤]
	그런데	[근데]	도리어	[되레]
	놓아 두어	[놔 둬]	그만두세요	[관두세요]
	나는	[난]	너를	[널]
	누구를	[누굴]	어디인지	[어딘지]
	좋으냐고	[좋냐고]	작으니?	[작니?]
(c)	사과는	[사관]	학교를	[학꼴]
	왔다는 소리	[왔단 소리]	가수인 것 같다	[가순 거 같다]
	작가입니다	[작갑니다]	재미있다	[재밌다]
	어디 있어	[어딨어]	마음	[맘]
	처음	[첨]	다음	[담]
	친구때문에	[친구땜에]	아무 말 하지마	[암말 하지마]
	아무리 싫어도	[암만 싫어두]	아니면 말고	[아님 말구]
	싫으면 그만둬	[싫음 관둬]	다 했으면 나가	[다 했음 나가]

큰일 났다	[클 났다]	그러니깐	[그깐]
그렇지	[그치/그지]	그렇지요	[그쵸]
놓아 둬	[내비 둬 or 냅 둬]	어디에다 놓아?	[어따 놔?]
넣을까	[늘까]	그걸 왜 사니?	[걸 왜 사니?]
그거 봐	[거 봐]	이리 내	[인 내]
이리 줘	[인 줘]		

8.3.2 Gaps between spelling and pronunciation

The current standard spelling conventions for the following words do not actually represent how they are often pronounced.

- Spelled with ㅗ but often pronounced ㅜ

그리고	[그리구]	자고 나서	[자구 나서]
먹고 싶다	[먹구 싶다]	먹어도 배고파	[먹어두 배고파]
빵도 사자	[빵두 사자]	아무리 해도	[아무리 해두]
바로 와	[바루 와]	앞으로	[앞으루]
위로 올라가	[위루 올라가]		

- Spelled with ㅓ but often pronounced ㅡ

꺼내	[끄내]	성질	[승질]
덜 덥다	[들 덥다]	하던 일	[하든 일]
오더라	[오드라]	아버지	[아브지]

- Spelled with ㅏ but often pronounced ㅓ (sometimes even spelled with ㅓ)

앉아	[앉어]	바빠요	[바뻐요]
알아	[알어]	아파서	[아퍼서]

- Spelled with ㅏ but often pronounced ㅐ

같아요	[같애요]	아기	[애기]
보자기	[보재기]	창피해	[챙피해]

- Spelled with ㅓ or ㅔ but often pronounced ㅣ

저희들	[지들]	너희들	[니들]
네 거	[니 꺼]	제 거	[지 꺼]

- Miscellaneous vowel sound changes

들러요	[들려요]	들르세요	[들리세요]
예쁘다	[이쁘다]		

- Spelled with a plain consonant but often pronounced with a tense consonant

버스	[뻐쓰]	배지	[빼찌]
잼	[쨈]	닦아요	[딲아요]
잘렸어	[짤렸어]	숙맥	[쑥맥]

- Loan words spelled one way but often pronounced differently

스웨터	[세타]	팬티	[빤쓰]
런닝셔츠	[난닝구]	브래지어	[브라자]

- Usually spelled without an extra ㄹ, but often pronounced with one

아프다기에	[아프다길래]
좋아 보이기에	[좋아 보이길래]
이거로	[이 걸로]
가려다가	[갈려다가 or 갈래다가]
가려면	[갈려면 or 갈래면]
보려는데	[볼려는데 or 볼래는데]
먹으려고	[먹을려고 or 먹을라고]
자르려고	[짤를려고 or 짤를라고]
하려고 해도	[할려고 해도 or 할라고 해도]

'Phonetic spelling' is sometimes employed for expressions that are used exclusively in speaking. One such form is -(더라)구요, which is usually written with a 구 to reflect its pronunciation even though it is really the suffix -고. Another form that is rarely used in writing is 뵙다. In fact, the correct spelling for its -요 form is not clear even to many native speakers (is it 뵈어요, 뵈요, or 뵈워요?). The official spelling is supposedly 뵈어요, which is what we use in this book.

Why can't we just write words the way we say them – 드럽다 instead of 더럽다 'be dirty,' 꼬매다 instead of 꿰매다 'sew,' and so on? You can if there is no danger of anyone judging you by how you spell things. In fact, 'phonetic spelling' is very common these days in personal notes and e-mail. However, it would be a mistake to write things in this way in important documents such as your résumé! Spelling is often considered to be an important indicator of whether someone is well educated or not.

Selected glossary

숙맥 *foolish person*	잼 *jam*	배지 *badge*
보자기 *wrapping cloth*	창피하다 *be embarrassed*	들르다 *stop by*
작가 *author*	꺼내다 *take (something) out*	도리어 *on the contrary*
성질 *disposition; temper*	한 눈 파는 사이 *while distracted*	

Vocabulary

9 Native and borrowed words

About 35 percent of Korean vocabulary is native (고유어) and about 60 percent can be traced to Chinese (한자어). For the most part, these Sino-Korean words were borrowed prior to 1945 and are now perceived to be fully 'Korean.'

In recent years, Korean has been borrowing heavily from western languages, especially English, in fields such as advertising, entertainment, sports, business management, and engineering. (Prior to 1945, western loan words (외래어) entered Korean indirectly via Japanese.)

9.1 Native Korean and Sino-Korean words

It is not unusual to find native Korean and Sino-Korean words with similar or overlapping meanings. When this happens, the native Korean word tends to be more colloquial, while the Sino-Korean word is usually more formal and literary (e.g., 엄마/아버지 versus the formal and impersonal 모친/부친). Occasionally, the Sino-Korean words take on a more specialized and narrower meaning – 손위 'someone older' and 손아래 'someone younger' versus 연상 (年上) 'older girlfriend/wife and 연하 (年下) 'younger boyfriend/husband.'

The majority of the vocabulary used in written materials such as newspapers, magazines, documents, and books is of Sino-Korean origin. The same is true of news broadcasts, lectures, and ceremonies, as well as just about any conversation on a topic that goes beyond ordinary daily life.

Take for example the verbs 죽다 and 돌아가시다, both of which mean 'die.' (The latter is an honorific verb; see *2.1.3*.) Although both words are common in personal conversation, neither would ever be used in a news broadcast or in formal writing. Such situations call for a Sino-Korean verb such as 사망하다 or the more indirect 승천하다, 작고하다, 타계하다, 별세하다, 유명을 달리하다, or 세상을 하직하다. Native but euphemistic expressions such as 목숨을 잃다 or 숨지다 may also be used.

The verbs 주다 and 드리다 work the same way. Both mean 'give,' with the latter being used to show deference to the referent of the indirect object; see **2.2**. Although these verbs are common in ordinary conversation, other situations require Sino-Korean expressions.

나는 형에게 토지 소유권을 **양도**했다.
I deeded my land title to my older brother.

그는 고아원에 백만원을 **기부**했다.
He donated ₩1,000,000 to an orphanage.

교장 선생님이 학생들에게 우등상장을 **수여**했다.
The principal awarded students certificates of excellence.

대통령이 장병들에게 위문품을 **하사**했다.
The President gave care packages to soldiers.

화장품 회사가 손님에게 기념품을 **증정**했다.
The cosmetic company presented customers with souvenirs.

A prescription drug may be accompanied by written Sino-Korean instructions that say 1 일 3 회 식후 복용. But this would sound strange in the spoken language, where you would say 하루에 세번 밥 먹고 나서 먹어 or, more formally, 하루에 세번 식사 하신 후에 드세요. A mother will say to her child, 단 걸 너무 많이 먹으면... 'If you eat too much sweet stuff...,' but a medical doctor will convey the same thought to his/her patient as 당분을 과도하게 섭취하면...

Here are further examples of the native versus Sino-Korean contrast.

Nouns and noun phrases:

Native	Sino-Korean	Meaning
맨날	매일	every day
더운물	온수	hot water
찬물	냉수	cold water
키	신장	height
무게	중량	weight
몸무게	체중	(body) weight
옷	의상, 의복	clothing
이, 이빨	치아	teeth
돈	자금, 금전	money, fund
남은 돈	잔액, 잔금, 잔고	balance (money)
맏딸	장녀	eldest daughter
맏아들	장남	eldest son
둘째딸	차녀	second eldest daughter
둘째아들	차남	second eldest son
사람	인간	human being
나이	연령	age
자리	좌석	seat

잠	수면	sleep
깊은 잠	숙면	sound sleep
새해	신년	new year
지난 해	작년	last year
올 해	금년	this year
다음 해	내년	next year
보내는 사람	발신인	sender
받는 사람	수신인	recipient
나가는 곳	출구	exit
들어가는 곳	입구	entrance
손님	고객	customer
남 or 다른 사람	타인	others
아이	아동	child
어른	성인	adult
죽은 사람	사망자, 고인	the dead
다친 사람	부상자	the wounded
믿음	신뢰	faith
몸	신체	body
지은이	저자	author
땅	토지	land

NOTE: 이빨 is familiar/casual; 인간 may be used derogatorily (어휴, 저 인간).

Verbs and verb phrases:

Native	Sino-Korean	Meaning
(값이) 떨어지다	(가격이) 하락하다	(price) to fall
(값이) 내리다	(가격이) 인하되다	
(값이) 오르다	(가격이) 인상되다	(price) to increase
(기온이) 오르다	(기온이) 상승하다	(temperature) to rise
(값이) 싸다	(가격이) 저렴하다	to be cheap
(인구가) 늘다	(인구가) 증가하다	(population) to increase
(실력이) 늘다	(실력이) 향상하다	(ability) to improve
줄다	감소하다	to decrease
들키다	발각되다, 적발되다	to be detected/caught

숨쉬다	호흡하다	to breathe
때리다	구타하다	to beat
말하다	언급하다	to mention
모으다	수집하다	to collect
(물건을) 사다	구입하다, 구매하다	to buy/purchase
이기다	승리하다	to win/gain a victory
(직장에서) 자르다 (직장에서) 잘리다	해고하다 해고당하다	to dismiss to be fired
자리에 앉다	착석하다	to be seated
모자라다	부족하다	to be insufficient/short
없애다	제거하다	to get rid of
빼다	제외하다	to exclude
(신문에) 나다/실리다	게재되다	to appear (in the press)
전기가/물이 끊기다 (소식이) 끊기다	단전/단수되다 (소식이) 단절되다	power/water to be cut off (news) to be cut off
차 (배, 비행기)에 타다	승차 (승선, 탑승)하다	to get in a car (ship, plane)
차에서 내리다	하차하다	to get out of a vehicle
물에 빠져 죽다	익사하다	to be drowned
다시 생각하다	재고하다	to reconsider
돈을 바꾸다	환전하다	to exchange (money)
돌려 주다	반환하다	to return
길을 넓히다	도로를 확장하다	to expand a road
다리를 놓다	교량을 건설하다	to construct a bridge
뿌리뽑다	근절하다	to eradicate

(시간이) 걸리다
   걸리는 시간
	(시간이) 소요되다
	   소요시간
		to take (time)
		   duration of a trip

(스키를) 빌려 주다	대여하다	to rent (skis)
(사람이) 짜다	인색하다	to be stingy
헷갈리다	혼동되다	to be confused/confusing
보태다	추가하다	to add/supplement

9.2 Loan words

Western loan words often end up contrasting with already existing native Korean and/or Sino-Korean words with similar meanings. When this happens, the loan words are generally associated with a more modern version of the concept.

Native Korean	Sino-Korean	Loan words	
춤	무용	댄스	*dance*
가게	상점	마트	*store, mart*
빵집	제과점	베이커리	*bakery*
술집	주점	빠, 클럽	*drinking bar*

NOTE: 빵 is a borrowing from Portuguese, but since it has been in the language
   for so long, it is considered native Korean.

In some cases, loan words are used to denote things for which there is no Korean word – 껌, 커피, 버스, 잼, 택시 are examples of this. In other cases, Korean words may be pushed aside by their borrowed equivalents – 사진기 by 카메라, 사증 by 비자, 포도주 by 와인, 정구 by 테니스, and so on.

Unless they have become fully Koreanized, foreign expressions tend to be more casual and colloquial. 파킹 'parking' and 컨셉 'concept' may be common among younger people when speaking casually, but they are to be avoided in formal writing and speech.

The following samples show just how freely fashion magazines use loan words these days.

떠나자, 1 박 2 일 **호텔 뷰티** 여행. 최근 내 시선을 사로잡은 것은 **웨스턴** 조선의 **홈스파 앤 푸드 패키지**. 해외 **리조트**의 고급 **스파**에서 사용하는 제품으로 **홈스파**도 즐기고 맛있는 음식도 먹는데다 **피트니스 클럽**에서 운동처방도 받고 **스트레칭**, **필라테스** 등의 **웰빙 클래스**도 수강할 있는 짧은 **웰빙** 여행이다.

Let's go for an overnight hotel beauty trip. What caught my eye recently is the 'Home Spa and Food' package from the Western Chosŏn. It's a short 'well-being' trip where you can enjoy the home spa using high-quality products that are used in overseas resort areas and enjoy delicious food. Furthermore, you can also get advice on your exercise plan from the fitness club and take 'well-being' classes such as stretching or pilates.

새롭게 **오픈**한 일식 **퓨전 레스토랑**은 수준급의 음식 맛만큼이나 **인테리어** 역시 고급스러워 **트렌드 세터**들까지 자주 찾을 만큼 벌써 입소문이 났다.

The newly opened Japanese fusion restaurant has an interior as great as its excellent-tasting food. So, it has already become well-known through word of mouth, attracting even the trend setters.

9.2.1 *Innovations in loan words*

Loan words often have a somewhat different meaning in Korean than in their language of origin, either because only one sense of the word was borrowed or because its meaning shifted after borrowing. For instance, 플라스틱 means only hard plastic while 비닐 ('vinyl') means only soft plastic. So when Koreans visit American supermarkets for the first time, they misunderstand what the cashier means by a plastic bag! Here are more examples of this sort.

린스	< rinse >	*conditioner*
스킨	< skin >	*toner*
팝송	< pop song >	*western pop songs*
빌라	< villa >	*townhouse*
콘도	< condo >	*time share*
커닝	< cunning >	*cheating on an exam*
서비스	< service >	*complimentary; free of charge*
미팅	< meeting >	*blind date*
부킹	< booking >	*pairing-off with a partner in a club*
스킨십	< skinship >	*romantic touch*
팬티	< panty >	*panties; boxers; briefs*
런닝셔츠	< running shirts >	*short-sleeve/sleeveless undershirt*
키친타월	< kitchen towel >	*paper towel*
이태리타월	< Italy towel >	*scrubbing cloth for skin*
콤비	< combi >	*sports coat*
잠바	< jumper >	*windbreaker, jacket*
파스	< PAS >	*medicated plaster, hot/cold patch*
사인	< sign >	*autograph; signature*

In addition, English loan words are sometimes combined in novel ways (see **10.5**).

백미러	< back mirror >	*rearview mirror*
핸드폰	< hand phone >	*cell phone*
에스라인	< S-line >	*curvaceous body*
커트라인	< cut line >	*passing score on an exam*
골인	< goal in >	*kicking a goal in a game*
오픈게임	< open game >	*game played before the main event*
애프터 서비스	< after service >	*after-sales service*
모닝콜	< morning-call >	*wake-up call*

비닐하우스	< vinyl house >	*greenhouse*
원룸아파트	< one-room apt >	*a studio; flat; efficiency*
오토바이	< auto-bi >	*motorcycle*
썬팅	< sun-ting >	*window tinting*
캠핑카	< camping-car >	*recreation vehicle (RV)*

Sometimes, parts of loan words are combined with other words to create new words:

| 오피스텔 | < office-(ho)tel > | *a place where one can do office work and sleep* |
| 웰빙버거 | < well-being burger > | *healthy burger* |

9.2.2 Phonetic changes to loan words

A loan word's pronunciation is refashioned to fit the sound pattern of Korean. The following changes are particularly common.

- The sound 'f' becomes ㅍ:

  팬 *fan*　　　　　카페인 *caffeine*　　　유니폼 *uniform*

- The sounds 'j,' 'z,' and sometimes 's' become ㅈ:

  엔진 *engine*　　　　비자 *visa*　　　　카지노 *casino*

- The sounds 'l' and 'r' merge into ㄹ at the beginning of a word:

  로션 *lotion*　　　　레이저 *laser*　　　라이벌 *rival*

- The sound 'sh' becomes ㅅ:

  샴푸 *shampoo*　　　샤워 *shower*　　　시트 *sheet*

- The sound 'th' becomes ㅅ in most cases (exception: 멕베드 Macbeth):

  스릴 *thrill*　　　　헬스 *health*　　　스미스 *Smith*

- The sound 'v' becomes ㅂ:

  베테랑 *veteran*　　　비타민 *vitamin*　　　인터뷰 *interview*

- Sequences of consonants are broken up with vowels (usually 으):

  클럽 *club*　　　　스탠드 *stand*　　　토스트 *toast*
  드라이브 *drive*　　스카프 *scarf*　　　유니폼 *uniform*

- A vowel (usually 으, but sometimes 이) is added to words that end in sounds such as 's,' 'z,' and 'ch':

  키스 *kiss*　　　　치즈 *cheese*　　　스포츠 *sports*
  스위치 *switch*　　이미지 *image*　　가스 레인지 *gas range*

Addition of the extra vowel is optional for words that end in the sounds 'p,' 't,' 'k,' or 'g':

테입/테이프 *tape*　　컷/커트 *cut*　　　　케익/케이크 *cake*

- Words that end in the sound 't' are spelled with a final ㅅ:

라켓 *racket*　　　에티켓 *etiquette*　　　인터넷 *Internet*

If the final ㅅ is followed by a suffix that begins with a vowel, it is pronounced as if it were 's' rather than 't': 인터넷 [인터넫] vs. 인터넷을 [인터네슬].

- The sounds 'p' and 'b' are neutralized into ㅂ; the sounds 'k' and 'g' are neutralized into ㄱ:

캡 *cap/cab*　　　백 *bag/back*

Because of this, Koreans may mistake 'Doug called' for 'Duck called' and Americans may hear 크랩버거 as 'crap burger' rather than 'crab burger'!

- The sound 'r' is dropped after a vowel (exceptions: 코르크 'cork,' 레퍼토리 'repertoire'):

코트 *court*　　　디저트 *dessert*　　　포크 *fork*
마트 *mart*　　　포스터 *poster*　　　레저 *leisure*

Because of these various changes, different borrowed words can end up with the same pronunciation in Korean: pan/fan 팬, passion/fashion 패션, coat/court 코트, folk/fork 포크.

9.2.3 *The grammar of loan words*

Most loan words are nouns that, like Sino-Korean nouns, can be converted into verbs by adding -하다, -나다, and so on as the need arises.

웰빙하다	*live a healthy life-style*	헬스하다	*exercise in a health club*
오바하다	*overreact; overinterpret*	드라이브하다	*go for a drive*
이메일하다	*do e-mail*	다운로드하다	*download*
폼나다	*look stylish*	펑크나다	*(appointment) gets broken*

NOTE: The @ in e-mail addresses is called 골뱅이, which is a type of fish that looks similar to the symbol.

Words that are adjectives in the original language tend to become nouns in Korean, and are then converted into descriptive verbs with the help of -하다.

쿨하다	*be cool*	스마트하다	*be smart*
섹시하다	*be sexy*	유머러스하다	*be humorous*

10 Word formation

A language's vocabulary is a work in progress. New words are constantly being added, sometimes through borrowing from other languages but more often by making adjustments to currently existing words.

10.1 Compounding

A particularly common strategy for word formation in Korean involves combining two or more elements to create a compound word.

10.1.1 Compound nouns

A very large number of Sino-Korean compounds consist of two roots. (These roots are often bound – that is, they cannot be used as words on their own.)

주차 (駐車)   운전 (運轉)   교통 (交通)

Many longer compounds can be created by combining two-item compounds with other words.

주차:	주차위반	*parking violation*	불법주차	*illegal parking*
	주차금지	*No Parking*	주차난	*parking difficulties*
운전:	운전면허	*driver's license*	음주운전	*driving while intoxicated*
	초보운전	*beginner's driving*	대리운전자	*designated driver*
교통:	교통사고	*traffic accident*	교통체증	*traffic congestion*
	대중교통	*mass transit*	교통신호	*traffic signal*
속도:	속도위반	*speed violation*	제한속도	*speed limit*
	경제속도	*economical speed*	속도계	*speedometer*
보험:	생명보험	*life insurance*	자동차보험	*car insurance*
	의료보험	*medical insurance*	보험료	*insurance premium*

The meanings of these long compounds can usually be predicted from their component parts:

불법주차	< *not-law-park-car* >	*illegal parking*
음주운전	< *drink-alcohol-move-turn* >	*driving while intoxicated*

Another type of compound noun is formed by combining two independent words of native Korean origin.

비: 비구름   *rain cloud*   비바람   *rain and wind; rainstorm*

        가을비   *autumn rain*   이슬비   *dew-like rain; drizzle*

Some compound nouns are hybrid in nature, consisting of words of different origin (e.g., loan word + Korean word, or vice versa).

메모지   *memo pad*   파격세일   *drastic sale*

청자켓   *denim jacket*   알콜중독   *alcohol addiction*

유머감각   *sense of humor*   도미노현상 *domino effect*

발레공연   *ballet performance*   문자메시지 *text message*

해외토픽   *newsy topics from abroad* 전신마사지 *whole body massage*

10.1.2 Compound verbs: noun + verb

A popular way to extend a noun's usage is to combine it with various special verbs to create a compound verb.

(a) Compound action verbs

하다: 한잔하다   *have a drink*   농구하다   *play basketball*

        밥하다   *cook rice*   조깅하다   *jog*

        망하다   *go to ruin*   파산하다   *go bankrupt*

가다: 이민가다   *emigrate*   유학가다   *go to study abroad*

        출장가다   *go on a business trip* 도망가다   *run away*

        피서가다   *get away from the   문병가다   *visit someone who
                   summer heat*   is sick*

(b) Compound descriptive verbs

하다: 정직하다   *be honest*   성실하다   *be sincere*

        용감하다   *be brave*   얌전하다   *be gentle/decent*

        알뜰하다   *be frugal*   부지런하다   *be diligent*

이다: 망신이다   *be a dishonour to*   꼴불견이다   *be unsightly*

        실망이다   *be disappointing*   대환영이다   *be very welcome*

        상극이다   *be incompatible with* 과학적이다   *be scientific*

지다: 그늘지다   *be shady/gloomy*   구석지다   *be off to one side*

        비탈지다   *be hilly*   야무지다   *be firm/hard-headed*

        건방지다   *be conceited/impudent* 끈덕지다   *be persevering*

10.1.3 Compound verbs: verb + verb

Pairs of verbs are often linked by means of -어/아, -어다/아다 or -고. There are hundreds of compounds of this type in Korean, but certain verbs occur more often than others in these patterns. These 'pivot verbs' are sometimes found in the initial position and sometimes in the second position.

(a) Pivot verb in the initial position:

갈-:	갈아입다	*change one's clothes*	갈아타다	*transfer (vehicles)*
	갈아신다	*change one's shoes*	갈아끼다	*replace (bulbs, etc.)*
내-:	내쫓다	*drive out; expel*	내보내다	*let out; expel*
	내몰다	*drive out; force out*	내버리다	*throw away*
알-:	알아보다	*recognize; inquire*	알아듣다	*catch (the meaning)*
	알아내다	*find out*	알아맞히다	*guess right*

(b) Pivot verb in second position:

가다:	대가다	*arrive in time for*	기어가다	*crawl on*
	잡아가다	*take (a suspect) to the police station*	쫓아가다	*go after; chase*
들다:	대들다	*defy; talk back*	스며들다	*penetrate; soak into*
	끼어들다	*intrude into*	접어들다	*approach; near*
	파고들다	*dig into; delve into*	오그라들다	*shrink*
보다:	지켜보다	*watch*	내려다보다	*look down; overlook*
	떠보다	*sound out a person*	눈여겨보다	*observe carefully*
	훔쳐보다	*steal a glance at*	흘겨보다	*squint at*

Some compounds may even consist of three verbs:

| 쳐들어가다 | < hit-enter-go > | *invade* |
| 말라비틀어지다 | < dry-twist-fall > | *shrivel up* |

10.2 Reduplication

Reduplication repeats all or part of a word to indicate emphasis, repetition, alternation, variety, or plurality (see ch. **13** for more examples).

• Emphasis:

우리 이 추억 **길이길이** 간직하자.
  Let's keep this memory for a long time.
승헌이는 운동, 공부, 노래 다 **고루고루** 잘 한다.
  Seunghun is equally good at sports, academics, and singing.

어제 산 장미가 벌써 **시들시들**하네.
The roses I bought yesterday are already wilted.

- Repetition:

면접 결과를 기다릴 때 마음이 **조마조마**했어요.
I felt uneasy (pit-a-pat, pit-a-pat) while waiting for the interview result.

이곳은 너무 시골이라 집들이 **띄엄띄엄** 있다.
This place is sparsely dotted with houses because it's a very rural area.

남의 일에 **꼬치꼬치** 캐묻지 마.
Don't try to find out every single detail of someone else's business.

- Alternation or variety:

티격태격 다투지 말고 좀 사이 좋게 지내라.
Don't bicker, and please get along with each other.

어제 술이 **곤드레만드레** 취해서 집에 갔어요.
I went home dead drunk yesterday.

내 친구는 남자 친구와의 일을 나한테 **미주알고주알** 다 얘기한다.
My friend tells me about things between her and her boyfriend to the last detail.

- Plurality:

끼리끼리 모인다더니...
People say birds of a feather flock together (isn't it so true).

구석구석 깨끗이 치우도록 해라.
Tidy up your room – every nook and cranny.

군데군데 청바지를 찢어서 입는 게 요즘 유행이야.
It's a trend these days to wear jeans after ripping them here and there.

10.3 Prefixation

Like their English counterparts (*un-*, *re-*, and so on), prefix-like elements in Korean occur at the beginning of a word and modify its meaning. The line between 'prefix + word' patterns and 'word + word' compounds is often hazy because many Korean prefixes evolved from full words and still have word-like meanings. Selected entries are presented throughout this chapter; for more illustrations and basic examples, see the *Handbook of Korean Vocabulary* by M. Choo & W. O'Grady (University of Hawaii Press, 1996).

가- (거짓 假) 'temporary; fake'

가건물 *temporary building*	가계약 *provisional contract*
가처분 *provisional disposition*	가입학 *provisional admission (to a school)*
가분수 *improper fraction*	가석방 *parole*

급- (급할 急) 'sudden; urgent'

급상승 *sudden rise* 급강하 *sudden drop (of temp.)*

급성장 *fast growth* 급회전 *sudden turn (of a car)*

급경사 *steep slope* 급선무 *urgent priority matter*

대- (큰 大) 'great; big; major' (opposite of 소 小)

대가족 *large family* 대문자 *capital letter*

대도시 *big city* 대성공 *great success*

대유행 *craze; fad* 대기업 *conglomerate*

대- (대할 對) 'with respect to; vis-à-vis'

대외 *with respect to foreign countries* 대일 *with respect to Japan*

대미외교 *policy toward the U.S.* 대미무역 *trade with the U.S.*

동- (한가지 同) 'same'

동시대 *same period/era* 동년배 *person of same age*

동업자 *business partner* 동질 *same quality; homogeneity*

되- 'again; back to source; in reverse'

되묻다 *ask again; ask back* 되팔다 *resell*

되씹다 *chew over and over again* 되새기다 *ruminate*

맹- (사나울 猛) 'fierce; violent'

맹활약 *being greatly active* 맹공격 *fierce attack*

맹연습 *rigorous practice* 맹훈련 *intense training*

무- (없을 無) 'not exist; have no…' (opposite of 유 有)

무면허 *unlicensed* 무기력 *lethargy; no energy*

무분별 *imprudence* 무차별 *indiscrimination*

반- (반대할 反) 'anti-; counter-'

반사회적 *anti-social* 반감 *antagonism; antipathy*

반작용 *reaction; counteraction* 반비례 *inverse proportion*

반- (반 半) 'half; semi-'

반세기 *half a century* 반자동 *semi-automatic*

반강제(적) *semi-compulsory* 반음 *a flat or sharp (in music)*

본- (근본 本) 'main; real; actual'

본회의 *main session (of the legislature)*   본바탕 *essence; intrinsic nature*

본보기 *example; model*   본마음 *one's real intention*

본체 *main body; true form*   본고장 *place of origin; home*

부- (도울 副) 'vice-; deputy-; subsidiary'

부사장 *company vice-president*   부총리 *deputy prime minister*

부교수 *associate professor*   부전공 *minor(field of study)*

부산물 *by-product*   부작용 *side effect*

부- (아닐 不) 'un-; not'

부자연 *unnaturalness*   부자유 *discomfort*

부적합 *incongruity*   부적절 *inappropriateness*

부도덕 *immorality*   부조화 *disharmony*

불- (아닐 不) 'un-; not'

불공정 *unfairness; injustice*   불안정 *instability*

불완전 *incomplete(ness)*   불구속 *nonrestraint*

불합격 *failure*   불균형 *imbalance*

NOTE: 不 is realized as 부 before ㄷ and ㅈ; it is 불 elsewhere (except 부실).

비- (아닐 非) 'un-; not'

비위생적 *unsanitary*   비현실적 *unrealistic*

비공개 *undisclosed; closed-door*   비양심적 *unscrupulous; unconscientious*

비주류 *non-mainstream*   비폭력 *nonviolence*

빗- 'slanted'

빗금 *slanted line*   빗장 *cross bar*

빗대다 *insinuate*   빗나가다 *go wide of the mark*

순- (순수할 純) 'pure; net'

순우리말 *pure Korean language*   순한국식 *pure Korean-style*

순이익 *net profit*   순살코기 *lean meat with no fat*

순백색 *sheet white; white as snow*   순도 (100%) *degree of purity*

악- (악할 惡) 'bad'

악영향 *bad influence*   악순환 *vicious cycle*

악조건 *adverse conditions*   악취미 *distasteful hobby*

악선전 *malicious propaganda*   악평가 *unfavorable critique*

역- (거스를 逆) 'reverse; counter'

역이용 *reverse use*   역이민 *reverse immigration*
역방향 *opposite direction*   역효과 *contrary/adverse effect*
역수출 *re-exportation*   역선전 *counterpropaganda*

유- (있을 有) 'possessing' (opposite of 무 無)

유죄 *being guilty*   유자격 *being qualified*
유권자 *eligible voter*   유지 *leading/influential figure*
유명세 *price of fame*   유명무실 *name only with no substance*

재 (다시 再) 're-; again'

재개발 *redevelopment*   재편성 *reorganization; rearrangement*
재입국 *reentry*   재정비 *putting in good order again*

저- (낮을 低) 'low' (opposite of 고 高)

저소득 *low income*   저금리 *low interest*
저지대 *low-lying land*   저자세 *low profile; modest attitude*
저개발 *underdevelopment*   저능아 *a feeble-minded child*

정- (바를 正) 'regular; full'

정회원 *regular member*   정교수 *full professor*
정육면체 *cube*   정비례 *direct proportion*

짓- 'randomly; roughly'

짓누르다 *squash*   짓밟다 *overrun; trample underfoot*
짓이기다 *mesh*   짓궂다 *be mischievous*

처- 'recklessly; at random'

처먹다 *eat greedily*   처넣다 *push in; shove in*
처바르다 *overapply (lotion)*   처박히다 *be cooped up inside*

총- (모두 總) 'overall; total'

총복습 *overall review*   총선거 *general election*
총인원 *total number of people*   총출동 *general mobilization*
총지출 *total expenditure*   총공격 *full-scale attack*

최- (가장 最) 'most; -est'

최강 *strongest*   최연소 *youngest*
최전방 *front line (military)*   최첨단 *spearhead; vanguard*
최우선 *highest priority*   최고학부 *highest institution of
                                            learning (university)*

치- 'upward'

치키다 *pull up (pants)*　　　　　　치밀다 *surge (emotion, anger)*

치솟다 *rise suddenly and swiftly*　　치뜨다 *lift up one's eyes*

현- (지금 現) 'present; current'

현상태 *present circumstances*　　　현정부 *current government*

현주소 *one's present address*　　　　현대통령 *President in office*

휘- 'round and round; recklessly'

휘젓다 *stir; swing*　　　　　　　　휘두르다 *brandish*

휘날리다 *flap/wave (in the wind)*　　휘몰아치다 *blow hard (wind); fall in whirls (snow)*

10.4 Suffixation

Unlike prefixes, which usually simply add to the meaning of a word, suffixes can modify both a word's meaning and its category.

10.4.1 Suffixes that create a noun

-개/게

찌개 *stew*　　　　　　　　　가리개 *screen, cover*

지게 *A-frame carrier*　　　　쪽집게 *tweezers*

-이

길이 *length*　　　　　　　높이 *height*

깊이 *depth*　　　　　　　　추위 *cold weather*

구이 *roasted meat, baked fish*　　시집살이 *living with one's husband's parents*

-기

밝기 *brightness*　　　　　　크기 *size, magnitude*

달리기 *running; race*　　　　줄넘기 *rope-jumping*

내기 *betting*　　　　　　　　술래잡기 *hide-and-seek*

-ㅁ/음 (-움 with some verbs that end with ㅂ):

모임 *meeting*　　　　　　　졸음 *drowsiness*

느낌 *sensation; feeling*　　외로움 *loneliness*

슬픔 *sorrow; sadness*　　　놀림 *teasing; making fun of*

10.4.2 Suffixes that create a descriptive verb

-답 'be like; be worthy of'

사람답다 *be humane*   학자답다 *be scholarly*

신사답다 *be gentleman-like*   어른답다 *be mature like an adult*

-맞 'give the impression of'

익살맞다 *be funny/comical*   궁상맞다 *be miserable-looking*

능글맞다 *be sly/sneaky*   능청맞다 *be sly/deceitful*

방정맞다 *be rash*   칠칠맞다 *be slovenly/untidy*

-스럽 'be suggestive of'

자연스럽다 *be natural*   만족스럽다 *be satisfying*

가증스럽다 *be detestable*   퉁명스럽다 *be blunt/brusque*

창피스럽다 *be embarrassing*   거추장스럽다 *be burdensome*

탐스럽다 *be appetizing/tempting*   정성스럽다 *be devoted with one's full heart*

-적 (-의 的) '-ic; -al; -ive'

공식적 *official*   상업적 *commercial*

기계적 *mechanical*   심리적 *psychological*

개인적 *personal*   충동적 *impulsive*

엽기적 *bizarre; grotesque*   현실적 *realistic; practical*

직선적 *straightforward*   일방적 *one-sided; unilateral*

NOTE: -적 is generally attached to Sino-Korean words that cannot combine with -하다. It is used in the following three types of pattern:

사람이 너무 충동**적이다**.   *She's too impulsive.*

충동**적인** 면이 마음에 든다.   *I like her impulsive side.*

충동**적으로** 내린 결정이다.   *It's an impulsively made decision.*

-롭 'be characterized by'

슬기롭다 *be wise/sensible*   지혜롭다 *be wise/resourceful*

자유롭다 *be unrestricted/free*   신비롭다 *be mysterious*

평화롭다 *be peaceful*   향기롭다 *be fragrant*

10.4.3 Suffixes that create an adverb

-껏 'to the best of'

능력껏 *to the best of one's ability*   재주껏 *to the best of one's talent*

요령껏 *to the best of one's judgment*   욕심껏 *as much as one desires*

-상 (위 上) '-wise; from the viewpoint of'

양심상 *for the sake of conscience*   체면상 *for honor's sake*

편의상 *for the sake of convenience*   사정상 *owing to circumstances*

예의상 *as a matter of courtesy*   교육상 *from the perspective of education*

역사상 *in history*   이론상 *from a theoretical point of view*

-(으)로

날로 *day by day*   참말로 *truly; indeed*

겉으로 *outwardly*   속으로 *inwardly; in one's heart*

대대로 *from generation to generation*   강제로 *by force*

Examples of the adverbial suffixes -리, -이/히, and -게 are presented in sentences because adverb-plus-verb combinations are best treated as 'chunks.'

-리

친구가 **멀리** 떠났어요.   *My friend has gone far away.*

달리 방도가 없습니다.   *There isn't any other way.*

전세계에 **널리** 알려졌다.   *It resounded through the world.*

공부를 **게을리** 하면 안 되지.   *You should not negelect your study.*

섣불리 덤볐다간 큰 코 다친다.   *If you make a foolhardy attempt, you will have a bitter experience.*

-이/히

이리 **가까이** 와요.   *Come up close here.*

내가 **끔찍이** 아끼는 후배예요.   *She's my junior who I care greatly about.*

서랍을 **샅샅이** 다 뒤져 봤어.   *I tried to ransack all the drawers.*

그 분의 겸손함은 **높이** 살 만하지.   *His modesty deserves high praise.*

우리 **영원히** 헤어지지 말자.   *Let's never break up.*

꾸준히 노력하면 성공할 거야.   *You'll succeed if you make constant efforts.*

딱히 뭐라고 설명하기가 어렵다.   *It's hard to pinpoint what it is exactly.*

무슨 생각을 그렇게 **골똘히** 해?   *What are you thinking so hard about?*

이 정도는 혼자 **거뜬히** 들 수 있어.   *I can easily lift this much by myself.*

은근히 화가 나는 거 있죠.   *I get mad in spite of myself.*

한 달 용돈이 **고스란히** 하루 기름값으로 다 나갔네.	*Oh dear, my monthly allowance got spent entirely on one day's gas.*
뻔히 알면서 왜 물어봐?	*Why do you ask when you already know it for sure?*

-게: (See *21.2.7.*)

짐 좀 **가볍게** 싸자.	*Let's pack the suitcase lightly.*
시간 없는데 **간단하게** 먹자.	*We don't have time; let's have a quick bite.*
차가 **겁나게** 달린다.	*This car is going so scarily fast.*
정말 **고맙게** 생각해요.	*I'm very grateful.*
눈물나게 고맙다.	*I'm so thankful that I could cry.*
정말 **미안하게** 생각해요.	*I feel bad (I owe you an apology).*
귀엽게 봐 주라.	*Go easy on me, please.*
시간이 **길게/지루하게** 느껴져요.	*It feels like eternity. (I am bored.)*
길게 쓰지 말고 **짤막하게** 써.	*Don't write a long one; write a short one.*
얼굴이 **까맣게** 탔어.	*My face got tanned very dark.*
까맣게 잊어버렸었어.	*I had totally forgotten.*
깨끗하게 단념해.	*Give it up completely.*
불편하겠다. 이리 **넓게** 앉아.	*You must feel uncomfortable. Sit over here using more space.*
어떤 벌이라도 **달게** 받겠습니다.	*I'll gladly accept any punishment.*
사과를 **두껍게/얇게** 깎는다.	*You're peeling a lot/little off the apple.*
딱 부러지게 얘기해.	*Say it decisively and firmly.*
배부르게 먹었어요.	*I've eaten enough; I'm full.*
책이 **불티나게** 팔린다.	*The books are selling like hot cakes.*
간만에 **빡세게** 공부 좀 했다.	*I studied awfully hard in a long time. [spoken/colloquial]*
뼈저리게 느끼고 있습니다.	*It sinks deep into my mind; I feel it keenly.*
시험이 너무 **쉽게** 나온 거 같애.	*The exam seems to be too easy.*
남 얘기라고 너무 **쉽게** 하지마.	*Don't speak lightly just because it's someone else's business.*
이 소설은 개인주의를 **신랄하게** 비판하고 있다.	*This novel poignantly criticizes individualism.*
좀 **싸게** 주세요.	*Please give me a little discount.*
너무 **비싸게** 산 거 같애.	*I think I paid too much for it.*
어렵게 내린 결정이에요.	*It was a difficult decision that I made.*

어렵게/부유하게 자랐다.	*He grew up in a poor/wealthy family.*
사진 예쁘게 나왔니?	*Has the photograph come out well?*
선물 예쁘게 포장해 주세요.	*Can you wrap the gift nicely?*
어리다고 우습게 보지 마.	*Don't underestimate me just because I'm young.*
젊게 사세요.	*Live young.*
그냥 좋게 생각해.	*Just think of it positively.*
커피 좀 진하게/연하게 타 주세요.	*Can you make my coffee strong/weak?*
옷을 춥게/얇게 입었다.	*You are not dressed warmly enough.*
춥게 자서 그런지 기침이 나네요.	*Maybe because I slept in a cold room, I'm coughing.*
안 보여요. 좀 더 크게 써 주세요.	*I can't see it. Could you write it bigger?*
내가 크게 한턱 낼게.	*I will treat you to a great meal.*
무릎에 파랗게 멍이 들었다 .	*My knee got bruised black and blue.*

Almost any descriptive verb (adjective) can be turned into an adverb by attaching -게. Some of the -리 and -이/히 adverbs above have -게 counterparts, but in many cases they are not interchangeable. For example:

멀리 떠났다.	멀게 느껴진다.
He has gone far away.	*I feel distant (from him).*
널리 알려졌다.	넓게 앉으세요.
It became known widely.	*Please sit using more space.*
길이 보존하자.	너무 길게 이야기하지 마세요.
Let's preserve it for a long time.	*Don't talk too long.*
굳이 갈 필요 없어.	굳게 약속했어.
You need not take the trouble to go.	*I made a solemn promise.*
분명히 여기 있었어.	분명하게 얘기했어.
It was here for sure.	*I made my point clearly.*

10.4.4 Suffixes relating to address terms

A variety of suffixes that are attached to terms of address carry implications about the speaker's relationship to the other person. As noted in chapter 3, the way in which you address others is an extremely sensitive matter in Korean. Considerable caution is therefore called for in the use of these suffixes.

-님: honorific suffix which is attached to proper names or certain titles (하느님 'God,' 부처님 'Buddha,' 부모님 'parents').

-씨 (성 氏): has multiple uses, which range from impersonal to romantic. When used improperly, it can offend people.

- Full name plus 씨 (진용주씨) is appropriate for impersonal use (for instance, in the bank when addressing customers), although it can be replaced by the more respectful -님 (진용주님).

- Either full name or first name plus 씨 is commonly used among young colleagues of similar age. It can also be used by an older person to address a younger person, but not vice versa.

- First name plus 씨 (which is less formal than full name plus 씨) is common among adults who are fairly close and who are about the same age but whose friendship began after college. It is also frequently employed by romantic partners, especially at the beginning of their relationship.

- Family name plus 씨 (김씨) is used for those who hold a menial job (김씨 아저씨). It is also neutrally used to refer to someone's family name (한국인 중에는 김씨가 제일 많다 'The Kims are the majority among Koreans').

-군, -양 (임금 君, 계집애 孃): used by a senior person to a much younger male/female (김군, 최양, 연지양).

-아/야: affectionately used for children or between very close friends of similar age or younger (희진아, 효리야, 자기야).

-(이)여: used in poems, religious prayers, advertisements, etc.

젊은이여 대망을 품으라.	*Young people, be ambitious.*
남성들이여!	*Males!*
하늘이시여!	*Father in heaven!*

10.4.5 Suffixes relating to people

-가 (전문가 家) 'professional person'

예술가 *artist*	사업가 *entrepreneur*
성악가 *vocalist*	역사가 *historian*
작곡가 *musical composer*	건축가 *architect*

-객 (손님 客) 'guest; person'

방문객 *visitor*	피서객 *summer tourist*
여행객 *tourist*	입장객 *visitor (to a public place)*

-관 (벼슬아치 官) 'government official'

경찰관 *police officer*	통역관 *interpreter*
시험관 *examiner*	검열관 *censor*

-내기 'person characterized by/seen as'

풋내기 *novice; greenie*   시골내기 *country bumpkin*

신출내기 *newcomer, novice*   보통내기 *ordinary person*

NOTE: 보통내기 (= 여간내기) is used in negated sentences only:
보통내기가 아니다. *He is no ordinary person.*

-돌이 'males characterized by/seen as' [spoken/colloquial]

떡돌이 *rice-cake loving boy*   곰돌이 *teddy bear*

공돌이 *factory boy*   짠돌이 *stingy boy*

-범 (범인 犯) 'criminal'

살인범 *murderer*   전과 2 범 *second-time offender*

유괴범 *kidnapper*   정치범 *political offender*

-사 (스승 師) 'professional; master'

이발사 *barber*   약제사 *pharmacist*

마술사 *magician*   선교사 *missionary*

요리사 *cook; chef*   간호사 *nurse*

-사 (선비 士) 'scholar; one who is officially qualified as'

비행사 *aviator*   영양사 *nutritionist*

회계사 *accountant; CPA*   투우사 *bullfighter*

-생 (날 生) 'student; birth'

초년생 *beginner; newbie*   90 년생 *person born in 1990*

유학생 *student studying abroad*   청강생 *auditor*

복학생 *student who is back in school (after military service)*   삼수생 *student preparing for college entrance exam for the third time*

-수 (손 手) 'person with a skill or role'

운전수 *driver*   소방수 *fire fighter*

일루수 *the first baseman*   유격수 *shortstop*

-순이 'females characterized by/seen as' [spoken/colloquial]

똑순이 *smart girl*   식순이 *kitchen maid*

짠순이 *stingy girl*   먹순이 *female eating-machine*

-아 (아이 兒) 'child; person'

행운아 *lucky person*   혼혈아 *child of mixed blood*

사생아 *illegitimate child*   정신지체아 *mentally retarded child*

-원 (관원 員) 'member; employee'

사무원 *office worker*	판매원 *salesperson*
경비원 *guard*	경호원 *bodyguard*
구조원 *rescuer*	교환원 *telephone operator*

-이 'person'

맏이 *the eldest child*	젊은이 *youngster*
멍청이 *air head; dunce*	절름발이 *person with a limp*
못난이 *fool*	지은이 *writer; author*

-인 (사람 人) 'person'

이방인 *foreigner; stranger*	외계인 *alien*
원시인 *primitive person*	현대인 *modern person*
지식인 *an intellectual*	직장인 *company worker*
대변인 *spokesperson*	보증인 *sponsor; guarantor*

-자 (사람 者) 'person; fellow'

지휘자 *(orchestra) director*	담당자 *person in charge*
소비자 *consumer*	시청자 *(TV) viewer*
탑승자 *passenger*	당첨자 *prize winner*
암살자 *assassin*	목격자 *witness*
중독자 *addict*	기회주의자 *opportunist*
영주권자 *permanent resident*	시민권자 *citizen*

-족 (무리 族) 'tribe; group'

올빼미족 *night people; owls*	얌체족 *selfish people*
꽃뱀족 *gold-digger*	제비족 *gigolos*
캥거루족 *grown-up children still living with their parents*	

-주 (주인 主) 'master; boss'

기업주 *boss of the enterprise; CEO*	경영주 *business owner; manager*
사업주 *business proprietor*	세대주 *head of a household*

-치 (어리석을 痴) 'imbecile'

백치 *moron*	천치 *idiot*
음치 *person who is tone-deaf*	길치/방향치 *person with a bad sense of direction*

-파 (물갈래 派) 'faction; clique'

인상파 *impressionists*   낭만파 *romantics*

보수파 *conservative force*   기분파 *people who are very generous*
                                                                         when they are in good mood

10.4.6 Suffixes relating to place or institution

-가 (거리 街) 'street'

주택가 *residential street*   홍등가 *red-light district*

상점가 *shopping street*   식당가 *restaurant row*

-방 (방 房) 'shop; store'

빨래방 *laundromat*   피씨방 *internet cafe*

찜질방 *sauna*   비디오방 *video room*

만화방 *cartoon reading room*   노래방 *singing room; karaoke*

-부 (나눌 部) 'section; department'

중심부 *center; central area*   국방부 *Department of Defense*

교육부 *Ministry of Education*   문화관광부 *Ministry of Culture*
                                                                         and Tourism

-사 (단체 社) 'company; corporation'

출판사 *publishing company*   신문사 *newspaper company*

방송사 *broadcasting company*   제작사 *manufacturer; producer*

-상 (장사 商) 'business; trade'

잡화상 *general store*   보석상 *jewelry store*

고물상 *junk store*   포목상 *linen store*

-석 (자리 席) 'seat'

운전석 *driver's seat*   커플석 *seat for a couple*

일반석 *general admission seat*   특(별)석 *reserved/special seat*

방청석 *seats for the public (at court,*   관중석 *seats for the audience (at*
          concert, etc.)   *ballpark, concert, etc.)*

-소 (곳 所) 'place; institute; facility'

환전소 *foreign exchange counter*   탁아소 *nursery; day care center*

이발소 *barber shop*   상담소 *office for consultation*

보건소 *public health center*   휴게소 *rest stop*

-실 (방 室) 'room; office'

실험실 *laboratory*   수술실 *operating room (OR)*
관리실 *management office*   자료실 *reference room*
냉장실 *cold-storage room*   냉동실 *freezer*

-원 (집 院) 'institution'

고아원 *orphanage*   수도원 *monastery*
양로원 *nursing home*   연수원 *training institute*
요양원 *rehabilitation center*   기도원 *prayer house*

-장 (곳 場) 'place (for an event)'

해수욕장 *swimming beach*   축구장 *soccer field*
경기장 *stadium; athletic field*   연회장 *banquet hall*
선착장 *harbor; port*   촬영장 *(cinema, film) set*

-지 (곳 地) 'place; land'

중심지 *center; central place*   거주지 *place of residence*
유적지 *historic site*   명승지 *famous scenic spots*
매립지 *land fill*   근원지 *place of origin*

-처 (곳 處) 'place; bureau'

구입처 *place for purchase*   거래처 *client; business connection*
접수처 *place for (school/job) appli-   응모처 *place for entering a contest,*
cation; information office*   *for a prize, etc.*

10.4.7   Suffixes relating to classification

-감 'material for; a suitable person'

신랑감 *prospective bridegroom*   신부감 *prospective bride*
경고감 *behavior that calls for warning*   눈요기감 *eye-candy*
사형감 *criminal deserving capital
punishment*

-기 (기계 機) 'type of machine'

계산기 *calculator*   식기세척기 *dish washer*
인쇄기 *printing machine*   전투기 *combat plane*

-기 (그릇 器) 'type of device; instrument'

분무기 *sprayer; vaporizer*   소화기 *fire extinguisher*
계량기 *gauge; meter; scale*   도청기 *wiretapping device; bug*
보행기 *baby walker*   보청기 *hearing aid*

-계 (경계 界) 'world; circle'

가요계 *pop music world*   영화계 *film world*

정계 *political world*   종교계 *religious world*

-과 (과목 科, 매길 課) 'department; section'

철학과 *Philosophy Department*   수학과 *Mathematics Department*

비뇨기과 *Urology Department*   인사과 *personnel division/office*

경리과 *accounting section*   총무과 *general affairs section*

-력 (힘 力) 'power; type of ability'

경제력 *economic power*   영향력 *influential power*

경쟁력 *competitive power*   어휘력 *one's capacity for vocabulary*

추진력 *driving force; positive drive* 가창력 *singing ability*

-류 (무리 類) 'kind; sort'

생선류 *class of fish*   면류 *noodles*

식품류 *groceries*   식기류 *tableware*

화장품류 *cosmetics*   가구류 *furniture*

보석류 *jewelry*   잡화류 *miscellaneous goods*

-면 (낯 面) 'aspect; newspaper section'

기술면 *technological aspect*   일면 *front page of the newspaper*

사회면 *page for local news*   경제면 *page for business news*

-물 (물건 物) 'type of stuff; thing'

해산물 *seafood*   건어물 *dried seafood*

인쇄물 *printed matter*   배설물 *excrement*

우편물 *mail; postal material*   유인물 *handout; leaflet*

-별 (다를 別) 'division; classification'

연도별 *division by year*   국가별 *division by country*

지역별 *division by region*   연령별 *division by age*

직업별 *breakdown by occupation*   색깔별 *division by color*

-성 (성품 性) 'nature; quality'

정통성 *orthodoxy*   처녀성 *virginity*

신빙성 *credibility*   일관성 *consistency; coherence*

게릴라성 *guerrilla style*   변태성 *abnormality; sexual perversion*

-식 (법 式) 'style; type; ceremony'

회전식 *revolving type (door)*   스파르타식 *Spartan style*
주관식 *essay-type (question)*   객관식 *multiple-choice type (question)*
약혼식 *engagement ceremony*   금혼식 *golden wedding anniversary*

-판 (책 版) 'edition'

문고판 *pocketbook edition*   번역판 *translated edition*
해적판 *pirated edition*   현대판 *modern edition/version*

-품 (물건 品) 'type of goods'

국산품 *domestic products*   수입품 *imported goods*
불량품 *defective goods*   재고품 *goods in stock; unsold goods*
중고품 *second-hand goods*   비매품 *articles not for sale*
식료품 *groceries*   혼수품 *articles necessary for marriage*

-풍 (모습 風) 'style; manners'

현대풍 *modern style*   집시풍 *gypsy style*
시골풍 *country manners*   학자풍 *scholarly*

-학 (배울 學) 'field of study'

언어학 *linguistics*   인류학 *anthropology*
통계학 *statistics*   사회학 *sociology*
천문학 *astronomy*   정치학 *political science*
의상학 *study of clothing*   경영학 *business administration*

-형 (틀 型) 'type; model'

표준형 *standard type*   천재형 *genius type*
혈액형 *blood type*   1998 년형 *the 1998 model*
마마보이형 *mama-boy style*   청순가련형 *pure and innocent type (girl)*

-형 (형상 形) 'shape; form'

사각형 *quadrangle*   계란형 *egg-shaped*
타원형 *oval-shaped*   V 자형 *V-shaped*

10.4.8 *Suffixes relating to monetary transactions*

-값 'price'

땅값 *land price*   기름값 *gas price*
점심값 *lunch money*   자리값 *price for a spot (at the beach, etc.)*
몸값 *ransom*   나이값(을 하다) *(act) one's age*

-권 (문서 券) 'ticket; coupon'

상품권 *gift certificate*　　　　　　　항공권 *airline ticket*

탑승권 *boarding pass*　　　　　　　　할인권 *discount coupon*

-금 (돈 金) 'money'

기부금 *contribution; donation*　　　　사례금 *honorarium; reward money*

축의금 *congratulatory money*　　　　　부조금 *congratulatory/condolence money*

비자금 *secret fund*　　　　　　　　　보증금 *security deposit*

계약금 *initial deposit; down payment*　중도금 *second deposit; partial payment*

보조금 *subsidy*　　　　　　　　　　비상금 *emergency money*

-료 (값 料) 'charge; fee'

통화료 *call charge*　　　　　　　　　전기료 *electricity charge*

수업료 *school fees; tuition*　　　　　구독료 *subscription charge*

연체료 *late fee*　　　　　　　　　　과태료 *monetary penalty*

임대료 *lease rent*　　　　　　　　　수수료 *service charge; commission*

-비 (비용 費) 'expenditures; cost'

생활비 *cost of living*　　　　　　　　교통비 *transportation costs*

치료비 *medical fee; doctor's bill*　　과외비 *private tutoring expenses*

유지비 *maintenance costs*　　　　　　수리비 *repair costs*

숙박비 *lodging expenses*　　　　　　인건비 *labor costs*

냉(난)방비 *cooling (& heating) costs*　양육비 *child-raising expenses*

-세 (세금 稅) 'tax'

자동차세 *auto tax*　　　　　　　　　통행세 *transit tax; toll*

재산세 *property tax*　　　　　　　　양도소득세 *capital gains tax*

인세 *royalties (on a book)*　　　　　부가세 *additional tax; surtax*

-세 (세낼 貰) 'rent'

삭월세 *monthly rental*　　　　　　　집세 *house rent*

방세 *room rent*　　　　　　　　　　자리세 *rent for a spot (in resort areas)*

10.4.9　Suffixes relating to language and writing

-어 (말씀 語)

모국어 *native language*　　　　　　　외국어 *foreign language*

유행어 *trendy phrase*　　　　　　　　수식어 *modifier (in grammar)*

동의어 *synonym*　　　　　　　　　　반의어 *antonym*

-장 (문서 狀) 'document; letter'

청첩(장) *wedding invitation card*   연하장 *New Year's card*

고소장 *written accusation*   일기장 *diary notebook*

독촉장 *(payment) demand note*   위임장 *power-of-attorney letter*

-담 (말씀 談) 'talk(s); tale'

성공담 *success story*   모험담 *adventure story*

경험담 *personal episodes*   정담 *friendly talk; tête-à-tête*

-서 (글 書) 'writing; document'

이력서 *résumé*   사직서 *letter of resignation*

계약서 *contract*   각서 *promissory note; written promise*

(신분)증명서 *identification card*   보증서 *letter of guarantee; warranty*

10.4.10 Suffixes relating to the speaker's perception and emotion

The following suffixes are used to express the speaker's 'negative' perception of things. They add an unpleasant negative connotation to the noun to which they are attached.

-투성이 'covered or smeared with'

오자투성이 *full of typos*   광고투성이 *covered with ads*

약점투성이 *full of weaknesses*   머리카락투성이 *hair all over*

-딱지

코딱지 *snot; nose dirt*   곰보딱지 *pockmarked person*

심술딱지 *nasty temper*   소갈딱지 *mind; thought*

NOTE: 소갈딱지 (= 소갈머리) is always followed by either 없다 with the meaning 'be stupid and thoughtless' or 좁다 with the meaning 'be terribly narrow-minded.'

-머리

그 성질머리는 여전하다.   *That terrible temper is still the same.*

버르장머리 한 번 고약하네.   *How terrible his manners are.*

인정머리하곤...   *How cruel she is; she has no heart.*

주변머리라고는 하나도 없다니까. *He has no adaptability whatsoever.*

이제 술이라면 넌덜머리가 난다.   *Alcohol really sickens me now.*

　(넌덜머리 = 진절머리)

-대가리 (대가리 is a familiar/casual version of 머리 'head')

멋대가리 *charm; taste*   맛대가리 *flavor; taste*

겁대가리 *fear; cowardice*   재미대가리 *fun; amusement*

NOTE: -대가리 is always followed by 없다 (맛대가리 하나도 없다 'be damn tasteless,' 재미대가리 없다 'be bloody boring,' etc.)

10.4.11 Suffixes relating to quantity/approximation

-량 (헤아릴 量) 'amount'

강수량 *amount of rainfall*   적설량 *amount of snowfall*

권장량 *recommended dose*   치사량 *fatal dose*

-쯤 'approximate size, amount, length of time, ability, etc.'

키가 180 쯤 되고 몸무게가 70 킬로쯤 된다.	*He is about 180 centimeters tall and weighs about 70 kilograms.*
아홉시간쯤 잤어.	*I slept for about nine hours.*
몇시쯤 됐어?	*What's the approximate time now?*
어디쯤 왔을까?	*I wonder where they are on their way here.*
이쯤에서 끝내는게 어떨까?	*How about ending it around here?*
20 대 초반/중반/후반쯤 돼 보인다.	*She looks like she is in her early/mid/late twenties.*
이 정도 추위쯤이야.	*Just this much cold is nothing.*
의사쯤 돼가지고 이런 것도 몰라?	*How can a doctor not know things like this?*

-경 (잠깐 頃) 'around, about (refers only to a time)'

십사일경 *around the 14th*   오후 두 시경 *around 2 p.m.*

화요일경 *around Tuesday*   2000 년경 *about the year 2000*

-께 'around, about (a certain time); near (a place)' [spoken/colloquial]

10 시께 *around 10 o'clock*   공원 정문께 *near the main gate of the park*

-분 (나눌 分) 'portion; amount'

이달분 *this month's amount*   일년분 *one year's worth*

갈비 일인분 *one helping of galbi*   (약) 이틀분 *(medicine) dose for two days*

-치 'a fixed quantity'

사흘치 *three-day supply*   두달치 *quantity for two months*

일년치 *one-year supply*   기대치 *level of one's expectation*

-어치 'worth'

값어치 *value; worth*   얼마치 *how many dollars' worth?*

(귤)만원어치 *₩10,000 worth of*   반푼어치 *the least amount*
　　　　(oranges)

NOTE: 반푼어치 is found only with one frequently used expression, 어림없다 'be impossible; no way.' By saying 어림 반푼어치도 없다, the meaning of impossibility is strongly emphasized – 'It's utterly impossible. It's nonsense.'

-짜리

만원짜리 지폐 *₩10,000 bill*   구백불짜리 가방 *₩900 bag*

방 두개짜리 아파트 *two-bedroom apt.*   아파트 20 평짜리 *20 p'yŏng apt.*

NOTE: 1[한] 평 = 35.57 sq. ft.

-째 'in entirety; as it is'

통째 *in its entirety; without cutting*   병째 *(drinking) out of a bottle*

그릇째 *all, including the container*   껍질째 *without peeling off the skin*

-꼴 'at the rate of; per unit' (can be replaced by -정도)

2000 원에 세 개니까 한 개에 약 700 원꼴이네요.
　Given that these are three for ₩2,000, each costs about ₩700.

일주일에 삼십 불이니까 하루 평균 약 4 불꼴이에요.
　Given that the weekly rate is $30, the average daily rate is approximately $4.

10.5 Abbreviations

Finding quick ways to say things is popular in Korean just as it is in English, and is often responsible for the creation of new expressions. One common strategy involves dropping the last part of the word/phrase.

왕싸가지 *rude person*   밥맛 *disgusting person/behavior*

인테리 *intellectual*   인플레 *inflation*

슈퍼 *supermarket*   프로 *program; professional; percentage*

다이아 *diamond*   런닝 *running shirt; undershirt*

추리닝 *training/sports clothes*   후라시 *flashlight*

매스컴 *mass communication*   알바 *part time job ('arbeit' in German)*
　　　　　　　　　　　　　　　　　　　(알바 < 아르바이트)

Another strategy eliminates the first part of the original word.

벤츠	< 머세디즈 벤츠 >	*Mercedes-Benz*
범생	< 모범생 >	*exemplary student*
업자	< 실업자 >	*unemployed person*
존심	< 자존심 >	*self-respect; pride*
간만에	< 오래간만에 >	*after a long time*

In addition, some compounds or phrases are shortened by retaining only a part (usually the first) of each component.

아점	< 아침 겸 점심 >	*brunch*
물냉	< 물냉면 >	*naengmyŏn noodles in cold soup*
비냉	< 비빔냉면 >	*naengmyŏn noodles mixed with spicy sauce*
입시	< 입학시험 >	*entrance exam*
열공	< 열심히 공부하다 >	*studying hard*
한영	< 한국어와 영어 >	*Korean and English (dictionary)*
의대	< 의과 대학교 >	*medical school*
급질	< 급한 질문 >	*urgent question*
남친/여친	< 남자친구/여자친구 >	*boyfriend/girlfriend*
선관위	< 선거관리 위원회 >	*election management committee*
공채	< 공개채용 >	*public hiring/employment*
조폭	< 조직 폭력배 >	*organized gangsters*
전교조	< 전국 교원 노동조합 >	*teachers' union*
자판기	< 자동 판매기 >	*vending machine*
택배	< 주택배달 >	*door-to-door delivery service*
민증	< 주민등록증 >	*identification card*

A somewhat similar process is also found with compounds formed with the help of loan words.

리모컨	< 리모트 컨트롤 >	*remote control*
에어컨	< 에어 컨디셔너 >	*air conditioner*
오므라이스	< 오므렛 라이스 >	*omelet rice*
디카	< 디지털 카메라 >	*digital camera*
몰카	< 몰래 카메라 >	*hidden camera*
컴맹	< 컴퓨터 문맹 >	*computer illiterate*
야깅	< 야간 조깅 >	*night-time jogging*

10.6 Some recently created expressions

The word formation processes discussed earlier in this chapter frequently create innovations in Korean vocabulary. In addition, the innovative and non-standard use of language that is popular among younger people often assigns new meanings to old words and expressions. Here is a sampling of comtemporary expressions that are widely used in colloquial speech, especially among young people.

공주병 정말 심하다. 그러니 **(왕)따**를 당해도 싸지. 저런 애는 **왕자병** 심한 애를 만나서 고생 좀 해 봐야 돼.

> *Her princess syndrome is really severe. He deserves to be ostracized being like that. She needs to date someone like her who has a serious prince syndrome to get a taste of her own medicine.*

요즘 튀는 배우들 중에는 **중고딩 (중딩 & 고딩)** 들이 많아요. 심지어는 **초딩**도 있구요. **대딩**만 해도 한물 갔어요.

> *Today's stand-out actors consist of mostly middle and high schoolers. There are even elementary schoolers. Even college students are a bit on the old side.*

여기는 **직딩**들이 자주 찾는 웹 사이트야.

> *This website is frequented by business people.*

요즘 한참 뜨는 배우예요. **얼짱**에 **몸짱**에 **맘짱**까지 완전 **캡**이죠.

> *He's the rising star these days. His face, body, and character are all top-notch.*

> NOTE: 맘짱 is a shortened form of 마음짱. The suffix -짱 is quite productively used if someone is a great cook, (s)he is a 요리짱; if someone is excellent in school, (s)he is a 공부짱; and so on.

오늘 기분 **짱이다**, 내가 한턱 거하게 **쏠**게. [쏘다]

> *I'm feeling awesome today, so I'll treat you to a great meal.*

백화점에서 세일을 크게 해서 **짱** 많이 샀어.

> *There was a big sale in the department store so we bought a ton of stuff.*

내가 저녁에 **문자 때릴**게. [때리다]

> *I'll text you in the evening.*

A: 저녁먹고 우리 영화하나 **때릴**까?

B: **당근이지**.

> *A: After dinner, do you wanna hit a movie?*
> *B: Of course.*

농담이 재미있기는 커녕 **썰렁하다**.

> *Your joke is far from being funny; it's cheesy.*

그렇게 안달만 하지 말고 이제 슬슬 **작업을 걸어** 봐.

> *Stop fidgeting like that and try to do something to show her that you're interested in her.*

어휴 열 받어. **뚜껑 열린다** 정말. [familiar/casual]
Oh, how infuriating. I'm about to blow my top.

그 교수한테 추천서 좀 써달라고 이메일 보냈는데 **씹혔어**. [familiar/casual]
I sent an e-mail to that professor asking for a letter of recommendation,
but it got completely ignored [chewed up].

A: 뭐? 그 교수가 수업시간에 너한테 **쪽 줬**다구? [familiar/casual]

B: 그래 그 노땅한테 **쪽 먹었**다. 완전 **쪽 팔렸**어. [familiar/casual]

  A: What? The professor embarrassed you in class?
  B: Yes, I got embarrassed by the old geezer. I was completely humiliated.

It would take another book to list the internet expressions that have developed
over the last decade and continue to be created on a daily basis. Speed is vital in
internet communication, and it is therefore not surprising that many innovations
are the product of abbreviation and clipping. For example, 안습이다 is the
clipped version of 안구에 습기가 차다 'the pupil gets moist,' which is used to
sarcastically mean 'how sad,' and 갑툭튀 is the shortened form of 갑자기 툭
튀어나온…, meaning 'popped out of the blue.'

11 Some vocabulary contrasts

No two languages present the world in exactly the same way, and it is common for one language to make distinctions that another ignores. This chapter focuses on some areas in which Korean makes contrasts in its vocabulary that have no direct counterpart in English.

11.1 Verbs of wearing

Unlike English, Korean uses different verbs for different types of 'wearing' – depending on the body part that is covered and also depending on how you put the article of clothing on. (Typical articles and accessories for each verb of wearing are provided below.)

11.1.1 Depending on the body part that is covered

- Things that are put on the torso as clothes: 입다

옷 *clothes*	바지 *pants*	웃도리 *top*
코트 *coat*	조끼 *vest*	잠바 *jacket*
스웨터 *sweater*	치마 *skirt*	앞치마 *apron*
팬티 *panties/boxers*	팬티 스타킹 *panty hose*	내복 *winter underwear*
수영복 *swim suit*	교복 *school uniform*	비옷 *rain coat*

밖에 추우니까 든든히 입어라. 바지 입고 조끼도 입고 코트도 입어.
> *It's cold outside, so bundle up. Put on the pants, the vest, and also the coat.*

- Things that are put on the feet: 신다

신발 *shoes*	양말 *socks*	구두 *dress shoes*
부츠 *boots*	운동화 *sneakers*	장화 *rubber boots*
실내화 *indoor shoes*	팬티 스타킹 *panty hose*	
판타롱/밴드 스타킹 *knee-length/thigh-length stockings*		

구두 신지 말고 운동화 신어. 그런데 바지를 입은 거니 신은 거니?
> *Wear sneakers, not dress shoes. By the way, are you wearing your pants as clothes or as shoes? (Your pants are too long!)*

NOTE: Both 입다 and 신다 can be used for 팬티 스타킹.

- Things that end up on or over the head: 쓰다

  안경 *glasses*   모자 *hat*   가발 *wig*
  가면 *mask*   우산 *umbrella*

  복면강도가 머리에 스타킹을 뒤집어 쓰고 들어 왔어요.
  The masked robber came in with a stocking over his head.

- Things that are put around the wrist, ankle, or waist: 차다

  시계 *watch*   팔찌 *bracelet*   발찌 *anklet*
  수갑 *handcuffs*   기저귀 *diaper*   총/칼 *gun/knife*

  보통 왼 손에 시계를 차고 오른 손에 팔찌를 차지요.
  People usually wear a watch on the left wrist and a bracelet on the right one.

- Things that are put around the shoulders: 걸치다

  숄 *shawl*   카디건 *cardigan*   코트 *coat*

  추울텐데 이 카디건 걸칠래?
  It must be cold; do you want to put this cardigan around your shoulders?

11.1.2 *Depending on the manner of putting something on*

- Things that are put on by 'tying' or 'buckling': 매다

  넥타이 *necktie*   벨트 *belt*   스카프 *scarf*

  오늘 금요일이니까 캐주얼하게 넥타이는 매지 말아야겠다.
  I think I better not wear a tie today because it's Friday and I want to be casual.

- Things that are put on by 'slipping on' or 'squeezing into': 끼다

  반지 *ring*   장갑 *gloves*   안경 *glasses*
  콘택트 렌즈 *contact lens*   팔찌 *bracelet*

  손가락마다 반지를 꼈어. 심지어는 엄지 손가락에까지.
  She has rings on each and every finger, including even her thumbs.

- Things that are put on by 'hanging': 걸다

  그 목걸이 거니까 우아해 보여요.
  You look elegant with the necklace on.

- Things that are put on by 'attaching': 달다 (or 부착하다 [written/formal])

  이름표/명찰 *name tag*   배지 *badge*   리본 *ribbon*

  세미나에 참석하시는 동안 모두 이름표를 부착해 주시기 바랍니다.
  We'd like all of you to wear name tags during the seminar.

  이름표를 다니까 사람들 이름 외우기에 편하네요. (다니까 < 달으니까)
  It's easy to memorize people's names because they have name tags on.

- Things that are put on by 'spraying': **뿌리다**

향수는 너무 많이 뿌리지 않고 적당히 뿌리는 것이 극히 중요하다.
  It's extremely important not to overdo one's perfume but to wear just the right amount.

- Things that are put on by 'wrapping around': **두르다**

앞치마 *apron*	수건 *towel*	두건 *bandana*
(실크) 스카프 *(silk) scarf*	(털) 목도리 *(wool) scarf*	숄 *shawl*

머리에는 두건을 두르고 목에는 수건을 둘렀더라구요.
  I saw him with a bandana around his head and a towel around his neck.

- Things that are put on by 'inserting': **꽂다**

머리에 핀을 꽂고 양쪽 귀 뒤에 꽃을 꽂았어요.
  She wore a pin in her hair and flowers behind both her ears.

- Things (accessories) that are put on in various manners: **하다**

넥타이 *necktie*	벨트 *belt*	스카프/목도리 *scarf*
팔찌/발찌 *bracelet/anklet*	귀걸이 *ear ring*	목걸이 *necklace*
리본 *ribbon*	머리핀 *hairpin*	가발 *wig*
가면 *mask*	앞치마 *apron*	브래지어 *bra*

큰 목도리를 하니까 귀걸이가 안 보인다.
  Because you wore a big scarf, I cannot see your ear rings.

- Any of the articles from above and other things that can be put on as part of formal attire, out of regulation, and so on: **착용하다** [written/formal]

유니폼 *uniform*	군복 *military uniform*	교복 *school uniform*
배지 *badge*	예복 *ceremonial clothes*	정장 *formal suit*
수영모 *bathing cap*	구명조끼 *life vest*	이름표/명찰 *name tag*

수영장에서는 반드시 수영모(자)를 착용해 주시기 바랍니다.
  Please be sure to wear bathing caps in the pool.

NOTE: 입다, 쓰다, 달다, etc. are used in non-formal situations: 수영모자 안 쓰고 수영하다 걸렸어 'I got caught while swimming without a bathing cap.'

As we have seen, more than one verb can be used with a particular item. This can come about due to differences in the formality of the situation (as in the case of 달다 vs. 부착하다 and 입다/쓰다/달다 vs. 착용하다). In addition, the choice of verb can vary depending on whether the speaker focuses on the body part that is covered or the manner of putting something on. So we can say 안경을 쓰다 because glasses are put on the head, but we can also say 안경을 끼다 because they are slipped on.

Finally, when there is more than one manner of wearing a certain item (usually accessories), 하다 may be used instead of a more specialized verb. Thus, we can say 넥타이를 매다 or 하다, 벨트를 매다 or 하다, 팔찌를 차다 or 하다, and so on.

11.2 Verbs of taking off

Verbs of taking off are not as diverse as verbs of wearing. There are just a few such verbs, and the choice among them is based on how something is taken off, as the examples below illustrate. (Perfume cannot be taken off and an umbrella is either folded, for which the verb 접다 is used, or shut down, for which 끄다 is used.)

- Things that are taken off by 'peeling' or 'lifting off': 벗다

옷 (any type of) garment	신발 (any type of) shoes	양말 socks
스타킹 stockings	브래지어 bra	안경 glasses
모자 hat	가발 wig	가면 mask
장갑 gloves		

  옷도 안 벗고 신발도 안 벗은 채 그냥 잠이 들었어요.
  He fell asleep without taking off his clothes or even his shoes.

- Things that are taken off by 'taking out': 빼다

반지 ring	귀걸이 ear ring	목걸이 necklace
팔찌 bracelet	장갑 gloves	시계 watch
안경 glasses	콘택트 렌즈 contact lens	벨트 belt
핀 pin	리본 ribbon	기저귀 diaper
배지 badge	이름표 name tag	

  찜질방에 갈 때는 반지하고, 목걸이, 귀걸이 전부 빼 놓고 가도록 해.
  Make sure to take the ring, necklace, and ear rings all off when you go to the sauna.

- Things that are taken off by 'untying': 풀다

넥타이 necktie	시계 watch	목도리 scarf
벨트 belt		

  답답할텐데 넥타이 푸세요.
  You must be feeling stuffy; why don't you take your necktie off?

- Things that are taken off by 'detaching': 떼다

  밖에 나갈 때는 배지하고 이름표를 떼자.
  Let's take off the badge and the name tag when we go out.

Notice that more than one verb can be used with certain items: 안경을 벗다 or 빼다, 장갑을 벗다 or 빼다, 시계를 풀다 or 빼다, and so on.

11.3 Verbs of playing

Unlike in English where the verb 'play' is used for all sorts of sports, games, and music, several different verbs are used in Korean. It is very important to note that 놀다 is an intransitive verb that means only 'play around without doing any type of purposeful activity' – the opposite of work. So, it cannot be used to describe participation in sports or games (with the exception of 윷놀다 'play *yut* sticks' – a traditional Korean game). Instead, as the next examples show, you must choose from a variety of other verbs based on the type of activity that is involved.

- Activities that involve hitting – keyboards, a ball, cards, etc.: 치다

드럼 *drum*	북 *Korean drum*	장구 *hour-glass-shaped drum*
기타 *guitar*	피아노 *piano*	탁구 *table tennis*
테니스 *tennis*	배드민턴 *badminton*	골프 *golf*
볼링 *bowling*	화투 *hwat'u/cards*	트럼프 *western cards*

피아노는 좀 치는데 기타는 못 쳐요.
I can play the piano a little bit, but I can't play the guitar.

화투칠 때는 낙장불입이죠.
When you play hwat'u, you cannot take your card back once you put it out.

- Activities that involve plucking strings: 켜다

바이올린 *violin*	첼로 *cello*	가야금 *Kayagŭm*

바이올린 켜는 소리가 정말 아름답다.
The violin sound is really beautiful.

- Activities that involve blowing: 불다

플룻 *flute*	피리 *pipe*	트럼펫 *trumpet*
색소폰 *saxophone*	나팔 *bugle*	호루라기 *whistle*

밤에 피리 부는 소리가 처량하게 들린다.
The sound of playing a pipe at night is sad.

- Playing musical instruments formally or professionally: 연주하다

다음 달에 국립극장에서 첼로를 연주할 예정입니다.
I will be performing cello at the National Theater next month.

- Activities that involve placing a piece in a board game: 두다

바둑은 좀 두는데 장기는 못 둡니다.
I can play paduk, but I don't know how to play chess.

- Activities involving various actions (running, kicking, hitting, etc.): 하다

농구 *basketball*	배구 *volleyball*	야구 *baseball*
축구 *soccer*	윷놀이 *yut-stick game*	게임 *game*
볼링 *bowling*	탁구 *table tennis*	테니스 *tennis*
골프 *golf*	배드민턴 *badminton*	화투 *hwat'u/cards*

NOTE: The words in the bottom two rows can also be used with 치다.

심심한데 농구하러 갈까?
We are bored; shall we go play basketball?

우리 화투하지 말고 윷놀이 하는 게 어때요?
How about playing yut-stick game instead of hwat'u?

- 윷: 놀다

저는 설날때마다 가족끼리 모여서 윷을 노는 게 참 재미 있어요.
I really love playing yut sticks with my family every New Year's Day.

11.4   Verbs of cleaning

Students in first-year Korean language classes often incorrectly say 얼굴을 청소했습니다 to mean 'I cleaned my face'! As we will see, verbs of cleaning are somewhat more specialized in Korean than in English.

- Surface washing or cleaning with water: 씻다 or 닦다

과일 *fruit*	채소 *vegetables*	쌀 *rice*
손 *hands*	얼굴 *face*	몸 *body*

과일은 깨끗이 씻어서 먹어야 돼요.
You should thoroughly wash fruit before eating it.

- Surface cleaning by wiping, brushing, scraping: 닦다

거울 *mirror*	차 *car*	유리창 *window glass*
식탁 *dining table*	접시 *plates*	책상 *desk*
과일 *fruit*	손 *hands*	얼굴 *face*
몸 *body*	이 *teeth*	

요즘 알바로 식당에서 접시 닦고 있습니다.
These days, I wash dishes in a restaurant as my part-time job.

- Cleaning of horizontal surfaces by wiping or mopping with a cloth: 훔치다

방 *room*	마루 *(wooden) floors*	책상 *desk*
식탁 *dining table*		

마른 걸레로 여기 마루 좀 훔쳐라.
Wipe this floor with a dry cleaning cloth.

- Gentle washing with hair soaked in water: 감다

샤워하면서 머리를 안 감는 사람도 있어요?
  Are there people who don't wash their hair while taking a shower?

- Washing face and hands: 세수하다

A: 세수 좀 해라. 얼굴이 그게 뭐니?

B: 어, 얼굴 닦았는데...
  A: Wash your face, please. Look at yourself.
  B: That's strange, I washed it...

- Washing automobiles: 세차하다

A: 세차 좀 해라. 차가 그게 뭐니?

B: 네, 그렇지 않아도 지금 차 닦으러 가는 길이에요.
  A: Why don't you wash your car? It's really bad.
  B: Yes, I'm actually on my way to get the car washed.

- Sweeping, vacuuming, mopping, etc.: 청소하다 or 치우다

집 *house*	방 *room*	복도 *hallway*
마당 *yard*	화장실 *bathroom*	욕실 *bathing room*
교실 *classroom*	계단 *stairs*	

방 청소는 내가 할테니까 너는 화장실 좀 깨끗하게 치워라.
  I'll clean the room, so you make the bathroom sparkly clean.

- Extracting smeared-in dirt, usually from a fabric, by squeezing or suctioning with the help of water (by hand or by machine): 빨다 or 세탁하다

옷 *clothes*	이불 *comforter*	담요 *blanket*
수건 *towel*	모자 *hat/cap*	운동화 *sneakers*
걸레 *cleaning cloth*	행주 *dish cloth*	

운동화를 어떻게 세탁기에 넣고 빠니? 손으로 빨아야지.
  How can you wash the sneakers in the washer? You should wash them by hand.

NOTE: 세탁하다 is usually used for professional (dry) cleaning while 빨래하다 is used for 'do laundry.'

- Doing the dishes (by hand): 설거지하다

설거지하기 너무 싫은데 우리 식기 세척기 하나 살까요?
  We hate doing dishes; shall we buy a dish washer?

- Cleansing by means of detergents or medicine: 세척하다

건강을 위해 위와 장을 세척하기도 한다.
  People sometimes have their stomach and intestines cleansed for their health.

12 Proverbs and idioms

Languages are made more lively and interesting by proverbs and idioms. Learning to use these sorts of items is especially important in Korean because they are very popular and very frequently employed.

12.1 Proverbs

Proverbs offer nuggets of advice that reflect a culture's practices and wisdom – whether it's 'The grass is always greener on the other side of the fence,' or the Korean equivalent 남의 떡이 커 보인다 'The other person's rice cake looks bigger.'

The following expressions are among the most commonly used. They are presented in Korean alphabetical order (가나다라순), followed by their English equivalent and, when appropriate, by their literal meaning in brackets. Helpful tips on how to use the proverbs can be found in *12.1.4*.

12.1.1 Proverbs with identical English equivalents

구르는 돌에는 이끼가 끼지 않는다.	*A rolling stone gathers no moss.*
눈에는 눈 이에는 이.	*An eye for an eye, a tooth for a tooth.*
늦었다고 생각할 때가 가장 빠르다.	*It's never too late to mend one's ways.*
뜻이 있는 곳에 길이 있다.	*Where there's a will, there's a way.*
로마는 하루 아침에 이루어지지 않았다.	*Rome was not built in a day.*
모르는 게 약이다.	*Ignorance is bliss.*
무소식이 희소식이다.	*No news is good news.*
빙산의 일각	*the tip of the iceberg*
뿌린 대로 거둔다.	*You reap what you sow.*
시작이 반이다.	*Beginning is half done.*
시장이 반찬이다.	*Hunger is the best sauce.*
아는 게 힘이다.	*Knowledge is power.*
오늘 할 일을 내일로 미루지 말라.	*Don't put off until tomorrow things that should be done today.*

천리길도 한걸음부터.	*A long journey starts with a single step.*
하늘은 스스로 돕는 자를 돕는다.	*God helps those who help themselves.*

12.1.2 *Proverbs with approximate English equivalents*

갈수록 태산이다.	*After a mountain is another mountain.*
고생 끝에 낙이 온다. (= 고진감래)	*Hard work pays off; No pain, no gain.*
구관이 명관이다.	*The devil you know is better than the devil you don't.*
그 아버지에 그 아들. (= 부전자전)	*Like father, like son.*
낮말은 새가 듣고 밤말은 쥐가 듣는다.	*Walls have ears.* [Birds hear your day-talk; mice hear your night-talk.]
눈 감으면 코 베어먹을 세상	*a dog-eat-dog world*
되로 주고 말로 받는다.	*Sow the wind and reap the whirlwind.*
두 손이 마주쳐야 소리가 난다.	*It takes two to tango.* [It takes two hands to clap.]
말이 씨가 된다.	*Self-fulfilling prophesy.*
바늘 도둑이 소 도둑된다.	*He that will steal an egg will steal an ox.*
발 없는 말이 천리 간다.	*Rumors spread like wildfire.* [Words without feet travel a thousand miles.]
불난 집에 부채질.	*Fanning the flames.*
빈수레가 요란하다.	*An empty barrel makes a lot of noise.*
사공이 많으면 배가 산으로 간다.	*Too many cooks spoil the broth.* [Too many boatmen take the boat to a mountain.]
세살 버릇 여든까지 간다.	*Old habits die hard.*
소 잃고 외양간 고친다.	*It's too late to shut the barn door after the horse is gone.* [One repairs the barn after the cow is gone.]
쇠 귀에 경 읽기	*Preaching to the deaf.*
쇠뿔도 단김에 빼야 한다.	*Strike while the iron is hot.*
아니 땐 굴뚝에 연기날까.	*There's no smoke without fire.*
열번 찍어 안 넘어 가는 나무 없다.	*If at first you don't succeed, try, try again.* [Chop ten times, any tree will fall.]
우는 아이 젖 준다.	*The squeaky wheel gets the grease.* [A crying baby gets milk.]

자라 보고 놀란 가슴 솥뚜껑 보고 놀란다.	*Once bitten, twice shy.* [A heart that was once scared of a mud-turtle will get scared of a kettle lid.]
쥐구멍에도 볕들 날이 있다.	*Every dog has his day.* [Sunlight may enter even a rat hole.]
친구따라 강남간다.	*Keeping up with the Joneses.*
티끌 모아 태산.	*Many a mickle makes a muckle.*
혹 떼러 갔다 혹 붙여 온다.	*Go for wool and come home shorn.* [One goes to remove a lump and comes back with another one.]
가다가 중지하면 아니 감만 못하니라.	*Don't start something unless you are going to finish it.*

12.1.3 Proverbs that are more or less unique to Korean

가만히 있으면 중간은 간다.	*If one keeps silent, one will at least be not wrong.*
개구리가 올챙이 적 생각 못한다.	*An upstart forgets his origins.* [The frog forgets his days as a tadpole.]
개천에서 용난다.	*A pauper becomes a king (beating the odds).* [A dragon may come from a creek.]
굿이나 보고 떡이나 먹지.	*Stay on the sideline and just watch the game.* [Just watch the show and eat the ricecake.]
기는/뛰는 놈 위에 나는 놈 있다.	*Don't be complacent with what you are; there's always someone better.* [For every crawling/running guy, there's a flying guy.]
꿈보다 해몽이 좋다.	*What it is depends on how it is interpreted* [The interpretation of a dream is better than the dream itself.]
남의 잔치에 감 놓아라 배 놓아라 한다.	*(S)he's calling the shots for someone else's business.* [(S)he's selecting fruit for someone else's party.]
낫 놓고 기역자도 모른다.	*(S)he is completely illiterate.* [Looking at a scythe, one doesn't even know the letter 기역 (which looks like the scythe).]
말 한마디로 천냥 빚을 갚는다.	*You can pay back a huge debt with a single word.*

모로 가도 서울만 가면 된다.	*It doesn't matter how you do things as long as you achieve the intended goal.* [All you need is to get to Seoul even if you detour.]
믿는 도끼에 발등 찍힌다.	*One gets stabbed in the back by someone who one trusts.*
뱁새가 황새를 따라가면 다리가 찢어진다.	*People ruin themselves by trying to imitate their betters.* [Small birds break their legs trying to follow big birds.]
병 주고 약 준다.	*You're toying with me.* [You gave me the disease and now the cure.]
사촌이 땅을 사면 배 아프다.	*One is jealous of one's cousin's success.*
설마가 사람 잡는다.	*It is dangerous to assume that something won't happen or didn't happen. (Anything is possible.)*
얌전한 강아지가 부뚜막에 먼저 올라간다.	*Quiet people are wilder.* [Well-behaved puppies go up on the kitchen countertop first.]
올라가지 못할 나무는 쳐다보지도 말라.	*Have a realistic goal.* [Don't even look at a tree you cannot climb.]
원수는 외나무 다리에서 만난다.	*Enemies are meant to run across a single lane bridge (a cruel coincidence).*
윗물이 맑아야 아랫물이 맑다.	*Be exemplary to your juniors.* [The downstream is clean only if the upstream is.]
작은 고추가 맵다.	*Small people are tough and smart.* [Small peppers are hot.]
젊어 고생은 사서도 한다.	*Pain while young is even desirable.*
지렁이도 밟으면 꿈틀한다.	*Even the meekest will lose his temper eventually.* [Even worms wiggle if stepped on.]
찬물도 위아래가 있다.	*Seniority rules even in drinking cold water.*
첫술에 배 부를까?	*Success doesn't come overnight.* [Will hunger be satiated with the first spoonful?]
핑계없는 무덤 없다.	*There is an excuse for everything.* [There is no grave without an excuse.]

12.1.4 How to use proverbs

In some cases, all that is needed is just a portion of the proverb, such as the boldfaced parts in the following examples; the rest is understood without being said.

닭 잡아 먹고 **오리발** 내민다.

One is denying something. [After eating chicken, one shows the duck feet.]

떡 줄 사람은 생각도 안하는데 **김칫국부터 마신다**.

You are counting your chickens (before they are hatched). [No one is even thinking about giving you the rice cake, but you are drinking Kimchi soup first.]

More often, proverbs are used in the following patterns, with necessary modifications to the original ending and sometimes with some added or substituted words.

- **-다는 거/말, -(이)라는 거/말**

부모님이 반대하신다고 언제까지 그 사람 몰래 만날 거야? **꼬리가 길면 잡힌다**는 거 모르니?

How long are you going to see him secretly just because your parents don't approve of him? Don't you know that 'prolonged wrongdoing gets caught eventually?'

열 길 물 속은 알아도 한 길 사람 속은 모른다는 말 이제 알 것 같아요. 단짝으로 지내던 친구가 저를 배신할 줄 어떻게 알았겠어요?

I think I now understand the saying, 'You know a 60-foot deep well but never know a 6-foot tall person.' How would I have known that my best friend would betray me?

구슬이 서말이라도 꿰어야 보배라는 말이 있지요. 연구를 많이 하면 뭐 합니까? 저널에 출판을 해야지요.

There is a saying, 'Three packs of pearls are nothing unless you string them together and turn them into treasure.' What's the point of doing a lot of research? You should publish it in a journal.

- **-다는데, -(이)라는데**

원숭이도 나무에서 떨어질 때가 있다는데, 조심하세요.

They say that 'even a monkey can fall from a tree.' So, be careful.

아 다르고 어 다르다는데 똑같은 말이라도 그렇게 기분 나쁘게 하니?

They say that even the same word can sound different depending on how one says it, but you are saying things in such an unpleasant way.

서당개 삼년이면 풍월을 읊는다는데 너는 요리사 남편을 두었으면서 어쩜 그렇게 요리를 못 하니?

They say that 'dogs at school can recite poems after three years,' so why is your cooking so bad when your husband is a chef?

같은 값이면 다홍치마라는데 기왕이면 모양이 예쁜 걸로 사지요.

They say that 'if the price is the same, pick a prettier/better-quality one,' so why don't we buy the one with the prettier design?

- -다더니, -(이)라더니

등잔 밑이 어둡다더니, 코 앞에 두고 여태 찾았네요.
Don't they say that 'right under the lamp is the darkest'? I've been looking for it all this time when it was right under my nose.

뭐 (똥) 묻은 개가 겨 묻은 개를 나무란다더니, 자기는 외박했으면서 나한테 늦게 들어 왔다고 야단이야.
Didn't I hear that 'The pot calls the kettle black. [A something-(shit)-covered dog scolds a husk-covered dog]'? You slept out, but are blaming me for having come home late.

호랑이도 제 말하면 온다더니, 우리 지금 네 얘기하고 있었는데.
'Speaking of the devil,' we were talking about you just now.

혹 떼러 갔다 혹 붙여 온다더니 문제를 해결하러 갔다가 오히려 더 큰 문제를 만들어 왔네.
Just like the saying, 'You go for wool and come home shorn,' you went out to solve a problem but came back with a bigger one.

싼게 비지떡이라더니, 지난 달에 오천원 주고 산 우산이 벌써 고장났어.
Just like I heard, 'If you buy cheaply, you pay dearly. [Cheap things are junk rice cake.],' the umbrella I bought for ₩5,000 last month is already broken.

- -다잖아, -(이)라잖아

가재는 게 편이고 초록은 동색이라잖아요. 다 끼리끼리 모이게 마련이에요.
Don't they say, 'Crawfish side with crabs' and 'The grass and the green are of the same color'? Birds of a feather always tend to stick together.

A: 이 길은 비가 와도 문제 없어. 10 년째 이 길로 다녔거든.
B: **돌다리도 두들겨 보고 건너라**잖아요. 그래도 조심하세요.
A: This road will be safe even when it rains. This is my tenth year traveling this road.
B: Don't they say, 'Look before you leap. [Tap even the stone bridge before crossing]'? Be careful nonetheless.

A: 짐이 별로 안 무거워요. 혼자 나를 수 있어요.
B: **백지장도 맞들면 낫다**잖아요. 이리 주세요.
A: My luggage is not that heavy. I can move it by myself.
B: You know, 'Two is better than one even to lift a sheet of paper.' Give it to me.

- **-다고, -(이)라고**

  배보다 배꼽이 크다고 저녁값은 만원인데 커피값이 이만원이에요.
  'The bellybutton is larger than the belly.' The dinner cost ₩10,000, but the coffee cost ₩20,000.

  하나를 보면 열을 안다고 이런 작은 일도 저렇게 성실히 하니 다른 일은 더 잘 할거예요.
  'You can tell ten things by looking at one exemplary case.' Looking at her treating this small matter so responsibly, I'm sure she will do other things even better.

  길고 짧은 건 대 봐야 안다고 실제 경기가 끝날 때까지는 어느 팀이 이길지 아무도 모른다니까요.
  They say 'It isn't over till it's over.' No one knows which team will win until the game is over, you know.

  가던 날이 장날이라고 모처럼 인사드리러 갔더니 안 계시더라.
  'What a coincidence to pick this day.' I went to say hello to her after a long time but she wasn't home.

  원두 커피를 좀 끓여야/내려야 되는데 종이 필터가 없네. **꿩 대신 닭**이라고, 이 키친타월이라도 써야겠다.
  I have to brew some coffee but don't have a paper filter. Well, just like the saying, 'Chicken, if you don't have pheasant,' I think I'll just use a paper towel.

- **...는 격이다** 'It's as if...'

  A: 스팸메일이 너무 많이 와서 이메일을 사용하지 말까 생각중이에요.
  B: **구더기 무서워서 장 못 담그는** 격이네요.
  A: I am thinking about stopping using e-mail because of too much spam mail.
  B: That's like 'Fearing maggots (something minor), *one gives up on making soy sauce* (something important).'

  A: 그 남자랑 잘 돼 가니?
  B: 말도 마. 결혼 약속한 사람이 있었대. 완전 **닭 쫓던 개 지붕 쳐다 보는** 격이 됐다.
  A: How is it going with that guy?
  B: Tell me about it. I didn't know he had a fiancée. I'm 'like a dog just looking up at the chicken on the roof after trying to chase it.'

  A: 여보, 당신이 진공 청소기 쓰더니 또 고장냈구나.
  B: 그럴리가 없는데. 내가 고장낸 거 아냐. **까마귀 날자 배 떨어지는** 격이네. (= 오비이락이네.)
  A: Darling, you just used the vacuum cleaner and it looks like you broke it again.
  B: No way. It wasn't me. It's as if 'the pear falls just as the crow flies out of the tree.' (Innocent behavior causes suspicion just due to its timing.)

- **-는 법이다**

A: 어제 똑같이 산 가방인데 친구 게 더 좋아 보이네.

B: **남의 떡이** 원래 **커 보이**는 법이에요.

  A: These are identical bags we bought together yesterday, but hers looks nicer.

  B: It's always like that: 'The other person's rice cake looks bigger.'

A: 벼락치기로 시험 준비를 했더니 역시 결과가 안 좋아.

B: 그러게 내가 미리미리 준비하랬잖아. **콩 심은 데 콩나고 팥 심은 데 팥 나**는 법이지.

  A: I crammed for the exam and sure enough, the result is no good.

  B: So, didn't I tell you to prepare in advance? You are supposed to 'reap what you sow (you cannot expect red beans where plain beans are sown).'

벼는 익을수록 고개를 숙이는 법이다. 이번에 승진했다고 너무 자만하지 말고 더 열심히 일하도록 해.

  'Truly great people are to be modest. [The rice stalk droops as it ripens.]' Just because you got promoted this time, do not become over confident but work harder.

- **-게/기 마련이다**

짚신도 제 짝이 있게 마련이니까 나도 좋은 사람 만날 수 있겠지?

  'Even straw shoes come in twos,' so I guess I'll be able to find my other half, right?

A: 똑같은 부하 직원이라도 같은 고향 출신을 더 챙기게 되네요.

B: 원래 **팔이 안으로 굽**게 마련이죠.

  A: They are all my staff, but I tend to favor those who are from my home town.

  B: I guess it's natural that 'one's arm bends inward.'

A: 왜 그렇게 짜증을 내며 말을 하니?

B: **가는 말이 고와야 오는 말도 곱**기 마련이야. 네가 먼저 짜증내며 말했잖아.

  A: Why are you speaking to me so irritably?

  B: 'You should speak kindly in order to be spoken to kindly.' You spoke to me that way first.

A: 직장 동료하고 오해가 있어서 사이가 안 좋았었는데 오해를 풀고 나니까 더 가까워졌어요.

B: 잘 됐네요. **비온 뒤에 땅이 굳**기 마련이지요.

  A: My relationship with a colleague soured because of a misunderstanding but we got even closer after the misunderstanding was cleared up.

  B: That's good. 'A relationship always solidifies after overcoming trouble. [The earth hardens after rain.]'

- -게 생기다 'It looks like…'

A: 남자친구 부모님이 갈비랑 잡채랑 음식을 잔뜩 해 오셨어요.
  저녁에 오셔서 좀 드실래요?
B: **원님 덕에 나팔 불**게 생겼네요. 네, 이따 갈게요.
  A: My boyfriend's parents came with plenty of kalbi and chapch'ae.
   Do you want to come over for dinner and have some?
  B: Looks like 'I can have a feast thanks to someone else. [I can
   blow a horn thanks to the governor.]' Yes, I'll come later.

두가지 일을 다 잘하고 싶었는데, 둘 다 제대로 못하고 있어. **두 마리
토끼 잡으려다 다 놓치**게 생겼어.
  *I wanted to do both things well, but I'm failing with both of them. 'I was trying to
  catch two rabbits, but it looks like I'm losing both of them.'*

엄마 아빠가 크게 다투셔서 당분간 집에서 밥 먹기 힘들 거 같애. **고래
싸움에 새우등 터지**게 생겼어.
  *Mom and Dad had a big fight, so I think it'll be difficult to eat at home for the time
  being. Looks like 'The shrimp's back will get torn by the whales' fight.'*

A: 호두 파이를 만들었는데 한번 드셔 보라고 가져 왔어요.
B: 고마워요. 잠깐만요. 어제 사과 두 상자를 샀는데, 한 상자 가져 가세요.
A: 어, 괜찮은데요....참, **되로 주고 말로 받**게 생겼네.
  A: I made walnut pie, so I brought some for you to try.
  B: Thank you. Wait. I bought two boxes of apples yesterday; please take one.
  A: Oh, it's okay. Well, it looks like I'm going to 'reap a lot more than I sowed.'

- -(이)다

저렇게 입으니까 사람이 달라 보이지 않니? 정말 **옷이 날개**다.
  *Doesn't she look so much better dressed like that? 'The clothes really make
  a difference. [Clothes are wings.]'*

아무리 급해도 우리 밥 먼저 먹고 하자. **금강산도 식후경**이야.
  *Let's eat first no matter how rushed we are. 'Even the beautiful Kŭmgang Mt. is
  best appreciated after a meal. (Nothing can be done properly when one is hungry.)'*

A: 아니, 수진이같이 얌전한 애가 어떻게 저런 날라리하고 사귈 수 있지?
B: 다 **제 눈에 안경**이지요.
  *A: My, how can someone so decent like Sujin go out with such a superficial and
   loose person?*
  B: Well, everybody has his/her own taste (beauty is in the eye of the beholder).'

● Others

털어서 먼지 안 나는 사람이 어디 있어요? 누구나 약점이 있기 마련이지요.

Who doesn't have skeletons in his closet? [There's no one without dust if you shake their clothes.] *It's natural that everyone has shortcomings.*

너는 **종로에서 뺨 맞고 한강에 와서 화풀이**하니? 왜 회사에서 화난 걸 갖고 집에 와서 그래?

Are you taking your anger out on the wrong person? [You got slapped on the face on Chong-no St. and are taking your anger out miles away at the Han River.] *Why are you bringing your work problems home?*

염불에는 마음이 없고 젯밥에만 마음이 있나봐요. 학회에 와서 관광하러 다닐 궁리만 하고 있으니 말이에요.

It seems like they 'have no interest in the prayer but only in the food offering.' They came to a conference, but are thinking only about sightseeing.

그 **자다가 봉창치는 소리** 좀 작작 해라. 말도 안 되는 소리 좀 이제 그만 하라구.

Please stop the 'out-of-the-blue and irrelevant remarks.' I mean, you should now stop talking nonsense.

차라리 **벼룩의 간을 내어 먹**지 동생이 무슨 돈이 있다고 돈을 꿔 달래냐?

How can you try to borrow money from your poor younger brother? It would be better to 'skin a flea for its hide [eat the liver of a flea].'

A: 여자친구한테 늦었다고 한마디 했다가 한 시간동안 설교를 들었어.

B: 하하, **되로 주고 말로 받**았구나!

A: I said a word to my girlfriend because she was late and I had to put up with one hour of her lecturing me.
B: Haha, 'you sowed the wind and reaped the whirlwind.'

부부싸움은 **칼로 물베기**라지만 너무 자주 싸우는 거 아니니?

They say that 'fights between a husband and a wife are like cutting water with a knife (don't have lasting results),' but still aren't you fighting too often?

도난사고를 이미 당했는데 **소 잃고 외양간 고쳐**야 무슨 소용 있겠어요? 미리 미리 도난경보장치를 달았어야지요.

We've already been robbed; what's the point of repairing the barn after losing the cow? We should have set the burglar alarm far in advance.

A: 한국어가 안 늘어서 걱정이에요.

B: 시작한지 두 달밖에 안 됐잖아요. **첫술에 배부르**겠어요?

A: I'm worried that my Korean is not improving.
B: It's been only two months since you started. You cannot expect to become full after just one bite.

12.2 Idioms

Idiomatic expressions – phrases and pieces of sentences such as 'head over heels' and 'pie in the sky' – add color and spice to language. Idioms of this sort are numerous in Korean and are a very important part of every-day speech.

12.2.1   Four-syllable Sino-Korean idioms

A particularly popular type of Korean idiom consists of four Sino-Korean roots. Following, in boldface, are some of the more commonly used expressions of this type.

거두절미하고 요점만 얘기하세요.
 'Leave out the beginning and the end,' and just give me the important points.

견물생심이라고 이렇게 예쁜 신발을 보니 너무 사고 싶다.
 'Seeing is wanting,' so now that I saw these beautiful shoes I want to buy them.

비행기 사고에서 **구사일생**으로 살아났어요.
 I had a 'narrow escape from death' in an airplane crash.

그 예쁜 얼굴에 애교까지 많다면 **금상첨화**일텐데.
 It'd be an 'added bonus [a flower on top of gold]' if she had an affectionate manner to go with her pretty face.

그 친구가 결혼을 한다고요? 저는 **금시초문**인데요.
 He's getting married? I'm 'hearing that for the first time.'

무슨 사고라도 당한 것은 아닐까 밤새 **노심초사**했어.
 Fearing she was in an accident, I was 'worried to death' all night.

여러 분야를 골고루 잘하는 **다재다능**한 사람입니다.
 He is a 'renaissance man' who can do many things equally well.

입사 초에는 두각을 나타내지 못했지만 입사 3년째부터 서서히
그 실력을 나타낸 **대기만성**형이죠.
 She was not outstanding when she first entered the company, but she is a 'late-bloomer type' whose talents started shining gradually from the third year.

동료들하고 잘 어울리지도 않고 항상 **독불장군**이야.
 Rarely associating with his co-workers, he's always a 'loner who wants everything his way.'

왜 자꾸 딴소리야? **동문서답**하지 말고 내 질문에 제대로 대답해.
 Why do you keep talking about something else? Stop 'giving an outrageously irrelevant answer [talking about west when I ask about east],' and answer my question properly.

게임이 **막상막하**네요. 어느 팀이 이길 지 감이 안 잡히는 데요.
It is a 'very close (neck and neck)' game. It's hard to tell which team will win.

주 5 일 근무제가 **만장일치**로 통과되었대요.
I heard that the five-day work week policy was 'unanimously' approved.

부모의 은공도 모르는 **배은망덕**한 딸이 되고 싶지 않아요.
*I don't want to be the 'ungrateful' daughter who does not appreciate
what her parents have done for her.*

십대들의 운전 부주의로 인한 사고가 **비일비재**한 것 같다.
Accidents that are caused by teenagers' reckless driving seem to be 'quite common.'

주위가 온통 스파이니 말도 함부로 못 하겠고 **사면초가**야.
*I can't even talk freely because there are spies all around me. I am surrounded
'by foes on all sides.'*

그 친구 사업 망하고 **설상가상**으로 병까지 걸려서 너무 안 됐어.
I feel bad because his business collapsed and 'to make things worse' he even got sick.

달리 방도가 없네요. **속수무책**이에요.
There is no other way. We 'can't do anything about it.'

이렇게 놀다간 **십중팔구** 시험에 떨어질 거야.
If we keep playing like this, then '10 to 1' we will fail the test.

다들 새로운 정책의 내용을 **아전인수**격으로 해석하고 있습니다.
Everybody is interpreting the content of the new policies in their own favor.

위아래도 몰라보고 완전 **안하무인**으로 행동하네.
*He's 'acting totally recklessly, showing no respect for anyone,'
even for those who are older or superior.*

저희는 **연중무휴**, 365 일 영업합니다.
We 'don't ever rest'; we're open 365 days a year.

화재의 원인은 아직 **오리무중**입니다.
We are still 'befuddled' about the cause of the fire.

이번 정책이 **용두사미**로 끝나지 않기를 바랍니다.
I hope this policy does not 'fade away [like a dragon head becoming a snake tail].'

유비무환이라고 지금부터 우리도 노년 준비를 해야 겠네.
*Since they say there are 'no worries after preparation,' we should also start
preparing for the later years.*

원래 친구라는 게 **유유상종**이죠. 비슷한 사람끼리 어울리기 마련이에요.
*'Birds of a feather flock together' naturally to become friends. Similar people tend
to get along.*

모두 **이구동성**으로 그 사람의 성실함을 칭찬하던데요.
I noticed 'everybody was in agreement' in praising his dependability.

우리는 일일이 말을 하지 않아도 상대방이 무엇을 원하는지 **이심전심**으로 알 수 있다.

Even if we don't say everything, we know what the other person wants 'through telepathy.'

한국인에게는 여름에 육개장, 삼계탕 등의 더운 음식을 먹는 **이열치열**의 관습이 있다.

Koreans have a custom of 'like cures like [governing heat with heat]' and of eating hot-temperature food such as yukkyejang and samgyet'ang in summer.

너도 이제 **이팔청춘**이 아니니까 몸 생각 좀 해서 마셔라.

You don't have the body of a 'teenager [16-year-old]' anymore, so drink sparingly.

죄를 지으면 언젠가는 벌을 받게 돼 있어. **인과응보** 아니니?

If we commit a crime, we are to be punished one day or another. Isn't that 'retribution'?

인생은 **일장춘몽**이라더니 정말 **인생무상**이에요.

They say that 'life is but an empty dream'; it's so true that 'life is futile.'

아름다워지고 싶거나 늙고 싶지 않은 것은 **인지상정**이다.

Wanting to become more beautiful or not wanting to age are 'natural desires of human beings.'

돈도 벌고 공부도 하고 **일석이조**예요.

Making money and studying is 'killing two birds with one stone.'

패키지여행하고 개인여행하고 **일장일단**이 있죠.

There are pros and cons to packaged vacations and self-planned vacations.

저는 **일편단심** 우리 남편밖에는 모르는 사람이에요.

My 'heart is focused only on' my husband.

검정고시로 대학도 나오고 **자수성가** 한 사람이야.

He went to college with a GED and 'succeeded without help from others.'

처음부터 네가 잘못했으니 이런 결과는 당연해. **자업자득**이야.

From the start it was your fault, so this result is totally expected. 'You reap what you sow.'

일이 어떻게 된 건지 **자초지종**을 얘기해 봐.

Tell me 'all the details of what happened.'

이제 희망도 없고 완전히 지쳐서 **자포자기** 상태예요.

Now that I have no hope and am completely exhausted, I'm 'in a state of utter despair.'

운동을 하겠다고 결심했는데 또 **작심삼일**이다.

I made up my mind to exercise but again my 'resolution was good for only three days.'

완전히 **적반하장**이네. 자기가 잘못해 놓고는 누구한테 큰 소리야?

How 'preposterous [to see a thief (who should be surrendering) lifting a weapon].'
You were the one who was wrong and who are you shouting at?

전화위복이라는 말이 있듯이, 이 시련을 잘 이겨내면 좋은 결과가 있을
거야.

*Just as there is a saying that 'misfortune turns into a blessing,' if you endure these
hardships then you will get good results.*

주객전도도 유분수지. 남의 집에 얹혀 살면서 큰소리야?

You have to know your place when you are lower on the totem pole. [Host and guest
are reversed.] *Are you yelling at the host family from whom you are getting a free
ride?*

사람이 정말 뭘 모르는 거 같아요. 한마디로 **천방지축**이에요.

He really doesn't seem to know anything. In a nutshell, he's 'brash and reckless.'

천생연분이란 하늘이 맺어 준 인연을 말한다.

'A match made in heaven' means a bond from the sky.

청산유수같은 말솜씨로 청중들을 압도했다.

He is dominating the audience with his 'talented and eloquent' speaking skills.

계획을 세웠으면 **초지일관** 밀고 나가도록 해.

If you set a plan, make sure you 'follow it through, from start to end.'

얼굴도 잘 생기고 성격도 좋고 운동도 잘하고 그야말로 **팔방미인**이시네요.

With your looks, personality, and athletic ability, you are really 'well-rounded.'

미안하긴. 나도 잘못했는데. **피장파장**이지.

No need to apologize. I was wrong too. We're all 'square.'

우유를 사러 슈퍼에 간 동생이 **함흥차사**예요.

My little brother, who went to the market to buy milk, 'hasn't come back for ages.'

12.2.2 *Idioms based on body parts*

깜짝이야. **간 떨어질 뻔 했다**. 들어온다고 인기척이라도 내야지. 너무
놀라서 **간이 콩알만해 졌**네.

*Oops. I was so startled that my liver almost fell out (my heart leaped into my throat).
You should have made some sound coming in. I got so scared that 'my liver shrank
to the size of a bean.'*

A: 여자 친구 선물로 이렇게 비싼 가방을 샀어? **간이 부었구나.** [간이 붓다]

B: 제 여자 친구가 워낙 **눈이 높거든요.** 더 비싼 걸 사주고 싶은
마음은 굴뚝 같지만 여유가 없어서요.

> A: *You bought this expensive bag for your girlfriend? You're crazy.*
>   *[Your liver must be puffed up.]*
>
> B: *My girlfriend has super taste. I 'want with all my heart' to buy her*
>   *a more expensive one, but I can't afford it.*

불고기 일인분이 요거밖에 안 돼요? **간에 기별도 안 가겠다.**

> *One serving of kalbi is only this much? My stomach [liver] won't even feel anything.*

눈 앞의 이익을 위해서 **간에 붙었다 쓸개에 붙었다 할** 사람이야.

> *He is a conniving person who will do anything to make a profit […who will*
> *stick to the liver and then to the gall].*

뭐 저런 애가 다 있어. 정말 **골 때리**네. 완전히 **내 배 째쇼야.** [familiar/casual]

> *How can there be such a person? He's ridiculous. He just doesn't give a damn,*
> *with this 'so-shoot-me' attitude.*

사람이 정말 훌륭해요. **고개가 절로 숙여지**는 그런 사람이에요.

> *She's really great. People cannot help bowing to her.*

누가 내 얘기하나 보다, **귀가 가려운** 걸 보니. [귀가 가렵다]

> *Someone must be talking about me. My ears are burning [itchy].*

오늘 나 **귀 빠진 날**인데 미역국도 못 먹었어.

> *Today is my birthday [the day when my ears came out], but I didn't even get*
> *to eat my seaweed soup.*

외국어를 배우는 목적은 **귀에 못이 박히도록** 자주 들었다.

> *I have heard about the purpose of learning a foreign language so many times*
> *that my ear drums are calloused.*

이번 한번은 **눈 감아 줄**테니까 다음부터는 조심하도록 해.

> *I will look the other way this time, but be careful next time.*

사원들이 모두 사장님 **눈에 들**려고 난리인데 나는 벌써 **눈 밖에 났**어.

> *Every employee tries to find favor in the boss's eyes, but I've already fallen out.*

집에 두고 온 아기가 **눈에 밟힌다.**

> *I can't stop thinking about the baby I left at home.*

내 **눈에 뭐가 씌웠**지. 그런 사람을 뭐가 좋다고.

> *I must have had wool over my eyes. What was there to like about him?*

너무 잠이 와서 잠깐 **눈을 좀 붙여**야겠어요.

> *I'm so sleepy that I better get some shut-eye.*

둘이 수업을 같이 듣다가 **눈이 맞아서** 사귀게 됐대요.

I hear that their eyes met while taking a class together and that the two are dating now.

요새 **눈코 뜰 새 없이** 바빠요.

I'm busy as hell these days [without time to open my eyes or nose].

내 친구하고 결혼할 사람이니까 **눈독 들이지** 마.

This is someone who is marrying my friend, so don't set your eyes on her.

친구 부모님은 **눈에 차지 않아** 하시지만 둘은 죽고 못 사는 사이야.

My friend's parents are not satisfied with him, but the two cannot live without each other.

이 길은 예전에 와 봐서 **눈에 익어요.**

I've been on this road before, so it looks familiar.

아버지가 **화가 머리끝까지 나셨어.** 당신 **눈에 흙이 들어가기 전에는** 외국인 사위 안 보시겠대.

Dad is so angry he's fuming from the ears. Until he enters his grave, he will never allow a foreigner as a son-in-law, he says.

머리에 피도 안 마른 게 어디서 어른한테 반말이야?

How dare you talk down to an elder when you're still wet behind the ears [...when the blood on your head hasn't yet dried]?

검은 머리 파뿌리 되도록 두사람 서로 사랑하며 행복하게 사십시오.

Until your hair turns all grey [until your black hair turns into green onion roots], live happily in love with each other.

어떻게 잘 보일까 **잔머리 굴리**지 말고 차라리 좋아한다고 말을 해.

Stop trying to come up with clever ideas to win favor from her; just tell her you like her.

굳게 믿고 있던 친구가 내 **뒤통수를 칠** 줄은 정말 몰랐어.

I had no idea that a friend I firmly trusted would stab me in the back [...would hit the back of my head].

너는 **배알도 없**니? 자존심도 없어?

Don't you have any guts? Don't you have any self-esteem?

그 친구하고는 성격이 잘 안 맞아 **발 끊**은지 오래됐어.

I didn't get along very well with that friend, so it's been a while since I cut off contact with her.

다음 달까지 끝내라는 최후통첩이 왔어요. **발등에 불이 떨어졌**어요.

The final notice said to finish by next month. A fire has been lit under me.

아이들이 너무 **속을 썩여**서 내 머리가 다 세었다.

My children caused me so much worry and heartache that my hair is all grey now.

어린 애가 **손버릇이** 아주 **나쁘다**.
The young kid has sticky fingers.

무슨 음식을 이렇게 많이 장만하셨어요? 정말 **손이 크**시네요.
You prepared so much food. You have very generous hands.

정말이라니까. 아니면 내 **손에 장을 지진다**.
I swear it's true. If not, I'll be a monkey's uncle [I'll boil stew in my hands].

빨리 **손을 쓰**지 않으면 환자의 목숨이 위태롭습니다.
If you don't take action right away, the patient's life will be in danger.

프로젝트가 이것 저것 **손이 많이 가**네요. 그래도 저희들 **손발이 잘 맞아**
즐겁게 하고 있습니다.
The project requires a lot of hands. Nevertheless, we work well together, so we're enjoying it.

인터넷이 접속이 됐다 안 됐다 해요. 컴퓨터를 한번 **손을 봐**야 겠어요.
The Internet connection is unstable. I must take a look at the computer.

그 사람 요새 주식에 **손을 대**고 있대요.
I hear he's dabbling in the stock market.

내 고집에 부모님도 **손 드**셨어요. [손들다]
My parents threw in the towel when trying to deal with my stubbornness.

A: 친구들한테 **손 내미**는 거 창피해서 더 이상 못하겠어. [손 내밀다]
B: 얼굴에 **철판 깔**고 한번만 더 부탁해 봐.
A: I can't beg my friends for help anymore because it's too embarrassing.
B: Try to have a thick skin [thick face] *and ask just one more time.*

A: 이 영화 정말 썰렁하다, 그냥 나가자.
B: 어떻게 **쪽 팔리**게 영화 중간에 나가냐? [familiar/casual]
A: This movie is really cheesy, let's just go.
B: How can we just leave in the middle – isn't it embarrassing (to lose face)?

나이 들어서까지 부모님한테 **손 벌리**기 싫어.
I don't want to ask my parents for help now that I'm older.

요즘 **입에 풀칠하**기 어려워요. 이러다 **입에 거미줄 치**겠어요.
These days it's hard to put food on the table. If this continues, you may find spider webs in the corners of my mouth (I may go hungry).

남편이 **입이 짧**아서 반찬을 매일 새로 해야 돼요.
My husband can never eat the same thing twice, so I have to cook a new side dish every day.

모처럼 와이프한테 선물을 하나 했더니 **입이 쫙 벌어졌어** (or **입이 귀밑까지 찢어졌어**).

> *I bought my wife a gift for the first time in a while and she's so happy that she can't stop smiling.*

A: 너는 **입이** 그렇게 **가볍니**? 그 새를 못 참고 남한테 얘기를 했어?
B: 사돈 남말하고 있네. 너는 뭐 **입이 무거**운지 아니? [입이 무겁다]

> *A: Why is your tongue so loose? You couldn't keep quiet for that long?*
> *B: Look who's talking. You can't even keep your mouth shut.*

이런 말 하려니 **입이** 잘 **안 떨어지**지만 너 이번 승진시험에서 떨어졌대.

> *It's difficult for me to say this, but I heard that you failed on the promotion exam.*

바지 좀 하나 사려고 했는데 **입에 맞는 떡이** 없네.

> *I wanted to buy a pair of pants, but there's nothing that suits my taste.*

A: 너는 어떻게 **엎어지면 코 닿을 곳에** 살면서 **코빼기도 안 비치냐**?
B: 야, 요즘 **내 코가 석자**라서 그래. 좀 봐 주라.

> *A: You live a stone's throw away, so why don't you even show your face?*
> *B: Yo, it's because I'm completely tied up with my own problems. Cut me some slack.*

이번 경기에서 상대팀 **코를 납작하게 만들어** 놓아야지. 그 잘난 체하는 **콧대를** 반드시 **꺾어** 놓을 거야.

> *During this game, I'll smash the other team's faces. I'm going to break their stuck up noses for sure.*

아 고소하다. 깨소금 맛이야. 그렇게 잘난 척하는 애는 한번 **큰 코를 다쳐**봐야 돼.

> *Yeah, it feels great. It serves her right. People like her with such a big head should have some bitter experiences.*

나한테 **미운털**이 박혔는지 나를 얼마나 이유없이 미워하는지 몰라요.

> *He hates me so much for no reason as if there's some ugly hair stuck on me.*

12.2.3 Idioms based on food, taste, eating, and cooking

또 한번 내 동생 **골탕 먹이**면 내가 가만히 안 있을 거야. **국물도 없**을 줄 알어.

> *If you play that prank on my brother again, you will hear from me. And you can be sure that you'll be dead meat.*

남자 친구랑 잘 돼가죠? 우리 언제쯤 **국수 먹**어요?

> *Things are going well with your boyfriend, right? When are we going to attend your wedding?*

너 **까마귀 고기**를 먹었냐? 지난번에 얘기해 줬는데 또 까 먹었어?
Why are you so forgetful? [Did you eat crow meat?] *Did you forget again what I told you last time?*

결혼하더니 **깨가 쏟아지**나봐요. 요즘 학교에서 통 안 보여요.
Having married, they seem to be having lots of fun together. We rarely see them at school.

빨리빨리 하지 왜 이렇게 **뜸을 들여**?
Why don't you do it quickly; why are you wasting time like this?

이번에는 **미역국 먹**지 않으려고 열심히 공부하고 있어요.
I am studying hard so I won't bomb on the test this time.

나는 경우없는 사람은 **밥맛**이야.
I hate people with no manners.

찬밥 신세 면하려면 취직해야겠어요. 저도 제 **밥값**은 해야죠.
I better get a job to avoid being treated badly [having to eat cold rice]. *I should earn my own food at least.*

완전 **콩가루 집안**이야. 떡해 먹을 집안이라구.
Their family is so messed up. It's really full of troubles.

콩밥 먹고 싶지 않으면 지금이라도 당장 자수하는 게 어때?
If you don't want to end up behind bars, why don't you go turn yourself in?

결혼해서 새살림 장만하는 **재미가 쏠쏠해**요.
Now that we're married, shopping for our new home is fun and exciting.

이 정도야 **식은 죽 먹기**죠. **누워서 떡 먹기**예요.
This is a piece of cake. It's a cake walk.

일은 항상 마무리가 중요해. **다 된 죽에 재 뿌리**지 (or **코 빠뜨리**지) 않도록 조심해.
Finishing well is always important. Make sure you don't ruin the finished product [by spraying ashes (or dropping snots) in the finished gruel].

A: 연 이틀 밤을 새우더니 완전히 **파김치**가 됐네. 그래, 시험은 잘 봤어?
B: **수박 겉 핥기**식으로 벼락치기했더니 완전히 **죽 쒔**지, 뭐.
  A: After staying up two nights in a row, you've gotten completely wiped out [you've turned into green onion gimchi]. *So, did you do well on the test?*
  B: I crammed in a very superficial way [like licking a watermelon skin (instead of eating the inside)], *so I bombed on the test* [I cooked gruel], *of course.*

죽이 되든 밥이 되든 한번 열심히 해 볼게요.
Whatever the outcome may be [whether it becomes gruel or rice], *I'll try my best.*

행사 준비는 내가 다 했는데 칭찬은 다른 사람이 듣고 완전히 **죽 쒀서
개 줬**네.

*I prepared everything for this event, but someone else received all the credit. I basi-
cally worked my guts out for someone else.* [I cooked gruel and gave it to a dog.]

국제영화제 통역을 맡아서 영화 배우도 보고 돈도 벌고 **꿩 먹고 알 먹기**야.

*Being a translator at the international film festival, I make money while also seeing
movie stars. It's like getting two for the price of one* [eating the pheasant and also
its egg].

걔 요새 **개밥에 도토리** 신세야. 친구들한테서 완전히 따돌림 받고 있어.

These days, that guy is ostracized. His friends are totally avoiding him.

노래방에 와서 그렇게 **꿔다 놓은 보릿자루**처럼 앉아있지 말고 신나게
좀 놀아봐.

You came to karaoke, so stop sitting around like a wall flower [like a borrowed
barley sack] *and come have some fun.*

그 사람 회사 **말아 먹**을 사람이야.

He is capable of destroying the company [mixing it with soup and eating it up].

여자친구한테 청혼했다가 **물 먹**었어요.

I proposed to my girlfriend and got rejected.

같은 회사에서 **한솥밥을 먹**은 지 오래돼서 정이 많이 들었어요.

Since we've been together for so long [eating from the same kettle] *at this
company, we've grown deeply attached.*

애가 너무 주책이 없어. 걔 여자친구는 아주 **한 술 더 뜨**고.

He's so indiscreet. And his girlfriend is even worse [...takes another spoonful].

12.2.4 *Idioms based on animals and insects*

질서라고는 하나없이 완전 **개판**이다.

With no order, this place looks like a damn mess.

글씨가 완전히 **개발새발**이네.

Your penmanship looks like someone wrote with their feet.

김교수, 부인하고 애들하고 호주로 보내 놓고 **기러기 아빠**로 살고 있대.

*I hear that Professor Kim is living as a wild goose dad, with his wife and kids sent
away to Australia (for the kids' schooling).*

그건 **돼지꿈**이 아니라 **개꿈**이네요.

That's not an auspicious dream, just a meaningless one.

야, 어쩌면 그렇게 노래를 못하냐? 꼭 **돼지 멱따는 소리**같다.

How can you be such a terrible singer? Your voice sounds like a dying pig.

너는 이제 독 안에 든 쥐다. 도망갈 꿈도 꾸지 마.
You're now a rat in a cage (completely trapped). Don't even think about escaping.

쥐뿔도 없으면서 있는 척하네.
She doesn't have any money [not even the rat's horn], *but pretends to.*

쥐꼬리만한 월급으로 다섯식구가 살려니 너무 힘들어요.
The few [rat-tail size] *dollars I call a salary make it impossible to feed 5 people.*

우물안 개구리처럼 살지말고 좀 시야를 넓혀라.
Stop living like a frog in a well and broaden your views.

동생이 취직시험 결과를 알아 보러 나가서는 꿩 구워 먹은 소식이에요.
My brother went out to get the results from his employment exam but is taking forever to return. (He must be running a marathon.) [He must have eaten barbecued pheasant.]

웬 대낮에 스킨십. 야, 닭살 돋는다.
Such a big public display of affection in plain daylight. It gives me goosebumps [chicken skin].

허리는 잘록한 게 개미허리인데 다리가 너무 무다리다.
Her waist is so small [like an ant's waist], *but her legs are like tree trunks.*

잠은 새우 잠자고 아침에는 겨우 고양이 세수만 하고 나왔어.
After a bad curled-up sleep [a shrimp's sleep], *I barely washed my face in the morning* [like a cat] *and came out.*

집세 낼 돈이 없어서 친구한테 빈대붙어 산 지 꽤 됐어.
It's been a while since I've been living like a parasite at my friend's place because I don't have money to pay the rent.

우리 아빠 고집은 아무도 못 꺾어. 황소고집이시거든.
Nobody else can overcome my father's stubbornness. He's stubborn as a mule.

그 쪽 피해는 우리측에 비하면 새 발의 피다 [= 조족지혈이다].
Their damage is like a scratch [blood on a bird's feet] *compared to ours.*

나같은 촌닭한테 누가 결혼신청을 하겠어요?
Who would ask a country bumpkin like me to marry them?

여자 제비(족)을 '꽃뱀(족)'이라고 하는 거 아세요?
Do you know that female gigolos are called 'flower-snakes (gold diggers)'?

12.2.5 Idioms based on miscellaneous other factors

여권을 분명히 여기다 잘 뒀는데 어디 갔지? 귀신이 곡할 일이네.
I'm sure I placed my passport here, but where did it go? God, this is impossible. [It's something that ghosts will cry over.]

네 와이프 정말 **쪽집게다**. 어쩜 그렇게 네 마음을 잘 알아 맞히니? 완전 **귀신**이다.

> *Your wife is so good at guessing. How does she read your mind so well? She's really a demon.*

걔 정말 **경우가 없**더라.부탁할 일 있을 때만 아는 척하고 아니면 인사도 안 해. 한마디로 **왕싸가지**야.

> *She has no manners. She only pretends to know me when she wants something; otherwise we're strangers to her. In one word, she's a bitch.*

올겨울 동남아여행은 아무래도 **날샌** 거 같다. 일이 너무 밀렸어. [날새다]
> *It seems like this winter's South East Asia trip is going to fall through. My work is too backed up.*

나한테 차를 빌려주면 너는 주차비 절약하고 나는 렌트비 절약하고. 결국 **누이 좋고 매부 좋은** 거 아니니?

> *If you let me borrow your car, you'll save your parking fee and I'll save my car rental fee. Isn't that ultimately good for both of us* [...good for the sister and also good for the brother-in-law]?

이번 작품은 틀림없이 **대박**이다.
> *The product will be a mega hit this time for sure.*

요새 직장에서 해고 당하고 형편이 **말이 아니**예요.
> *He was fired recently, so his financial situation is really bad.*

말 돌리지 말고 용건만 말해.
> *Stop beating around the bush and come to the point.*

너 그렇게 **물불 안 가리**고 다이어트 심하게 하다 병 난다.
> *If you take your diet too far* [through fire and water], *then you'll get sick.*

그 여배우는 한 때 잘 나갔었는데, 지금은 **한물갔어**.
> *That actress was once in high demand, but now she's all washed up.*

이번 유럽 여행계획은 완전히 **물 건너 갔어**.
> *My plan for the Europe trip this time totally fell through.*

버는 만큼 다 써버리면 언제 돈을 모으냐? **밑 빠진 독에 물 붓기**지.
> *If you spend everything you earn, when are you going to save? It's like trying to fill a bottomless barrel with water.*

걔라면 말도 마. 나는 완전히 **학을 떼**었어. 걔 이름만 들어도 **신물이 난다**.
> *That guy, let me tell you. I've gotten totally sick of him. Even the sound of his name makes me sick to my stomach* [gives me acid].

A: 쟤, 왜 저렇게 기분이 **저기압**이지?

B: 남자친구한테 **바람 맞았**대.

> *A: Why is she so down?*
> *B: I heard that she got stood up by her boyfriend.*

남편이 **바람을 피우**는 지 부인이 **바가지**를 많이 긁는 거 같아요.

> *I think the wife is nagging the husband a lot, maybe because he's having an affair.*

관광지에서는 **바가지 요금**을 조심해야 돼요. 까딱하다간 **바가지 쓰**거든요.

> *You need to be aware of inflated prices at tourist attractions. If you aren't careful,*
> *you can easily get ripped off.*

너무 **비행기 태우**지 마세요. 저도 알고 보면 못 하는 거 많아요.

> *Don't inflate my ego too much. You'll find out that there are many things I can't do.*

좀 더 신중하게 생각하고 결정했어야 하는데 제가 **생각이 짧**았어요.

> *I should have thought it over more thoroughly and decided, but I was thoughtless.*

어쩌면 너넨 둘이 그렇게 **죽이 척척 맞냐**?

> *How can you two guys get along so well?*

그렇게 벼락치기로 공부하면 금방 다 잊어버릴 텐데. 완전 **초치기**네!

> *If you cram like that, you'll quickly forget everything. Aren't you trying to*
> *memorize everything at the last SECOND?!*

2년 동안 사귄 여자친구하고 깨끗하게 **쫑냈**어.

> *I cut it off completely with my girlfriend, who I've been dating for 2 years.*

너무 화가 나서 오빠하고 **한바탕 했**어.

> *Because I was feeling so angry, I had a big fight with my brother.*

그 친구 완전히 **형광등**이야. 항상 못 알아듣고 혼자 딴 소리 해.

> *He's so terribly slow in catching on [like a fluorescent light]. He's always*
> *the only one who doesn't understand things and talks nonsense.*

오늘 미팅이 있어서 머리에 **힘 좀 줬**는데 이거 너무 튀는 거 아니니?

> *I paid some special attention to my hair for today's blind date, but does it stand*
> *out too much?*

12.2.6 *Figurative uses of verbs*

아빠한테 들키면 큰일인데. 동생을 **구워 삶**아야지, 이르지 말라고.

> *It'll be bad if I get caught by my dad. I better butter my sister up not to tell.*

아버지는 피곤하신지 벌써 **골아 떨어지**신 거 같아요.

> *Dad seems to have conked out; he must be tired.*

잘 알지도 못하면서 왜 **넘겨짚**고 그래?

> *Why do you jump to a conclusion without knowing the situation well?*

쟨 좀 **덜 떨어지**지 않았니? 모자라도 한참 **모자란다**.
 Isn't he a little retarded? He's seriously lacking something upstairs.

잘못은 자기가 해놓고 왜 나한테 **덮어 씌우**는거야?
 He was the one who was wrong, so why is he shifting the blame to me?

어떻게 얼굴색 하나 안 변하냐, 뻔뻔스럽게? 정말 **두껍다**.
 How can she be so shameless not to even show it on her face? She's so thick-skinned.

공부고 뭐고 다 **때려치우**고 취직이나 할까봐.
 I think I'll drop my studies and whatever, and just get a job.

선을 볼 생각이 있는지 좀 **떠 보**세요.
 Feel him out to see if he's interested in having a blind date to meet his future spouse.

일년 재수했는데 이번에 또 **미끄러졌**대.
 She tried the entrance exam for a second year but failed again this time, I heard.

너 요즘 왜 이렇게 **삐딱하**니? 뭐가 불만이야?
 Why are you so uncooperative these days? What's your problem?

그 사람이 실수한 게 명백한데도 모두들 그를 **싸고 돌**았다.
 His mistake is clear, but everybody is shielding and protecting him.

그런 말 했냐고 물어봤더니, 딱 **잡아떼**더라. 완전 오리발이야.
 I asked him if he said it, but he completely denied it. He just wouldn't admit it.

너 너무 **밟**는 거 아니니? 이러다 딱지 떼겠다.
 Aren't you going too fast? You're going to get a ticket speeding like this.

저 배우 몸매 **끝내준다**. 정말 잘 **빠졌다**. 완전 에스라인이야.
 That actress' figure is amazing. She's really curvaceous. She has an hour-glass figure.

부장님한테 잘 해라. 한번 **찍히**면 다시 눈에 들기 힘들어.
 Be respectful to the department head. Once you fall out his graces, you will never be the same in his eyes.

네가 뭐 그리 대단하다고 데이트 신청도 거절하고 **튕기**니?
 How come you're so special that you need to play hard to get, refusing to date the guy?

동생한테 한바탕 **퍼부**었더니 속이 시원하다. [퍼붓다]
 I feel refreshed now that I unloaded my anger on my sister.

그렇게 뒤에서 남을 **씹**으면 속이 후련하니?
 Do you get some kind of satisfaction from talking [chewing] behind someone's back like that?

오랜만에 보니 **훤해졌**네요. 무슨 좋은 일 있어요?
 I haven't seen you for a while, but you are looking better than ever. Did something good happen?

13 Sound symbolism

Korean is noted for its rich and vivid sound symbolism – the use of speech sounds to mimic the sounds of nature and to capture subtle impressions about appearance, texture, and other sensory experiences.

It may not be enough to say 가슴이 내려 앉았어 'My heart sank,' when 가슴이 "철렁" 했어 is so much more descriptive thanks to the way 철렁 dramatically portrays a sinking feeling. Why say 하루종일 웃는 얼굴이야, when 하루종일 싱글벙글이야 better describes a face that is 'all smiles'? And of course nothing captures the image of a child's angelic smile better than 방글방글. The vivid and graphic image of these expressions can only be imagined and visualized; it is often difficult to adequately translate them into English.

13.1 How sound symbolism works

Sound-symbolic expressions typically function either as adverbs or as verbal nouns (in combination with a noun suffix -이 or with special verbs such as -이다, -하다, -대다, and -거리다).

- 찌개가 **보글보글** 끓는다.   *The stew is bubbling.*
- **깜박**이   *car signal light*
- 신호등이 **깜박**인다.   *The traffic light is blinking.*
- 길이 **미끌미끌**하다.   *The road is slippery.*
  쾅하는 소리가 났어요.   *There was a thud.*
- 문이 자꾸 **덜컹**댄다/**덜컹**거린다.   *The door rattles repeatedly.*

When one hears a sound-symbolic adverb, one can predict what type of verb is to follow. If you hear 벌떡, for instance, you know it's the image of someone swiftly getting up or standing up, so it can only be followed by a verb such as 일어나다. 텅 describes how utterly empty something is, so the verb that follows must be 비다. 쑥쑥 is the sound/image created by something growing by leaps and bounds, so it is followed by verbs such as 자라다, 크다, or 올라가다.

It is therefore often unnecessary to end the sentence with a verb. When you hear 뚝, you know it's the sound of something suddenly stopping or dropping. If a mom tells a crying baby 뚝!, the omitted verb is 그쳐 'stop.' And if the news headline says 전국기온 뚝 'the nation's temperature *ttuk*,' the missing verb can only be 떨어졌다 'dropped.' (Verbs are often omitted in headlines as well as in written advertisements, where brevity is vital.)

시청률 **쑥쑥**	*Viewing rate grows rapidly.*
수재 복구비 **꿀꺽**	*Repair fund for flood damage swallowed.*
추석물가 **들썩**	*Prices jump for Chusŏk.*
전국이 **꽁꽁**	*The nation freezes up hard.*
주름이 **확**!	*Wrinkles disappear suddenly.*

Many impressionistic adverbs and nouns appear in two or more related shapes. Those containing the 'dark' vowels 어, 에, 여, 우, 위, 유, 워, 웨, 으, 이, and 의 tend to connote something bigger, heavier, slower, and deeper, which can sometimes be seen as negative. In contrast, those that contain the 'bright' vowels 아, 애, 야, 오, 외, 요, 와, and 왜 indicate something small, light, swift, and gentle, which is often seen to be positive. Here are some cases that illustrate the contrast between these two types of vowels.

With bright vowels:

김치가 **새콤**한 게 맛있다.
The kimch'i is soury and delicious.

눈이 **반짝반짝** 빛난다.
Her eyes are twinkling.

피부가 **촉촉**하다.
Her skin is moist.

아이들이 **종알**댄다.
The kids are chattering.

똑딱똑딱 시계소리
tick tock, the sound of a clock

With dark vowels:

김치가 **시큼**한 게 맛없다.
The kimch'i is soury and tasteless.

번개가 **번쩍번쩍** 친다.
The lightning is flashing.

담요가 **축축**하다.
The blanket is damp.

어른들이 **중얼**댄다.
The adults are mumbling.

뚝딱뚝딱 망치소리
tuk tack, the sound of a hammer

Initial consonants too can form the basis for sound-symbolic contrasts. Plain consonants (ㅂ, ㄷ, ㄱ, ㅈ, ㅅ) can be replaced by their tense or aspirated counterparts to express emphasis or a strong feeling. The tense consonants (ㅃ, ㄸ, ㄲ, ㅉ, ㅆ) sound tight, crisp, and intense, while the aspirated consonants (ㅍ, ㅌ, ㅋ, ㅊ) call to mind something harsh.

박박 문질러, 더 **빡빡**, 좀 더 세게 **팍팍** 좀 문질러 봐.
  Scrub it, scrub it more, try to scrub it harder.

수박을 **작은/조그만** 걸로 하나 사. 더 **짝은/쪼끄만** 거 없어?
  Buy a small watermelon. Do you have a tinier one?

전기가 나가서 방이 **깜깜**해요. 온 동네가 불빛 하나 없이 **캄캄**해요.
  The electricity went out, so the room is dark. The whole neighborhood is pitch dark without a single light.

There are three major types of sound-symbolic expressions: those that describe sounds (의성어), those that describe outer appearance (의태어), and those that describe feeling and touch (의정어). A few expressions fall on the border line, making it difficult to see which category they belong to. The following division is based on our best judgments for presentational purposes.

13.2 Onomatopoeia (의성어)

Onomatopoeia, the use of speech to mimic the sounds of nature, is far more widespread in Korean than in English. Some of the more frequently used onomatopoeic expressions follow. (Remember that sounds are often perceived differently across cultures – Koreans hear 멍멍 while Americans hear *bow-wow*.)

13.2.1 Animal sounds

개/강아지 *dog/puppy*	멍멍 *bow-wow*
고양이 *cat*	야옹야옹 *meow meow*
돼지 *pig*	꿀꿀꿀꿀 *oink oink*
사자/호랑이 *lion/tiger*	으르렁 *growl, snarl*
새 *birds*	짹짹 *tweet, chirp*
생쥐 *mouse*	찍찍 *squeak squeak*
소 *cow*	음메 *moo*
수탉 *rooster*	꼬꼬댁 꼬꼬꼬꼬... 꼬끼오 *cock-a-doodle-doo*

Metaphorical uses:

무서워서 **끽소리/찍소리**도 못 했어.
  I was so scared that I couldn't say a word.

아웅다웅 하지 말고 친하게 지내도록 해.
  Stop fighting like cats and try to get along with each other.

사이좋게 지내지 못하고 왜 그렇게 서로 **으르렁**대니?
  Why are you wrangling with each other, and not able to get along?

13.2.2 Human sounds

• Laughing

너무 웃겨서 **까르르 까르르** 배꼽을 잡았어.
  It was so funny that I laughed very hard until my stomach hurt.

저 뒤에서 공부 안 하고 **낄낄**거리는 학생 누구야?
  Who is that student in the back giggling and not studying?

만화가 웃긴가 봐. 보면서 계속 **키득**거린다.
That cartoon must be funny. He keeps chuckling while reading it.

너는 뭐가 좋다고 그렇게 **해해**거리냐?
What makes you so silly to keep you smiling like that?

NOTE: For online chatting, ㅎㅎㅎ indicates a loud laugh
and ㅋㅋㅋ a suppressed laugh.

- Sleeping

아빠가 **드르렁드르렁** 코를 고셔서 한 잠도 못 잤어.
My dad was snoring so loudly I couldn't get any sleep.

아기가 **새근새근** 잘 잔다.
The baby is sleeping well, making gentle breathing sounds.

피곤했는지 **식식거리며** 잔다.
He must have been tired because he's sound asleep.

너는 공부는 안 하고 맨날 **쿨쿨** 잠만 자니?
How can you not study and just sleep like that all the time?

- Eating/Drinking

고소한 빵 냄새에 침이 **꿀꺽** 넘어갔지만 꾹 참았어.
The smell of bread baking made my mouth water, but I suppressed it.

떡을 한 입에 **꿀떡** 삼켰다.
I swallowed the rice cake in one gulp.

목이 말라 냉수를 **벌컥벌컥** 들이켰다.
My throat was dry so I chugged cold water.

아기가 이가 나서 사탕을 **오도독 오도독** 깨물어 먹어요.
The baby has teeth, so he crunches the candy.

짭짭대지 말고 조용히 먹어.
Stop making that smacking noise with your mouth and eat quietly.

홀짝홀짝거리지 말고 **쭈욱** 들이켜.
Stop sipping and drink it down like a man.

라면을 한 젓갈에 **후르륵** 다 먹었다.
I finished the ramen in one big slurp.

- Speaking/Shouting

왜 이렇게 **꽥꽥** 소리를 지르고 야단이야. 나 귀 안 먹었어.
Why are you screaming like crazy? I'm not deaf.

그렇게 **딱딱**거리지 말고 좀 좋은 말로 하면 안되겠니?
Can't you talk more nicely instead of speaking so harshly?

뭘 잘했다고 **빽빽**거려? 조용히 해.
What did you do that gives you the right to have a loud mouth? Shut up.

저희끼리 **속닥속닥**하다가도 내가 가면 입을 닫아버려요.
They whisper amongst themselves, but whenever I appear they close their mouths.

그렇게 **수군**거리지 말고 한 사람이 크게 얘기해 보세요.
You guys stop mumbling unintelligibly like that and have one person speak out.

밖에 무슨 일이 있나 봐요. **웅성웅성**하네요.
There must be something going on outside. People are chattering.

그동안 쌓였던 불만을 **주절주절** 늘어 놓더라.
He was releasing his pent-up complaints one after another.

그 사람은 무슨 불만이 그렇게 많은지 항상 **투덜**거려요.
*There seem to be so many things that he's dissatisfied about;
he grumbles all the time.*

- Crying

목이 아프도록 **엉엉** 울었어.
I bawled so hard my throat hurt.

아기가 어디가 아픈 지 하루종일 **징징**거린다.
The baby must be sick because he has been whimpering all day.

감기가 걸린 거니? 우는 거니? 왜 그렇게 **훌쩍훌쩍**대니?
Did you catch a cold? Or are you crying? Why are you sniffling?

흑흑, 이야기가 너무 슬퍼요. [literary writing]
Boo-hoo, the story is so sad.

- Bodily noise

건강해야지. 그렇게 늘 **콜콜**해서 어떡하니?
You should be healthy. I'm worried that you are so fragile all the time.

짐이 너무 무겁다고 **끙끙**대더라.
He was groaning, saying that the luggage was too heavy.

독감으로 일주일 내내 **끙끙** 앓았어.
I was sick with the flu all week, moaning and groaning.

아무 데서나 방구를 **뿡뿡** 뀌고 매너가 완전히 꽝이야.
He has no manners; he farts regardless of where he is.

관리인이 **씩씩**거리며 뛰어들어왔다.
The usher ran in, heaving and panting.

속이 좀 **출출**하네. 배에서 **쪼르륵/꼬르륵** 소리가 난다.
I'm sort of hungry. My stomach is grumbling.

감기가 오나 봐요. 아침부터 **콜록콜록** 기침이 나요.
I must be catching a cold. I've been coughing since the morning.

13.2.3 Sounds involving inanimate objects and forces

부엌에서 무슨 **달가닥**거리는 소리 못 들었어?
Did you hear the rattling noise in the kitchen?

하루종일 **따르릉 따르릉** 전화통에 불이 났어요.
'Ring-ring,' the phone's been ringing off the hook all day long.

땡하면 떨어진 거고 **딩동댕**하면 합격한 겁니다.
A buzz means you're wrong and the chime means you can advance.

똑똑 노크를 하지 그렇게 **쾅쾅** 두들기니? 문 부서지겠다.
Why don't you knock instead of banging on the door? You'll break the door down.

바스락거리지 말고 가만히 좀 앉아 있어.
Stop shuffling around and sit still.

기름을 많이 넣고 **바싹** 튀기면 **바삭바삭**해서 맛있어요.
If you use a lot of oil and deep-fry it, then it'll be crispy and tasty.

그렇게 **북북** 찢지말고 가위로 똑바로 오려 봐.
Stop ripping it and cut it neatly with scissors.

자동차들이 필요이상으로 **빵빵**거린다.
The cars are honking their horns more than necessary.

문이 자꾸 **삐걱**거려요.
The door keeps squeaking.

남들이 알까봐 **쉬쉬**하는 거 같아요.
He seems to be hushing it up in case other people find out.

정성껏 길렀던 머리가 **싹둑싹둑** 잘려 나갔다.
The hair that I put so much effort into growing was snipped off strand by strand.

날씨가 추워지려나 봐요, 바람이 **쌩쌩** 부네요.
The weather must be getting cold. The wind is blowing hard.

사과가 **아삭아삭**하지 않고 **푸석푸석**해서 맛이 없다.
The apple doesn't taste good because it's soggy, not crunchy.

와글와글대던 소리가 쥐 죽은 듯이 딱 끊어졌다.
The cacophonous noise of people suddenly died down.

아이들이 장난이 심해서 매일 **와당탕통탕/와당탕쿵쾅** 난리예요.
The unruly kids are boisterously thumping around every day.

차에 실어 놓았던 물건들이 **와르르** 무너졌어요.
The luggage I had stored in the car came crashing down.

비가 **주룩주룩** 쏟아지는데 우산도 없이 어떻게 나가?
It's raining cats and dogs, so how can I go out without an umbrella?

범인은 자기 잘못을 뉘우치며 닭똥같은 눈물을 **줄줄** 흘렸다.
　The criminal was shedding big tear drops as he lamented his past mistakes.

슬리퍼를 그렇게 **질질** 끌며 다니지 마라.
　Stop going around dragging your slippers like that.

하루 종일 **쫄쫄** 굶었더니 눈에 뵈는 게 없네.
　After starving to death the whole day, I can eat just about anything.

찰싹하고 따귀 때리는 소리가 났다.
　There was a sound as if someone got slapped in the face.

찰칵 소리가 났는데 사진이 안 찍혔어요.
　It sounded like it took the picture, but it didn't.

수영장에 사람이 너무 많아서 그냥 **첨벙**거리다 왔어.
　There were too many people in the pool, so I just splashed around in the water.

물이 **콸콸** 쏟아지지 않고 **찔끔찔끔** 나오네요.
　Water is dripping out, not pouring out.

너무 세게 치지 말고 가볍게 **톡** 건드려 봐.
　Don't hit it too hard; try to softly tap it.

땅바닥에 **털썩** 주저앉았다.
　He sat down on the ground with a plop.

In the following examples, the sounds are less directly associated with the action or state described by the sentence but still evoke some aspect of meaning for Koreans.

우리도 **떵떵**거리고 살 때가 올 거야.
　There will be a time when we can live grandly.

사람이 **똑** 부러지지 못하고 너무 우유부단하다.
　She can't crack down and be firm; she's too indecisive.

걔 때문에 속이 **부글부글** 끓어.
　I'm boiling with anger because of him.

시간이 너무 **빠듯**하다.
　It's too tight; there's not enough time.

컴퓨터라면 **빠삭**해요.
　If it's the computer, I'm fairly familiar with it.

이번 일의 성과에 대해 가슴이 **뿌듯**합니다.
　I feel happy and satisfied about the results from the recent project.

어렸을 때는 **왈가닥**이더니 **꽁**한 성격으로 바뀌었어.
　She was boisterous when she was little, but now she is glum and introverted.

너는 그 **욱**하는 성격이 문제야.
　The problem with you is your hot temper.

무슨 **꿍꿍이**가 있는 게 틀림없어.
There is definitely an ulterior motive.

오늘도 **땡땡이** 치고 학교에 안 갔구나, 너!
You played hookie again, didn't you?!

직장 동료가 우리 몰래 회비를 **쓱싹**했어.
My company co-worker embezzled the club membership fees.

13.3 Mimetic expressions (의태어)

Mimetic expressions attempt to convey the speaker's impression of appearances and behaviors through the choice of particular speech sounds. Some expressions of this type may have both onomatopoeic and mimetic effects.

13.3.1 Impressions of appearance

강아지가 신문을 **갈기갈기** 찢어 놓았지 뭐예요.
The dog shredded the newspaper into pieces, you know.

얼굴에 **거뭇거뭇**하게 주근깨가 생겼어.
Freckles appeared on my face, creating dark spots here and there.

구질구질하게 이렇게 더러운 데서 어떻게 자?
It's grotty, how can I sleep in this messy place?

나도 모르게 눈물이 **글썽글썽**해지네요.
I can't control the tears building up in my eyes.

피부가 **까무잡잡**해서 건강해 보여요.
Her skin is nice and dark, so she looks healthy.

서류가 **꼬깃꼬깃** 다 꾸겨졌다.
The document got wrinkled all over.

얼음이 **꽁꽁** 얼었네요.
The ice is frozen all the way through.

세수도 못해서 얼굴이 **꾀죄죄**하다.
I didn't even get to wash my face, so it looks grimy.

운동화가 **너덜너덜**해졌어. 하나 사야겠다.
The sneakers are worn out and tattered. I'll have to buy new ones.

좁은 동네에 집들이 **다닥다닥** 붙어 있다.
The houses are clustered together in the small town.

방학동안 여기저기 군살이 **더덕더덕** 붙었어요.
I gained weight all over during the vacation.

세수 좀 해라. 눈에 눈곱이 **덕지덕지** 끼었네.
Wash your face. You still have crud stuck all over in your eyes.

얼굴이 **동글동글**해서 아주 어려 보여요.
His face is nice and round, so he looks very young.

책상 위가 **뒤죽박죽** 정신이 하나도 없다.
The desk is so cluttered I can't find anything.

치아가 약간 **들쑥날쑥**하시네요. 교정을 받아 보실 생각 없으세요?
Your teeth are slightly crooked. What do you think about getting braces?

먹고 잠만 자니까 **뒤룩뒤룩** 살이 찐다.
I do nothing but eat and sleep, and I'm getting fatter and fatter.

미끈하게 잘 빠졌다.
He has a nice body.

백화점에 사람이 **바글바글**하더라.
The mall was bustling with people.

저게 뭐가 날씬한거니, **바싹** 마른 거지.
That's not slender, but skinny to the bone.

임산부처럼 배가 **불룩** 튀어나왔네.
My stomach is bulging as if I'm pregnant.

파마가 너무 **빠글빠글**하게 나왔다.
The perm came out too curly.

너무 더워서 땀이 **뻘뻘** 난다.
It's so hot I'm sweating bullets.

줄이 **삐뚤삐뚤**하게 그려졌네.
The line came out squiggly.

집이 정말 **으리으리**하더라.
The house is so luxurious, I noticed.

생글생글 웃는 모습이 귀여워요.
Her pleasantly smiling face is cute.

그 남자배우는 **씩** 웃을 때가 제일 멋있어요.
That actor is most handsome when he flashes a big smile.

나는 **얼룩덜룩**한 무늬 보다는 단색이 좋더라구요.
I prefer a single color to a multi-colored design.

새로 산 화장품이 피부에 안 받나 봐. 얼굴에 **오돌도돌** 뭐가 난다.
I think my skin is allergic to the new make-up. My face is breaking out in a rash.

아이가 양 볼이 **오동통**해서 아주 귀여워요.
The kid's cheeks are so chubby, it's cute.

코가 **오똑**한 게 잘 생겼다.
He's good looking with a high nose.

남자가 **우락부락**한 게 좀 무섭게 생겼어.
The guy looks rough, so he appears a bit scary.

가을에는 **울긋불긋**한 단풍이 정말 볼만해요.
The leaves changing color in the fall are worth seeing.

길이 **울퉁불퉁**해서 잘못하다간 넘어지겠다.
The road is bumpy, so you might fall if you're not careful.

나무에 감이 **주렁주렁** 달린게 탐스러워 보인다.
The blossoming persimmon clusters on the tree look delicious and tempting.

하와이는 길이 **쭉쭉** 뻗지 않고 **꼬불꼬불**하다.
The roads in Hawaii are winding, not straight.

옷이 다 말랐으면 **차곡차곡** 개어 놓아라.
When the clothes are dry, neatly fold them.

보석을 너무 **치렁치렁** 달면 천박해 보이지 않니?
If you have too much jewelry hanging from you, won't you look cheap and superficial?

팽팽/탱탱하던 피부가 **쪼글쪼글**해 진다.
My once tight and toned skin is turning wrinkly.

눈이 신나게 **펑펑** 쏟아진다.
It's snowing hard; it's exciting.

뚱뚱하긴요. **포동포동**한 게 귀엽기만 하네요.
What do you mean 'fat'? His chubbiness is just cute.

살이 빠져서 꽉 끼던 청바지가 **헐렁헐렁**해졌다.
I lost weight, so my blue jeans that used to be tight became big and baggy.

키가 **호리호리**하게 크고 얼굴도 그만하면 미인이에요.
She's tall and slender, and has a fairly beautiful face.

어디 아팠어요? 그동안 얼굴이 **홀쭉**해졌네요.
Were you sick? Your face got smaller (from your losing weight).

머리가 **희끗희끗**한 게 적어도 40 대 중반은 됐을 거야.
His few grey hairs show that he must be at least in his mid 40s.

13.3.2 *Impressions of behavior/motion/manner*

윗분들 말씀 **고분고분** 잘 듣도록 해.
  Make sure you obediently listen to your superiors.

저 사람은 아부가 심해. 과장님만 보면 늘 **굽실거려**.
  *That person brown-noses a lot. Whenever the director is around,
  he sucks up to him (bowing constantly).*

수상하게 왜 남의 집을 **기웃**거리지?
  I wonder why he is suspiciously snooping around other people's houses?

아차, **깜빡**했다.
  Oops, I totally forgot [I blinked].

우리 아빠는 내 동생이라면 완전 **껌뻑** 죽으셔.
  My dad would give his life when it comes to my brother.

성격이 너무 **꼬장꼬장**해서 피곤해.
  His personality is so straight and strong that it is tiring.

이렇게 **꼼지락**거리다가 또 늦겠다.
  We'll be late again if we act this slow and clumsy.

너무 졸려서 강의시간 내내 **꾸벅꾸벅** 졸았어요.
  I was so drowsy that I was nodding off through the entire lecture.

지렁이가 **꿈틀꿈틀**하는 게 너무 징그럽다.
  It's so disgusting the way worms wiggle.

알았다는 듯이 고개를 **끄덕끄덕**한다.
  He's nodding his head as if in agreement.

침착하지 못하고 왜 이렇게 **덜렁**대니?
  Why can't you be calm; why do you act so carelessly?

준다고 그렇게 **덥석** 받는 게 어디 있어?
  How can you snatch it so quickly just because someone offered it?

계단에서 넘어져 갖고 **데굴데굴** 굴러 떨어졌어.
  He fell and rolled down the stairs.

급해서 발을 **동동** 구른다.
  He is in such a hurry he can't stop moving around.

누구를 찾는지 계속 **두리번**거리네요.
  He keeps looking around as if he's looking for somebody.

나는 **뚱**한 사람보다는 **나긋나긋**한 사람이 좋더라.
  I prefer a soft and gentle person over a glum and untalkative one.

알지도 못하는 사람하고 **맹숭맹숭** 앉아서 무슨 얘기를 해요?
  What can I talk about, sitting awkwardly with someone I don't even know?

군고구마에서 김이 **모락모락** 나네요.
The steam is rising from the baked sweet potato.

사과나무가 **무럭무럭** 잘 자란다.
The apple tree is growing rapidly.

나는 한 때만 유명했다가 잊혀지는 **반짝가수**는 되기 싫어.
I don't want to be a flash-in-the-pan type of singer.

백화점에서 오늘 하루만 **반짝세일**을 한대요.
I heard that there's a surprise one-day sale at the department store today.

눈길에 뒤로 **벌렁** 자빠졌어.
I slipped and fell flat on my back on the snowy road.

뭐가 무섭다고 그렇게 **벌벌** 떨어?
What's so scary that you're trembling like that?

너무 화가 나서 손이 **부들부들** 떨린다.
I am so angry that my hands are shaking.

아침부터 비가 **부슬부슬** 오네요.
It's been drizzling since morning.

왜 이렇게 **비실비실** 기운이 없니?
Why do you mope around with no energy?

비틀비틀하는 거 보니까 운전하면 안 되겠다.
Seeing you staggering and wobbling, there's no way you can drive.

그 사람은 도대체 **빠릿빠릿**한 구석이 없고 느려 터졌어.
That person does nothing energetically and is terribly slow with everything.

담배만 **뻐끔뻐끔** 피우고 앉아 있지 말고 나가서 일자리 좀 찾아 봐.
Stop sitting around puffing on your cigarette and go look for a job.

이 일에 대해서 입도 **뻥끗**하지마, 알았지?
Don't say a word about this, okay?

하루종일 **뾰로통**해서 말도 안 해요.
She doesn't even talk, sulking and pouting all day.

부모님이 깨시지 않게 방에 **살금살금** 들어갔어요.
I tip-toed in, so my parents wouldn't wake up.

우는 아이를 **살살** 달래야지 그렇게 **윽박**지르면 어떡해요?
How can you scold him so harshly when you should be comforting the crying kid?

바람이 **솔솔** 불어 아주 시원하다.
The gentle breeze is very refreshing.

졸려서 눈이 **스르르** 감긴다.
My eye lids are slowly drooping because I'm sleepy.

이제 날씨도 선선해졌으니 운동을 **슬슬** 시작해 볼까?
Now that the weather is getting cooler, shall we slowly start exercising?

나도 대강 알고 있으니까 **시시콜콜** 다 얘기할 필요 없어.
You don't have to give me all the trivial details because I generally know what it's about.

남기지 말고 **싹싹** 먹어 치우자.
Let's not leave any food and eat everything on the plate.

가서 잘못했다고 **싹싹** 빌어 봐.
Go and desperately try to beg for forgiveness.

종업원들이 다 **싹싹**하고 친절해요.
All the waiters/waitresses are so pleasant and kind.

아기가 **아장아장** 걷는 게 너무 귀엽네요.
The baby's toddling around is very cute.

계속 일어섰다 앉았다 **안절부절**못하고 있어요.
He's restlessly getting up and down.

어물어물하다간 그 남자 다른 여자한테 뺏긴다.
If you don't make yourself clear and dawdle, you will lose that man to some other girl.

노는 친구들하고 어울려 다니며 **어영부영**하다가 대학 진학을 못했어요.
Idling away my time while getting along with academically non-serious friends, I failed to go to college.

얼렁뚱땅 넘어가지 말고 태도를 확실하게 해.
Don't behave so evasively and take a definitive position.

허리가 너무 아퍼서 **엉금엉금** 기어다닐 정도예요.
My back hurts so much that I have to crawl around.

너무 추워서 **오들오들** 떨린다.
It's so cold that I'm shivering.

우물쭈물하지 말고 딱 부러지게 설명을 드려.
Stop stammering around and give her a clear-cut explanation.

학생들이 시험문제가 어려워서 **쩔쩔**매던데요.
I noticed that the students were having a rough time because the test was so hard.

쫀쫀하게 뭘 그런 사소한 일에 신경을 쓰고 그래?
Why are you so sensitive about such a trifling matter?

허둥대지 말고 **차근차근** 말해 봐요.
Stop rushing and try to explain it to me slowly and carefully.

아빠가 너무 화가 나서 **펄쩍펄쩍** 뛰셨어.
My dad was so angry that he was jumping up and down.

너 술 취했구나, **해롱해롱**하는 거 보니까.
You must be drunk because I see you acting silly.

급해서 **허겁지겁** 나오느라고 아침도 못 먹었어요.
I was in such a rush leaving home this morning that I couldn't even have breakfast.

늦게 일어나서 **허둥지둥**하지 말고 일찍 일어나.
*Wake up early and don't get yourself all flustered by rushing because
you woke up late.*

물에 빠져 **허우적**대는 걸 살려 줬다.
I saved the drowning person who was splashing around.

무슨 일이라도 난 듯 **헐레벌떡** 뛰어가던데요.
I saw him running along panting and puffing as if something had happened.

불이 **활활** 잘 탄다.
The fire is burning well.

무슨 급한 일이 있는지 **후다닥** 뛰어나가던데요.
I saw him rushing out hurriedly, maybe because he has something urgent.

몸살기운이 있는지 온몸이 **후들후들** 떨려.
My whole body is shivering; I must be having flu symptoms.

걱정일랑 **훌훌** 털어 버리고 여행을 떠나 보는 게 어때?
Shed your worries completely and why don't you take a trip?

하루종일 굶었더니 다리가 **휘청**거린다.
My legs are unsteady after not having eaten all day long.

이가 **흔들흔들** 빠질 거 같아요.
The wobbly tooth looks like it's about to come out.

이렇게 돈을 **흥청망청** 쓰다간 곧 알거지 되겠다.
If we mindlessly splurge money like this, we will soon end up as bums.

저 사람이 아까부터 우리를 **힐끗힐끗** 곁눈질로 쳐다보네.
That person has been glancing at us from the corner of his eye.

13.4 Expressions denoting feeling and touch (의정어)

13.4.1 Impressions of feeling

기억이 **가물가물**한데요.
My memory is hazy. (I can't remember it clearly.)

누가 내 얘기하나 보다, 귀가 **간질간질**해.
My ears are tingling [tickling], so someone must be talking about me.

여행하고 싶어서 몸이 **근질근질**해요.
I'm itching to go traveling.

(생선)회를 먹고 나면 항상 속이 **느글느글**해.
I feel nauseous everytime after I eat raw fish.

밥이 너무 **꼬들또들**해서 못 먹겠어요.
I don't think I can eat the rice because it's too dry and hard.

그 사람만 보면 가슴이 **두근두근** 뛰어.
My heart starts beating fast everytime I see him.

국 좀 **따끈따끈**하게 데워 주세요.
Please make the soup piping hot for me.

꼭 나를 두고 하는 말인 것 같아서 **뜨끔**했어.
*I was feeling guilty [I had a stinging feeling] because
he sounded like he was talking about me.*

하루종일 머리가 **띵**하다.
I've been having a dull headache all day.

정신이 **말똥말똥**한 게 잠이 안 온다.
I can't sleep because I'm wide awake.

차멀미가 나는 지 속이 **매슥**거려요.
I think I'm having motion-sickness from the car ride; I'm feeling nauseous.

목이 너무 말라서 **바짝바짝** 탄다.
I'm so thirsty that my throat is burning.

마음이 **싱숭생숭**해서 일이 손에 잘 안 잡혀요.
My mind is scattered and wandering, so I can't work.

하마터면 죽을 뻔했어. 지금 생각해도 **아찔**하다.
I almost died. I still feel jumpy when I think about it.

알다가도 모르겠어요. 정말 **알쏭달쏭/아리송**해요.
I think I know it, but I don't. It's really vague and perplexing.

어질어질한 게 머리가 빙빙 돈다.
I'm so dizzy that my head is spinning.

마취가 안 풀려서 아직도 **얼얼**해.
I'm still feeling the effects of the anesthetic, so I still feel numb.

짐을 좀 날랐더니 온몸이 **욱신욱신** 쑤신다.
After moving some luggage, my whole body is aching.

몸살감기 걸리려나 봐. 자꾸 **으슬으슬** 추워.
I must be catching the flu. I keep feeling cold.

머리가 **지끈지끈**하다.
My head is pounding.

짜릿한 감동을 주는 그런 영화예요.
That's the type of film that moves and electrifies you.

창피해서 얼굴이 **화끈** 달아오르는 거 있지.
My face suddenly started burning, you know, because I was feeling embarrassed.

13.4.2   Impressions of touch

겨울이라 그런가? 얼굴이 **까칠까칠**해졌어요.
I wonder whether it's because it's winter. My face became very dry.

말랑말랑하던 빵이 밤새 **딱딱**해졌네요.
The nice and soft bread became rock hard overnight.

차를 항상 **반들반들**하게 닦아 갖고 다닌다.
He always keeps his car super shiny.

지성피부라서 얼굴에 개기름이 항상 **번들번들**해요.
I have oily skin, so my face is always greasy.

살결이 정말 **보들보들**하다.
Your skin is really silky smooth.

얼굴만 **빤드르르**하게 생겨 갖고 완전 날라리야.
*The only thing going for her is her sleek-looking face; she's
a really superficial playgirl.*

가죽이 부드럽지가 않고 아주 **뻣뻣**하네요.
The leather is very stiff, not soft.

인절미가 **쫄깃쫄깃**한 게 맛있다.
This sweet-rice cake is good because it's chewy.

14 Numbers

Like English, Korean makes use of two types of numbers – cardinal numbers, which are used for simple counting (e.g., *one book*, *two books*, etc.), and ordinal numbers, which are used to indicate order or position in a series (e.g., *first place*, *second place*, and so on).

Unlike English, Korean makes use of two sets of numbers, one native Korean in origin and the other Sino-Korean. Native numbers stop at 99, but Sino-Korean numbers can be as long as 16 digits.

14.1 Native Korean numbers

14.1.1 Native Korean cardinal numbers

1	하나	2	둘	3	셋	4	넷	5	다섯
6	여섯	7	일곱	8	여덟	9	아홉	10	열
20	스물	21	스물하나	30	서른	40	마흔	50	쉰
60	예순	70	일흔	80	여든	90	아흔	99	아흔아홉

NOTE: When followed by a counter, 하나, 둘, 셋, 넷, and 스물 change their form to 한 (개), 두 (개), 세 (개), 네 (개), and 스무 (개), respectively. For some counters such as 장, 잔, 달, 단, and 대 (see *14.3.1*), 세/네 alternates with 석/넉, mostly in the speech of senior adults.

14.1.2 Native Korean ordinal numbers

Native Korean ordinal numbers are formed by adding -째 to the cardinal number – except for 첫째 'first.'

첫째, 둘째/두째, 셋째/세째, …열한째, 열두째, …스무째, 스물한째,…

When the number occurs with a counter/classifier (see *14.3.1*), -째 is attached after the counter.

오늘 사과 세 개째 먹는다.	*This is the third apple that I'm eating today.*
다섯 달째 소식이 없어요.	*There's no news for the fifth month in a row.*
벌써 여덟 병째야.	*It's the eighth bottle already.*
벌써 몇 번째 얘기를 했는지 몰라.	*I already told him for the umpteenth time.*

14.2 Sino-Korean numbers

14.2.1 Sino-Korean cardinal numbers

1 일 (一)	2 이 (二)	3 삼 (三)	4 사 (四)	5 오 (五)
6 육 (六)	7 칠 (七)	8 팔 (八)	9 구 (九)	10 십 (十)
20 이십	21 이십일	30 삼십	40 사십	50 오십
60 육십	70 칠십	80 팔십	90 구십	99 구십구

NOTE: Chinese characters are provided in parentheses.

Unlike English, which breaks down long numbers into three-numeral units, Korean organizes long numbers into four-numeral chunks. (Nonetheless, when writing large Arabic numbers, Korean uses commas to group numerals into sets of three, just as English does.)

English:

9,|6 0 1,|2 3 4,|5 0 0,|7 8 9
trillion   billion   million   thousand

9 trillion, 601 billion, 234 million, 500 thousand, 789

Korean:

9,|6 0 1,2|3 4,5 0 |0,7 8 9
　조　　　　억　　　　　만

9 조　　6,012 억　　3,450 만 0,789
[구**조** 육천십이**억** 삼천사백오십**만** 칠백팔십구]

To keep the groupings clear, it is useful to remember particular reference points such as 'thousand' 천 and 만 'ten thousand,' and so on.

일	one
십	ten
백	hundred
천	**thousand**
(일)**만**	**ten thousand**
십만	hundred thousand
백만	**million**
천만	ten million
(일)**억**	**one hundred million**
십억	**billion** *(UK 1,000 million)*
백억	ten billion *(UK 10,000 million)*
천억	one hundred billion *(UK 100,000 million)*
(일)**조**	**trillion** *(UK one billion)*

$1 (일불)   =   approx. ₩1,000 (천원)

$10 (십불)   =   ₩10,000 (만원)

$100 (백불)   =   ₩100,000 (십만원)

$1,000 (천불)   =   ₩1,000,000 (백만원)

$10,000 (만불)   =   ₩10,000,000 (천만원)

$100,000 (십만불)   =   ₩100,000,000 (일억원)

$1,000,000 (백만불)   =   ₩1,000,000,000 (십억원)

14.2.2 Sino-Korean ordinal numbers

Sino-Korean ordinal numbers are formed with the help of the prefix 제- as in 제 12 부 'the twelfth episode.' However, except in formal writing, 제- is usually omitted and the bare Sino-Korean number is used in combination with various counters to indicate order.

1 페이지/쪽	*page 1*
2 과	*lesson 2*
3 편	*volume 3*
5 번	*number 5*
(시험, 경기) 1 등	*top score (in an exam, game)*
일급 (호텔)	*first class (hotel)*
(장기, 바둑) 2 급	*second rank (in chess, paduk)*
(보물) 1 호	*(treasure) #1*
(태권도) 5 단	*fifth rank (in T'aekwŏndo)*
(창립) 25 주년	*twenty-fifth anniversary (of the foundation)*
10 대 (대통령)	*10th (president)*
(야구, 드라마) 9 회	*9th inning (in baseball), 9th episode (in a drama)*
(입학시험, 파티) 2 차	*the second round (entrance exam, partying)*
(아파트) 15 층	*15th floor (of an apt.)*
(고등학교) 2 학년	*second grade (in high school)*
(음반) 4 집	*Vol. #4 (music CD)*
(한국인) 2 세	*second generation (Korean)*

14.3 Native versus Sino-Korean numbers

In most cases, there is a strict division of labor in the use of native Korean numbers and Sino-Korean numbers. For example, native Korean numbers are used for counting (small numbers) and for o'clock (세시 '3 o'clock'), while Sino-Korean numbers are employed for minutes, dates, months, years, money, and so forth (16 절지 '8 ½ by 11 size paper,' 24 금 '24 K gold,' and so on).

In some cases, both types of numbers can occur with the same counter, creating sharp contrasts in meaning.

Native number (quantity)		Sino-Korean number (order)	
한 페이지/쪽	*one page*	일 페이지/쪽	*page 1*
두 과	*two lessons*	이 과	*lesson 2*
세 편	*three volumes*	삼 편	*volume 3*
다섯 번	*five times*	오 번	*number 5*

Very rarely, either number can be used for the same concept, but this is correlated with a contrast in speech style.

Native number (colloquial)	Sino-Korean number (written/formal)	
사진 두 장	사진 2 매	*two photos*
스무 살	20 세	*20 years old*
아들 하나 딸 셋	1 남 3 녀	*one son, three daughters*
세째 아들	3 남	*third son*
다섯 식구	5 인가족	*a family of five*

The rest of this section focuses on how the functions of the two sets of numbers are divided up.

14.3.1 Counting

Native numerals are used for counting smaller units. For larger quantities, Sino-Korean numerals are used, often in combination with native numbers. There is a tendency for Sino-Korean numbers to be used for multiples of 10, starting from 20, even when there is a native Korean counterpart.

1	종이 한 장 *one sheet of paper*
10	" 열 장
20	" 스무 장 or 이십 장
21	" 스물 한 장
125	" 백 스물 다섯 장 or 백 이십 오 장
1,502	" 천 오백 두 장 or 천 오백 이 장

1	학생 한 명 *one student*
10	" 열 명
70	" 일흔 명 or 칠십 명
99	" 아흔 아홉 명 or 구십구 명
52,309	" 오만 이천 삼백 아홉 명 or 오만 이천 삼백 구 명

Counters *(or Classifiers)*

Numbers usually occur with counters such as 장 for thin/flat objects like sheets of paper, 명 for people, 마리 for animals, and so on, all of which indicate the type of element being counted. (When counting large numbers, things/persons are usually counted by twos, as in 둘 넷 여섯 여덟 열 열둘 열넷 열여섯 열여덟 스물... (using only even numbers). The following counters are frequently used.

Counters for inanimate things

갑/보루 (a pack/carton of cigarettes): 담배 한 갑/보루

개 (3-D objects in general , 'default classifier' when nothing else fits): 빵 한 개
    one piece of bread, 쓰레기통 두 개 *two garbage cans*

권 (bound material): 잡지 한 권 *one magazine*, 만화책 열 권 *ten cartoon books*

그루 (tree): 소나무 한 그루 *one pine tree*

대 (machines and large appliances): 차/세탁기두 대 *two cars/washing machines*

대, 개비 (tiny slender objects): 담배 한 대 *one cigarette*, 성냥 두 개비 *two matches*

매 (sheets of paper) [formal/written]: 이력서 1 매 *one copy of a résumé*

벌 (clothes, silverware): 정장 한 벌 *one formal suit*, 수저 두 벌 *two spoon*
    & chopstick sets

부 (periodicals such as magazines, multi-page documents): 월간지 한 부
    one monthly magazine, 신청서 한 부 *one application document*

송이/다발 (stem/bouquet): 장미 두 송이/다발 *two stems/bouquets of roses*

자루 (long slender objects): 연필 한 자루 *one pencil*

장 (thin, flat objects): 도화지 열 장 *10 sheets of drawing paper*

점 (pieces of art): 그림 한 점 *one picture*

채 (buildings): 집 한 채, 건물 아홉 채 *nine buildings*

척 (ships): 배 한 척 *one boat*, 잠수함 세 척 *three submarines*

첩 (pack of herbal remedy): 한약 스무 첩 (= 한 제) *20 packs of Chinese medicine*

켤레 (pair of shoes, socks, gloves): 운동화 한 켤레 *one pair of sneakers*,
    양말 세 켤레 *three pairs of socks*

통 (letters in an envelope): 편지 세 통 *three letters*

NOTE: Unlike most other counters, 매 can be used with Sino-Korean numbers – 사진
2 매, 이력서 1 매.

Counters for food

그릇, 공기 (a bowl of rice, etc.): 국 두 그릇 *two bowls of soup*, 밥 한 공기
   one bowl of rice

단 (a bunch of vegetables): 파 세 단 *three bunches of green onion*,
   시금치 두 단 *two bunches of spinach*

대 (a rib bone): (소)갈비 (돼지갈비, 닭갈비) 한 대 *one beef (pork, chicken) rib*

모 (tofu, jelly): 두부/도토리묵 한 모 *one cake of tofu/acorn jelly*

모금 (a sip, a puff): 물 한 모금 *a sip of water*, 담배 두 모금 *two puffs on a*
   cigarette

분 (one serving): 불고기 3 인 분 *three servings of pulgogi*

송이 (bunch): 포도 다섯 송이 *five bunches of grapes*

숟갈, 젓갈 (a bite): 밥 한 숟갈 *one spoonful of rice*, 국수 한 젓갈 *one chopstick-*
   ful of noodles

알: (small round-shaped things) 포도 두 알 *two grapes*, 계란 다섯 알 *five eggs*

잔 (liquids in a glass/cup): 차 두 잔 *two cups of tea*, 술 한 잔 *one drink*

컵 (liquids, etc. in a cup/glass): 물 한 컵 *one glass of water*, 쌀 한 컵 *one cup of rice*

접시 (main dish): 요리 세 접시 *three dishes of gourmet food*

쪽 (small slice): 사과 한 쪽 *one piece of apple*, 마늘 세 쪽 *three slices of garlic*

통 (round-shaped fruit, etc.): 수박 세 통 *three watermelons*,
   마늘 한 통 *one bulb of garlic*

포기 (a head of cabbage): 배추 한 포기 *one head of cabbage*

NOTE: Sino-Korean numbers are used for counting servings (불고기 3 인분).

Counters for animate things

명 (people): 학생 세 명 *three students*, 모르는 사람 두 명 *two strangers*

분 (honorific form of 명): 손님 세 분 *three guests*

쌍 (a couple, a pair): 연인/부부 한 쌍 *one romantic/married couple*

마리 (animals, fish, birds): 물고기 한 마리 *one live fish*, 새 여러 마리 *several*
birds

Counters for miscellaneous things

건 (agenda items, assembly bills): 강도 사건 다섯 건 *5 robbery incidents,*
　의안 열 건 *10 assembly bills*

곡 (pieces of music): 노래 일곱 곡 *7 songs*

대 (injections, beatings): 주사/매 한 대 *one injection/beating*

통 (phone calls, rolls of film): 전화 네 통 *4 phone calls,* 필름 여덟 통 *8 rolls of film*

편 (movies, musicals, poems): 영화 네 편 *4 movies,* 시 두 편 *two poems*

가지 (sorts): 고기 반찬 세 가지 *3 kinds of meat dishes,*
　나물 아홉 가지 *9 kinds of cooked vegetable dishes*

Four types of counting expressions

When a numeral such as 두 combines with a noun such as 사과 in counting, four different patterns are possible.

- 사과 두 개 is the most common pattern. Particles like -이/가 and -을/를 can be attached to either or both elements.

  식탁 위에 사과(가) 두 개(가) 있어요.
  　There are two apples on the dining table.

- 사과 둘 is not uncommon, but is usually restricted to small numbers and to countable nouns (one to five, with one being the most common and natural). Particles can be attached to either or both elements.

  비빔밥 하나 주세요.
  　Please give me one bibimbap.

  딸을 넷을 낳고 아들 하나를 낳았어.
  　She had one son after four daughters.

  학생 둘이 졸업하고 셋이 새로 들어 왔다.
  　Two students graduated and three new ones arrived.

- 두 사과 is uncommon and restricted in many ways. The number must be smaller than ten and the noun usually must be followed by 다 'all.'

Acceptable	Unacceptable/strange-sounding
두 차로 갑시다. *Let's go in two cars.*	두 차를 샀다. *I bought two cars.*
세 닭이 다 병이 났다. *All three chickens got sick.*	세 닭을 키운다. *I am raising three chickens.*
두 강아지가 다 예쁘다. *The two puppies are both cute.*	두 강아지가 뛰어왔다. *Two puppies came running.*
네 커피가 다 코나예요. *All four coffees are Kona.*	네 커피를 샀다. *I bought four coffees.*

Exceptionally, the following cases are natural even with bigger numbers.

열아들 안 부럽다.
　I don't envy those with many sons. (I am satisfied with my daughter.)
열다섯 집이/학교가/나라가 모였다.
　Fifteen families/schools/countries got together.

- 두 개의 사과 is used mostly in formal speech or writing.

한 잔의 차	*one cup of tea*
열 권의 책	*ten books*
5 개 국가의 수상	*prime ministers of 5 countries*

14.3.2 Units of measurement

Sino-Korean numbers are used for the metric system as well as for some American units of measurement. Native numbers are employed only for a few traditional Korean units of measurement. (All Arabic numerals are to be read as Sino-Korean numbers, unless otherwise specified.)

Temperature (기온/온도)

섭씨 Centigrade (vs. 화씨 Fahrenheit)
　섭씨 0 도는 화씨 32 도이다. *0 degrees Centigrade is 32 degrees Fahrenheit.*
　최저 기온 (영상) 2 도 *low temperature, two degrees (above zero)*
　현재 기온 15 도 *current temperature, 15 degrees*
　체감 온도는 영하 5 도이다. *Perceived temperature with windchill is 5 below zero.*

Length/distance (길이/거리)

Metric units: 킬로(미터), 미터, 센티(미터), 밀리(미터)

165 센티 키의 남자 *a man of 165 cm in height*

500 미터 달리기 *500 m race*

제한속도 100 (킬로) *speed limit 100 km*

강수량 400 밀리 *precipitation, 400 mm*

비가 100 밀리미터이상 내렸습니다. *It rained more than 100 mm.*

1 킬로는 0.6 마일이다. *1 km = 0.6 mile*

American unit: 인치 (used for waist, chest, & hip sizes)

허리 29 (인치) *29-inch waist,* 가슴둘레/엉덩이둘레 35 (인치) *35-inch chest/hip*

Modern Korean units:

For female clothes : 44 (XS), 55 (S), 66 (M), 77 (L)

For mostly male clothes: 90 (XS), 95 (S), 100 (M), 105 (L)

Traditional units:

자 (약 30.3 cm): 옷감 일곱 자 *200 cm wide cloth,*

     여섯 자짜리 장롱 *180 cm wide dresser*

뼘 'hand's width': 길이가 두 뼘 정도 된다. *The length is about two hands' width.*

치 (only for idioms): 한 치의 양보도 없다. *There's not an inch of concession.*

NOTE: The sizes for female clothing (44, 55, etc.) are read as [사사], [오오], etc., but the ones for male clothing (90, 95, etc.) are usually read as [구십], [구십오], etc.

Area (면적)

Metric units: m^2 (평방미터 or 제곱미터)

Traditional units: 평 is commonly used. (1[한]평 = 35.57 sq. ft.)

30[삼십/서른]평짜리 아파트 *a 1,000 sq. ft. apt*

대지 200 평 *7,100 sq. ft. of land*

건평 72[칠십이/일흔두]평 *2,500 sq. ft. interior*

Volume (체적/부피)

Metric units: 리터, 밀리리터, 씨씨 (cc)

우유 1 리터는 100 씨씨다. *One liter of milk is 100 cc.*

500 씨씨짜리 오렌지 쥬스 *a 500 cc (carton of) orange juice*

Traditional units (not commonly used): 말 (= 4 gallons), 되

(쌀) 한 말 = 열 되

Weight (중량/무게)

Metric units: 킬로(그램), 그램

  1 킬로그램은 약 2 파운드정도 된다. *1kg = about 2 lbs.*

  몸무게가 5 킬로나 늘었다. *I gained 5 kg!*

Traditional unit: 근 (= 600 grams), 관 (= 3.75 kg)

  소고기 한 근 *600 grams of beef,* 돼지고기 반 근 *300 grams of pork*

  고추 한 관 *3.75 kg of red pepper* 마늘 두 관 *7.5 kgs of garlic*

As of July 2007, a new and revised measurement system has been implemented, prohibiting the use of traditional units such as 평, 근, 관, 돈, as well as some American units such as 인치.

Prohibited units	Mandated metric alternatives	
(아파트) 1 평	3.3 m^2 (apartment)	
(소고기) 한 근	600 g (beef)	
(감자) 한 관	3.75 kg (potato)	
(금) 한 돈	3.76 g (gold)	
1 인치	2.54 cm	
For example:		
20 평짜리 아파트	66 제곱미터짜리 아파트	*710 sq. ft. apt.*
20 인치짜리 티브이	50.8 센티짜리 티브이	*20 inch TV*
두 돈짜리 금반지	7.84 그램짜리 금반지	*7.84 gram gold ring*

14.3.3 Time, date, and age

Both native and Sino-Korean numerals can be used for time, dates, and ages. A particularly notorious case involves telling time, which requires a native number for o'clock but a Sino-Korean number for minutes. Rather than trying to memorize the rule, it makes sense to simply remember an example – 7 시 20 분 [일곱 시 이십 분]. The following table summarizes the use of Sino-Korean and native Korean numbers with respect to their various functions. (All Arabic numerals are to be read as Sino-Korean numbers, unless otherwise specified.)

Time/date/age	Numerals	Examples
Hours	Native:	한 시간, 여덟 시간 NOTE: Sino-Korean numerals are used for 24 시간, 48 시간, etc.
O'clock	Native:	오후 한 시 *1:00 PM* 오전 열한 시 *11:00 AM*
Minutes/Seconds	Sino:	34 분 52 초
Century	Sino:	21 세기
Year	Sino:	2006 년 *the year 2006 or 2006 years*
Month	Sino: Native:	6 [유]월 *June* 11 월 *November* 6 개월 *6 months* 11 개월 *11 months* 여섯 달 *6 months* 열한 달 *11 months*
Day	Sino: Native:	6 일 *6th day* or *6 days* 31 일 *31st day* or *31 days* 하루 *1 day* 이틀 *2 days* 사흘 *3 days* 나흘 *4 days* 닷새 *5 days* 엿새 *6 days* 이레 *7 days* 여드레 *8 days* 아흐레 *9 days* 열흘 *10 days* 보름 *15 days or 15th day* NOTE: 엿새 , 이레, 여드레, and 아흐레 are used mostly by senior adults.
Week	Sino:	4 주(일)
(X) night (X) days	Sino:	7 박 8 일 하와이 여행 *7 night-8 day trip to Hawaii*
(X) years old	Native: Sino:	서른 살 *30 years old* 쉰 한 살 *51 years old* 20 세 미만 관람불가 *No admission under 20.* 60 세 환갑 *sixtieth birthday* 70 세 고희 *seventieth birthday*
Born in (X) year	Sino:	1990 년생 [천구백구십년생] 90 년생 [구십년생 or 구공년생] (연년생 *children born within a year of each other*)
Stages of life (every 10 years)	Sino:	10 대 [십대/일공] *teenage* 20 대 [이십대/이공] *twenties*

NOTE[1]: Two different calendars are used –양력 (solar calendar) for most dates and 음력 (lunar calendar) for certain special days such as 추석 and 구정 (Chinese New Year's Day).

NOTE[2]: The day you are born, you are one year old in terms of Korean age. To indicate American age, which is used for all legal purposes, 만- is used (만 20 세/살). An American age of 20 corresponds to a Korean age of either 21 or 22.

14.3.4 Arithmetic and fractions

Sino-Korean numbers are used for arithmetical calculation, fractions (분수), decimals (소수), and multiplication tables (구구단). But native numbers are used for numerical comparison in general.

- Arithmetical calculation: Sino-Korean numbers

2 더하기 (+) 2 는 4	4 빼기 (–) 2 는 2
2 곱하기 (x) 2 는 4	4 나누기 (÷) 2 는 2

  NOTE: Informal calculation of small quantities can be done with native numbers:
  다섯에서 셋을 빼면 둘이다. *If you subtract 3 from 5, it is 2.*

- Fractions (분수) and decimals (소수): Sino-Korean numbers

½	2 분의 1 (or 2 분지 1 [uncommon/old-fashioned])
2 ¼	2 와 4 분의 일
1 ½	1 과 2 분의 1
0.314	영점 삼일사
2.0	이점 영

- Multiplication tables (구구단)

구일은 구	9 x 1 = 9	구이(는) 십팔	9 x 2 = 18
구삼(은) 이십칠	9 x 3 = 27	구구(는) 팔십일	9 x 9 = 81

- Numerical comparison: Native numbers

두배	*two times as much*
두배 반	*two and a half times as much*
열배	*ten times as much*

  NOTE: Fractional or larger numbers used for comparison (especially multiples of 10, starting from 20) are Sino-Korean: 4.2 배, 삼십배, 백배, etc.

14.3.5 Money and currency

Sino-Korean numerals are used.

연봉이 오만 불이다.	*The annual salary is $50,000.*
월급은 사백만 원 정도 된다.	*The monthly salary is about ₩4,000,000.*
십만 원짜리 수표 두 장	*two cashier's checks of ₩100,000 each*
6 불 25 전 (= 육 달러 이십오센트)	*$6.25*

NOTE: The traditional monetary unit 푼 is found in idioms like 한 푼도 없다 'I am penniless.'

14.3.6   Numbers relating to transportation

Sino-Korean numerals are used.

지하철 6 호선	*Subway line 6*
지하철 1 구간	*Subway route 1*
26 번 버스	*Number 26 bus*
28-1 [이십팔 다시 일] 번 버스	
288[이백팔십팔 번 or 이팔팔] 버스	

14.4   Expressions of quantity

14.4.1   Approximate quantities

감자가 **서너 개** 있을 거예요.	*I'm pretty sure that we have 3–4 potatoes.*
강의실에 남자 **너댓 명**이 있었어요.	*There were 4–5 men in the lecture room.*
공사가 **이삼일**이면 끝날 겁니다.	*The construction will end in 2–3 days.*
대략 서른 살 정도 됐을 거예요.	*He is probably about 30 years old.*
약 5 킬로 **정도** 될 겁니다.	*It will probably be about 5 km.*
차로 **한** 십분**쯤** 걸릴 거예요.	*It will take about 10 minutes by car.*
근 보름동안 물만 마셨어.	*I had nothing but water for about 15 days.*
십사일**경** 만나자.	*Let's meet around the 14ᵗʰ.*
몇 시**쯤** 만날까?	*About what time shall we meet?*
비가 50 밀리**가량** 오겠습니다.	*The precipitation will be about 50 mm.*
못 들어도 **몇**백불은 들 겁니다.	*It will probably cost several hundred dollars at least.*
기온은 10 도 **안팎**으로 쌀쌀하겠습니다.	*It will be chilly with the temperature hovering around 10.*
40 도를 **웃도는** 폭염	*sweltering heat of over 40 degrees (C)*
20 도에서 23 도 **사이**	*temperatures between 20 and 23*
인구는 4 천 5 백만 **내지** 5 천만 정도 된다.	*The population is about 45 to 50 million.*

14.4.2   Non-numerical expressions of quantity

• One and only (with the prefix 단- 單)

단독주택	*single-family home*
단층집	*single-story house*
단칸방	*small single room*

- Several; many (with the prefix 수- 數)

  수천 번   *several thousand times*

  수십 개   *several dozen (apples)*

  수개월   *many months*

  수년간   *for many years*

- Many; all sorts of

  뭇 남성들의 시선을 한 몸에 받았다.
  > *She monopolized attention from all sorts of men.*

- Most

  대부분의 사람들이 다 선호하는 스타일이다.
  > *It's a style that most people like.*

- Some

  일부 사원들의 반발이 심하다.
  > *Some of the company employees are strongly opposed.*

- Half; quarter

  수입이 **(절)반**으로 줄더니 이제 **반의 반**도 안 되겠다.
  > *My income was reduced to half and now is probably less than a quarter.*

- Majority of

  과반수/대다수의 찬성이 필요하다.
  > *We need the majority's approval.*

- Minority of

  찬성하는 사람은 **극소수**에 불과합니다.
  > *Those who agree are no more than a tiny minority.*

  소수민족 *minority race*

- Just

  갖고 싶은 것 **딱** 3 가지만 골라 봐 .
  > *Pick just three things that you want to have.*

  여동생이 이제 **갓** 스물이에요.
  > *My younger sister has just turned twenty.*

- More than; not more than; less than

  50 킬로 **미만/이하**의 사람들은 헌혈을 할 수 없습니다.
  > *Those weighing less than/not more than 50 kg cannot donate their blood.*

  한 달 수입이 오천불 **이상** 됩니다.
  > *The monthly income is over $5,000.*

  학생이 열 명이 **넘는다/안 된다**.
  > *There are more/fewer than ten students.*

14.4.3 Markers of plurality

- Reduplicated words

  김과장님 생일 파티에 **누구누구** 갔습니까?
  Who all went to the birthday party for section chief Mr. Kim?

  친구 집들이에 **뭐뭐** 사갔어요?
  What kind of things did you buy and take to your friend's house-warming?

  하와이에 가면 **어디어디**를 꼭 봐야 되는 지 알려 주세요.
  Please let me know what places we should see when we visit Hawaii.

  한국가는 비행기가 **언제언제** 뜹니까?
  On which days are there planes going to Korea?

- -들

  친구들하고 언제 놀러들 와라. 다들 잘 있지?
  Come over with your friends sometime. Are they all doing well?

- 등 [formal/written]

  이 음식점은 고등어 조림, 아구찜 등 생선요리를 잘 합니다.
  This restaurant is good for fish like broiled mackerel, steamed angler (fish), etc.

Grammar

15 Verb types

Verbs make up the single most important class of words in Korean, and are the elements through which many of the language's most important semantic contrasts are expressed.

15.1 Action verbs versus descriptive verbs

The category of verb in Korean is more comprehensive than in English, encompassing both words that denote actions (*action verbs*) and words that denote states (*descriptive verbs*). The latter may be called 'adjectives,' but they must be distinguished from English adjectives since they can carry tense marking.

15.1.1 How to distinguish between the two types of verbs

- Action verbs form their present tense in the -다 style, as -ㄴ/는다.

  병헌이가 낮잠을 **잔다**.   *Byoung-hun is taking a nap.*
  성아가 김밥을 **먹는다**.   *Sung-ah is eating a seaweed roll.*

  In contrast, descriptive verbs form their present tense without a suffix, as -다.

  영화가 **재미있다**.   *The movie is fun.*
  거리가 **한산하다**.   *The street is quiet and empty.*
  하늘이 **맑다**.   *The sky is clear.*

- Action verbs and compound verbs ending in 있다/없다 have the present tense adnominal form -는.

  낮잠을 **자는** 병헌이   *Byoung-hun, who is taking a nap*
  김밥을 **먹는** 성아   *Sung-ah, who is eating a seaweed roll*
  재미있는 영화   *fun movie*

  In contrast, descriptive verbs have the present tense adnominal form -ㄴ/은.

  한산한 거리   *quiet and empty street*
  맑은 하늘   *clear sky*

A small number of words can function as either action verbs or descriptive verbs.

키가 크다. *He's tall.*   키가 아직도 큰다. *He's still growing.*
시간이 늦다. *It's late.*   (학교에) 늦는다. *You're getting late (for school).*

15.1.2 How to convert descriptive verbs into action verbs

- By adding -어 지다

Descriptive verb	Action verb
짧다; 길다	짧아지다; 길어지다
춥다; 덥다	추워지다; 더워지다
까맣다	까매지다
예쁘다	예뻐지다

요새 여성들의 치마가 점점 짧아진다.
  These days, women's skirts are getting shorter and shorter.

날씨도 따뜻해지고 낮도 많이 길어졌어요.
  The weather has gotten warmer and the day time has gotten a lot longer.

피부가 하얗더니 햇빛에 점점 까매진다.
  Her white skin is gradually darkening under the sun.

원래도 예뻤지만 더 예뻐졌네요.
  You were pretty before, but have gotten even prettier.

- By adding -어 하다 to certain verbs denoting psychological states

Descriptive verb	Action verb
좋다; 싫다	좋아하다; 싫어하다
반갑다; 귀찮다	반가워하다; 귀찮아하다
피곤하다	피곤해하다
-고 싶다	-고 싶어하다

Whereas a descriptive verb talks about an inner feeling, the corresponding action verb evokes an external manifestation of the feeling – perhaps a smile in the case of 반가워하다 'be glad' or a frown in the case of 귀찮아하다 'feel bothered.'

In talking about psychological states, either a descriptive verb or an action verb is possible when the subject is the speaker.

정말 부럽다. 내가 얼마나 부러워하는지 아니?
  I am so envious. Do you know just how much I envy you?

However, things work differently for other types of subjects. You can ask another person about his/her inner feelings using a descriptive verb, as in 많이 섭섭했죠? 'You were very much disappointed, right?' However, the action verb is required for commands, as in 너무 섭섭해하지 마세요. 'Don't be too disappointed.' Moreover, only the action verb is possible with a third person subject.

할머니가 많이 반가워 하시지?
  Grandma was so glad to see you, wasn't she?

언니가 동유럽으로 배낭여행을 가고 싶어해요.
  My sister wants to go backpacking in eastern Europe.

The difference between X 가 좋아요 **and** X 를 좋아해요

X 가 좋아요 is ambiguous between 'X is good' and 'I like X.' So 고기가 좋아요 can mean either 'the meat is good in quality' or 'I like meat.' In contrast, X 를 좋아해요 can only mean 'I like X.'

  Moreover, there is a difference between two expressions even when they both mean 'I like X': X 가 좋아요 can be based on temporary feelings, but X 를 좋아해요 always makes a general statement about liking. Therefore, 날씨가 좋아요 is an acceptable way to say 'I like the weather,' as one looks out at the sky, but 날씨를 좋아해요 is not. (비오는 날씨를 좋아해요 'I like rainy weather' is fine because it is based on general experience, not on a one-time feeling.) Upon walking into a store and finding a nice bag, one can say 이 가방이 좋아요 'I like this bag' or 이런 가방을 좋아해요 'I like this type of bag,' but not 이 가방을 좋아해요.

15.2 Intransitive verbs versus transitive verbs

Intransitive verbs denote actions and states that have a single principal participant – the subject.

개가 사납게 짖는다.   *The dog is barking fiercely.*
아기가 정말 귀여워요.   *The baby is so cute.*

Transitive verbs denote actions or states involving two principal participants – the subject and the direct object. (The subject is not overtly expressed in the second sentence.)

친구가 책을 잃어버렸다.   *My friend lost the book.*
매일 아침 우유를 마십니다.   *I drink milk every morning.*

15.2.1 A difference between English and Korean

Many verbs in English can be either intransitive or transitive (e.g., 'The door opened/He opened the door'), but only very few can be used in both ways in Korean.

Verbs	Intransitive use	Transitive use
움직이다 *move*	몸이 안 움직인다. *My body won't move.*	몸을 못 움직이겠어. *I can't move my body.*
멈추다 *stop*	차가 갑자기 멈췄다. *The car stopped suddenly.*	차를 갑자기 멈췄다. *He stopped the car suddenly.*

The following table contains verbs that can be both intransitive and transitive in English, but require two distinct forms in Korean. The suffixes (-이, -히, etc.) that are responsible for the intransitive–transitive alternation in these examples are discussed in more detail below.

English Verbs	Intransitive	Transitive
decrease	줄다 *(X) decreases*	줄이다 *decrease (X)*
increase	늘다 *(X) increases*	늘리다 *increase (X)*
attach	붙다 *(X) sticks*	붙이다 *attach (X)*
boil	끓다 *(X) boils*	끓이다 *boil (X)*
melt	녹다 *(X) melts*	녹이다 *melt (X)*
freeze	얼다 *(X) freezes*	얼리다 *freeze (X)*
burn	타다 *(X) burns*	태우다 *burn (X)*
wake up	깨다 *(X) wakes up*	깨우다 *wake (X) up*
open	열리다 *(X) opens*	열다 *open (X)*
close	닫히다 *(X) closes*	닫다 *close (X)*

Intransitive

바지가 좀 줄었다.
  The pants got a little shorter.
라면이 아직 다 안 끓었어.
  The ramen hasn't boiled all the way yet.
고기가 좀 탔네요.
  The meat burned a little.
차문이 열렸어요.
  The car door is open.

Transitive

(바지를) 아직 더 줄여야겠어.
  I need to shorten the pants more.
(라면을) 좀 더 끓이자.
  Let's boil the ramen a little more.
(고기를) 일부러 태운 거예요?
  Did you burn the meat on purpose?
(차문을) 누가 열었지요?
  Who opened the car door?

15.2.2 Noun–verb compounds

A similar contrast is found with certain noun–verb compounds, where 되다 or 나다 is used for the intransitive version and 하다 or 내다 for the transitive version.

Nouns			Intransitive	Transitive
시작 *beginning* 준비 *preparation* 예약 *reservation* 녹음 *recording*			되다	하다
열 *heat; anger* 끝 *end* 힘 *energy* 겁 *timidity* 소문 *rumor* 고장 *break-down* 신경질 *irritability* 기운 *energy* 사고 *accident* 시간 *time* 짜증 *irritated feeling*			나다	내다
생각 *thought* 기억 *memory*			나다	하다

NOTE: These patterns can be used with or without a particle on the noun – either 겁나다/겁내다 or 겁이 나다/겁을 내다. See *15.3.3* for more discussion of 되다 versus 하다.

Intransitive	*Transitive*
예약됐습니까?	언제 예약을 하셨는데요?
Has it been reserved?	*When did you reserve it?*
녹음이 안 됐어요.	녹음을 다시 해 보세요.
It's not recorded.	*Try and record it again.*
애기가 아직 안 끝났어.	이제 애기를 그만 끝내자.
Our conversation is not finished yet.	*Now let's stop and end our conversation.*
컴퓨터가 고장났어요.	컴퓨터를 또 고장냈어요?
The computer broke down.	*Did you break the computer again?*
전화번호가 생각났어요.	전화번호를 기억해요?
The phone number came to my mind.	*Do you remember the phone number?*
요새 시간이 안 나요.	시간을 좀 내 보세요.
I don't have time these days.	*Try to make some time.*

15.3   Special sub-types of intransitive verbs

Several sub-types of intransitive verbs are identified based on the presence of particular suffixes and/or special verbs.

15.3.1   *Intransitive verbs with the suffix* -이/히/기/리

A limited set of transitive verbs form their intransitive counterparts with the help of the suffixes -이, -히, -기, or -리. A few examples are presented in the table below, followed by examples of their various uses.

Transitive verbs		Intransitive verbs with -이/히/기/리	
덮다	*cover (X)*	덮**이**다	*(X) be covered*
섞다	*mix (X)*	섞**이**다	*(X) be mixed*
바꾸다	*switch (X)*	바뀌다	*(X) be switched* (뀌 < 꾸이)
잠그다	*lock (X)*	잠기다	*(X) be locked* (기 < 그이)
꽂다	*insert (X)*	꽂**히**다	*(X) be inserted*
뽑다	*pick (X)*	뽑**히**다	*(X) be picked*
찍다	*photograph (X)*	찍**히**다	*(X) be photographed*
묻다	*bury (X)*	묻**히**다	*(X) be buried*
끊다	*cut (X) off*	끊**기**다	*(X) be cut off*
뜯다	*pluck (X)*	뜯**기**다	*(X) be plucked*
안다	*hug/caress (X)*	안**기**다	*(X) be hugged/caressed*
듣다	*hear (X)*	들**리**다	*(X) be heard*
찌르다	*poke/stab (X)*	찔**리**다	*(X) be poked/stabbed*
끌다	*pull (X)*	끌**리**다	*(X) be pulled*

Uses of intransitive verbs with -이/히/기/리

- **Passive**

  Passives turn a transitive sentence around and present it from the perspective of the one who is affected by the action rather than the one who performs it.

  청소년들이 이 책을 많이 읽습니다. (transitive)
  Many teenagers read this book.
  이 책이 청소년들에게 많이 읽힙니다. (passive)
  This book is read by many teenagers.

  고양이가 쥐를 잡았다. (transitive)
  The cat caught the mouse.
  쥐가 고양이한테 잡혔다. (passive)
  The mouse was caught by the cat.

견인차가 내 차를 끌어 갔다. (transitive)
> *The tow truck towed my car.*

내 차가 견인차에 끌려 갔다. (passive)
> *My car was towed by the tow truck.*

The 'by' in 'by many teenagers' and similar phrases is usually expressed by -에게/한테 (with an animate noun) and -에 (with an inanimate noun). However, it is expressed by -에 의해(서) in order to avoid ambiguity in cases where -에게/한테 can be interpreted as 'to someone' instead of 'by someone' – as in 누군가에게 팔렸다 'sold to someone' versus 누군가에 의해 팔렸다 'sold by someone.'

The passive form can also be used to express adversity, indicating that someone is negatively affected by an action. Unlike typical passive sentences, these patterns may include -을/를 marked nouns.

소매치기한테 지갑을 털렸어요.
> *I got robbed of my wallet by a pickpocket.*

우리 대표선수가 상대편에게 약점을 잡혔다.
> *Our key player had his weakness discovered by the opposing team.*

- **Potential/uncontrollable**

Verbs marked by -이/히/기/리 can also be used to indicate that something happens out of one's control. When used in this way, the verb is usually in the present tense.

글씨가 너무 작아서 잘 안 보여요.	*I can't see the writing because it's too small.*
눈치(가) 보인다.	*I feel uneasy (about what he's thinking).*
이제 마음이 놓인다.	*I feel relieved now.*
여기는 고기가 잘 안 잡힌다.	*I can't really catch fish here.*
일이 손에 안 잡힌다.	*I can't seem to be able to work.*
밥이 안 먹혀요.	*I can't seem to be able to eat.*
졸려서 눈이 자꾸 감긴다.	*I'm so sleepy that my eyes keep falling shut.*
나는 잘 웃는 사람한테 끌려.	*I get attracted to those who laugh a lot.*
문이 안 열린다.	*The door won't open. (I can't open it.)*
너무 떨린다.	*I'm so nervous. (I can't help it.)*
얘기가 곧이 안 들려요.	*The story doesn't sound right to me. (I can't believe it.)*

The transitive counterparts of these verbs (without -이/히/기/리) indicate that the action is under one's control. Notice the following contrasts.

아무리 감을 **잡**으려고 해도 도대체 감이 안 **잡혀**요.
> *No matter how hard I try to figure it out, I can't possibly do that.*

신경 안 **쓰**려고 해도 자꾸 신경이 **쓰이**네요.
I try not to be concerned, but it keeps bothering me.

밥을 좀 **먹어**야 되는데 밥이 통 안 **먹혀**요.
I must eat some food, but I just can't seem to be able to.

- **Idiosyncratic uses**

  The following patterns have no transitive counterparts and are best treated as
  fixed expressions. Some have passive-like meanings and others express uncontrollable situations or feelings.

스트레스가 쌓인다.	*Stress keeps building up.*
난처한 입장에 놓였다.	*I've been put in a difficult position.*
시간에 얽매이지 말고 천천히 해.	*Don't be pressured by the clock, and take your time.*
기가 막힌다.	*I'm at a loss for words. (It's ridiculous.)*
교통이 많이 막힌다.	*The traffic is jammed.*
그런 방법은 이제 먹히지가 않아.	*Such a method doesn't work any more.*
친구집에 얹혀살고 있어요.	*I'm living at my friend's house as a parasite.*
하루 종일 집에 틀어박혀 있었어.	*I was cooped up at home all day.*
항상 시간에 쫓기게 돼.	*I find myself always crunched for time.*
차가 밀린다.	*The traffic is backed up.*
일이 많이 밀렸어요.	*I'm behind in my work.*
추위가 풀렸다.	*The cold weather turned warm.*
졸업생들이 잘 풀린다.	*The graduates are finding good jobs.*
감기가 잔뜩 걸렸어요.	*I have a full-blown cold.*
그 일이 자꾸 마음에 걸린다.	*That incident weighs constantly on my mind.*
그런 행동은 법에 걸린다.	*That kind of behavior is against the law.*
성공은 노력여하에 달렸다.	*Success depends on one's efforts.*
쪽 팔린다.	*It's embarrassing.* [familiar/casual]
TV를 통해 얼굴이 많이 팔렸다.	*His face became exposed to the public through TV.*

15.3.2   Intransitive verbs with 지다

지다, which is linked to the main verb by -어/아, can be used with a limited
number of verbs. (지다 can also be used to turn a descriptive verb into an action
verb; see *15.1.2*.)

Transitive verbs	Intransitive verbs with 지다
쏟다 *pour (X)*	쏟아지다 *(X) be poured*
찢다 *tear (X)*	찢어지다 *(X) be torn*
세우다 *establish (X)*	세워지다 *(X) be established*
부수다 *break (X)*	부서지다 *(X) be broken*
전하다 *convey (X)*	전해지다 *(X) be conveyed*
끄다 *turn (X) off*	꺼지다 *(X) be turned off*

NOTE: A small number of intransitive verbs can be formed by either a suffix or 지다:
찢기다 or 찢어지다 for 찢다 'tear' and 믿기다 or 믿어지다 for 믿다 'believe.'

Uses of intransitive verbs with 지다

- **Passive**

파도가 모래성을 허물었다. (transitive)
The wave destroyed the sand castle.
모래성이 파도에 허물어졌다. (passive)
The sand castle was destroyed by the wave.

검찰이 사건의 진상을 밝혔다. (transitive)
The prosecutor revealed the true picture of the case.
사건의 진상이 검찰에 의해 밝혀졌다. (passive)
The true picture of the case was revealed by the prosecutor.

NOTE: With the 지다 and 되다 passives, the formal-sounding X 에 의해
is used instead of X 에게/한테 to express 'by someone.'

- **Potential/uncontrollable**

지다 can indicate that something happens in a way that is out of one's control.
When used in this way, the verb is usually in the present tense.

접시가 잘 깨진다.	*The dish breaks easily.*
통조림이 안 따진다.	*This can won't open. (I can't open it.)*
계획이 틀어졌어요.	*The plan fell through.*
이 옷은 잘 안 빨아져요.	*This dress doesn't wash well.*
믿기지 않는다. 정말 안 믿어져.	*It's unbelievable. I can't believe it.*
머리가 점점 벗겨져요.	*My hairline is gradually receding.*
요즘은 책이 통 안 읽어진다.	*I can't seem to be able to read these days.*
칼이 안 들어서 고기가 안 썰어져.	*The meat won't cut well because the knife is dull.*
이 칫솔은 이가 잘 닦아져/닦여.	*This tooth brush brushes well.*
안 기다리려해도 자꾸 기다려진다.	*I can't help but wait (for him) even if I try not to.*

아침에 절로 눈이 떠진다.   *My eyes pop open automatically*
                                                  in the morning.

The transitive counterparts of these verbs (without 지다) indicate that the action is under one's control. Notice the following contrasts between a transitive verb and its intransitive counterpart with 지다.

아무리 눈을 **뜨**려고 해도 눈이 안 **떠져**요.
   No matter how hard I try to wake up, my eyes won't open.

전화를 내가 **끊**은 게 아니라 전화가 그냥 **끊어졌**어요.
   I didn't hang up the phone, but it just got cut off.

과일 통조림을 좀 **따**야 되는데 이게 안 **따지**네요.
   I have to open this canned fruit, but it won't open.

- **Idiosyncratic uses**

   The following patterns have no transitive counterparts and are best treated as fixed expressions. Some of these denote uncontrollable actions and states.

   전철이 끊어졌다/끊겼다.   *The subway has shut down (for the day).*

   발랑 까졌다.   *She's wild and brash.*

   잠이 쏟아진다.   *I'm having a huge wave of drowsiness.*

   입이 안 떨어져요.   *I can't seem to be able to open my mouth*
                                                  (to say anything).

   차마 발이 안 떨어져.   *I can't seem to be able to move my feet*
                                                  (to leave).

15.3.3   *Intransitive verbs with* 되다

Some Sino-Korean nouns that combine with 하다 to form a transitive verb can occur with 되다 to create an intransitive verb.

Transitive with 하다	Intransitive with 되다
해결하다 *solve (X)*	해결되다 *(X) be solved*
사용하다 *use (X)*	사용되다 *(X) be used*
왜곡하다 *distort (X)*	왜곡되다 *(X) be distorted*
기대하다 *expect (X)*	기대되다 *(X) be expected*

Uses of intransitive verbs with 되다

- **Passive**

   대화 중에 누군가가 그 사람의 이름을 거론했다. (transitive)
      Someone mentioned his name during the conversation.

   대화 중에 누군가에 의해 그 사람의 이름이 거론되었다. (passive)
      His name was mentioned by someone during the conversation.

유괴범이 어린아이를 납치했습니다. (transitive)
  A kidnapper abducted the child.
어린아이가 유괴범에 의해 납치되었습니다. (passive)
  The child was abducted by a kidnapper.

- **Potential/uncontrollable**

긴장되는데요.	*I'm getting nervous.*
자꾸 걱정이 되네요.	*I keep getting worried.*
도저히 이해가 안 돼요.	*I can't possibly understand.*
이번 한국여행이 많이 기대됩니다.	*I'm looking forward to this trip to Korea.*
공부를 해야 되는데 공부가 잘 안 돼요.	*I have to study, but I can't seem to be able to.*
아무리 용서를 하려고 해도 용서가 안 돼요.	*No matter how hard I try to forgive him, I just can't.*

15.3.4 Other special intransitive verbs

Some nouns combine with 당하다 'suffer/undergo' or 받다 'receive' to create compound intransitive verbs with a passive-like meaning.

- With 당하다

강간당하다	*be raped*	사기당하다	*be swindled*
배반당하다	*be betrayed*	거절당하다	*be rejected*
무시당하다	*be ignored*	고소당하다	*be sued*
실연당하다	*be lovelorn*	왕따당하다	*be alienated*

- With 받다

사랑받다	*be loved*	칭찬받다	*be praised*
존경받다	*be respected*	처벌받다	*be punished*
멸시받다	*be despised*	비난받다	*be criticized*
간섭받다	*be interfered with*	상처받다	*be hurt/broken-hearted*

In addition, two special verbs – 속다 and 맞다 – are worth noting since they have a passive meaning in the absence of any suffix or auxiliary.

지영이가 사기꾼한테 속았다.	*Jiyoung got deceived by the swindler.*
동생이 형한테 맞았다.	*The younger brother got hit by the older brother.*

15.4 Special sub-types of transitive verbs

Like intransitives, transitive verbs can be organized into several subclasses based on the presence of particular suffixes and/or special verbs.

15.4.1 Transitive verbs with the suffix -이/히/기/리/우/구/추

A limited number of native Korean transitive verbs are formed from intransitives with the help of the suffixes -이, -히, -기, -리, -우, -구, or -추. So, whereas 울다 means 'cry,' 울리다 is a transitive verb with the meaning 'make someone cry.' In other cases, there is also a significant shift in meaning: 서다 means 'stand' or 'stop,' but its transitive counterpart 세우다 means 'establish' or 'pull over.' Additional examples are presented in the table below.

Intransitive verbs (with subject only)	Transitive verbs with -이/히/기/리/우/구/추 (with subject & direct object)
붙다 *(X) sticks* 속다 *(X) be deceived*	붙이다 *attach (X)* 속이다 *deceive (X)*
식다 *(X) cools off* 넓다 *(X) be wide*	식히다 *cool (X) off* 넓히다 *widen (X)*
굶다 *(X) starves* 웃다 *(X) laughs*	굶기다 *starve (X)* 웃기다 *make (X) laugh*
날다 *(X) flies* 오르다 *(X) rises*	날리다 *make (X) fly* 올리다 *raise (X)*
차다 *(X) be filled* 깨다 *(X) wakes up*	채우다 *fill (X)* 깨우다 *wake (X) up*
돋다 *(X) sprouts/comes out*	돋구다 *stimulate/whet (X)*
늦다 *(X) be late* 맞다 *(X) fits*	늦추다 *delay (X); loosen (X)* 맞추다 *make (X) fit*

When the verb is transitive to begin with, the suffix -이/히/기/리/우/구/추 adds another element to its meaning – typically an indirect object. So, instead of someone doing something on his own, (s)he directly or indirectly causes someone else to do it.

Transitive verbs (with subject & direct object)	Transitive verbs with -이/히/기/리/우/구/추 (with subject, direct object, & one other)
먹다 *eat (X)* 보다 *see (X)*	먹이다 *feed (X) to (Y)* 보이다 *show (X) to (Y)*
입다 *wear (X: clothes)* 읽다 *read (X)*	입히다 *dress (Y) in (X)* 읽히다 *make (Y) read (X)*
신다 *wear (X: shoes)* 감다 *wash (hair)*	신기다 *put (X) on (Y)* 감기다 *wash (Y's) (hair)*
알다 *know (X)*	알리다 *inform (Y) of (X)*
쓰다 *wear (X: hats)*	씌우다 *put (X) on (Y's head)*

Uses of transitive verbs with -이/히/기/리/우/구/추

• Causative

The following examples are divided into two groups: one with the sense of causing SOMEONE to do something (as is the case for all the verbs in the second table above and some in the first table) and the other with the sense of causing SOMETHING to happen. The 'causative' meaning is clear in the first type, but is less evident in the second type, which often is hardly distinguishable from simple transitives.

Causing someone to do something:

승진하려고 웃사람들한테 돈을 **먹였**대요.	*I heard that he bribed his superiors to get promoted.*
형제간에 싸움을 **붙였**어요.	*They made the two brothers get into a fight.*
아이를 의자에 **앉히**세요.	*Have the child sit in a chair.*
교수가 학생들에게 책을 많이 **읽힌**다.	*The professor makes students read a lot.*
아기 신발 좀 **신겨** 줘라.	*Help the baby put the shoes on.*
아빠가 나한테 그 일을 **맡기**셨다.	*Father put me in charge of the matter.*
누가 내 동생을 **울렸**지?	*Who made my younger sister cry?*
아기를 너무 많이 **재우**지 마세요.	*Don't let the baby sleep too much.*

Causing something to happen:

요새 요가에 재미를 **붙였**어요.	*I've taken an interest in yoga these days.*
전통문화에 관심을 **기울이**고 있다.	*I am focusing my interest on traditional culture.*
저민생선에 밀가루를 **묻혀** 놓아.	*Have the sliced fish floured.*
너무 뜨거워서 좀 **식혀**야겠어요.	*It's too hot, so I better cool it off a bit.*
남기지 말고 다 먹자.	*Let's eat it all and not leave anything.*
얼음 좀 **얼려**야겠어요.	*I think I should make some ice.*
값 좀 그만 좀 **올리**지.	*I wish they would stop raising the price.*
남의 일에 왜 그렇게 핏대를 **올리**니?	*Why do you get so angry over other people's business?*
도박으로 집을 **날렸**어.	*I lost my house through gambling.*
어떻게 친구 마음을 **돌릴** 수 있을까?	*I wonder what I can do to change my friend's mind?*
시계 좀 **맞춰** 놓자.	*Let's set the watch.*
날짜를 좀 **늦출**까요?	*Shall we delay the date a little?*

All of the above patterns have counterparts without the suffix -이/히/기/리/우/구/추. This leads to contrasts such as the following.

아기가 너무 많이 **자**네요. 그만 **재우**세요.
  The baby is sleeping too much. Stop letting him sleep.

형제간에 싸움이 **붙었**어요. 누가 싸움을 **붙인** 거예요?
  The two brothers got into a fight. Who made them get into a fight?

요즘 나는 요가에 재미가 **붙었**어. 너도 한 번 재미를 **붙여** 봐.
  I got interested in yoga these days. Why don't you try to take an interest in it too?

시계가 안 **맞는**다. 좀 **맞춰** 놓자.
  The watch is not correct. Let's set it.

우리만 **알**고 있지 말고 다른 사람들한테도 **알리**자.
  Let's inform other people too, instead of keeping the information to ourselves.

커피가 한 방울도 안 **남았**네. 좀 **남기**지.
  Not a drop of coffee is left. I wish you had left a little for me.

친구 마음을 아무리 **돌리**려고 해도 마음이 돌아오지를 않네요.
  I try very hard to change my friend's mind, but her mind won't change.

얼굴에 뭐가 **묻었**네요. 뭘 **묻힌** 거예요?
  You have something on your face. What do you have your face covered with?

- **Idiosyncratic use**

  The following patterns (all noun–verb combinations) don't have non-causative counterparts and are best treated as fixed expressions.

  치사하게 남의 **약점을 들먹이냐?**   *How shameful of you to bring up my weaknesses.*

  네가 얼마나 강한지 **본때를 보여 줘.**   *Teach them a lesson to show how strong you are.*

  시계를 **전당포에 잡혔어.**   *I pawned my watch at the pawn shop.*

  그 사람은 **돈을** 너무 **밝혀요.**   *He's obsessed with money.*

  오늘 손님이 없어서 **파리 날린다.**   *There are no customers, so no business today* [letting just the flies fly].

  투수로 **이름을 날렸다.**   *He won his fame as a pitcher.*

  졸업 후에 **전공을 살리**고 싶어요.   *I want to put my college major to use after graduation.*

  너 남자친구하고 **입맞추는** 거 봤어.   *I saw you kissing your boyfriend.*

  알리바이를 위해 서로 **입을 맞췄다.**   *We all told the same story as our alibi.*

15.4.2 Transitive verbs with -게 하다

The meaning expressed by -게 하다 is always causative – making or letting someone do something. (When it comes to making someone do something, the verb 하다 can be replaced by 만들다.) This pattern is fully productive – it can be used with any verb.

선생님이 그 학생을 집에 일찍 가게 하셨다.
    The teacher had the student go home early.

너무 오래 기다리게 하지 말고 빨리 오세요.
    Come quickly and don't make us wait too long.

방을 너무 춥게 해서 감기가 들었어.
    She made the room too cold, so I caught a cold.

뜻하지 않은 비행기 연착이 우리로 하여금 시간을 낭비하게 만들었다.
    The unexpected delay of the airplane made us waste our time.

When both the -이/히/기/리/우/구/추 form and the -게 하다 form are permitted, the former tends to express more direct causation than the latter (e.g., 먹이다 'feed' vs. 먹게 하다 'make/let someone eat').

In addition, the -이/히/기/리 forms often have simple transitive or idiomatized uses and cannot alternate with the -게 하다 forms, which have only a causative use.

맛이 죽인다.   *It has a killer taste.*

종을 울렸다.   *They rang the bell.*

얼굴을 붉혔다.	*She blushed/reddened.*
과거를 숨겼다.	*He hid the past.*
죽어가는 물고기를 살렸다.	*I saved the dying fish.*
사투리 쓴다고 놀려요.	*They make fun of my regional accent.*

15.4.3 Transitive verbs with 시키다

In the case of a small set of nouns, the verb 시키다 can replace 하다 to express a causative meaning.

피곤하니까 나한테 **말 시키**지 마. 아무**말**도 **하**고 싶지 않아.
I'm tired, so don't make me talk. I don't want to say anything.

음식을 직접 **하**지 않고 항상 **시켜** 먹는다.
She doesn't cook food, but has it delivered all the time.

다른 사람들 **조심시키**기 전에 너부터 **조심해**.
You be careful first before making other people be careful.

본인부터 **소개하**고 여자친구도 **소개시켜** 주세요.
Introduce yourself first and have your girlfriend introduce herself to us as well.

우리는 치열하게 서로 **경쟁했**다. 선생님이 우리를 **경쟁시켰**다.
We competed fiercely. Our teacher made us compete.

NOTE: Other nouns that can be used in these patterns include 공부 'study,' 구경 'sightseeing,' 긴장 'nervousness,' 노래 'singing,' 승진 'promotion,' 연습 'practice,' 일 'work,' 해산 'dispersal/dispersing,' and 확신 'confirmation.'

15.4.4 Transitive verbs with -뜨리다

The auxiliary verb -뜨리다 is used to form the transitive counterpart of a small set of intransitive verbs that contain -지다.

과자가 다 **부서졌**다. 더 **부서뜨리**지 마.
The biscuit got all crumbled. Don't crumble it up more.

뭐 **빠진** 거 없니? 하나도 **빠뜨리**지 말고 챙겨.
Is there anything missing? Don't miss anything; pack everything.

컵이 식탁에서 **떨어졌**어요. 누가 컵을 **떨어뜨렸**어요.
The cup dropped from the table. Someone dropped it.

벌써 소문이 **퍼졌**다. 누가 소문을 **퍼뜨렸**지?
The rumor spread already. I wonder who spread the rumor.

접시가 그냥 **깨졌**어. 내가 **깨(뜨리)**지 않았어.
The plate just broke. I didn't break it.

NOTE: Both 깨다 and 깨뜨리다 are transitive with the meaning 'break.'
The -뜨리다 in this case simply has an intensifying effect.

16 Tense and Aspect

Tense situates a state or event in time (past, present, or future), while aspect expresses the way it is viewed (ongoing, repeated, completed, and so on). Verbal forms are often given names – such as 'past tense' or 'future tense.' However, these names are somewhat misleading, since most forms have several functions beyond the one from which their name is derived. (The same is true in English, where the so-called 'present tense' can be used to express the future, as in *She arrives tomorrow at 3:00*, for example.) As you proceed, it is important to bear in mind the distinction between the name typically used to identify a verb's form and the various uses to which that form is put.

16.1 Tense and aspect on sentence-final verbs

16.1.1 The basic form

The most basic verb form is used primarily to express present-time states and actions. Except for action verbs in the 한다 style, for which -ㄴ/는 is inserted (e.g., 본다, 듣는다), it involves no special marking.

- With descriptive verbs, the basic form denotes a present state.

내 동생은 키가 작다.	*My younger brother/sister is short.*
머리가 너무 짧아요.	*My hair is too short.*

- With action verbs, the basic form is used not only to express present-time actions but also, depending on the context and/or the meaning of the verb, habitual actions, past actions that continue to the present, future actions, and processes in progress, as the following examples illustrate.

지금 밥 먹는다.	*I'm eating right now.*
매일 아침 해변가를 달린다.	*I run along the beach every morning.*
두 달째 여기 살아요.	*I've been living here for two months now.*
다음 주에 출장간다.	*I'm going on a business trip next week.*
국수가 불어요.	*The noodles are getting soggy.*

16.1.2 -어 있다 (or -아 있다)

Used to express a continuing present state that results from a completed action, this form is found with only a small number of *intransitive* action verbs that imply definite end points. (있다 is replaced by 계시다 for an honorific subject.)

몸은 학교에 와 있지만 마음은 딴 데 가 있다.
My body is at school, but my mind is somewhere else.

외국에 나와 있어서 국내사정을 잘 모릅니다.
Being outside the country, I'm not familiar with the domestic situation.

계속 서 있었더니 다리가 쑤신다.
My legs are hurting after standing up for a long time.

문이 열려 있어서 누가 있는 줄 알았어요.
I thought/knew someone was here because the door was open.
(See 22.3.2 for the ambiguity of 알다 between 'know' and 'think.')

잠든지 알았더니 아직도 깨어 있었니?
I thought you fell asleep, but you're still awake?

여행간다고 잔뜩 부풀어 있어요.
She's so elated about the trip.

아버지가 일주일째 병원에 입원해 계세요.
Father has been hospitalized for a week.

16.1.3 -고 있다

This form, which can combine with any action verb, mainly indicates an action in progress. (있다 is replaced by 계시다 for an honorific subject.) It expresses:

- With most action verbs: ongoing or habitual action

일주일째 비가 오고 있다.	*It's been raining for a week.*
그림을 그리고 있습니다.	*I'm painting.*
아침으로 빵을 드시고 계셔.	*She's been eating bread for breakfast.*

  있다 can be replaced by 앉아 있다 and 자빠졌다, literally 'be sitting down' and 'be lying down,' to indicate the speaker's dissatisfaction toward the person's action.

종일 티브이만 보고 자빠졌어.	*He's doing nothing but watching TV all day.*
정말 웃기고 앉아 있어.	*She's being ridiculous.*

- With verbs of wearing or contact: either ongoing action or present state resulting from a completed action

빨간 넥타이를 매고 있어요.	*He's putting on (or wearing) a red tie.*
흰색 구두를 신고 있다.	*She's putting on (or wearing) white shoes.*

| 이름표를 달고 있습니다. | *He's putting on (or wearing) a name tag.* |
| 이 가방 좀 잠깐 들고 있을래? | *Would you hold this bag for a minute?* |

To unambiguously express an ongoing action, -고 있는 중이다 can be used:

| 넥타이를 매고 있는 중이에요. | *I'm in the middle of putting a tie on.* |

* With verbs of cognition: present state resulting from a completed activity

| 잘못을 깨닫고 있다. | *She realizes her faults.* |
| 뭔가 오해하고 있는 것 같아요. | *He seems to misunderstand something.* |

-어 있다 (continuing state) vs. -고 있다 (continuing action)

학교에 와 있다.	*He's at school.*
학교에 오고 있다.	*He's on his way to school.*
할아버지가 아직 살아 계시다.	*Grandfather is still alive.*
할아버지가 한국에 살고 계시다.	*Grandfather is living in Korea.*

16.1.4 -었 (or 았/ㅆ)

Frequently called the 'past tense,' this form denotes a past state for descriptive verbs.

* Past state

| 나도 왕년엔 멋있었다. | *I too was cool-looking in the old days.* |
| 날씨가 아주 포근했어요. | *The weather was quite nice and warm.* |

* With 멀다: past or non-past states

고등학교 때 집이 아주 멀었어요.	*My house was very far from my highschool.*
도착하려면 아직 멀었니?	*Are we far from being there?*
저녁 아직 멀었어요?	*Is dinner far off?*
내 요리실력은 너한테 아직 멀었다.	*My cooking is far inferior to yours.*

For action verbs, -었 is used not only for past actions, but also for completed actions or processes that result in a present state. The individual verb's meaning can help determine which interpretation is appropriate. Hence 결혼했다 can mean 'got married,' focusing on the past event, or 'is married,' focusing on the present state resulting from the past event. But 공을 찼다 'kicked the ball' can only denote a past action and 잘 생겼다 'is handsome' can only denote the present state. (생기다 is an action verb, meaning 'get formed/ created.')

Here is a summary of the meanings that -었 can be used to express when it appears with an action verb.

- Past action (including actions that are just completed or continuing to the present)

친구가 직장을 옮겼다.	*My friend changed companies.*
지금 막 도착했습니다.	*I've just arrived.*
여기서 지금껏 살았다.	*I've lived here up till now.*

- Completed action/process followed by a continuing 'present' state: Each sentence has both meanings but typically, the present state meaning is prominent.

잠이 완전히 깼어.	*I got totally awakened.* *I am totally awake.*
약국이 문을 닫았어요.	*The pharmacy closed.* *The pharmacy is closed.*
빨간 가방을 메었어.	*She put a red purse on her shoulder.* *She has a red purse on her shoulder.*
오늘 줄무늬 셔츠 입었니?	*Did you put a striped shirt on today?* *Are you wearing a striped shirt today?*
감기 걸렸어요.	*I caught a cold.* *I have a cold.*
나 너무 살쪘지?	*I got very fat, right?* *I'm very fat, right?*
화났니?	*Have you gotten angry?* *Are you angry?*
준비 다 됐어요?	*Have you gotten all set?* *Are you all set?*
옷이 다 젖었다/말랐다.	*The clothes got all wet/dry.* *The clothes are all wet/dry.*
고기가 딱 알맞게 익었다.	*The meat got perfectly cooked.* *The meat is perfectly cooked.*
라면이 좀 불었어요.	*The ramen got soggy.* *The ramen is soggy.*
이가 한 개 썩었어.	*One tooth got decayed.* *One tooth is decayed.*
얼굴이 많이 부었어요.	*My face got puffed up.* *My face is puffed up.*
장미가 다 시들었다.	*The roses got all withered.* *The roses are all withered.*
부인이 꽤 늙었어요.	*His wife got quite old.* *His wife is quite old.*

잘 알았습니다.	*I got it.*
	I understand.
귀 먹었어?	*You became deaf?*
	Are you deaf?
눈이 멀었구나/삐었구나!	*She became blind!*
	She's blind!

- Present state only

아이가 엄마를 닮았네요.	*The child resembles his mother.*
정말 잘/못 생겼다.	*He's really good/bad looking.*

When these verbs, except 잘/못 생겼다, occur in the basic (present tense) form, they have a progressive or future meaning.

자꾸 화가 나요.	*I keep getting angry.*
살찐다, 그만 먹어.	*You're going to get fat; stop eating.*

How then do you refer to a past state such as 'He was angry?' There are two possibilities. One is to use the -었더라 ending (see *16.1.6*) if you just want to say 'He was angry (when I saw him)' without committing yourself to what the current situation is.

화가 많이 났더라.	*He was really angry when I saw him.*
얼굴이 부었더라구요.	*Her face was puffed up when I saw her.*

On the other hand, if you want to indicate a past state that is over, a second -었 is required, creating the suffix -었었 (see *16.1.5*).

화가 많이 났었어요.	*He was really angry (but no longer is).*
얼굴이 부었었어요.	*Her face was puffed up (but no longer is).*

-었다 vs. -어 있다 for certain verbs

-어 있다 focuses more on how things are now rather than on what was done, but both forms express more or less the same thing – a present state resulting from a completed action.

눈이 많이 부었다.	*Your eyes are very puffed up.*
눈이 많이 부어 있다.	" "
열쇠가 주머니에 들었어.	*The key is in the pocket.*
열쇠가 주머니에 들어 있어.	" "

-었다 vs. 고 있다 for verbs of wearing/contact

-고 있다 focuses more on how things are now rather than on what was done, but both forms express more or less the same thing – a present state resulting from a completed action.

겨울옷을 입었어요.	*She's wearing winter clothes.*
겨울옷을 입고 있어요.	" "
등산화를 신었어요.	*She's wearing hiking boots.*
등산화를 신고 있어요.	" "
큰 가방을 들었다.	*He's holding a big satchel.*
큰 가방을 들고 있다.	" "

- Completed action or state in the future

혼자 가면 갔지 같이는 안 갈래.	*I would go if I can go by myself, but I don't want to go with him.*
친구들이 많이 왔으면 좋겠다.	*It would be nice if many friends came.*
너 이제 아빠한테 혼났다.	*Now you're going to get scolded by Dad.*
나는 이제 죽었구나.	*Oh no, I'll be dead meat.*
커피를 다섯잔이나 마셨으니 오늘 잠은 다 잤다.	*I won't be able to sleep tonight now that I've drunk five cups of coffee.*

16.1.5 -었었

With descriptive verbs, there is generally only a subtle difference between -었 and -었었, with both denoting 'past state,' but the latter creates a more distant feeling.

옛날엔 날씬했(었)어요.	*I used to be slender.*
올겨울도 추웠지만 작년 겨울은 더 추웠(었)어.	*It was cold this winter, but last winter was even colder.*
어렸을 때도 똑똑했(었)는데 지금도 아주 똑똑해.	*She was smart when she was little, and she still is very smart.*

With action verbs, the difference can be sharper. There, -었었 expresses:

- A more remote past than what is indicated by a single -었, thereby implying an experience prior to a past reference time.

전에 잠깐 만났었어요.	*I had met him briefly before.*
전화했을 때 이미 떠났었어.	*I had already left when you called.*

- Circumstances implying discontinuation of a situation

신혼여행 갔었습니다.	*They went on their honeymoon, but are back.*
신혼여행 갔습니다.	*They went on their honeymoon (and are still gone).*
지난주에 병원에 입원했었어.	*I had been hospitalized last week.*
지난주에 병원에 입원했어.	*I got hospitalized last week (and am still in the hospital).*
결혼을 했었습니다.	*I was married before.*
결혼을 했습니다.	*I got married and still am.*
엄마를 닮았었어요.	*I used to look like my mom.*
엄마를 닮았어요.	*I look like my mom.*
감기가 걸렸었습니다.	*I had a cold.*
감기가 걸렸습니다.	*I have a cold.*
잘 알았었습니다.	*I used to know it well.*
잘 알았습니다.	*I got it. I understand.*

16.1.6 -더, -었더

This form is used for a less assertive retrospective report of a past or continuing action or state ('I saw...,' 'I noticed...,' 'I heard...'), based on a perception, impression, casual observation, or hearsay. It is very commonly used, but only in the spoken style since it presupposes a particular person to speak to. It can occur in either the 해요 or 해 style. (-더 may be pronounced -드 – see **8.3**.)

	해요 style (존댓말)	*해* style (반말)
Statement	-더라구요, -데요, -던데요	-더라, -데, -던데
Question	-던가요	-디, -던

NOTE: The -데(요) and -던데(요) endings are often accompanied by rising intonation.

-더 does not occur with the more formal 합니다 style. Expressions such as 갑디다 and 갔읍디다, with the -ㅂ/읍디다 ending, are old-fashioned and are used only among old folks.

- -더 with either descriptive or action verbs

코요테 새 노래가 참 신나더라.	*I noticed Koyote's new song is very upbeat.*
새 앨범이 5집이던가요?	*Was her new album the fifth one?*
부인이 참 예쁘더라.	*His wife is a beauty, I noticed.*
성격은 별로라던데요.	*Her personality is not very good, I heard.*
걔 공부 진짜 열심히 하더라.	*I saw him studying really hard.*

이번 시험에는 꼭 합격하겠던데.	*It seemed like he'd definitely pass the test this time.*
도서관에 그 책이 없더라구요.	*I noticed the library didn't have that book.*
오다 보니까 밖에 비가 오데요.	*On my way, I saw it raining hard.*
비가 많이 오디/오던?	*Was it raining hard?*
오늘 못 온다더라.	*I heard that he can't come today.*
왜 못 온다던가요?.	*Why did he say he can't come?*

The -더 form is inappropriate for a report based on lengthy experience or something that one is sure about. Therefore, it usually is not used to talk about oneself or a close family member. For this reason, the following sentences sound strange.

Unacceptable/strange-sounding

내 동생은 참 말을 안 듣더라.	*My brother never listens, I noticed.*
우리 엄마는 요리를 잘 하시더라.	*My mom is a great cook, I noticed.*
우리 남편은 정말 착하더라.	*My husband is really nice, I noticed.*

However, -더 is perfectly fine for reporting one's own feelings from one's own perspective ('I find/found myself…').

나는 김치 볶음밥을 잘 만드는 여자가 좋더라.
  I find myself liking women who can make good Kimch'i fried rice.

나는 이런 치마는 잘 안 입게 되더라.
  I find myself not wearing skirts like this.

기가 막혀서 말이 안 나오더라.
  That was so unbelievably ridiculous that I found myself speechless.

너무 맛이 없어서 못 먹겠더라구요.
  It was so bad that I found myself unable to eat it.

기분 나쁘더라. 정말 화가 나더라.
  I was upset. I found myself getting really angry.

- -었더 with only action verbs

The -었더 form is NOT used with descriptive verbs in sentence-final position (although it is found on descriptive verbs in non-final positions; see 16.2.2). Hence, we can say 지루하더라 'I found it boring,' 시끄럽더라 'It was noisy, I noticed,' 맛있더라 'I found it delicious,' and so on, but NEVER 지루했더라, 시끄러웠더라, or 맛있었더라.

-었더 is used only with action verbs to report an action/process that is already completed at the time of observation. The following pairs illustrate the contrast between -었더 and -더.

밖에 비 왔더라.	*I noticed that it had rained.*
밖에 비 오더라.	*I noticed that it was raining outside.*
들어 왔더라구요.	*I saw that he had come in.*
들어 오더라구요.	*I saw him coming in.*
장미가 다 시들었더라.	*I saw the roses all withered.*
장미가 시들더라.	*I saw the roses withering.*
얼굴이 퉁퉁 부었더라구요.	*I saw her face all puffed up.*
얼굴이 퉁퉁 붓더라구요.	*I noticed her face was getting all puffy.*

16.1.7 -을, -겠

A variety of forms involving -을 (ㄹ after a verb stem ending in a vowel) or -겠 are used to talk about the future, but they are not 'pure' future tense markers. Rather, as the following examples show, they are more directly associated with the expression of intention and conjecture, which indirectly evokes the future.

- **-을래(요)** 'I am going to…; Are you going to…?'

언제 또 만날래?	*When are you meeting him again?*
그 사람 이제 그만 만날래요.	*I'm going to stop meeting him from now on.*

- **-을게(요)** 'I will…; Let me…'

숙제 꼭 낼게요.	*I'll be sure to turn in the homework.*
제가 도와 드릴게요.	*Let me help you.*

- **-을까(요)?** 'Shall I/we…; Will you/(s)he …I wonder?'

제가 언제 들를까요?	*Shall I drop by sometime?*
다음달까지 끝낼 수 있을까요?	*Will we be able to finish it by next month?*
너희들끼리 갈 수 있을까?	*Will you be able to go by yourselves?*
그 친구들이 파티에 올까요?	*Will they come to the party, I wonder?*
내일 정말 눈이 올까?	*Will it really snow tomorrow?*

- **-었을까(요)** 'Will you/(s)he have…-ed?; I wonder whether…'

그 친구 지금쯤 도착했을까?	*Will he have arrived by now?*
서운했을까요?	*I wonder whether she was upset.*

- **-을 거, -겠** 'I will…; Will you…?; You /(s)he… will probably…'

목요일쯤 떠날 거예요.	*I'll leave around Thursday.*
오전에 떠나실 겁니까?	*Will you be leaving in the morning?*

이제 괜찮을 거예요.   *You'll probably be okay now.*

자주 연락 드리겠습니다.   *I'll be in touch often.*

엄마가 기다리시겠다.   *Mom must be waiting for us.*

- **-었을 거, -었겠** (Conjecture about a past/completed event or state)

A: 이제 다 고쳤겠지요?   *I guess they've fixed it by now?*

B: 아직 못 고쳤을 거예요.   *I doubt that they have.*

A: 표 사느라고 힘들었겠지?   *I bet it was difficult to buy the ticket, right?*

B: 많이 힘들었을 거야.   *I'm sure it was.*

> **-을게요 (promissory) vs. -을 거예요 (plan): 'I will…'**
>
> To someone who will be waiting for your call, you say 전화할게요, but to others you say 전화할 거예요. -을게요 is used if the speaker's intentions are in any way the listener's personal concern. To your mother or spouse, who is concerned about your health, you promise with 담배 끊을게 'I promise I will quit smoking.' To most others, you would simply talk about your plan by saying 담배 끊을 거야 'I'm going to quit smoking.'

16.1.8 -을 거 *versus* -겠

When used to express conjecture, the two forms can differ in meaning. -을 거 is for conjecture based on knowledge, reasoning, factual support, or substantial evidence, while -겠 indicates conjecture based on feelings, emotions, casual judgment, or circumstantial evidence.

이 고추 매울 거예요. 내가 먹어봤어요.
These peppers will be hot. I tried them.

색깔 보니까 고추가 맵겠어요.
Their color tells me that the peppers are going to be hot.

일기예보에서 오늘 비 올 거래요.
The weather forecast says it'll rain today.

하늘 보니까 비 오겠어요.
The look of the sky tells me that it's going to rain.

-겠 is often used to express sympathy or concern, but -을 거 is used for neutral and objective information.

Sympathy/concern	*Neutral guess/conjecture*
피곤하시겠어요.	피곤하실 거예요.
You must be tired.	*You'll be tired.*
전화비 많이 나오겠네요.	전화비 많이 나올 거예요.
Your phone bill will be large, I'm afraid.	*Your phone bill will be large.*

Sympathy/concern

수업에 늦었겠네요.
He must have been late for class.

천천히 먹어라, 배탈나겠다.
Eat slowly, you're going to get sick.

감기 들겠다, 조심해.
You're going to catch a cold, be careful.

Neutral guess/conjecture

수업에 늦었을 거예요.
He was probably late for class.

(no appropriate -을 거 form)

(no appropriate -을 거 form)

Questions containing -겠 are often answered with the -을 거 form.

A: 이 정도 갖고 되겠어요? *Will this much be enough?*
B: 될 거예요. *It'll be enough.*

16.1.9 Only -겠, not -을 거

Unlike -을 거, which is mostly used to express a neutral intention/conjecture, -겠 often expresses a variety of other things, including the following.

- Courteous requests/questions
  좀 앉으시겠습니까? *Would you sit down, please?*
  주문하시겠어요? *Would you like to order?*
  음료수는 뭘로 하시겠어요? *What would you like to drink?*

  NOTE: Less formally, one could say: 앉으실래요, 주문하실래요, etc.

- Courteous promise
  다시 전화 드리겠습니다. *I'll call again.*
  맛있게 먹겠습니다. *I'll enjoy the food.*

  NOTE: Less formally, one could say: 전화 드릴게요, 먹을게요, etc.

- Other courteous/formulaic expressions
  처음 뵙겠습니다. *How do you do?*
  실례하겠습니다. *Excuse me.* (when entering a place)
  그럼 이만 줄이겠습니다. *Let me stop here.* (in letter writing)
  이따 다시 오시면 고맙겠습니다. *I'll be grateful if you come back later today.*
  잘 알겠습니다. *I understand.*

- Formal reports in weather forecasts or meetings
  내일 낮 기온은 오늘과 비슷하겠습니다.
  Tomorrow's daytime temperature will be like today's.
  총장님의 환영사가 있겠습니다.
  There will be a welcoming speech from the president of the university.
  잠시 후 연예가 소식을 전해 드리겠습니다.
  In a moment, we'll give you the entertainment news.

- Ability/possibility

  이거 다 먹겠니?

  Will you be able to eat it all?

  그 사람이 이 시간에 퍽이나 집에 있겠다.

  Fat chance that he'll be home at this time.

  설마 지금껏 안 먹었겠어요?

  Could he still not have eaten? (I doubt it.)

  누가 일이 이렇게 나빠질지 알았겠어요?

  Who would have known that things will get this bad?

- Hypothetical/idiomatic expressions

  졸려 죽겠다/미치겠다.

  My eyelids feel so heavy that I'm dying/going crazy.

  집에 전화가 없어서 답답해 못 살겠다.

  Having no phone in the house drives me so crazy that I can't stand it.

  너무 웃어서 배꼽 빠지겠다.

  My stomach hurts [my belly button is going to come out] *from laughing too much.*

  음식을 많이 차려서 상다리 부러지겠어요.

  You prepared so much food that we might need a bigger table
  [this table is going to break].

  웬일이야? 내일은 해가 서쪽에서 뜨겠다.

  What's going on? The sun will rise in the west tomorrow.
  (to indicate something unexpected but good has happened)

  좀 조용히 얘기 해. 귀청 떨어지겠다.

  Talk quietly please. You are deafening me [my ear(drums) will fall out].

  왜 한숨을 푹푹 쉬고 그래? 땅 꺼지겠다.

  Why do you keep sighing so deeply? The ground might sink.

  별 상식 없는 사람 다 보겠네요.

  What a person lacking in common sense he is.

16.2   Tense and aspect on non-final verbs

This section focuses on whether a verb in non-final position is marked separately for tense/aspect and, when it is, how its interpretation relates to the tense/aspect of the final verb.

16.2.1   Conjunctive constructions (see ch. 21)

Here, there are two possibilities.

- The internal verb is not marked for tense/aspect, but relies on the final verb for its interpretation.

  비 **오기** 전에 왔어요.   *I came before it rained.*

  그동안 책 **쓰느라고** 바빴어요.   *I've been busy writing a book for a while.*

  운전하면서 먹을 거예요.   *I'll eat while I drive.*

  눕자마자 잠이 들었어요.   *I fell asleep as soon as I lay down.*

  샤워하는데 전화가 왔어요.   *The phone call came as I was taking a shower.*

  비행기표 **사서** 보내 줄게.   *I'll buy the air ticket and send it to you.*

  눈이 많이 **와서** 비행기가   *It snowed a lot, so the airplane got delayed.*
    지연됐어요.

- Both verbs carry tense/aspect.

  눈이 많이 **왔기 때문에** 비행기가 지연됐어요.
    Because it snowed a lot, the airplane got delayed.

  기분이 몹시 **나빴지만** 꾹 참았어요.
    I patiently held my feelings in, although I was very upset.

  저녁에 **외식할 거니까** 일찍 들어 와.
    Come home early because we're going to eat out this evening.

  Tense/aspect marking on the inner verb in patterns such as the following dramatically changes the meaning of the sentence.

  학교에 **갔다가** 서점에 들렀어.   *I went to school, then dropped by a bookstore.*
  학교에 **가다가** 서점에 들렀어.   *On the way to school I dropped by a bookstore.*

16.2.2   Adnominal constructions

The adnominal suffixes (-는, -은, -던, -을, etc.) that connect a clause with a noun also provide information about tense/aspect. (See **22.2** for more on adnominal expressions.)

-는 is used to indicate:

- With action verbs and compound 있다/없다 verbs: Present tense or simultaneity with the event in the main clause.

  옆집에 사는 사람을 만났다.   *I met a person who lives next door.*

  사고나는 장면을 목격했습니다.   *I witnessed the accident taking place.*

  일리있는 말을 했어요.   *He said something that has a good point.*

  전례없는 일입니다.   *It's something without precedent.*

- Fixed expressions

  쉬는 시간 *break (time)*   노는 날 *day off*

  먹는 물 *drinking water*   (못) 쓰는 거 *(un)usable thing*

  택시타는 곳 *taxi stop*   있는/없는 집 *rich/poor home*

-은 (or ㄴ) is used to indicate:

- With descriptive verbs: Present state

  따끈한 차 *hot tea*   차가운 냉수 *cold water*

  작은 소망 *humble wish*   군인인 너 *you who are in the military*

- With most action verbs: Past tense, or a time prior to the event in the main clause.

  여행가서 찍은 사진이야.
  These are photos that I took when I went on a trip.

  한 달 전에 부친 소포가 어제야 도착했어요.
  The package that they mailed a month ago arrived just yesterday.

  이미 본 영화를 또 빌려 왔어요.
  He rented a movie that we had already seen.

- With some action verbs that denote a process: Present state resulting from a completed process.

  젖은 수건 *wet towel*   살찐 고양이 *fat cat*

  잘 익은 복숭아 *well-ripened peach*   화난 사람 *angry person*

  불어 터진 라면 *totally soggy ramen*   감기 걸린 사람 *person who has a cold*

- With verbs of wearing/contact: Present state resulting from a completed action.

  안경 낀 학생   *the student who is wearing glasses*

  파란 우산을 든 꼬마   *the kid who is holding a blue umbrella*

  체크남방에 청바지를 입은 남자   *the man who is wearing a plaid shirt with blue jeans*

-던 and -었던 are used to indicate:

- With descriptive verbs: -던 is used for a situation that continued for a while but has changed; -었던 represents the past state at a certain point of time. There is only a subtle difference between the two forms.

착하던/착했던 친구가 많이 변했다.
  The friend who used to be nice has changed a lot.

물을 안 갈아 줬더니 예쁘던/예뻤던 꽃이 다 시들었다.
  I didn't change their water, so the flowers that used to be beautiful are all withered.

- With action verbs: -던 represents a past habit or a suspended action. In contrast, -었던 indicates a completed action from a retrospective viewpoint. In the following cases, the difference can be subtle.

예전에 살던/살았던 집이에요.   *That's the house where I used to live.*

내가 다니던/다녔던 학교야.   *That's the school that I used to attend.*

전에 좋아하던/좋아했던 노래다.   *That's the song that I used to like.*

Depending on the nature of the verb, however, -던 may indicate a temporarily suspended action and -었던 may indicate a one-time only event.

친구들과 만나던 까페   *the café where I used to meet with friends*
친구들과 만났던 까페   *the café where I had met with friends once before*

빨간 옷을 입던 친구   *the friend who used to wear red clothes*
빨간 옷을 입었던 친구   *the friend who had worn red clothes once before*

내가 먹던 사과   *the apple I was eating* (but temporarily stopped)
내가 먹었던 사과   *the apple I had eaten before*

NOTE: Regardless of the verb type, both -던 and -었던 denote only a past habit if the verb occurs with 즐겨.

내가 즐겨 먹던 사과   *apples I used to enjoy eating*
친구들과 즐겨 만났던 까페   *the café where I used to enjoy meeting friends*
빨간 옷을 즐겨 입었던 친구   *the friend who used to enjoy wearing red clothes*

-을 (or ㄹ) is used to indicate:

- A future event with respect to the event denoted by the final verb

피자 먹을 사람은 이리로 모여.
  Gather here, those who are going to eat pizza.

오늘 볼 시험 준비를 하고 있었어요.
  I was preparing for an exam to be taken today.

- Fixed expressions

  볼 일 *things to take care of*   잘 시간 *time for bed*

  먹을 거 *things to eat*   죽을 고생 *hell of a difficult experience*

- Intention or conjecture

  두 달 안에 끝마칠 계획입니다.   *I'm planning to finish in two months.*

  아무래도 늦을 모양이에요.   *It looks like he's probably going to be late.*

  올 사람은 다 온 것 같습니다.   *I think everyone who's coming came.*

-었을 (or 았을) is used to indicate:

- Conjecture about a past event that has not been verified

  어제쯤 도착했을 편지가 왜 아직 안 올까요?

  I wonder why the letter that should have arrived by yesterday is not here yet.

  병원에 갔으면 하루만에 나았을 병이야.

  It's a sickness that would have been healed in a day if you had gone to the hospital.

Special case: -을 때 vs. -었을 때 'when…'

  -을 때: simultaneous with the action in the main clause
  -었을 때: completed prior to the action in the main clause

어제 백화점에 갈 때 길에서 고등학교 동창을 만났다.

  I ran into my high school friend on my way to the department store yesterday.

어제 백화점에 갔을 때 고등학교 동창을 만났다.

  I ran into my high school friend when I went to the department store yesterday.

지난번에 올 때 아무 것도 안 사 갖고 왔어요.

  Last time when I was coming, I didn't bring anything.

지난번에 왔을 때 집에 아무도 없었어요.

  Last time when I came, there was no one at home.

16.3 More aspect-related contrasts

A variety of important aspect-related contrasts are marked by suffixes, auxiliary verbs, or a combination of the two.

16.3.1 Beginning/changing into

- -기 시작하다 'begin'

  비가 내리기 시작한다.   *It's beginning to rain.*

  태권도를 배우기 시작했어요.   *I began learning t'aekwŏndo.*

- **-게 되다** 'become; come to'

  친하던 친구하고 사이가 서먹서먹하게 됐어요.
  > *My relationship with my once close friend became awkward.*

  무서워하던 선생님을 좋아하게 됐다.
  > *I came to like the teacher that I once feared.*

- **-어지다** 'become'

해가 점점 길어진다.	*The days are getting gradually longer.*
허리가 많이 가늘어졌다.	*Your waist has become very slender.*
십년은 더 젊어지신 거 같아요.	*You look like you've gotten at least 10 years younger.*

16.3.2 Continuation

- **-어 가다** 'gradually (from present to future)'

밥이 다 돼 간다.	*The rice is getting almost done.*
사랑이 식어 간다.	*Our love is gradually cooling off.*
살아 가다 보면 좋은 날이 올거야.	*If you keep on living, better days will come.*
회사가 쓰러져 가고 있대요.	*They say the company is gradually collapsing.*

- **-어 오다** 'gradually (from past to present)'

슬슬 배가 고파 온다.	*I'm gradually getting hungry.*
지금까지 잘 참아 왔어요.	*We've stood up well until now.*

16.3.3 Completion

- **-고 나다** 'have finished'

한잠 자고 나면 괜찮을 거야.	*You'll feel better after taking a nap.*
다들 떠나고 나니까 빈집같다.	*The house feels empty after everyone has left.*
방부터 치우고 나서 공부해야지.	*I better clean the room first before I study.*

- **-고 말다** 'finally end up doing'

결국 들키고 말았어.	*I ended up getting caught.*
물고기가 끝내 죽고 말았어요.	*The fish ended up dying in the end.*
이 일은 반드시 해내고 말거야.	*I'm going to complete this no matter what.*

- **-어 내다** 'make it all the way; manage to complete'

  수술 후 통증이 심했을 텐데 잘 견뎌 냈어.
  > *The pain after your surgery must have been bad, but you did a good job managing it.*

맡은 임무를 잘 해 낼 수 있을까 모르겠어요.
  I wonder whether I'll be able to manage to complete the assigned mission.

범인을 어떻게 해서든지 찾아 내야 됩니다.
  We must find the criminal at all costs.

- **-어 치우다** 'get rid of completely'

단숨에 숙제를 해 치웠다.   *I dashed through my homework.*

어제 남은 음식을 먹어 치웠어요.   *I ate up all the leftovers from yesterday.*

그렇게 무능한 사람은 갈아 치워.   *Get rid of such an incompetent person.*

- **-어 버리다** 'do completely (to one's regret or relief)'

어떡해요? 비행기를 놓쳐 버렸어요.
  What should I do? I missed my plane.

아이스크림이 다 녹아 버렸다.
  The ice cream melted completely.

그렇게 경우없는 사람은 그냥 무시해 버리세요.
  Just completely ignore such a rude person.

나쁜 기억은 싹 지워 버리는 게 건강에 좋아요.
  It's healthy to completely erase bad memories.

16.3.4 Completion followed by an enduring result

- **-어 놓다, -어 두다** 'complete something (and keep the resulting state)'

With 놓다 the emphasis is on the completion of an action, whereas with 두다 it is on the purposeful retention of the result of an action.

비행기표를 미리 예약해 놓을까/둘까?
  Shall I make a reservation for the airline ticket in advance?

컴퓨터 그냥 켜 놓으세요/두세요.
  Just leave the computer on, please.

이따 배고플테니까 지금 많이 먹어 놔/둬. (놔 < 놓아)
  Eat big now, since you'll be hungry later.

차를 길에 세워 놓고/두고 어디 갔어?
  Where did he go, with his car parked in the driveway?

세일할 때 많이 사 놓으려구요/두려구요.
  I'm trying to stock up on things when there's a sale.

빨래는 비눗물에 담가 놓으세요/두세요.
  Keep the laundry soaking in the soapy water.

- **-어 놓다 only** (with exclusive focus on the completion of an action)

  강아지가 신발을 물어뜯어 놓았어요.
  The puppy has chewed up my shoes.

  뺑소니 운전사가 사고쳐 놓고 도망갔어요.
  A hit-and-run driver had an accident and ran away.

  그 친구가 거의 다 된 일을 망쳐 놓았어.
  He ruined the work that was almost finished.

  내일까지 고쳐 놓겠대요.
  They said they'll fix it by tomorrow.

  간다고 약속해 놓고 이제 와서 딴소리하면 어떡해?
  How can you change your mind now, after you promised to go?

- **-어 두다 only**

  그냥 자게 내버려 두세요.
  Just leave him alone so he can sleep.

  다시 한 번 말해 두겠는데 다음부터는 늦지 않는 게 좋을 거다.
  Let me tell you once again: You better not be late from now on.

16.3.5 Experience

- **-어 보다 'try'**

  이 안경을 한 번 써 보세요.   *Try these glasses on.*

  그 음식점에 저도 가 봤어요.   *I've been to the restaurant too.*

- **-는/은 적이 있다 or 없다** 'have an (or no) experience of' (일 can replace 적.)

  가끔 학교버스를 놓치는 일이 있습니다.
  I sometimes miss the school bus.

  밥은 한 번도 굶은 적이 없어요.
  When it comes to a meal, I've never skipped one.

  택시 탔다가 바가지 쓴 적이 한두 번이 아니다.
  This is not the first time I took a taxi and got ripped off.

  고속도로에서 운전하다가 타이어가 터진 일이 있다.
  I once got a flat tire while driving down the highway.

- **-어 본 역사가 없다** 'never experienced (emphatic)'

  평생 거짓말은 해 본 역사가 없다.   *I have no history of lying.*

  그런 말은 들어 본 역사가 없어.   *I've never heard of such a thing.*

  복권에 당첨 돼 본 역사가 없어요.   *Never in my life have I won a lottery.*

16.3.6   Habit

- **-곤 하다** 'usually do; used to'

  스트레스가 쌓이면 운동을 하곤 합니다.
  I usually exercise whenever I get stressed.

  외로울 땐 혼자서 바닷가에 가곤 했다.
  Whenever I felt lonely, I used to go to the ocean by myself.

- **-어 버릇하다** 'make a habit of'

  이제부터 아침에 일찍 일어나 버릇을 해야겠어요.
  I think from now on I should make a habit of getting up early in the morning.

  잘 못하는 일도 자꾸 해 버릇하면 잘하게 돼.
  If you keep doing something that you may not be good at, you'll become good at it.

16.3.7   Repetition

- **-어 대다** 'do continuously'

  그렇게 떠들어 대니 목이 안 쉴 수가 없지.
  How can your voice not go hoarse when you babble on like that?

  스키장 가자고 졸라 대는 바람에 할 수 없이 갔다 왔어요.
  I had no choice but to take them skiing because they were pestering me for it.

- **-어 쌓다** 'repeat excessively'

  아이가 계속 울어 쌓는다.   *The child is crying non-stop.*

  정말 잘 먹어 쌓는다.   *You really do keep eating.*

17 Modality

Modality involves information about a wide range of contrasts that reflect speakers' attitudes and intentions. Like tense and aspect, modality is expressed with the help of verbal inflection and/or auxiliary verbs.

17.1 Requests, suggestions, permission, and prohibition

17.1.1 Requests

- **-어(라)** (commands)

  제발 방 정돈 좀 해라.
    Get the room organized, please.

  여기 낙지소면 하나하고 소주 한 병 주세요.
    We'd like one order of octopus noodles and a bottle of soju.

- **(좀) -어 줘** '(Please) … for me'

  내일 아침 7 시에 좀 깨워 줘요.
    Please wake me up at 7 a.m. tomorrow morning.

  학교 정문 앞에 세워 주세요.
    Please drop me off right in front of school.

- **-면 한다/고맙겠다/감사하겠습니다** 'It would be nice if you…'

  아빠, 저 돈 좀 부쳐 주셨으면 하는데요.
    Dad, can you send me some money?

  다음부터는 시간을 꼭 지켜 줬으면 고맙겠어요.
    It would be nice if you are punctual in the future.

- **(좀) -어 줄래/주시겠어요?** 'Would you …for me?'

  여자 향수 좀 보여 주실래요?
    Would you show me women's perfumes?

  밥 한 공기 추가하고 물 좀 갖다 주시겠어요?
    Would you bring me another bowl of rice and some water?

- **(좀) -어 주실 수 있을까요?** 'Would it be possible to…for me?'

  죄송하지만, 라디오 소리 좀 줄여 주실 수 있을까요?
    Excuse me, but would it be possible to turn down the radio for me?

  너무 비싼데 좀 깎아 주실 수 있어요?
    It's too expensive for me; can you give me a discount?

17.1.2 Suggestions (advice/instructions)

- **-는 게 어때?** 'How about...?'

지도에서 찾아보는 게 어때?	*How about looking it up on the map?*
저녁값은 각자 내는 게 어떨까요?	*How about going Dutch on the dinner?*
한번 더 만나보는 게 어떻겠니?	*How about meeting him one more time?*

- **-지 그래?** 'Why don't you...?'

신문에 구인광고를 내지 그래?	*Why don't you put out the want ad?*
병원에 좀 가 보지 그러세요?	*Why don't you go to the hospital?*

- **-을 필요/거 없다** 'No need to...'

치료 받을 필요 없어요.	*I don't need any medical treatment.*
너무 신경쓸 거 없어.	*No need to be concerned so much.*

- **-면 된다** 'All you need is to...'
  (Be careful not to use this pattern to ask for permission! See the following box.)

관리비는 이 달 말일 안으로 입금하시면 됩니다.
  You can pay the maintenance fee at the bank before the end of this month.

김치찌개는 김치하고 돼지고기를 썰어 넣고 그냥 끓이면 돼요.
  All you need for Kimch'i stew is to put in chopped up Kimch'i and pork, and just boil them.

- **-도록 해** 'Make sure that...'

앞으로는 좀 더 일찍 일어나도록 해.
  Make sure that you get up a bit earlier from now on.

출근 시간에 절대 늦지 않도록 하세요.
  Make sure that you are never late for your work in the morning.

- **-을 것** (in written instructions)

신분증을 반드시 지참할 것.
  You must carry your ID.

모든 서류를 다음 주 월요일까지 제출할 것.
  All documents must be submitted by next Monday.

17.1.3 Permission

- **-어도 된다/괜찮다** 'may; can'

좀 입어 봐도 돼요?	*May I try these (clothes) on?*
반말해도 괜찮아.	*You can be casual when you talk with me.*
미리 예약하지 않아도 됩니까?	*Is it okay for us not to make a reservation in advance?*

The difference between -어도 된다 and -면 된다

English speakers tend to use the -면 된다 pattern to ask for permission, but that is a mistake. To ask for permission to go to the restroom, 화장실 가도 돼요? should be used, NOT 화장실 가면 돼요? -면 된다 is employed for instructions or directions – 비오면 연기하면 돼 'you can postpone if it rains,' 시청가려면 여기서 좌회전 하시면 됩니다 'To go to the city hall, you should make a left turn here.' It may also be used to request confirmation of what you are required to do (수요일까지 내면 돼요? 'Will it do if I submit it by Wednesday?'). To ask for permission to be late, you should say 금요일까지 내도 돼요? 'May I submit it by Friday?'

- **-면 안 돼?** 'Would it be not okay if...?'

  장례식에 안 가면 안 돼요?　　　　*Can I not go to the funeral?*

  합석 좀 하시면 안 될까요?　　　　*Could you share the table with (others)?*

- **-을 수 있을까?** 'Will it be possible...?'

  전화 좀 쓸 수 있을까요?　　　　*May I use the phone?*

  같이 좀 앉을 수 있을까요?　　　　*May I sit with you?*

17.1.4 Prohibition

- **-지 마** 'Don't...'

  다시는 나한테 전화하지 마.　　　　*Don't ever call me again.*

  너무 긴장하지 마세요.　　　　*Don't be too nervous.*

- **-면 안 된다** 'You must not...'

  진통제를 과용하시면 안 됩니다.　　*You must not overuse pain killers.*

  여기서 좌회전하면 안 돼요.　　　　*You cannot make a left turn here.*

- **-어선 안 된다** 'You should not...'

  한약 드시는 동안 돼지고기를 입에 대셔선 안 됩니다.
  　You should not eat pork while you're taking Chinese medicine.

  이 말은 절대 아무한테도 해선 안 돼요.
  　You must not tell anyone this.

- **-을 수 없다** 'You are not allowed to...'

  박물관내에서 사진 찍을 수 없습니다.
  　You are not allowed to take pictures in the museum.

  이 곳에서는 수영할 수 없습니다.
  　Swimming is prohibited here.

  도서관 안에서는 음식을 먹을 수 없습니다.
  　You are not allowed to eat in the library.

17.2 Obligation, ability, and possibility

The dividing lines for obligation, ability, and possibility are not always clear-cut, so there may be some overlap in the examples that follow.

17.2.1 Obligation (necessity)

- -어야 한다/된다 'must; have to'

  항상 다른 사람의 말을 경청해야 한다.
  One must always listen when other people speak.

  백불 갖고 일주일을 살아야 돼요.
  I must survive on 100 dollars this week.

  당분간 허리띠 졸라매야(되)겠어요.
  We'll have to tighten our belts for the time being.

- -지 않으면 (or 안 -면) 안 된다 'must; have to'

  올 안으로 취직하지 않으면 안 돼요.
  I must find a job before the year is over.

  나는 하루도 커피를 안 마시면 안 돼.
  I have to have coffee every single day.

- -지 않을 수가 (or 안 -을 수가) 없다 'have no choice but to'

  도움을 청하지 않을 수가 없었어요.
  I had no choice but to ask for his help.

  잔소리를 안 할래야 도저히 안 할 수가 없어요.
  I can't possibly help but complain, even if I try not to.

- -는/을 수밖에 없다 'have no choice but to'

  아무래도 직장을 그만두는 수밖에 없다.
  I have no choice other than to quit the job.

  방세가 너무 비싸서 아파트를 옮기는 수밖에 없겠어요.
  The rent is too expensive, so we'll have no choice other than to move to a different apartment.

  도움을 청할 수밖에 없었어요.
  I had no choice but to ask for his help.

17.2.2 Ability

- -을 수 있다 'can; be able to'

  왼손으로 테니스 칠 수 있어?
  Can you play tennis with your left hand?

  마감일까지 제출할 수 있을까요?
  Will we be able to submit it by the deadline?

제가 도울 수 있는 한 최선을 다해 도와 드리겠습니다.
  I'll help you as best I can.

될 수 있는 대로 교통이 편리한 집을 구하려고 해요.
  As far as possible, I'm trying to find a place with an easy commute.

- 못- 'cannot; be unable to'

아기가 아직 못 걸어요.
  The baby can't walk yet.

수영은 할 수 있는데 골프는 잘 못 쳐요.
  I can swim, but I can't play golf well.

  NOTE: Inability is usually expressed by 못-; -을 수 없다 is used for prohibition or impossibility rather than inability (see *17.1.4 & 17.2.3*).

- -을 줄 안다/모른다 'know how to…'

김치 담글 줄 아세요?
  Do you know how to make Kimch'i?

어떻게 너는 먹을 줄만 알고 요리할 줄은 모르니?
  How come you only know how to eat, but not how to cook?

운전은 할 줄 알지만 길을 잘 몰라요.
  I know how to drive, but I'm not good with directions.

17.2.3 *Possibility*

- -수(가) 있다/없다 'There is a/no possibility…'

제 꾀에 제가 넘어 가는 수가 있다.
  It's possible to be outwitted by one's own cleverness.

어떻게 그럴 수가 있어? 있을 수 없는 일이다.
  How can it be? It's impossible.

표가 매진돼서 할 수 없이 내일 표를 예약했어요.
  Tickets were sold out, so I had no choice but to reserve one for tomorrow.

방문이 열리지 않아서 별 수 없이 창문으로 들어 갔다.
  The bedroom door wouldn't open, so I had no choice but to go in through the window.

- -지도 모른다 'may; be possible'

그 소문이 맞는지도 모른다.   *That rumor may be true.*
남자친구가 아닐지도 몰라요.   *He may not be a boyfriend.*
여행갔는지도 몰라.   *She might have gone on a trip.*

- **-리가 없다** 'cannot be; no way'

그렇게 순진한 애가 거짓말을 할 리가 없어. 설마 그럴리가.
It's impossible for such an innocent kid to tell a lie. No way.

네가 시험에 떨어졌을 리가 없어.
There's no way that you failed the exam.

17.3 Regret, desire, and doubt

17.3.1 Regret

- **-었어야 한다/된다** 'should have…'

진작 병원에 갔어야 해요.
You should have seen a doctor much earlier.

밤늦게 커피를 마시지 말았어야 되는데…
I shouldn't have had coffee late at night.

못 오면 못 온다고 얘기를 해 줬어야지.
If you couldn't come, you should have told me so.

- **-을걸 (그랬다)** 'I wish I had…'

엄마한테 좀 더 잘해 드릴걸 그랬어요.
I wish I had been a better daughter to my Mom.

사랑한다고 고백할걸.
I wish I had confessed to her that I love her.

규칙적으로 건강검진을 받았더라면 좋았을걸.
I wish I had gotten regular health check-ups.

- **-지 (그랬어)** 'I wish you had…'

여행가서 사진 좀 많이 찍지 (그랬어).
I wish you had taken more pictures during the trip.

곧바로 경찰에 신고를 하지 그랬어.
You should have made a report to the police immediately.

- **-면 -었을텐데** 'would have…if …'

내가 미리 알았으면 무슨 조치를 취했을텐데.
I would have taken some measures if I had known about it in advance.

차라리 아무 것도 몰랐으면 좋았을텐데.
I'd rather have known nothing about it.

- **-는 건데 …** 'should have…'

길을 물어보고 가는 건데 잘못했어.
It's my mistake. I should have asked for directions beforehand.

작년에 운전면허 시험을 보는 건데 그랬어. 그 때 봤어야 하는 건데.
I should've taken the driver's license exam last year. I should've taken it then.

- **-게 아닌데 'shouldn't have…'**

술 마시고 운전하는 게 아닌데.
I shouldn't have driven a car after drinking.

잘 자리에 그렇게 많이 먹는 게 아니었는데.
I shouldn't have eaten so much right before going to bed.

17.3.2 Desire (wish)

- **-고 싶다, -고 싶어한다 'would like to; want'**

어떤 집에서 살고 싶니?
What kind of house would you like to live in?

정원이 크고 바다가 보이는 집에서 살고 싶어.
I want to live in a house with a big yard and an ocean view.

내 동생은 가수가 되고 싶어한다.
My younger brother wants to become a singer.

- **-었으면 좋겠다/한다 'It would be nice if…'**

평생 하와이에서 살았으면 좋겠다.
It would be nice to live in Hawaii forever.

전공을 바꿨으면 합니다.
I think I would like to change my major.

잠 좀 실컷 잤으면 원이 없겠다.
I wouldn't have any other wish if I could sleep as much as I like.

17.3.3 Doubt

- **-을라고?**

설마 지금까지 안 먹었을라고?
I strongly doubt that they haven't eaten until now. (How can they not have?)

그런 잉꼬부부가 설마 부부싸움을 할라고요?
I doubt that such a happily married [macaw] couple fight – surely they don't.

17.4 Degree

17.4.1 'Nearly/almost'

- **-을 뻔했다 'almost happened'**

어젯밤에 더워서 미칠 뻔했어.
It was so hot last night that I almost went insane.

고기 굽다가 하마터면 화상을 입을 뻔했어요.
I almost got burnt while barbecuing the meat.

- **-을락 말락 한다** 'almost happening'

머리가 천장에 닿을락 말락 한다.   *Your head is almost touching the ceiling.*

속치마가 보일락 말락 해.   *Your slip is almost showing.*

- **-다시피 됐다** 'became close to...'

차 사고로 거의 죽다시피 됐어.
She's near death due to a car accident.

부도로 인해 회사가 거의 파산하다시피 됐습니다.
The company is close to bankruptcy due to the bounced payment.

- **-다시피 한다** 'almost as if...'

완전히 제 집 드나들다시피 하는구나.
He goes in and out of this place like it's his own house.

일년을 도서관에서 살다시피 했어.
I almost lived in the library for a year.

17.4.2 Deserving quality

- **-을 만하다**

요즘 볼 만한 영화가 뭐 있어요?
Are there any good movies (worth seeing) lately?

그 식당 부페가 먹을 만하던데요.
I tried that restaurant buffet; it was quite good (well worth trying it).

그런 행동을 하다니 비난받을 만하네요.
They deserve to be criticized for behaving like that.

힘은 좀 들지만 그럭저럭 견딜 만해요.
It's a bit tough but somehow manageable. I'm okay handling it.

17.5 Evidentiality

A variety of verb forms are used to indicate how speakers have come to think or know what they say or report and how committed they are to its truth. Use of these forms allows speakers to strengthen or soften the impact of their statements and to distance themselves from what they say.

17.5.1 They say... (hearsay)

Because the information is 'second-hand,' the speaker is not responsible for whether it is true. (See **22.1** for quoted clauses.)

- **-댄다, -다더라(구요), -답니다**

기름값이 또 올랐댄다.	*They say that the price of gas went up again.*
요새 부동산 경기가 안 좋대요.	*I hear that the real estate market is slow these days.*
부인이 많이 아프다더라.	*I heard that his wife is very sick.*
위암이라더라구요.	*They say it's stomach cancer.*
항암치료를 받고 있답니다.	*I heard that she's receiving chemotherapy.*

17.5.2 Seems like; feels like; I think...

The following forms can express a guess or opinion in a less assertive way.

- **-거 같다**

성격이 괴팍해서 친구들하고 잘 못 어울리는 거 같아요.
It seems like he's so picky that he doesn't get along with his friends.

아무래도 핸드폰을 잃어버린 거 같다.
I think I lost my cell phone.

말은 안 해도 많이 힘들었던 거 같아요.
It seems like she had a tough time even though she doesn't talk about it.

경기가 무승부로 끝날 거 같은데요.
I bet that the game will end in a tie.

- **-듯 하다/싶다**
  (less commonly used than -거 같다; often employed in written language)

눈이 충혈되고 눈꼽이 낀 걸 보니 결막염에 걸린 듯 합니다.
Looking at your red and runny eyes, it seems like you might have conjunctivitis.

자꾸 멀미가 날 듯 해서 더이상 운전 못하겠다.
I don't think I can drive any more because I feel like I'm getting car-sick.

절대적인 의미의 남녀평등이란 불가능할 듯 싶다.
I think that equality between men and women in the absolute sense may be impossible.

- **-지 싶다, -을까 싶다**

좀 늦어도 괜찮지 싶어.
I think it might be okay to be a little bit late.

벌써 도착했지 싶은데 모르겠다.
I think they already arrived, although I'm not sure.

어제 소개팅한 남자한테서 전화가 오지 않을까 싶은데.
I feel like I may be getting a phone call from the guy who I met on a blind date yesterday.

17.5.3 *Looks like; appears; I get the impression that…*

The following forms are somewhat more assertive than the preceding ones because their use presupposes some type of observable evidence.

- **-나 보다, -은가 보다**

엄마 설겆이 하시나 봐.	*Looks like Mom is doing the dishes.*
결혼할 사람인가 보다.	*Looks like he's her fiancé.*
사는 게 좀 어려운가 봐요.	*It looks like she's not doing well financially.*
어디 외출했나 보다.	*Looks like they went out somewhere.*
시험문제가 어려웠나 봅니다.	*It looks like the exam questions were tough.*

  NOTE: In the present tense, action verbs usually occur with -나 보다 (자나 보다) and descriptive verbs with -은가 보다 (작은가 보다); in the past tense, both types of verbs occur with -나 보다 (잤나 보다, 작았나 보다).

- **-어 보인다** (based on immediate sensory experience)

빵이 맛있어 보인다.	*The bread looks delicious.*
나이에 비해 젊어 보여요.	*He looks young for his age.*
좀 외로워 보였어요.	*She looked a little lonely.*

  NOTE: This is used only with descriptive verbs.

- **-게 생겼다** (based on subjective judgments)

  천상 처음부터 일을 다시 하게 생겼다.
  > *Looks like we'll have to start all over again.*

  일이 이렇게 많으니 밤새우게 생겼네요.
  > *With this much work, it looks like we'll have to stay all night.*

  입장 곤란하게 생겼어.
  > *Looks like I'll be put in a difficult position.*

  마음씨 좋게 생겼다.
  > *He appears to have a kind heart.*

- **-모양이다**

  (based on indirect evidence, including appearance or second-hand information)

상대가 마음에 안 드는 모양이야.	*Looks like he doesn't like her date.*
지금 막 끝난 모양이에요.	*It looks like it's just finished.*
아예 안 올 모양이다.	*Looks like he's not coming at all.*
피곤한 모양이에요.	*It looks like he's tired.*
무척 바빴던 모양입니다.	*It looks like she was very busy.*

- **-겠다** (see *16.1.8*)

  이 사과는 색깔 보니까 정말 맛있겠어요.
  > *I bet this apple is delicious, looking at its color.*

어제 늦게까지 일하느라 피곤했겠다.
You must have been tired working till late last night.

17.5.4 I am almost certain...; probably...

The following forms imply a fairly reliable source or a general belief that one concurs with. For this reason, they are relatively assertive.

- **-을 거다** (see *16.1.8*)

  아무리 설득해 봐도 소용없을 거다.
  It'll probably be useless to try to persuade her.

  성수기에는 비행기표 구하기가 힘들 거예요.
  I'm pretty sure that it'll be hard to find a plane ticket during peak travel season.

- **-을텐데**

  교통이 복잡할텐데 지하철 타고 가세요.
  I'm sure the traffic is heavy, so take the subway.

  결혼 준비하느라 바쁠텐데 이번 프로젝트에 너무 신경쓰지 마세요.
  You must be busy with your wedding preparations, so don't worry about this project.

- **-을 걸** (with a rising intonation)

  출퇴근시간이라 교통이 복잡할 걸.
  I'm sure the traffic will be bad because it's rush hour.

  택시보다 지하철이 더 빠를 걸요.
  I'm pretty sure that the subway will be faster than a taxi.

17.5.5 Summary of evidential patterns

The following table offers a summary of the evidential patterns discussed above.

	With an action verb (...it will rain)	With a descriptive verb (...it hurts)
'I hear...'	비 온댄다	아프댄다
'It seems like...'	비 올 거 같다	아픈 거 같다
	비가 올 듯 하다	아픈 듯 하다
	비 올까 싶다	아프지 싶다
'It looks like...'	비 오려나 보다	아픈가 보다
	non-applicable	아파 보인다
	비 오게 생겼다	아프게 생겼다
	비가 올 모양이다	아픈 모양이다
	비 오겠다	아프겠다
'I am almost certain...'	비 올 거야	아플 거야
	비 올 텐데	아플 텐데
	비 올 걸	아플 걸

17.6 Special verb-endings expressing the speaker's attitude

The following verb-endings are frequently used in colloquial speech.

17.6.1 Explanatory/emphatic

- -는/은 거다 is extremely common; it creates the following effects.

(a) Inviting the listener to be engaged in the conversation. Use of -는/은 거다 implies an unstated reason for asking the question, and invites something more than a simple to-the-point response:

정말 괜찮은 거예요?
  Are you really alright? (If not, I can do something for you...)

그 사람하고 결혼까지 생각하고 있는 거니?
  Are you thinking about even marrying him? (You got to be kidding!)

혹시 마음에 두고 있는 사람이 있는 거야?
  Do you by any chance have someone in mind? (Why are you avoiding this guy?)

(b) Presenting the story in a dramatic way (in the present tense), invoking the listener's attention to what is to follow:

아침을 해 놓았다고 좀 먹고 가라고 하시는 거예요. (늦었는데...)
  You know, she was telling me to eat before leaving, saying that she fixed breakfast for me. (I was late...)

나보고 그 사람하고 결혼을 하라는 거다. (그게 말이나 되니?)
  They were telling me to marry him, you know. (Does that even make any sense?)

수업시간에 끄덕끄덕 졸고 있는데 선생님이 딱 보고 계시는 거야.
  I was dozing off during class and guess what – the teacher was looking at me.

-는/은 거 있지 is also commonly used for a similar effect.

모두 내 얼굴만 쳐다보는 거 있죠.
  You know what? Everyone was staring at me!

전자렌지에 커피를 데워 놓고 까맣게 잊어버린거 있지.
  You know what? I totally forgot I had coffee warmed up in the microwave.

정신없이 바쁘다 보니 여권 만료일이 지난 거 있지.
  Having been so incredibly busy, I didn't even realize that my passport expired.

(c) Making the sentence more tangible and clear. The situation being described can be verified while the sentence is being uttered:

파인애플은 이렇게 자르는 거야. *You are to cut pineapples like this.*

여기서 뭐 하는 거야?   *What are you doing here?*

빨래하는 거야.   *I'm washing clothes (as you can see).*

- **-다는 거 아니니?**

  This is used for dramatic presentation of new or surprising information.

  내가 부동산 중개인이 됐다는 거 아니니?

    I've become a real estate agent. Can you believe it?

  제가 이번에 승진한다는 거 아닙니까?

    I'm getting promoted this time. Can you believe it?

- **-단/냔/잔/란 말이다, -다/냐/자/라구요, -다/냐/자/라니까, & -다/냐/자/라니?**

  These are employed with the quoting pattern (see **22.1**) to repeat what one has already said or sometimes just to say something in an emphatic way.

  A: 어떻게 그렇게 내 일에 무관심할 수가 있어?

  B: 무관심한 게 아니라 **바쁘다니까.**

  A: 그래도 그렇지. 좀 관심 좀 **가져보란 말야.**

  B: **알았다니까.** 잔소리 좀 이제 그만 **하라구.**

  A: **잔소리라니?** 이게 잔소리로 밖에 안 들리니?

    A: How can you be so indifferent and show no concern for what I do?
    B: It's not that I'm being indifferent. I told you that I'm busy.
    A: Even so, you should show some interest, I'm telling you.
    B: Okay, I said I got your point. No more nagging please.
    A: Nagging? Does it sound like nothing but nagging to you?

17.6.2 *Exclamatory and beyond*

- **-네** (spontaneous emotional reaction)

  이 옷 못 보던 건데, 색깔이 참 예쁘네요.

    I haven't seen that dress before; its color is really pretty.

  하와이는 본토에 비해 물가가 비싸네.

    Things are expensive in Hawaii compared to the mainland.

- **-데** (general exclamation)

  모자가 잘 어울리는데!   *The hat looks very good on you!*

  이 오징어볶음 정말 맛있는데요!   *This panbroiled cuttlefish is really delicious!*

- **-구나, -군요** (first realization)

  너 왔구나.   *Oh, you're here.*

  네가 그 영수네 반 친구구나.   *Oh, you're that classmate of Youngsoo's.*

  하와이는 공기가 정말 좋군요.   *The air quality in Hawaii is really good.*

- **-다** (no audience intended)

  저 강아지 너무 귀엽다!   *That puppy is so cute!*

  커피 향기 진짜 좋다.   *The aroma of the coffee is really good.*

- **-구만** (casually noticing something that wasn't expected)

화난 거 아니구만.	*Hey, she's not angry.*
문이 잠겼구만.	*Oh, the door's locked.*

- **-담, 는담** (lightly expressing a complaint or dissatisfaction)

그렇게 남을 헐뜯는 법이 어디 있담?	*How can he back-bite me like that?*
뭘 그렇게 비싸게 받는담?	*Why do they charge so much?*
뭘 그렇게 꾸물거린담?	*Why is she so slow (like a snail)?*

- **-을라** (warning or showing endearing concern)

우산 갖고 가라. 비 맞을라.	*Take an umbrella with you. You're going to get rained on.*
그렇게 뛰어가다 넘어질라.	*You're going to fall, running like that.*
깨진 유리 만지지 마. 다칠라.	*Don't touch the broken glass. You're going to get hurt.*

18 Negation

18.1 How to negate statements and questions

18.1.1 Short versus long negation

Except for a very small number of verbs that have an inherently negative counterpart (있다 ~ 없다, 알다 ~ 모르다, etc.), there are two basic ways to negate a verb in Korean. One is to place 안/못 in front of the verb (short negation) and the other is to attach -지 않다/못하다 at the end of the verb (long negation). The table below presents examples involving an action verb, a descriptive verb, and the copula verb. (n/a = non-applicable)

	Short negation		Long negation	
	with 안	with 못	with -지 않다	with -지 못하다
가요	안 가요	못 가요	가지 않아요	가지 못해요
비싸요	안 비싸요	n/a	비싸지 않아요	n/a (see *18.1.2*)
(책)이에요	(책)이 아니에요	n/a	n/a	n/a

Notice that the action verb 가다 allows both short negation and long negation, as does the descriptive verb 비싸다 (although not with 못). The copula verb (책)이다 allows only short negation by 안, whose spelling changes to 아니. (The contrast between 안 and 못 is discussed in *18.1.2*.)

Meaning-wise, short negation and long negation are usually interchangeable. However, the short form is more direct and therefore more colloquial, while the long form is less direct and is more frequently used in formal writing.

In long negation, a particle can be added after -지 in order to emphasize the verb – 불이 났을 때 빠져 나오지를 못했어 'I couldn't escape when there was a fire.' Short negation is more widely used than long negation, but the latter often sounds more natural with verbs that are three or more syllables in length.

아름답지 않다. (rather than 안 아름답다.) *It's not beautiful.*

학자답지 않다. (rather than 안 학자답다.) *She's not scholarly.*

Nonetheless, short negation sounds natural with certain highly frequent multi-syllable verbs.

안 좋아한다. (or 좋아하지 않는다.) *I don't like it.*

안 어울린다. (or 어울리지 않는다.) *They don't look good together.*

안 잘라진다. (or 잘라지지 않는다.)   *It (the meat) won't cut.*

안 깨끗하다. (or 깨끗하지 않다.)   *It's not clean.*

안 보고 싶다. (or 보고 싶지 않다.)   *I don't want to see it.*

18.1.2 안 *versus* 못

안 expresses the meaning of 'don't intend,' 'does not,' and 'is not,' while 못 is typically used to express inability as well as the meaning of 'definitely not' or 'be impossible.'

불어를 일부러 안 썼어.
  I deliberately didn't use French.

불어를 못 썼어. (이해할 수 있는 사람이 없어서.)
  I couldn't use French. (Because there was no one who could understand me.)

안 can be used with any verb, but 못 is usually not employed for either short or long negation involving descriptive verbs. In the case of certain descriptive verbs denoting desirable qualities, the use of 못 in long negation (-지 못하다) expresses the lack of such qualities or the speaker's dissatisfaction with the negative state of affairs.

넉넉하지 못하다. *He's not well-to-do.* 똑똑하지 못하다. *She's not smart.*

정직하지 못하다. *She's not honest.*   너그럽지 못하다. *He's not generous.*

NOTE: The -하지 in -하지 못하다/않다 may sometimes be contracted to -치 for frequently used expressions – 똑똑치 못하다, 만만치 않다 'It's no easy matter.'

The descriptive verb 못하다 by itself means 'be not as good as,' as in 동생이 형만 못하다 'The little brother is not as good as the older brother.'

18.1.3 *Fixed expressions in which the choice of negative is frozen*

조퇴해야지 **안 되겠다**.   *I think I'll have to leave work early.*

가지 **않으면 안 돼요**.   *I must go.*

사고를 당했다니 정말 **안됐다**.   *I hear they had an accident; it's too bad.*

칼이 너무 **안 들어요**.   *The knife is too dull.*

걔 정말 **못생겼다**.   *He's really bad-looking.*

이런 **못난** 자식.   *Oh, you fool.*

저런 **되지 못한** 자식.   *What a bastard.*

걔 정말 **못됐다**.   *He's really a brat.*

  "   **못돼 먹었다**.   "

  "   **돼먹지 못했다**.   "

그런 말 하면 **못 쓴다**.	*You shouldn't say such a thing.*
걔네집 **못 산다**.	*His family is poor.*
돈이라면 **맥을 못 춘다**.	*If it's money, she can't resist.*

- Not ~ but ~

가수가 **아니고/아니라** 배우다.	*He's not a singer but an actor.*
영화배우지 가수가 **아니다**.	*He's an actor, not a singer.*

- Neither ~ nor ~

가수도 **아니고** 영화배우도 **아냐**.	*She's neither a singer nor an actress.*
예쁘**지도 않고** 애교스럽**지도 않다**.	*She's neither pretty nor affectionate.*
차가 막혀 **오(지)도 가(지)도 못해**.	*I'm stuck in traffic, unable to move forward or backward.*

- It's no ~

어제 오늘 일이 아니에요.	*It's no recent matter.*
홀몸이 아니야.	*She's pregnant* [no single body].
장난이 아니다.	*It's no joke.*

18.1.4 How to negate complex verb constructions

- 'Verb + verb' compounds are treated as one unit.

먹어 봤어.	**못** 먹어 봤어.	or	먹어 보지 못했어.
I tried (the food).	*I haven't tried (the food).*		
보고 싶어요.	**안** 보고 싶어요.	or	보고 싶지 않아요.
I want to see it.	*I don't want to see it.*		
좋아 보인다.	**안** 좋아 보인다.	or	좋아 보이지 않는다.
You look good.	*You don't look good.*		
사 주었다.	**못** 사 주었다.	or	사 주지 못했다.
I bought it for him.	*I couldn't buy it for him.*		
가야 됩니다.	**안** 가도 됩니다.	or	가지 않아도 됩니다.
I have to go.	*I don't have to go.*		

- 'Bound noun + verb' compounds are treated as one unit.

약하다.	**안** 약하다.	or	약하지 않다.
He's weak.	*He's not weak.*		
깨끗해요.	**안** 깨끗해요.	or	깨끗하지 않아요.
It's clean.	*It's not clean.*		

- 'Free standing noun + verb' compounds are treated as two units.

배고파.   배 **안** 고파.   or   배고프지 않아.
  I'm hungry.   *I'm not hungry.*

축구한다.   축구 **못** 한다.   or   축구하지 못한다.
  I play soccer.   *I can't play soccer.*

NOTE: 'Noun + 있다' is negated as 'noun + 없다', as in 재미있다/재미없다 (except 필요하다, whose negated counterpart is 필요없다).

18.1.5   Negative prefixes for Sino-Korean nouns

금- [禁]: 금연 *no smoking*   금주 *no drinking*

몰- [沒]: 몰염치하다 *be shameless*   몰상식하다 *be senseless and absurd*

무- [無]: 무면허 *unlicensed*   무인도 *deserted island* [no person island]

미- [未]: 미혼 *unmarried*   미성년자 *under age (minor)*

부- [不]: 부조화 *disharmony*   부적합하다 *be inappropriate*

불- [不]: 불분명하다 *be unclear*   불평등하다 *be unequal/unfair*

비- [非]: 비무장지대 *demilitarized zone* 비경제적이다 *be uneconomical*

18.2   How to negate commands and proposals

-지 말다 is used for the negation of commands and proposals. (말다 is an irregular verb, as the following examples show.)

걱정(하지) 말아요/마.   *Don't worry.*

추월하지 마시오.   *Do not pass.*

이메일로 하지 말고 카드로 보내자.   *Let's send a card instead of an e-mail.*

담배꽁초를 함부로 버리지 맙시다!   *Let's not toss cigarette butts everywhere!*

The principal use of 말다 is to negate commands and proposals, but there are also cases where it is used to negate other verb forms.

가지 말아야겠어요.   *I think I shouldn't go.*

비 오지 말았으면 좋겠어요.   *I hope it won't rain.*

밥 먹다 말고 어디가?   *Where are you going in the middle of eating?*

가든지 말든지 마음대로 해.   *Do as you wish – go or not.*

갈까 말까 망설이는 중이에요.   *I'm vacillating over whether to go or not.*

그 가게는 가나마나야. 물건이 없어.   *No use going to that store. They don't have much stuff.*

18.3 Negative form, but positive meaning

- **-잖아(요)** 'you know'

Originally a contracted form of -지 않아, -잖아 is used to seek confirmation or agreement, not to negate. (It is pronounced with a falling or level contour.)

전화 오잖아.   *The phone is ringing, you know.*

전화 왔잖아.   *There was a phone call, you know.*

The -잖아(요) form is very assertive and can be used (with an exasperated tone) when one is highly annoyed.

참견하지 말라 그랬잖아.
  I told you to mind your own business.

먹기 싫은데 왜 자꾸 먹으래? 싫다잖아.
  Why do you keep bugging me to eat when I don't want to? I told you I don't want to.

- **-어야 되는 거 아니니** 'you know'

Frequently used, this is a way to strongly remind someone what (s)he should do or should have done. (It is pronounced with a falling or level contour.)

가야 되는 거 아니니.   *You have to go, you know.*

약속을 했으면 지켜야 될 거 아냐.   *She should keep her promise since she made it, you know.*

신경을 좀 썼어야 될 거 아니에요.   *You should have shown some concern, you know.*

- **그렇게... -을 수가 없다** 'very...'

그렇게 바싹 말랐을 수가 없어. (= 너무너무 바싹 말랐어.)
  She's way too skinny.

연기를 그렇게 잘 할 수가 없어. (= 연기를 아주 잘 해.)
  He's an incredibly good actor.

경치가 그렇게 아름다울 수가 없어요. (= 경치가 무척 아름다워요.)
  The scenery is incredibly beautiful.

- **얼마나...-는/은지 모른다** 'very...'

얼마나 많이 샀는지 몰라. (= 정말 많이 샀어.)
  I bought so much stuff.

얼마나 바빴는지 몰라요. (= 너무너무 바빴어요.)
  I was so very busy.

열이 얼마나 높은지 몰라요. (= ...굉장히 높아요.)
  She has a very high fever.

- -기 짝이 없다 'very…' (used only for negative conditions)

  미안하기 짝이 없다. (= 정말 미안하다.)
  I'm terribly sorry.

  불편하기 짝이 없네요. (= 굉장히 불편하네요.)
  It's awfully inconvenient/uncomfortable.

- **Double negation**

  As in English, two negatives can create a positive. It is useful to treat each of the following examples as a simple fixed expression.

  없는 게 없어요. (= 다 있어요.)   *They have everything.*

  비극이 아닐 수 없다. (= 비극이다.)   *It's a tragedy.*

  하지 않을 수 없다. (= 해야 된다.)   *I have to do it.*

  가지 않으면 안 돼. (= 가야 돼.)   *I have to go.*

18.4   Expressions that require negative verbs

Certain expressions can be used only if the verb is negated (or at least has a negative meaning).

다시는 너를 못 볼 줄 알았어.
I didn't think I could ever see you again.

미처 상상도 못 할 일이야.
It's beyond the stretch of my imagination.

아직(껏) 여자 친구도 없냐?
Don't you have a girlfriend yet?

이 비디오 카메라는 성능이 **별로** 안 좋은 거 같아요.
This camcorder doesn't seem to have very good performance.

요즘은 **그리/그다지** 바쁘지 않습니다.
I'm not that busy these days.

면종류를 **과히** 좋아하지 않는 편이에요.
I kind of don't like noodles that much.

드라마 결말이 어떻게 됐는지 **전혀** 몰라요.
I have zero idea as to how the drama ended.

남자친구가 먼저 사과할 기미가 **도무지** 안 보여.
I don't see the slightest inkling of my boyfriend's intention to apologize to me first.

무슨 말을 하는지 **도무지** 알아 들을 수가 있어야지.
I couldn't possibly understand what he was saying.

담배에 중독이 돼서 **도저히** 못 끊겠어.
I can't possibly quit smoking because I'm addicted to it.

시차가 바뀌어서 잠이 **좀처럼** 오질 않아요.
I can hardly sleep because of jet lag.

이 소문 퍼뜨리면 **절대** 안 된다.
You should not spread the rumor by any means.

무슨 바쁜 일이 있는 지 **영** 전화를 안 받아요.
He may be busy with something; he doesn't answer the phone at all.

호주로 유학간 그 친구한테서 **통** 소식이 없어.
There's been no news whatsoever from the friend who moved to Australia to study.

이번에 들어온 신입사원이 **여간** 똑똑한 게 아냐.
The recently hired guy in our office is extremely smart [smart beyond ordinary].

물이 안 나와서 **이만저만** 불편한 게 아니에요.
There's a water stoppage, so I can't describe just how inconvenient things are.

고통을 **이루** 다 말로 표현할 수 없다.
I can't possibly describe the pain in words.

중요한 전화 기다리느라 **꼼짝** 못 해.
I can't budge because I'm waiting for an important phone call.

부모님 은혜를 **결코** 잊어선 안 된다.
We should never forget what our parents have done for us.

일이 밀려서 **조금도** 쉴 틈이 없어요.
I don't have even a minute for a break because of the backlog of work.

그건 **한낱** 변명에 지나지 않는다.
That's nothing but an excuse.

네 자존심을 상하게 할 생각은 **추호도** 없었어.
I didn't mean to hurt your pride, not in the least.

내 말이 **채** 끝나기도 전에 전화를 끊어 버리는 거 있지.
You know what? He hung up on me before I even finished what I was saying.

미래는 **아무도** 모른다.
No one knows the future.

맥주 겨우 두 잔**밖에** 안 마셨어.
I had no more than two glasses of beer.

듣(지)도 보(지)도 못하던 이름인데요.
That's a name I neither heard of nor saw.

19 Particles

Particles (also called suffixes) are typically attached at the end of a noun or a noun phrase. Some carry information about grammar (is the noun a subject or direct object?) and others carry information about meaning, including subtle nuances that are expressed in English by means of stress, intonation, and so on.

19.1 Omission of particles

Unless they carry information that cannot be inferred from other sources, particles may be omitted. The most frequently omitted ones are -이/가, -을/를, and -의, but given the right context, it is also possible to leave out certain other particles as well.

이 책(은) 선생님(께) 갖다 드려.　　*Take this book to your teacher.*

친구(의) 동생(이) 학교(에) 갔어요.　*My friend's younger sister went to school.*

When permitted, most particle omission takes place only in colloquial speech, not in formal writing. In fact, particles should be retained in any kind of writing, since they can do the work of pauses and intonation when it comes to breaking sentences into smaller chunks.

마이클과 동규는 비자 인터뷰를 하러 대사관에 갔다. (in writing)

마이클하고 동규, 비자 인터뷰하러 대사관 갔다. (in speaking)

　Michael and Tongkyu went to the Embassy to do a visa interview.

Even in speaking, particles are best retained for the purpose of rhythmic balance and the syntactic grouping of words when the sentence is long. The short sentences in the first column sound natural without particles but if the same particles are omitted in the second column, the sentences would sound lopsided.

차 없어.	여자친구가 차**가** 없어.
I don't have a car.	*My girlfriend doesn't have a car.*
전기 나갔다.	아파트 전체에 전기**가** 나갔다.
The power went out.	*The power went out in the entire apartment complex.*
소문 벌써 퍼졌어요.	소문**이** 인터넷을 통해서 벌써 퍼졌어요.
The rumor spread already.	*The rumor spread already via the Internet.*

19.2 -이/가

The particle -이/가 is primarily used to mark a subject, but it can also mark certain non-subjects.

19.2.1 Use of -이/가 to mark subjects

Subjects marked by -이/가 can be divided into two types – those with no added meaning and those with an added meaning.

- *With no added meaning*

  -이/가 indicates a 'neutral' subject.

한국 경제가 크게 발전했다.	*The Korean economy made great progress.*
(네가) 먼저 가.	*(You) go first.*
식당(이) 잘 돼요.	*The restaurant has good business.*

  This type of subject is commonly omitted when its referent can be inferred from the context. (This is especially true when the referent is a person.) Even when the noun is retained, the particle can easily be omitted.

- *With an added meaning*

  -이/가 adds a sense of focus, newness, or exhaustive listing ('this and only this') to the subject. This type of subject CANNOT be omitted.

A: 죄송합니다.	*I'm sorry.*
B: 아닙니다. **제가** 죄송하죠.	*Not at all. I'm the one who is sorry.*
A: 어느 나라가 월드컵을 주최했죠?	*Which country hosted the World Cup?*
B: **한국과 일본이** 했어요.	*Korea and Japan did.*

The following pairs of examples illustrate the contrast between the two types of subjects. The first subject in each pair is neutral – it does not receive any phonetic focus and refers to a specific entity. In contrast, the second subject has an added meaning – it is focused (with high pitch). Moreover, when it is a common noun (rather than a name or a pronoun), it refers to a general class rather than to a single thing.

식당(이) 잘 돼요.	*The restaurant has good business.*
식당이 잘 돼요.	*Restaurants (not other things) have good business.*
자두(가) 맛있어요.	*This plum is delicious.*
자두가 맛있어요.	*Plums (not other fruit) are delicious.*

In all the examples considered so far, -이/가 can be replaced by the honorific particle -께서 when the referent of the subject is worthy of special deference (see

2.4). This is possible only when -이/가 occurs on a subject; it cannot happen when -이/가 is used to mark a non-subject, as in the next set of examples.

19.2.2 Use of -이/가 to mark non-subjects

In addition to its role as subject marker, -이/가 has several other functions. It can appear on:

- The noun that precedes 되다 and 아니다

고등학교 동창이 **원수가** 됐다.	*My high school friend has become my enemy.*
미국에 온 지 근 **20 년이** 된다.	*It's almost 20 years since I came to the U.S.*
회계사가 아니라 변호사예요.	*He's not a CPA, but an attorney.*

- The direct object of verbs such as 있다, 없다, and 필요하다

나한테 좋은 **생각이** 있어요.	*I have a good idea.*
현금이 별로 없어요.	*I don't have much cash.*
무엇보다도 **시간이** 필요하다.	*I need time more than anything.*

- The direct object of certain psychological verbs

요리 잘하는 **남자가** 좋더라.	*I find that I like men who are good cooks.*
몸매 좋은 **사람이** 부러워요.	*I envy those who have a nice figure.*
지네가 제일 무서워요.	*I'm most scared of centipedes.*
지구 **온난화가** 두렵습니다.	*I fear global warming.*
아리조나 **기념관이** 보고 싶어요.	*I'd like to see the Arizona Memorial.*

  NOTE: If these verbs are converted into action verbs by attaching -어 하다, as in 무서워하다 and 두려워하다, the particle has to change to -을/를 (지네를 무서워한다; see section *15.1.2*.)

- Focused possessors

동생이 집이 더 크다.	*The younger brother's house is bigger.*
엄마가 머리가 아프세요.	*My mom's head hurts.*

- Emphatic negation

별로 나가고 **싶지가** 않어.	*I don't really want to go out.*
시계가 **정확하지가** 않다.	*The watch is not accurate.*

Use of -이 as a name particle

The particle -이 is added to a Korean first name that ends in a consonant, usually when the person being referred to is a child or a close friend/sibling of a similar age or younger.

미선이가 석훈이를 만나러 왔어.
   Miseon came to see Seokhoon.

영미하고 소영이하고 싸웠대.
   I heard that Youngmee and Soyoung had a fight.

A: 이거 진석이 모자예요?
B: 아니, 기철이거야.
   A: Is this Jinseok's hat?
   B: No, it's Kichul's.

A: 선영이가 현진씨한테 청혼했다며?
B: 아니야. 현진씨가 선영이한테 청혼을 했지.
   A: I heard that Sunyoung proposed to Hyunjin, is that true?
   B: No, that's not true. It was Hyunjin who proposed to Sunyoung.

NOTE: The name particle is attached only to Korean names, not to foreign names: 마이클이 윌리엄을 만나러 왔어. 'Michael came to see William.' (The -이 in '마이클이' is a subject particle.)

19.3 -은/는

The particle -은/는 is known to be difficult for English speakers, and perfect mastery cannot be achieved in a short period of time. However, the following information should be helpful in understanding its fundamentals.

   Put simply, -은/는 has two basic uses:

- Marking a topic that appears at the beginning of the sentence and that indicates what the sentence is about.

- Marking an element that is to be contrasted with other elements.

When used on a word that is not at the beginning of the sentence, -은/는 is always contrastive, as in 영희가 얼굴은 예쁘다. When it appears on an element at the beginning of a sentence, it can mark a topic or it may signal a contrast – sometimes both, depending on the context and the content of the sentence. The following interpretations are based on the most likely scenario.

오늘은 정기 휴일입니다.   *Today is a regular holiday.* (topic)
오늘은 바빠서 안 돼요.   *TODAY is not possible because I'm busy.* (contrast)

얼굴은 동그래요.	*Her face is round.* (topic or contrast)
얼굴은 예쁘다.	*Her FACE is pretty.* (contrast)
돈은 중요하죠.	*Money is important, of course.* (topic)
돈은 있어요.	*MONEY, I have.* (contrast)

The element marked by -은/는 often corresponds to the subject of the sentence, but sometimes it occurs in addition to a subject as in:

| 한국은 가을이 아름답다. | *In Korea, autumn is beautiful.* |
| 산은 설악산이 최고예요. | *As for the mountains, Sŏrak Mt. is the best.* |

19.3.1 Uses of -은/는 when it marks a topic

- To set the stage for the rest of the sentence, by indicating what it is to be about

이 케익은 직접 만드셨어요?	*This cake, did you make it yourself?*
윤호는 오늘 넥타이를 맸어.	*As for Yunho, he was wearing a tie today.*
여름에는 냉면이면 그만이다.	*In summer, naengmyŏn is all you need.*
붙고 떨어지고는 운에 달렸다.	*Passing or failing the exam depends on luck.*

- To express old information (either known to both the speaker and the listener, or part of the shared background)

| A: 떡은 누가 먹었어? | *The rice cake, who ate it?* |
| B: 떡이 있었어? 나는 못 봤는데. | *Was there a rice cake? I didn't see it.* |

| A: 스타워즈는 정말 대작이야. | Star Wars *is really a masterpiece.* |
| B: 스타워즈가 어떤 영화인데? | *What kind of movie is* Star Wars? |

  NOTE: 'Rice cake' and 'Star Wars' are NEW information to B and therefore don't appear with -은/는 in his utterances.

| 차는 어떤 걸로 사실 생각이세요? | *As for the car, what kind are you planning to buy?* |

- To define or make a broad statement

사람은 이성적 동물이다.	*Men are rational animals.*
하와이는 지상낙원이다.	*Hawaii is paradise on earth.*
한국은 삼면이 바다로 둘러싸인 반도다.	*Korea is a peninsula surrounded by the ocean on three sides.*

- To change the topic

  음식이 어때? 값은? 식당 분위기는?
  How's the food? How about the price? What about the ambience of the restaurant?

19.3.2   Uses of -은/는 when it marks a contrast

-은/는 is used to highlight points of contrast. Notice that the two elements marked by -은/는 are being contrasted in the following sentences.

오늘은 수업에 가지만 내일은 못 갈 것 같다.
> *I'm going to class TODAY, but I don't think I'll be able to TOMORROW.*

외제차는 비싸지만 국산차는 비싸지 않아요.
> *IMPORTED CARS are expensive, but the KOREAN-MADE ones are not.*

꽃은 샀지만 케익은 내가 구웠어.
> *I bought the FLOWERS, but I baked the CAKE.*

Sometimes, the elements being contrasted do not appear in the same sentence.

A: 백합 열 송이만 주세요.
B: 백합은 없는데요. (다른 꽃들은 있지만…)
> *A: Please give me ten lilies.*
> *B: LILIES, I don't have any. (Although I have other flowers…)*

A: 한국어가 어려워요?
B: 어렵지는 않아요. (그렇지만 공부할 게 너무 많아요.)
> *A: Is Korean difficult?*
> *B: It's not DIFFICULT. (But there's a lot to study.)*

In English, this type of information is usually expressed with the help of dramatic intonation, but in Korean the particle -은/는 is powerful enough to do the job itself (although it is often accompanied by high pitch).

Contrastive -은/는 can occur (often contracted) in many different positions in the sentence.

조금은 이해할 수 있어.	*I can understand A LITTLE.*
제 생각엔,…	*In MY opinion,…*
남편감으론 별로야.	*He's not great as a HUSBAND.*
요새 같아선…	*If it's like THESE days…*
먹어선 안 된다.	*You must not EAT this.*
깨끗은 해.	*It's CLEAN (but…).*
도와는 줄게.	*I'll HELP you (but…).*
좋긴 좋다.	*As for quality, it's GOOD.*
운동을 날마다 하기는 어렵다.	*Exercising EVERY DAY is tough.*
전적으로 나쁘다고는 할 수 없다.	*We can't say that it's TOTALLY bad.*

It is sometimes unclear whether a sentence-initial -은/는 marks a topic or a contrast. Depending on which element is focused, a sentence such as 공부는 성아가 잘한다 can have different interpretations:

공부는 **성아가** 잘 한다. (공부 is a topic. The sentence is about study in general; 성아, not other people, is good academically.)

공부는 성아가 잘 한다. (공부 is contrastive. 성아 is good academically, but not at some other things.)

If the noun marked by -은/는 is not at the beginning of the sentence, however, it can only have one interpretation:

성아가 **공부는** 잘한다. (공부 is contrastive: 성아 is good academically, but not at some other things.)

There is a big difference in meaning and nuance between a noun marked by -은/는 and one marked by -이/가.

얼굴은 예쁘다.   *She has a pretty FACE (but a lousy personality, bad figure, poor brain, or something else that is bad).*

얼굴이 예쁘다.   *She has a pretty face.*

The following table provides a summary of different uses of -이/가 and -은/는 with respect to the subtle cue of phonetic focus.

The different uses of -이/가 and -은/는 with respect to phonetic focus:		
	Unfocused (low pitch)	*Focused (high pitch)*
-이/가	neutral subject	exclusive ('this and only this')
-은/는	topic	contrast

19.4 -을/를

The prototypical function of -을/를 is to mark a direct object, but it can also be used in a variety of other ways.

19.4.1 Use of -을/를 to mark direct objects

The particle -을/를 is primarily used to mark a direct object whose referent is the 'undergoer' of the action denoted by the verb.

책을 주문했어요.   *I ordered the book.*

Often, a noun that functions as a direct object in Korean occurs with a preposition in English.

대학을 졸업했다.   *He graduated **from** college.*

친구를 기다리고 있습니다.   *I am waiting **for** my friend.*

새 차 사는 것을 포기했어요.   *I gave up **on** buying a new car.*

19.4.2 Use of -을/를 to mark non-direct objects

In addition to its role as direct object marker, -을/를 can be used to mark:

- A destination (instead of 에)

  외국을 자주 나간다.   *They often go abroad.*

  할머니는 작은집을 가셨어요.   *Grandmother went to uncle's place.*

- Purpose of a movement

  남해안으로 여행을 떠났어요.   *She left for a trip to the south coast.*

  영화구경을 갈까?   *Shall we go for a movie?*

- The noun that describes a property of a direct object (instead of -로)

  차를 외제를 샀어.   *I bought a car, a foreign-made one.*

  구두를 높은 걸 샀어.   *She bought the shoes, ones with high heels.*

- The indirect object of certain verbs for added exclusiveness (instead of -에게/한테/께)

  책을 그 친구를 주었어.   *I gave the friend the book.*

  돈을 할아버지를 드렸어요.   *I gave Grandfather the money.*

- Duration of an action or state

  근 일주일을 아팠어요.   *I was sick for almost one week.*

  두 시간(동안)을 걸었다.   *I walked for two hours.*

- Quantity

  친구가 너 만나러 세번을 왔었다.   *Your friend came to see you three times.*

  오늘 커피 세 잔을 마셨어요.   *I drank three cups of coffee today.*

  한 시간에 90 마일을 달렸어.   *We drove 90 miles in one hour.*

- Emphatic negation

  다리가 움직이질 않아.   *My legs won't move.*

  아이가 통 말을 듣질 않는다.   *The child doesn't listen at all.*

  NOTE: -질 is a contracted form of 지를. Contraction is normally reserved for casual speech (see ch. **8**) and not for writing, but it is used here because emphatic negation is typically very colloquial.

19.4.3 Some fixed patterns involving -을/를

The following bold-faced patterns, which are usually employed for formal and written language, are fixed expressions that include -을/를.

오늘 자정**을 기해서** 새 법이 효력을 발휘한다.
  As of midnight tonight, the new law goes into effect.

동서양을 **막론하고** 부모의 자식에 대한 사랑은 한이 없다.
Whether it's the East or the West, parents' love for their children is endless.

이기고 지고를 **떠나서** 경기를 마음껏 즐깁시다.
Aside from who wins and who loses, let's enjoy the game to the fullest.

한라산을 **비롯해서** 제주도 곳곳을 여행했다.
We visited every site on Jeju Island, including Halla Mountain.

이번 시합의 우승을 **위해서** 일 년간 열심히 준비했습니다.
In order to win this game, we practiced hard for the entire year.

탐험대가 북극을 **향해서** 출발했습니다.
The expedition began its voyage toward the Arctic.

19.5 -도

-도 helps express emphasis as well as the meaning of 'also,' 'even,' and 'indeed.' It cannot co-occur with -이/가 or -을/를, but it does occur in combination with other particles. Here is a summary of its basic uses.

- 'Also'

그 영화도 봤다.	*I saw the movie too.*
그 음식점에도 가 봤어요.	*I've been to that restaurant also.*

- 'Even'

밥은 커녕 물도 못 먹었어요.	*I didn't even have water, let alone a meal.*
꿈에도 몰랐어요.	*I didn't know, not even in my wildest dreams.*
벼룩이도 낯이 있지.	He's so shameless. [Even a flea has a shame.]
얼마 먹지도 못했어요.	*I didn't even eat much.*
네 말은 이제 콩으로 메주를 쑨대도 안 믿는다.	*I don't believe what you say any more* [even if you say you make soybean paste out of soy].

- 'Indeed'

너는 참 샘도 많다.	*You are very jealous indeed.*
해수욕장에 사람도 많더라.	*There were indeed lots of people at the beach.*
많이도 먹는다.	*You really do eat a lot.*
불행하게도 여행 중 사고를 당했습니다.	*Unfortunately, an accident happened during their trip.*

- 'Not only ~ but also'; 'neither ~ nor'

놀기도 잘 놀고 공부도 열심히 해요.
Not only does she play hard, she also studies hard.

쥐도 새도 모르게 처리하도록 하세요.
  Take care of it secretly [so not even the mice or the birds know about it].

춥지도 덥지도 않고 딱 좋습니다.
  It's just right, not too cold or too hot.

19.6 -의

The particle -의 links two nouns, the first of which often denotes a possessor, as in 남편의 직장동료 'husband's colleague.' It can also be used when no possession is involved, as in 연상의 여인 'older woman (as a romantic partner).' In most cases, -의 is omitted within compound nouns, even in formal writing, as in 한국문화 'Korean culture,' 해외토픽 'newsy topics from abroad,' and 물건 가격 'prices of things.'

However, there are cases where -의 must be retained at all times.

- In fixed formal expressions

  천고마비의 계절   *the season of high sky and fat horses (autumn)*
  성공의 비결   *secrets of success*
  표현의 자유   *freedom of speech*
  불변의 진리   *unchangeable truth*

- In fixed expressions of other types

  스승의 날 (5 월 15 일)   *Teachers' Day* (May 15th)
  선물의 집   *gift store*
  사랑의 기쁨   *joy of love*
  연하의 남자   *younger man (as a romantic partner)*
  남의 집, 남의 눈, etc.   *other's house, other's eyes (attention), etc.*
  반의 반   *a quarter portion*

- Following another particle

  둘만의 약속   *promise between just the two of us*
  자식으로서의 도리   *one's duty to one's parents*
  하와이에서의 추억   *memory of our time in Hawaii*
  한국으로부터의 소식   *news from Korea*

- When followed by coordination involving -와/과

  너와 나의 차이점   *the difference between you and me*
  존과 메리의 책   *John and Mary's book*

19.7 -에

-에 is one of the most frequently used particles in Korean. It has multiple meanings and uses, usually centered around the expression of location in space or time.

19.7.1 Uses of -에 involving space

- Location where someone/something exists

  학교 근처에 살아요.   *I live in the vicinity of school.*

  얼굴에 뭐가 묻었어.   *You have something on your face.*

  양복을 옷걸이에 걸어 두세요.   *Leave the suit hanging on a hanger.*

  답안지에 이름을 쓰세요.   *Put your name down on the answer sheet.*

- Destination

  학교에 갔다.   *She went to school.*

  친구들을 생일 파티에 초대했어.   *I invited friends to my birthday party.*

  동창들이 모두 학교에 모였다.   *All of the alumni gathered at school.*

  개도 우리 그룹에 포함시키자.   *Let's have him join our group.*

  NOTE: 뛰다 and 걷다, which are simple manner of motion verbs, call for -까지 where -에 might otherwise be expected. 학교까지 뛰었다/걸었다 (학교에 뛰었다/걸었다 is unacceptable).

- Inanimate recipient

  화초에 물을 주었다.   *I gave water to the plant.*

  학교에 등록금을 냈다.   *I paid tuition to the school.*

  은행에 돈을 맡겼어요.   *I entrusted money to a bank.*

  NOTE: For animate recipients, -에게/한테 should be used instead of -에 (see **19.9**).

-에 and -에다(가)

For emphasis in colloquial speech, -에 can sometimes be followed by -다(가) when marking a recipient.

차에다 갖다 놓자.   *Let's take it to the car.*

팔에다 문신을 새겼어요.   *He got a tattoo on his arm.*

손에다 발라 봐.   *Try it (the cream) on your hand.*

종이컵에다 마시자.   *Let's drink it in a paper cup.*

전자렌지에다 데워 먹자.   *Let's warm it up in the microwave before eating it.*

냉장고에다 붙여 놓으세요.   *Stick it on your refrigerator.*

- Abstract point

추위에 어떻게 지내세요?	*How are you doing in this cold weather?*
이제 유학 생활에 익숙해졌어.	*I've got used to the life of studying abroad.*
성공은 노력여하에 달려있다.	*Success depends on your efforts.*
테니스에 관심이 많다.	*She has a lot of interest in tennis.*
공부에 전념하고 싶습니다.	*I'd like to concentrate on studying.*
사업에 실패했어요.	*He failed in his enterprise.*
지역사회 발전에 공헌이 컸습니다.	*They contributed to the development of our local community.*
퇴근시간에 맞춰서 회사로 갈게.	*I'll go to your office just as you get off work.*

- Addition/enumeration

과로에 영양실조래요.
I was told that I have malnutrition on top of exhaustion from overwork.

전기료에다 전화비를 합하면 백 불이 넘는다.
It's over $100 if you add the phone bill to the electricity bill.

복더위에 후덥지근한 장마까지 겹쳐서 사람들의 불쾌지수가 높다.
People are highly irritable because of the muggy rainy spell on top of the dog-day heat.

19.7.2 Uses of -에 involving time, cause/means, and per/for

- Time and/or age

새벽에 잠이 깼어.	*I got woken up very early in the morning.*
내일 저녁 일곱 시 반에 만나자.	*Let's meet at 7:30 p.m. tomorrow.*
칠십에 돌아가셨어요.	*She died at the age of 70.*

- Cause/means

더위에 지쳤어.	*I got worn out by the heat.*
바퀴벌레에 질렸어요.	*I'm fed up with cockroaches.*
못에 찔렸어요.	*I got poked by a nail.*
바람에 모자가 날라갔다.	*The hat got blown away by the wind.*
천둥소리에 깜짝 놀랐다.	*I got startled by the sound of thunder.*
술에 취했다.	*She got drunk from the alcohol.*
거짓말에 속아 넘어갈 뻔했어.	*I almost got fooled by the lie.*
차가 돌에 맞았다.	*My car got hit by a stone.*
누군가의 발에 밟혔어요.	*I got stepped on by someone's foot.*

옷이 땀에 젖었다.	*The clothes got soaked with sweat.*
모기에 (or 모기한테) 물렸어요.	*I got bitten by a mosquito.*

- Per/for

시계가 하루에 일 분씩 더 간다.	*This watch is fast by one minute per day.*
버스가 몇 분에 한 대씩 있습니까?	*How often [per how many minutes] does the bus run?*
애인을 일주일에 두 번 정도 만나.	*I meet my boyfriend about twice a week.*
대구가 세 마리에 만원이에요.	*The codfish is ₩10,000 for three.*
아파트가 3 억에 팔렸다.	*The condo sold for ₩300,000,000.*
숙면이 건강에 최고예요.	*Good sleep is the best thing for one's health.*
친절에 감사드립니다.	*I'd like to thank you for your kindness.*
그 아버지에 그 아들이다.	*Like father, like son.*

19.7.3 *Some fixed patterns involving -*에

정치에 **대해서**는 문외한입니다.
   With regard to politics, I'm a lay person.

그 일에 **관해** 아는 바가 없습니다.
   I know nothing about that matter.

외국어에 **관한 한** 자신있습니다.
   I'm confident as far as foreign languages are concerned.

경우에 **따라** 다르겠죠.
   It will depend on the situation.

최근 연구에 **따르면** 적당한 양의 카페인이 몸에 좋다고 합니다.
   According to a recent study, a moderate amount of caffeine is good for our health.

예년에 **비하면** 날씨가 별로 안 더운 편이야.
   Compared to previous years, the weather is kind of not that hot.

일기예보에 **의하면** 주말에 태풍이 온대요.
   According to the weather forecast, a typhoon will arrive during the weekend.

일시적 현상에 **불과하다**.
   It's no more than a temporary phenomenon.

그것은 헛소문에 **지나지 않는다**.
   That's nothing but a false rumor.

외국생활에 **있어서** 외로움을 이기는 방법을 터득하는 것이 필요하다.
   When it comes to living in foreign countries, it's necessary to learn how to overcome loneliness.

> Verbs that require -에 in Korean, but take a plain direct object in English:
> 수영복이 몸에 꼭 맞는다.   *The swimsuit **fits the body** perfectly.*
> 이 곳 음식이 **입맛에 맞는다**.   *The food here **suits my taste**.*
> **질문에 대답해**.   ***Answer the question**.*
> 조심스럽게 **배에 접근했다**.   *We **approached the boat** cautiously.*
> 내년에 **대학에 입학한다**.   *I **enter college** next year.*

19.8 -에서

The primary uses of -에서 are to indicate a starting point (concrete or abstract) and to mark the location of an activity.

- Starting points (concrete)

  한국에서 편지가 왔어.   *A letter came from Korea.*

  우리 집은 끝에서 두 번째 집이야.   *Our house is the second one from the end.*

  매일 30 분에서 한 시간 정도   *Make sure that you exercise from 30 minutes*
  운동하도록 하세요.   *to one hour every day.*

- Starting points (abstract)

  그 기사를 신문에서 읽었어요.   *I read the article in the newspaper.*

  비용은 회사에서 부담한다.   *The company bears the expense.*

  독창성은 진정한 호기심에서   *Originality starts from true curiosity.*
  비롯됩니다.

  교육적 관점에서 좋지 않다.   *It's no good from an educational point*
                                        of view.

- Location of an activity

  학교 앞 시계탑에서 기다릴게.   *I'll wait at the clock tower in front of school.*

  공원에서 시간을 좀 때웠어.   *I managed to kill some time in the park.*

  거실 소파에서 잠이 들었어요.   *I fell asleep on the sofa in the living room.*

> **-에 versus -에서 for location**
>
> -에 is used to indicate a location where someone/something exists or where an action ends up, while -에서 is used to represent a location where an activity actually takes place. (By 'activity,' we mean 'doing something,' including even sleeping. Whatever the activity involves, it must take place INSIDE the location.)
>
> | | |
> |---|---|
> | 자리에 앉으세요. | *Please be seated.* |
> | 자리에서 떠들지 마세요. | *Don't make noise while seated.* |
> | 밖에 비가 온다. | *It's raining outside.* |
> | 밖에서 만날까요? | *Shall we meet outside?* |
>
> In some cases, both -에 and -에서 are allowed with a negligible difference in meaning.
>
> | | |
> |---|---|
> | 미국에/미국에서 살아요. | *I live in America.* |
> | 호텔에/호텔에서 묵었어요. | *We put up at a hotel.* |
> | 학교에/학교에서 모였다. | *We gathered at school.* |
> | 학교 앞에/앞에서 세워 주세요. | *Please drop me off in front of school.* |

19.9 -에게(서)/한테(서)

-에게(서) is usually used in written/formal language, whereas -한테(서) is colloquial.

19.9.1 -에게/한테

The basic function of these particles is to indicate 'to someone,' as in 나한테 왔다 'She came TO ME.' They contrast with -에, which is used for 'to a place,' as in 학교에 왔다 'She came TO SCHOOL.'

- Animate recipients (-께 is used for honorific recipients.)

시민들에게 광고지를 나눠 주었다.	*They distributed flyers to the citizens.*
강아지한테 장난감을 주었다.	*I gave a toy to the puppy.*
남한테 책임을 돌리지 마.	*Don't shift responsibility to others.*
어른들께 안부 전해 주세요.	*Please give my regards to your parents.*
너한테 미쳤어, 홀딱 반했어.	*He's crazy about you, totally smitten.*
그 책 저한테 있어요.	*The book is with me. (I have the book.)*
그 사람한테 필요한 건 시간이야.	*What's necessary for him is time.*
남에게 뒤떨어지고 싶지 않아요.	*I don't want to fall behind others.*

> -에게 vs. -한테 vs. -께 vs. -더러/보고 for an animate recipient
> At the beginning of a letter, only -에게 and -께 are used:
>   영채에게   *Dear Youngchae*
>   김교수님께 *Dear Professor Kim*
> -더러/보고 is used only for 'telling' verbs (usually in colloquial quoted speech)
> for an intended recipient of the message:
>   영진이보고 나한테 전화 좀 하라고 전해 줄래요?
>   *Would you tell Yongjin to call me?*
>   엄마더러 직접 오시라고 해.
>   *Tell your Mom to come herself.*

- Animate agent 'by (someone)'
  너한테 완전히 속았다.   *I've been completely duped by you.*
  독사한테 물렸어요.   *I got bitten by a poisonous snake.*
  일반인에게 많이 읽히는 책입니다. *It's a popular book among the general public.*

19.9.2 -에게(서)/한테(서)

Addition of -서 to -에게/한테 'to someone' changes its meaning to 'from someone.' The -서 is optional, however, and the interpretation ('to someone' or 'from someone') is usually determined by the context. Recall that -에서 is used for 'from (a place)'; see **19.8**.

- 'From (someone)'
  도서관에서 빌린 게 아니라 친구한테(서) 빌렸어.
    I borrowed it from a friend, not from the library.
  시댁에서 막 나오는데 남편한테(서) 전화가 왔어요.
    *As I was just coming out from my in-laws' place,
    a phone call came from my husband.*
  전문가에게 조언을 구하도록 합시다.
    Let's get some advice from an expert.

19.10 -(으)로

The two most basic uses of -(으)로 are to indicate a direction (왼쪽으로 'toward the left') and a means or instrument (차로 'by means of car'). However, it has multiple other more or less related meanings and uses.

19.10.1 -(으)로 *involving direction, change, and choice*

- Direction

  밖으로 나갈까?   *Shall we go outside?*

  어디로 옮겨요?   *Where are you moving it to?*

  NOTE: In the examples below, -(으)로 is appropriate but -에 is not, because the
  precise destination point is not clear. (See *19.7.1* for the use of -에 to mark a
  destination.)

  오른쪽으로 가세요. (ok)   오른쪽에 가세요. (not acceptable)

  아파트로 이사갔다. (ok)   아파트에 이사갔다. (not acceptable)

- Change

  이 거 백 원짜리로 좀 바꿔 주시겠어요?
    Can you change this into ₩100 coins?

  논문을 영어로 번역하고 있어요.
    I'm translating my dissertation into English.

  두 달만에 몸무게를 70 킬로로 줄였다.
    I reduced my weight to 70 kg in two months.

  차를 새 거로 바꿨어요.
    I replaced my car with a new one.

- Choice

  어느 예식장으로 정할까?   *Which wedding hall shall we decide on?*

  아침은 빵으로 때우자.   *Let's just take care of breakfast with bread.*

  같은 걸로 두 개 주세요.   *Give me two of the same.*

  일회용으로 사자.   *Let's buy a disposable one.*

  없던 일로 하지요.   *Let's forget that it happened.*

  다음주 토요일로 정할까요?   *Shall we make it next Saturday?*

  담배를 끊기로 했습니다.   *I decided to quit smoking.*

  성인 100 명을 대상으로 설문   *We carried out a survey, targeting*
    조사를 실시했다.   *100 adults.*

- 'As (someone)'

  선교사로 한국에 5 년간 있었다.   *I was in Korea for five years as a missionary.*

  식당에서 종업원으로 일합니다.   *I work as a waiter in a restaurant.*

  회장으로 1 년을 지냈습니다.   *I spent a year as president.*

  그 사람이 사윗감으로 적격이야.   *He is perfect son-in-law material.*

  너 나를 뭘로 보는 거야?   *Who do you take me for?*

19.10.2   Uses of -(으)로 involving means, cause, time, and manner

- Means/instrument ('by means of; with')

차로 갈까, 비행기로 갈까?	*Shall we go by car or by airplane?*
젓가락으로 먹는 게 더 편해요.	*It's easier to eat with chopsticks.*
카드로 지불해도 되겠습니까?	*Will it be okay if I pay with my credit card?*
두부는 콩으로 만든다.	*Tofu is made with beans.*
극장이 학생들로 붐비네요.	*The theater is crowded with students.*
한국말로 여러분의 생각을 자주 표현하세요.	*Try to express your thoughts in Korean frequently.*
우리 대화로 오해를 풀어 보자.	*Let's try to solve our misunderstanding by communicating.*
70 마일로 가다가 걸렸어.	*I got caught driving at 70 miles an hour.*
어느 길로 오셨어요?	*Which road did you take to get here?*
우리 팀이 3 대 1 로 이겼어.	*Our team won by 3 to 1.*

- Cause/source

과로로 쓰러졌대.	*I hear that she passed out from exhaustion.*
직장암으로 돌아가셨어요.	*He died of colon cancer.*
도박으로 망했다.	*He went bankrupt from gambling.*
집안일 핑계로 모임에 안 나갔어.	*With the excuse of a family matter, I didn't go to the meeting.*
사고 소식으로 온 식구가 슬픔에 잠겼다.	*Everyone in the family was overwhelmed with sadness by the news of the accident.*

- Time

한국어 실력이 날로 늘고 있어요.	*Your Korean is improving day by day.*
환율이 시시각각으로 변합니다.	*The exchange rate changes every second.*
아침저녁으로 제법 선선해요.	*It's quite chilly in the mornings and the evenings.*

- Manner

양가 부모님께 정식으로 인사드렸어요?
  Have you formally introduced one another to each of your parents?

강제로 선을 보게 하는 법이 어디 있어요?
  How can you force me to go on a blind date for an arranged marriage?

즐거운 마음으로 일합시다.
  Let's work with a happy attitude.

19.10.3 Some fixed patterns involving -(으)로

언니로서 동생에게 한마디 하겠는데...
  Let me tell you one thing as your older sister...

태풍으로 인해 인명피해가 많았습니다. [written/formal]
  There was a great loss of life due to the typhoon.

사고로 말미암아 앞을 못 보게 되었다. [written/formal]
  He became blind because of the accident.

자주 바뀌는 정책은 국민들로 하여금 불만을 토로하게 만들었다.
  Frequent changes in public policy made people complain. [written/formal]

한국 갔다 올 때 하와이로 해서 왔어요.
  I came back from Korea by way of Hawaii.

말씨로 봐서 성격이 차분한 것 같아요.
  Judging from her way of speaking, she seems to have a calm personality.

생긴 거로 보나 실력으로 보나 그 사람이 최고야.
  Based on either his looks or his ability, he is the best.

19.11 -와/과, -하고, and -(이)랑

The two most basic functions of these forms are to coordinate nouns and to express accompaniment. -와/과 is usually used in written/formal language, while -하고 and -(이)랑 are used more colloquially. (The contrast between -와/과 and -하고 parallels that between -에게 and -한테.) -(이)랑 has a more spoken flavor.

19.11.1 'And' type coordination

외국인이 좋아하는 한국의 대표적 음식은 갈비와 빈대떡입니다.
  Foreigners' favorite Korean foods include Kalbi and Pindaettŏk (Korean pancakes).

죄와 벌은 책으로 읽었는데 전쟁과 평화는 영화로 봤어요. (-와/과 only)
  As for Crime and Punishment, *I read the book, but as for* War and Peace, *I saw the movie.*

시댁 어른들하고 친정 부모님이 오셨어요.
  My husband's family and my parents came over.

빵이랑 과자랑 마실 거랑 잔뜩 샀어.
  I bought tons of stuff, including bread, cookies, and beverages.

좋기도하고 섭섭하기도하고 그래요.
  I have mixed feelings – glad on the one hand and sad on the other.

NOTE₁: Nouns can also be conjoined by 및 in formal writing or very formal speech, except when they refer to a person – 상품 교환 및 환불 가능 'Merchandise can be exchanged or refunded,' or 섭취방법 및 주의사항 'Directions for use and warnings.'

NOTE₂: 그리고, which is employed primarily to combine sentences, can also be used to combine nouns (짜장 하나, 짬뽕 둘, 그리고 탕수육 하나 주세요. 'One tchajang, two tchamppongs, and one sweet-and-sour pork, please.').

19.11.2 Accompaniment

The meaning of accompaniment that is expressed by -와(과)/하고/이랑 does not always translate as 'with' in English – it is sometimes equivalent to 'to,' 'from,' or even nothing at all.

- 'With' in English

상대방 대표와 악수를 나눴습니다.	*He shook hands with the representative of the other party.*
동료들과 협력해서 이벤트를 성공적으로 마쳤다.	*I finished the event successfully, cooperating with my colleagues.*
친구들과 이별하게 돼서 슬프다.	*I feel sad having to part with friends.*
저하고 아주 가까운 사이에요.	*He's on very close terms with me.*
남자 친구하고 헤어졌어요.	*I broke up with my boyfriend.*
친구하고 교대로 운전할 거예요.	*I'll take turns driving with a friend.*
우리 차가 앞차하고 부딪쳤어요.	*Our car collided with the car in front of us.*
면접 날짜가 친구 결혼식하고 겹쳤어.	*My interview date overlaps with my friend's wedding.*
내 친구는 연예인이랑 사귄다.	*My friend goes out with an entertainer.*
친구랑 한 시간 동안 통화했어.	*I talked one hour on the phone with a friend.*
나도 너랑 같은 생각이야.	*I agree with you.*

- 'To' in English

언니하고 아주 친해요.	*I'm very close to my sister.*
아빠하고 어쩜 저렇게 비슷하니?	*Isn't he so similar to Dad?*

- 'From' in English

남편하고 이혼했어요.	*I got divorced from my husband.*
생각한 거하고 전혀 다르네요.	*It's totally different from what I thought.*

- 'Into' in English

퇴근하는 길에 개하고 마주쳤어.	*I ran into him on my way home from work.*

- No preposition in English

정신과 의사와 상담해 보세요.	*Try to consult a psychiatrist.*
오빠와 결혼할 사람이에요.	*She's someone who'll marry my brother.*
순이하고 영희하고 많이 닮았다.	*Suni and Younghee look very much alike.*

-에(게)/한테 (one-way relationship) **vs. -와/과/하고/이랑** (reciprocal relationship)

남편한테 전화했어요.	*I phoned (or made a call to) my husband.*
남편하고 전화했어요.	*My husband and I talked on the phone.*
엄마한테 연락했어요.	*I contacted Mom.*
엄마하고 연락했어요.	*Mom and I were in touch.*
저를 형에게 비교하지 마세요.	*Don't compare me to brother.*
저를 형과 비교하지 마세요.	*Don't compare me and brother.*
구두가 치마에 잘 어울린다.	*The shoes look good for the skirt.*
구두가 치마랑 잘 어울린다.	*The shoes and the skirt go well (together).*

19.11.3   *Some fixed patterns involving -와/과*

In the following patterns, which are mostly found in formal language, -와/과 is usually appropriate. (The last two allow -와/과 only.)

모든 사람**과 더불어** 화평하게 지냅시다.
  Let's get along harmoniously and peacefully with everyone.

이것은 진품**과 다름이 없습니다.**
  This is exactly the same as the original (the genuine article).

지난 번 경우**와 마찬가지로** 우리 팀이 역전승을 거뒀다.
  Our team came from behind to win the game, just like in our last match.

우리의 계획**과 반대로** 일이 진행됐어요.
  The project went contrary to how we planned it.

어린아이**와 같이** 마음이 순수하다.
  She has a childlike innocence.

결혼**과 동시에** 직장을 그만두었습니다.
  I quit my job at the same time that I got married.

19.12   -만, -뿐, and -밖에

19.12.1   *-만 'only; just'*

100 불만 깎아 주세요.	*Can you give me just a $100 discount?*
그 친구는 명품만 좋아해요.	*She likes only brand-name products.*
빨리만 한다고 좋은 게 아냐.	*Being just fast is not necessarily good.*
일은 안 하고 먹기만 해.	*He only eats, without working.*
좋기만 하다.	*It looks just fine to me. (Who says it's not?)*

NOTE: -만 has two other uses. With time expressions, it indicates 'after an interval of' (오랜만이에요 'It's been a long time,' 십 년 만에 왔어요 'I came back after 10 years of being away'). At the end of a sentence, -만 does the job of conjunctive 'but' (주제넘습니다만, 제 생각에 그 방법은 옳지 않은 것 같습니다 'I may be out of line, but that plan doesn't sound right to me').

19.12.2 -뿐 *'only; just'*

뿐 is usually used in the following patterns.

남은 게 이것뿐이에요?
  Is this all that's left?

바쁜 사람은 비단 너뿐(만)이 아니야.
  You're not the only busy person.

소설뿐(만) 아니라 시도 씁니다.
  She writes poems as well, not just novels.

이 제품은 가격이 저렴할뿐더러 성능도 우수합니다.
  This product has high performance as well as a low price.

이삿짐을 옮기기만 했을뿐 정리는 아직 안 했어.
  I only moved my things (furniture, etc.), but haven't put them in order yet.

커피를 좋아한다뿐입니까? 없으면 못 살아요.
  It's not just that she likes coffee. She can't live without it.

19.12.3 -밖에 *'(nothing) but'*

-밖에 must be used with an accompanying negative. There is usually an expectation of some kind that is not satisfied in the eyes of the speaker or with respect to general standards.

맥주 한 잔밖에 못 마셔요.	*I can't drink more than one glass of beer.*
포기하는 수밖에 없겠어요.	*There'll be no choice but to give up.*
초저녁이야. 일곱 시밖에 안 됐어.	*The night is still young. It's only 7:00 p.m.*
일밖에 모르는 사람이야.	*She cares about nothing but her work.*
너무 이기적이다. 저밖에 몰라.	*He's so selfish. He cares only about himself.*

-만 vs. -밖에

Other than the fact that -밖에 must be followed by a negative expression, the difference in meaning between the two is not always clearcut. -만 is usually appropriate when the choice is made 'willingly,' while -밖에 is more appropriate when the choice is made unwillingly or reluctantly.

건강 생각해서 그냥 한 잔만 마셨어.
   I had only one drink being mindful of my health.
술이 모자라서 한 잔밖에 못 마셨어.
   I had only one drink because there was not enough liquor.
만 원만 쓰고 나머지는 저금하려고요.
   I'm going to spend just ₩10,000 and put the rest into my savings.
만 원밖에 안 썼는데 돈이 벌써 다 떨어졌어요.
   I spent just ₩10,000 but I'm already out of money.

In other cases as well, they are often not interchangeable.

Use only -밖에, not -만: 'all I have; all that's left; all I can; and so on'

돈이 천 원밖에 없어. *I only have ₩1,000 (no more).*
사과 한 개밖에 안 남았다. *We only have one apple (no more).*
한 잔밖에 못 마십니다. *I can have only one drink (no more).*

Use only -만, not -밖에: in commands or proposals.

안주만 먹지 말고 술도 좀 들어요.
   Don't just eat the side dishes; have some drinks.
운전해야 되니까 한 병만 시키자.
   Let's order just one bottle because we have to drive.

19.13 -부터

- Starting from; beginning with

기초부터 확실히 다지세요.	*Be sure to get a firm grasp of basics first.*
뭐 마실 거부터 시키자.	*Let's order something to drink first.*
어려서부터 물을 두려워했어요.	*I've been afraid of water since I was little.*

다음 달부터 요리학원에
   등록해야겠어요.
	I think I should register for cooking school,
	   starting from next month.

- Starting point: combined with -(에)서 or -(으)로

도서관에서부터 걸어 왔어요.	*I walked from the library.*
집을 처음(서)부터 다시 지었어요.	*We rebuilt the house from scratch.*
오빠로부터.	*Your brother.* (signature in letter-writing)

피해자로부터 손해배상 청구서가
   날라왔다.
	A written claim for damages came flying in
	   from the victim.

NOTE: None of the instances of -부터 in the above examples can be replaced by -에서.

-에서 vs. -부터

Both -에서 and -부터 indicate some sort of a starting point but they are interchangeable only when there is an end point expressed by -까지.

주차장에서/부터 사무실까지 *from the parking lot to the office*

10 살에서/부터 15 살까지 *from 10 to 15 years old*

2 월 말에서/부터 3 월 중순까지 *from the end of February to the middle of March*

In other cases, only one is possible:

Use only -에서, not -부터: 'from (a point)' – without an end point expressed by -까지

브라질에서 편지가 왔다. *A letter came from Brazil.*

집에서 떠났다. *She left from home.*

1 시간에서 2 시간 정도 *from one hour to two hours*

맨끝에서 두 번째 집 *the second house from the very end*

Use only 부터, not -에서: 'first; starting from; since; from (a person)'

밥부터 먹자. *Let's eat first.*

내일부터 비 온대요. *I hear that it will rain starting from tomorrow.*

처음부터 다시 하자. *Let's start over from the beginning.*

언제부터 자는 거야? *Since when are you sleeping?*

오빠로부터 (or 오빠한테서) 편지가 왔어요. *A letter came from my brother.*

Both are possible, but they differ in meaning in the following case:

제 1 과에서 시험 문제가 나온다. *The exam is based on chapter one.*

제 1 과부터 시험 문제가 나온다. *The exam starts from chapter one.*

19.14 -까지

- 'To; until' (end point in time or space)

  어젯밤 늦게까지 책을 읽었어요.
  I was reading till late last night.

  영업시간은 오전 8 시부터 오후 5 시까지입니다.
  Our business hours are from 8 a.m. to 5 p.m.

  돌아와서부터 지금까지 줄곧 잠만 잔 거 있죠.
  You know, I've been doing nothing but sleeping from when I got back up till now.

  여기서부터 집까지 바래다 줄게.
  I'll escort you from here to your house.

- 'And even'

  세탁기, 냉장고, 그리고 침대까지 새로 샀다.
  I bought a new washer, a new fridge, and even a new bed.

  가족에 친척에 친구들까지 초대했어요.
  She invited her family, her relatives, and even her friends.

- 'Even; as far as'

대학까지 졸업하고 어떻게 그렇게 무식할 수가 있어요?
  How is it possible to be that ignorant, even after graduating from college?

목숨까지(도) 바칠 각오가 돼 있습니다.
  I'm ready to sacrifice even my life.

눈총을 사면서까지 만나고 싶지 않다.
  I don't want to date her so much that I'd be hated for it by others.

주량이라고 할 거까지는 없고 소주 한 병정도 마십니다.
  *I won't go as far as calling it my 'Churyang' (resistance to alcohol),
  but I can drink about one bottle of soju.*

19.15   -조차 and -마저

These particles are somewhat similar to -까지 in that they express the meaning 'even; as far as.' However, there are also differences: -조차 is reserved for 'even the most basic or the most expected thing,' while -마저 and -까지 are used to indicate 'even the last.' Both -조차 and -마저 are used only for undesirable situations, but there is no such restriction on -까지.

- 'Even the most basic': -조차 is most natural

이름조차도 기억이 안 나요.
  I can't remember even her name.

너무 피곤해서 손가락 까딱하기조차 싫다.
  I am so tired that I don't even want to lift a finger.

누가 들어오는 거조차 모르고 잠을 잤어요.
  I slept without even knowing that someone came in.

- 'Even the last': -마저/까지 is more natural than -조차

심지어 그는 양심마저 팔아버렸다.
  He went as far as selling out his conscience.

막차까지 놓쳤으니, 어떻게 집에 가지?
  I missed even the last bus/train; how am I going to get home?

- Undesirable situation in general: any of -조차/마저/까지

운동은커녕 밥 먹을 시간조차 없어요.
  I don't even have time to eat, let alone time to exercise.

이혼한 사실을 가족들까지 모르고 있는 것 같아요.
  Even his family members don't seem to be aware of the fact that he got a divorce.

결혼식에 가장 친한 친구마저 안 온 거 있죠.
  Even my closest friend didn't come to my wedding, you know.

- Desirable situation: only 까지 is natural

유엔 사무총장까지 지내신 훌륭한 분이세요.
He's a great man who even served as the Secretary-General of the United Nations.

5 캐럿짜리 다이아까지 받았대요.
She even received a five-carat diamond ring.

그 남자는 못 하는 게 없어, 심지어 요리까지도.
There's nothing he cannot do well, including even cooking.

19.16 -(이)나

- The best of the remaining choices (not used with past tense)

빵이나 먹지 뭘 밥을 해요?
Why don't we just eat bread; what are you making rice for?

참견말고 걸레질이나 하시지.
Why don't you stop butting in and just do the mopping?

잠도 안 오고 애인도 없고 빨래나 하자.
I can't sleep, nor do I have a girlfriend, so let me just do the laundry.

이번 달에는 좀 힘들고 다음 달에나 될 거 같은데요.
It won't be ready this month; it will have to be next month, I'm afraid.

얘기는 나중에 하고 빨리 먹기나 해.
You can talk later, so go ahead and just focus on eating.

- Emphasis on quantities that are more than expected

성수기라 그런지 왕복 항공료가 천 불이나 하는 거 있죠.
Perhaps because it's high season, the round trip airfare is as high as $1,000.

맥주를 자그마치 일곱 병이나 마셨어요!
I drank as many as seven bottles of beer!

-씩이나 expresses even stronger emphasis on something that is more than expected.

네? 천 불씩이나 해요? 그렇게 비싸요?
What? A thousand dollars? That expensive?

일곱 병씩이나 마셨으니 필름이 끊길 수밖에.
No wonder you were totally wasted, having drunk SEVEN bottles.

It can also be used casually for unexpected things that don't involve quantity.

그냥 와도 되는데 뭘 선물씩이나...
You didn't have to bring anything; what's this gift for?

아무거나 시키지 뭘 갈비씩이나...
Anything should be fine; you don't have to order (the expensive) Kalbi.

무슨 중병이 걸렸다고 병문안씩이나...
What is this visit to check on her health for, as if she has some serious illness?

- Approximation (of quantity) in questions

| 그런 가방 얼마나 해요? | *How much is a bag like that?* |
| 학생이 몇 명이나 돼요? | *How many students are there?* |

- For indefinite pronouns (see *3.2.5*)

  누구나, 언제나, 아무나, 아무거나

- '(Either)...or' (See *21.1.3* for the conjunctive version -으나.)

태권도나 합기도를 배워 봐라.	*Try to learn either taekwondo or hapkido.*
집이나 사무실로 연락 주세요.	*Give me a call at home or at my office.*
이거나 그거나 (똑같애).	*Either this or that; they are much the same.*

  NOTE: '(Either...) or' can be expressed by the word 또는 in formal language.
  곳에 따라 눈 또는 비가 오겠습니다.
  Depending on the area, it will either snow or rain.
  시장 또는 백화점에서 구입할 수 있습니다.
  It can be purchased either at a market or at a department store.

19.17 Miscellaneous other particles

- **-씩** 'each; respectively; apiece'

날마다 8 시간씩 일합니다.	*I work eight hours each day.*
한 사람 앞에 세 장씩 나눠 드려.	*Give out three sheets for each person.*
전화번호는 한 자리씩 읽는다.	*Phone numbers are read digit by digit.*
부페에서는 한 번에 조금씩 가져다 먹는 게 좋아.	*It's good to bring and eat a small amount each time when you dine at a buffet.*

- **-마다** 'each; every'

집집마다 에어컨이 다 있다.	*Each house has an air conditioner.*
다섯 시간마다 한 알씩 드세요.	*Take one tablet every five hours.*
전화할 때마다 집에 없더라.	*She's not at home every time I call.*

- **-들** 'plural -s'

It is unnecessary for most nouns to be marked for plurality as long as the context is clear, as in 사람이 많다. However, -들 must be kept when the noun is accompanied by a demonstrative, as in 그 사람들, 그 학생들, and so on – unless a plural numeral is included, as in 그 두 학생. In addition, it can be attached to adverbs, to connectives, and even to the verb at the end of a sentence to indicate the plurality of the subject noun.

| 왜들 안 와요? | *Why don't you guys come?* |
| 편히들 쉬세요. | *You all have a good rest.* |

가면서들 먹어라.　　　　　　*Eat them on your way back.*

들어오세요 들.　　　　　　*You all come in please.*

- **-끼리** 'among; by themselves' (exclusiveness in a group activity or gathering)

우리끼리 얘긴데, 팀장이 너무 거만한 거 같지 않아요?
Between ourselves, isn't the boss too stuck-up?

가족끼리만 모이기로 했는데 친구를 데려 오면 어떡해?
Just our family members were going to get together, so how come you brought your friends?

원래 끼리끼리 모이게 마련이죠.
It's always the case that birds of a feather flock together.

- **-(이)야** 'if it be'

닭 한 마리쯤이야 혼자 먹을 수 있지.
If it's a matter of one chicken, I can finish it up by myself, of course.

말이야 쉽지만 행동으로 옮기기는 쉽지 않아요.
If it's talk, it's easy, but it's not easy to put the words into action.

생기기야 잘 생겼죠.
If it's looks, he is good-looking, of course.

- **-(이)야말로** 'indeed; be THE one'

그 사람이야말로 우리 부서에서 꼭 필요한 인물이지.
He is indeed an indispensable person in our department.

나야말로 이렇게 TV 보고 있을 때가 아니지. 내일이 시험인데.
I am the one who shouldn't be watching TV like this. I have an exam tomorrow.

- **-은/는커녕** 'far from; on the contrary; let alone'

반에서 일등은커녕 10등 안에도 못 들겠다.
Far from being at the top of the class, I doubt that you'll be even within the top ten.

편지는커녕 전화 한 통도 없어요.
There's not even a phone call from her, let alone a letter.

올 여름에는 피서는커녕 수영장도 한 번 못 갔어.
This summer, I couldn't even go to the swimming pool once, let alone go on a summer vacation.

예쁘기는커녕 호박이 따로 없더라.
Far from being pretty, I found her to be just like a pumpkin (ugly).

NOTE: 커녕 can be replaced by 말할 것도 없고 or 고사하고, provided that 예쁘기는 is changed to 예쁜 건.

- **-따라** 'of all times'

  그날따라 사람이 너무 많았어요.   *Of all days, it was that day that it was*
  so crowded.

  금년따라 유난히 비가 많이 온다.   *This year, there's an unusual amount of rain..*

- **-깨나** 'to some extent' [spoken/colloquial]

  고집깨나 센데요.   *She's quite stubborn.*

  심술깨나 부리게 생겼다.   *He looks somewhat cross-tempered.*

  돈깨나 있는 사람인 거 같애.   *It seems like he's got some money.*

20 Comparison

Nothing is absolute in life; it's all a matter of comparison. This chapter focuses on how similarities and differences are expressed in Korean.

20.1 How to express equality and similarity

20.1.1 'As...as'

Many of the following expressions are figurative (involving exaggeration to some extent), which can add an interesting flavor to language.

- **-만하다** 'be as...as; be like...'

딸이 엄마만하네요.	*The daughter is as tall as her mother.*
방이 손바닥만하다.	*The room is small, like the size of one's palm.*
목소리가 모기소리만해요.	*Her voice is small, like that of a mosquito.*
콩알만하다.	*It's as tiny as a bean.*
코딱지만하다.	*It's tiny, like a piece of snot.* [familiar/casual]

- **-만큼** 'as...as'

  영화가 책만큼 잘 됐네요.
    The movie is as well made as the book.

  사랑없는 결혼만큼 불행한 게 어디 있겠어요?
    Can there be anything as unfortunate as a marriage without love?

  양심이라곤 손톱/눈곱/털끝만큼도 없다.
    She doesn't have an ounce of conscience, not even the slightest amount.

  노력한 만큼 성적을 받게 돼 있어.
    You're supposed to receive as much credit as the effort you put in.

  먹을 만큼만 시켜, 너무 많이 시키지 말고.
    Order just as much as you'll be able to eat; don't order too much.

- **-정도** 'about as much as; to the extent that'

걔도 네 키 정도 돼.	*She's about as tall as you are.*
그 사람도 제 주량 정도예요.	*He can drink about as much as I can.*
인사불성이 될 정도로 마셨다.	*He drank until he became unconscious.*
발디딜 틈도 없을 정도로 꽉 찼다.	*It's so crowded that there's no place to step.*

- **-같다, -같이, -같은** '(be) as…as; (be) like…'

방이 돼지우리 같다.	*The room is like a pigsty.*
일이 산더미 같다.	*I have a mountainous amount of work.*
얼굴이 백지장 같다.	*Your face looks as pale as a sheet of white paper.*
찰거머리 같다.	*She's like a leech.*
물에 빠진 생쥐 같다.	*I look completely soaked, like a drenched mouse.*
하늘이 무너지는 거 같다.	*I feel devastated, as if the sky is falling.*
고목나무에 매미 붙은 것 같다.	*She's like a tiny locust stuck to that big guy (a giant tree).*
살얼음판을 걷는 것 같다.	*I feel nervous, as if I'm walking on a thin ice.*
앓던 이 빠진 것 같다.	*I feel relieved, as if a rotten tooth came out.*
고치니까 감쪽같다.	*It's as good as new now that it's repaired.*
나도 너같이 자유로웠으면 좋겠다.	*I wish I were as free as you are.*
불여우같이 생겼다.	*She looks as cunning as a sly fox.*
양같이 순해요.	*He's soft and meek like a sheep.*
꿀 먹은 벙어리같이 말을 안 해.	*He won't talk, like a mute who ate honey.*
약속을 항상 칼같이 지킨다.	*She keeps her appointments sharp and precise like a knife.*
잠꼬대 같은 소리 그만 해.	*Stop that nonsense sleep-talk.*
우뢰와 같은 박수	*thunderous applause*
날아갈 것같은 기분이야.	*I feel so light that I think I can fly.*

- **-듯 하다, -듯(이)** '(be) as…as; (be) as if…'

거짓말을 밥 먹듯 한다.	*He lies all the time, as often as he eats.*
굶기를 밥 먹듯 해.	*She goes hungry as frequently as she eats.*
돈을 물 쓰듯 써요.	*She splurges money like water.*
땀이 비 오듯 쏟아진다.	*Sweat is pouring down like rain.*
뛸듯이 기뻤어요.	*I was so happy I could leap with joy.*
마파람에 게 눈 감추듯 다 먹었네.	*You ate as quickly as a scared crab closes its eyes in the rainy southern wind.*
변덕이 죽 끓듯 해요.	*She's as capricious as boiling porridge.*
(찬)물을 끼얹은듯 조용하다.	*It's as quiet as if someone splashed cold water.*
불을 보듯 뻔하다/자명하다.	*It's as clear and obvious as watching a fire.*
책이 날개 돋힌듯 팔린다.	*The book sells well, as if it has wings.*

강건너 불구경하듯 한다.	*They show no concern, as if they're watching a fire on the other side of the river.*
아무 일도 없었다는 듯이...	*As if nothing happened...*
가물에 콩 나듯	*as rare as beans sprouting in a drought*
구렁이 담 넘어가듯	*just like a snake slithers over a fence (in a surreptitious manner)*
다람쥐 쳇바퀴 돌듯	*like a squirrel running around the rim of a sieve (stuck in a routine)*
번갯불에 콩 볶아 먹듯	*just like beans get roasted by lightning (super quickly)*

● **-처럼** 'like; as...as'

이 술도 저 술처럼 독하네요.	*This liquor is as strong as that one.*
밖이 대낮처럼 환하다.	*Outside is as bright as broad daylight.*
사람들이 벌떼처럼 몰려든다.	*People are swarming in like bees.*
사방이 쥐 죽은 것처럼 고요하다.	*Everywhere is as quiet as a mouse [as if a mouse died].*

20.1.2 *'Be the same; be no different'*

네 차하고 내 차하고 색깔이 **같다**.
Your car and my car have the same color.

부인**이나** 남편**이나 똑같다**.
The wife and the husband are the exact same type.

우리는 오랫동안 알고 지내서 가족**이나 진배없다/다름없다**.
We are no different from family because we have known each other for a long time.

20.1.3 *'Be similar; be much the same'*

● Written/formal expressions

타사제품이 본사제품과 **유사하다**.
The other company's products are similar to ours.

최근 녹차 시장의 치열한 경쟁은 전쟁터를 **방불케 한다**.
The recent fierce competition in the green tea market reminds us of a war zone.

그 두 대학은 사회과학 분야에서 **쌍벽을 이룬다**.
Those two universities are the two greatest in social science.

국산차가 요즘은 외제차**와 견줄** 만하다.
Cars made in Korea these days can measure up to foreign-made ones.

이 기업은 기술면에서 세계 유수기업들**과 어깨를 겨룬다/나란히 한다**.
This company is on a par with the world's most prominent companies when it comes to its technology.

- Spoken/colloquial expressions

  호두 속살은 마치 사람 두뇌하고 **흡사하다**.
  The inside of a walnut is similar to the human brain.

  포도 주스는 와인하고 맛이 **비슷하다**.
  Grape juice tastes similar to wine.

  둘의 농구실력이 **비까비까하다**.
  The two's basketball skills are neck-and-neck.

  버드와이저**나** 하이트**나** 그게 **그거다** (or 거기서 거기다).
  Budweiser and Hite are about the same.

  다들 실력이 **그만그만하다**.
  Everyone's ability is just about the same.

  형**하고** 동생**하고** 키가 **맞먹는다**.
  The older brother and the younger brother are about the same height.

- Idiomatic expressions

  두 팀 선수진이 **막상막하**예요.
  The two teams are neck-and-neck in terms of the quality of their players.

  34 살 노처녀나 35 살 노총각이나 **피장파장**이지 뭐.
  A 34-year-old single woman and a 35-year-old single guy are no different, you know.

  두 이론이 **대동소이**하다.
  The two theories are six of one and half dozen of the other.

  두 학교가 별 차이 없어요. **오십보백보**예요.
  There's little difference between the two schools. They're about the same.

  다들 서로 잘났다고 다투지만 내가 보기엔 **도토리 키재기**다.
  They all argue that they're better than the others, but they are all about the same as far as I can see. [It's like a height contest among acorns.]

- Resemblance in appearance

  웃을 때 모습이 할머니**와** 꼭 **닮았다**.
  She looks exactly like Grandma when she laughs.

  아들이 아버지를 쏙 **뺐다** (or 빼다 박았다). [spoken/colloquial]
  The son is a carbon copy of his father.

20.1.4 'Be no less than'

현재 일본의 한류열풍은 동남아 지역**에 못지않다**.
The recent wave of Korean pop-culture in Japan is no smaller than the one in South East Asia.

우리 팀 실력이 그쪽 팀한테 한 치도 기울지 않는다.
Our team's skill is not in the least inferior to the other team's.

20.2 How to express differences

- **More/less**

  언니가 **더/덜** 예쁘다.
  The older sister is more/less beautiful.

  지하철이 **훨씬** (더) 빠르다.
  The subway is much faster.

  동생이 **훨** 똑똑하다. [spoken/colloquial]
  The younger sister/brother is way smarter.

  이 집이 **백배** (더) 맛있어요. [spoken/colloquial]
  This restaurant food is 100 times more delicious.

  이 색상이 **한층** (더) 고상합니다. [written/formal]
  This color is much more elegant.

  등록금 낼 돈도 없는데 **하물며** 차 살 돈이 있겠어?
  He doesn't even have money to pay for his tuition, much less for clothes.

- **Than**

  사진**보다** 실물이 잘 생겼다.
  He is better looking in real life than in pictures.

  내가 가는 거**보다** 네가 오는 게 어때?
  How about you coming rather than me going?

  예상했던 것**보다** 시험이 좀 어려웠어요.
  The exam was more difficult than what we expected.

  자유 없이 사**느니** 차라리 죽는 게 낫다.
  I'd rather die than live without freedom.

  너를 시키**느니** 내가 한다. 앓**느니** 죽지.
  I'd rather do it myself than ask you to do it. Better to die than suffer.

- **Be better 낫다; be not as good as 못하다**

  이쪽 게 (더) **낫다/나아요**.   *This one is better.*

  사람이 짐승**만도 못하다**.   *He's worse than a brute.*

  이번 수상은 전 수상**보다 못하다**.   *The current prime minister is not*
                                       as good as the previous one.

- **In comparison to; compared with**

  우리 회사가 타 회사**에 비해** 기술이 부족하다/월등하다.
  Our company lacks/excels in technology compared with other companies.

  나는 너**에 비하면** 아주 게으른 편이야.
  I am really lazy compared to you.

- **Can't compare; be beyond comparison; pales in comparison**

  시중 와인 맛은 양조장에서 음미하는 와인과 **비교가 안 된다**.
  The taste of wine from the market can't compare to wine from the brewery.

  집에서 정성스럽게 싼 도시락은 어느 유명음식점 음식**에 댈 게 아니다**.
  Lunch packed at home with love is beyond comparison with food from any famous restaurant.

  걔는 나한테/나하고 **상대가 안 된다**.
  He's no match for me.

  추진력으로 말할 것 같으면 나는 너**한테 게임이 안 된다**. [spoken/colloquial]
  Speaking of driving force, I can't compete with you.

  그 회사 라면은 이 라면**에 쩹도 안 된다**. [familiar/casual]
  The taste of that company's ramen is nothing near this one.

  우리 팀의 현재 공격력으로는 상대팀**한테 어림도 없다**.
  Our team's current offense can't match our opponent's.

  그 남자는 내 이상형 **근처도 못 간다**.
  That guy doesn't come even close to my ideal type of man.

  저 배우는 내 여자친구에 비하면 **저리가라다** (or **아무것도 아니다**).
  That actress cannot hold a candle to my girlfriend.

  미모가 춘향이 **뺨친다**.
  When it comes to beauty, she puts Cleopatra [Chunhyang] to shame.

- **Be inferior to**

  승부 근성은 미스터 최**한테 아직 멀었다**.
  You are far inferior to Mr. Choi's fighting spirit.

  운동 실력은 내가 그 친구**한테 한참 밀린다**.
  My athletic abilities are far behind that guy's.

  동생 외모가 형**한테 기운다/빠진다**.
  The little brother's looks are not as good as his big brother's.

  남편 학벌이 부인**한테 좀 딸린다**.
  The school the husband graduated from is not as good as the one the wife is from.

  탁구는 내가 형**한테 좀 꿀린다**. [male speech]
  When it comes to table tennis, I have to give in to my big brother.

20.3 How to express superlatives

- **The -est**

  학생들 중에서 **제일 똑똑**하다.
  He's the smartest among all the students.

  금강산이 **가장** 아름다운 산으로 손꼽힌다. [written/formal]
  Kŭmgang Mt. is considered to be the most beautiful mountain.

최- (最): combines with many Sino-Korean roots.

최신유행 *the latest fashion*   최대의 효과 *the greatest outcome*

최상급 *superlative (degree)*   최악의 경우 *if worst comes to worst*

맨-: combines with a few native-Korean nouns denoting location or sequence.

맨 처음 *the very first*   맨 나중 *the very last*

맨 아래 *the very bottom*   맨 오른쪽 *rightmost*

- Indirect expressions

누구보다도 성실하다.   *He's as sincere as anyone.*

타의 추종을 불허한다.   *He's second to none.*

둘째가라면 서럽다.   *I'm second to none.*

따라올 자가 없다.   *She's second to none.*

그 분야에 독보적인 존재이다.   *He's unrivaled in his field.*

꽃중의 꽃은 장미죠.   *The flower of flowers is the rose, of course.*

둘도 없는 친구예요.   *She's my one and only best friend.*

여름에는 냉면이면 그만이다.   *Naengmyŏn is the best in summer.*

스트레스 푸는 데는 노래방이   *Nothing can beat karaoke when it*
    왔다지. [spoken/colloquial]   *comes to stress busters.*

그 영화 짱이다. [slangy]   *That movie is tops.*

20.4 How to express proportions and gradation

- -에 따라 'in proportion to; accordingly'

능력에 따라 대우를 받는다.
  Everyone is treated in proportion to their abilities.

평균수명이 길어짐에 따라 고령화 문제가 심각하게 대두되고 있다.
  As the average life span increases, aging emerges as a serious problem.

국제유가가 폭등함에 따라 주식시장이 활기를 띠고 있다.
  The stock market is showing signs of life as the international price of oil soars.

- (-면) -을수록 (더) 'the more…, the more…'

잠은 잘수록 더 오는 법이다.
  It's natural that the more you sleep, the sleepier you get.

생각하면 생각할수록 약이 올라요.
  The more I think about it, the more exasperated I get.

친한 사이일수록 더 예의를 지켜야 되는 거 아닌가요?
  Shouldn't people be more polite to someone close?

21 Conjunctives

Conjunctives typically attach to verbs. They are used to combine clauses into longer sentences and to express various meanings relating to background, time, cause, purpose, and so on. (Adnominal patterns that express these types of meanings are also included in this chapter.)

21.1 Combination of equal-status clauses

21.1.1 'And'

- **-고** (with descriptive verbs)

  방이 넓고 깨끗하다.   *The room is spacious and clean.*

  광어가 물이 좋고 싱싱합니다.   *The flounder is new and fresh.*

- **-(으)며** [formal/written]

  원기회복에 좋으며 부작용이 전혀 없습니다.
  : *It's good for restoring energy and has no side effects at all.*

  이번 지진으로 부상자가 많이 발생했으며 재산 피해도 많았습니다.
  : *Many were injured and a lot of property damage was incurred by the recent earthquake.*

21.1.2 'And whatever'

- **-(이)고...-(이)고**

  약혼식이고 결혼식이고 간편하게 해.
  : *Make the ceremonies for the engagement, the wedding, and whatever, simple.*

  과자고 빵이고 뭐 좀 먹고 시작합시다.
  : *Let's eat some cookies, bread, and whatever, before we begin the work.*

- **-(이)고 나발이고** [familiar/casual]

  여행이고 나발이고 돈이 있어야지.
  : *I have to have money for travel and whatever.*

  다이어트고 나발이고 더 이상 힘들어서 못 하겠다.
  : *Diet and whatever, it's too hard to do it any longer.*

- **-(이)고 뭐고**

  피서고 뭐고 시간이 있어야 가죠.
  : *I can't go for a summer getaway and whatever else, without time.*

12 시가 넘어서 지하철이고 뭐고 다 끊어졌다.
It's past midnight so the subway and whatever else are all closed.

• -(이)다 뭐다

논문이다 뭐다 정신없이 한 학기가 간 거 있죠.
With the dissertation and things, the semester just flew by without my realizing it.

망년회다 뭐다 불려다니다 보니 술을 너무 많이 마셨어요.
Being invited to end-of-the-year parties and the like, I drank too much.

• -(이)며…-(이)며; -하며…-하며

책이며 가방이며 다 잃어 버렸어요.
I lost the books, the bag, and everything.

생긴 거하며 걸음걸이하며 완전히 아빠다.
In terms of his looks, his walk, and everything, he is a complete Dad junior.

• -(이)니…-(이)니

독일이니 영국이니 안 가 본 데가 없어요.
Germany, England, and wherever, there's no place she hasn't been.

• -느니…-느니 (attaches to a report style ending -다/냐/라/자)

경주가 좋다느니 설악산이 좋다느니 의견이 분분해요.
Some say Kyŏngju is good and others say Sŏrak Mt. is good; opinions vary.

주말에 오라느니 주중에 오라느니 이랬다 저랬다 하네요.
They go back and forth, telling me to come on weekends and then on weekdays.

• -(으)랴…-(으)랴

책 쓰랴 학생들 가르치랴 바쁜 정도가 아니에요.
I am beyond busy writing a book, teaching students, and things like that.

21.1.3 'Or'

• -거나

머리가 아프거나 열이 나면 조퇴하고 오도록 해.
Leave work early and come home if you have a headache or fever.

그 선생님은 학생들이 듣거나 말거나 혼자 얘기해요.
That teacher talks regardless of whether students listen to him or not.

• -(으)나

자나 깨나 불조심해.   *Whether asleep or awake, watch out for fire.*

오나 가나 말썽이야.   *He's a troublemaker no matter where he goes.*

이 약은 먹으나 마나예요.   *This medicine does nothing, whether I take it or not.*

비가 오나 눈이 오나 하루도   *Rain or shine [rain or snow], she exercises without*
거르지 않고 운동을 해요.   *skipping a single day.*

● **-던가**

학교에 있던가 집에 있던가 둘 중에 하나일 거야.
  He will be at school or at home, either of the two.

뭐 해서 밥 먹지? 그냥 국에 말아 먹던가 해야겠다.
  What should I eat rice with? I guess I better eat it mixed with soup or something.

● **-든(지)**

네가 오든지 내가 가든지 그 때 상황 봐서 하자.
  Whether you come or I go, let's play it by ear.

밥을 먹든지 말든지 상관 안 해.
  I don't care whether you eat or not.

심심하면 신문을 읽든지 (해).
  If you're bored, read a newspaper or something.

빵이든 뭐든 좀 드셔야지요.
  You should eat something, whether it's bread or anything.

● **-다든지...-다든지** (-다 changes to -라 for the verb -이다)

전화가 온다든지 누가 찾아 온다든지 하면 즉시 연락해, 알았지?
  Let me know immediately if there's a phone call or someone looking for me, okay?

수박이라든지 참외라든지 뭐 그런 거 없어요?
  Do you have watermelon or melon, or something like that?

● **-(이)랄지...-(이)랄지** [spoken/colloquial]

인삼차랄지 생강차랄지 국산차로 아무 거나 한잔 주세요.
  Give me Korean tea, like ginseng tea, ginger tea, or anything like that.

21.1.4 'Not only...but also'

● **-도...-고...-도**

피아노도 잘 치고 노래도 잘 불러요.
  She's not only a good piano-player but also a good singer.

성적도 우수하고 대인관계도 원만합니다.
  He has a high GPA and also gets along well with people.

● **-을 뿐더러, -을 뿐(만) 아니라**

머리가 우수할 뿐더러 노력도 많이 해요.
  She is not only smart, but also hard-working.

물건이 많을 뿐(만) 아니라 값도 싼 거 같아요.
  It seems that they not only have a lot of stuff, but their prices are cheap as well.

● **-거니와, -(으)려니와**

시간도 없거니와/없으려니와 만나고 싶지도 않아요.
  Not only do I have no time, but I don't want to see him either.

꽃은 비싸기도 하려니와/하거니와 금방 시들어서…
Flowers are not only expensive but they wither so soon, so…

돈도 돈이려니와/돈이거니와 시간도 문제야.
Money is a problem, so is time.

● **-만…-게 아니라**

이 식당은 음식맛만 좋은 게 아니라 종업원들도 참 친절해.
This restaurant not only has good food, but their employees are really kind as well.

컴퓨터에만 관심이 있는 게 아니라 자동차에도 관심이 많아요.
He is not only interested in computers, but also in cars.

● **(-이)자, (-이)요**

처음이자 마지막이다.   *This is the first and the last.*

시인이요 학자다.   *She is a poet and a scholar.*

21.2 Combination of unequal-status clauses

In what follows, we will look at conjunctive patterns where one of the clauses is subordinate, providing additional information about the main clause (when the action occurred, why it occurred, and so forth). The dividing lines for the various clause types ('sequence' versus 'reason,' 'background' versus 'sequence,' etc.) is sometimes blurry, but they will do for the purposes of exposition.

21.2.1 Background

The following patterns give speakers a way to attract the listener's interest and to provide the information needed to draw relevant inferences.

● **-는데/은데**

To draw the listener's interest and attention:

저 한국 가는데 뭐 부탁할 거 없어요?
I'm going to Korea; do you have anything to ask of me?

부탁드릴 게 한 가지 있는데 좀 들어 주시겠어요?
I have one favor to ask of you; would you do it for me?

장모님께 드릴 생일선물을 찾는데 뭐가 좋을까요?
I'm looking to buy a gift for my mother-in-law's birthday; what do you recommend?

어제 백화점에 갔었는데 세일을 크게 하더라구요.
I went to the department store yesterday and saw that they were having a big sale.

To have the listener draw relevant inferences:

지금 좀 피곤한데…(다음에 하면 안돼요?)
I'm a bit tired right now… (can I do it later?)

차가 막히던데…(어떻게 이렇게 일찍 도착했니?)
> *I noticed that the traffic was slow… (how did you arrive this early?)*

한국 생활이 벌써 15 년인데…(한국말 유창한 거야 당연하지.)
> *I've lived in Korea 15 years already…(my Korean should be fluent, of course.)*

잡채 만드는데…(와서 먹어라.)
> *We're making chapch'ae…(come over and eat it.)*

NOTE: -는 데 (written with an intervening space): 'in doing…'
> 잡채 만드는 데 뭐뭐 들어가지? *What goes into making chapch'ae?*

• -니까, -었더니

Both are used (only with first person, except in questions) to indicate situations in which one discovers something. Usually, -었더니 is not natural for a state that is brought about without the subject's action – only -니까 is appropriate for the first three sentences below. (-니 can be used instead of -니까, but is less common and less colloquial.)

집에 없는 거 보니까 학교에 갔나 보다.
> *He's not home; looks like he's gone to school.*

친구랑 한 잔 하다 보니까 벌써 12 시가 넘은 거 있죠.
> *I was drinking with a friend and before I knew it, it was past midnight.*

요즘 경제가 안 좋다 보니까 사람들 인심도 많이 각박해졌어요.
> *The economy is so bad these days that people have become very ungenerous.*

막상 가 보니까/봤더니 생각보다 어려운 점이 많더라구요.
> *When I actually went there, I noticed that many things were tougher than I thought.*

알고 보니까/봤더니 연인사이가 아니라 그냥 친구래요.
> *As I found out, they are not romantic partners but just friends.*

계산해 보니까/봤더니 이 달에는 수입보다 지출이 더 많았어요.
> *I did calculations and found out we had more expenses than income this month.*

기껏 찾아 놓으니까/놓았더니 필요없대.
> *I managed to find it for him after much trouble; and now he says he doesn't need it.*

병원에 가니까/갔더니 의사가 뭐래요?
> *You went to the hospital; so what did the doctor say?*

• -은 즉, -건대

그쪽 얘기를 들어 본 즉, 억울하게 누명을 썼더라구요.
> *As I heard the other side's story, I found out that they were falsely accused.*

내가 장담하건대 그 영화는 반드시 히트할 거야.
> *I guarantee the movie will be a hit.*

내가 예언하건대 1 년 안에 큰 지진이 발생할 것이다.
> *I predict there will be a big earthquake within a year.*

21.2.2 Time: simultaneity

- **-(으)면서** 'while; as'

  The two clauses that are connected by these forms typically share a subject. (으며 can be used instead of 으면서 but is less common and less colloquial.)

  음악을 들으며 공부하는 버릇이 있다.
  I have a habit of studying while listening to music.

  잠꼬대를 하면서 잘 자더라.
  I saw you sleeping very well while sleep-talking.

  일찍 들어 오겠다 그러면서 급히 나갔어요.
  He went out hurriedly, saying that he'll be home early.

  경기가 악화되면서 해외여행 인구가 부쩍 줄었다.
  As the economy worsened, the number of people traveling abroad plummeted.

- **-을 때, -을 적에** 'when'

  여행갈 때 비상금을 꼭 챙겨 가세요.
  Make sure to take emergency money when you travel.

  피곤할 때는 항상 찜질방에 가는 게 습관이 됐어요.
  Going to a sauna every time I feel tired has become my habit.

  시간 있을 때마다 한국어를 공부하려고 합니다.
  I intend to study Korean whenever I have time.

  어렸을 적에 친구들과 숨바꼭질을 자주 했다.
  I often played hide-and-seek when I was little.

- **-동안(에), -사이(에)** 'during'

  -동안 can be for any amount of time, but -사이 is usually a short while.

  공사하는 동안 출입을 삼가해 주시기 바랍니다.
  Please keep out of the place during construction.

  계산대에서 기다리는 동안 호기심에 책을 들쳐보기 시작했다.
  I started leafing through the book out of curiosity while waiting at the cashier's.

  친구가 일을 보는 사이/동안 서점에 가서 시간을 때웠다.
  I went to a bookstore and killed time while my friend was taking care of her errand.

  눈 깜짝할 사이에 벌어진 일이에요.
  It's something that happened in the blink of an eye.

- **-중에, -도중에** 'in the middle of'

  Both indicate that something occurs in the middle of an action, but -도중에 emphasizes that the action expressed in the first clause is interrupted.

  바쁘신 중에 시간을 내 주셔서 감사합니다.
  Thank you for taking time out for me when you are busy.

수업하는 중에 전화가 왔다.
> *There was a phone call in the middle of class.*

통화하는 도중에 전화가 그냥 끊기더라구요.
> *During our phone conversation, the phone just got cut off.*

말씀하시는 도중에 죄송합니다만...
> *I'm sorry for interrupting during your conversation, but...*

NOTE: The same meaning can be expressed by a compound noun.
(수업중에, 통화 도중에, 말씀 도중에, and so on.)

● **-어서**

젊어서는 참 예뻤는데 이제 많이 늙었다.
> *She was very pretty when she was young, but she's really aged now.*

아주 어려서 미국에 왔대요.
> *I hear that he came to the States when he was very little.*

10년만에 박사가 돼서 돌아왔대요.
> *I heard that she came back in ten years with a Ph.D.*

새벽 2시가 넘어서 들어왔어요.
> *He came home after 2:00 in the morning.*

● **-시** [written/formal]

Combined with Sino-Korean nouns, -시 functions as a conjunctive.

개봉 후 보관 시 직사광선을 피해 주십시오.
> *When storing after opening, avoid direct sunlight.*

카드 도난 사고 발생 시 카드 회사에 즉시 연락하십시오.
> *Inform the credit card company immediately when the card is stolen.*

이착륙과 활주 시에는 컵받침을 접어 놓으십시오.
> *Keep the tray folded during takeoff, landing, and taxiing.*

21.2.3 Time: sequentiality

● **-고** (with action verbs)

약을 먹고 잠이 들었어요.	*She took the medicine and fell asleep.*
졸업하고 바로 취직했어.	*He graduated and got a job right away.*
방석 깔고 앉으세요.	*Please use the cushion and sit down.*

● **-어(서)**

Unlike clauses connected by -고, which express separate events that happen to be in sequence, use of -어서 indicates that something is shared by the two actions. That something can be a direct object, a location, a co-participant, expertise, a posture, and so on.

차를 고쳐서 팔았어요.	*I fixed the car and sold (it).*
저녁은 나가서 먹자.	*Let's go out and eat dinner (outside).*
친구 만나서 술 한잔 했어.	*I met a friend and had a drink (with him).*
의대 나와서 대학병원에 있다.	*He graduated from medical school and is at a university hospital (with his expertise).*
이 정도야 누워서 떡먹기죠.	*This much is a piece of cake. [It's lying down and eating rice cake (lying down).]*

The difference between -고 and -어서

In English, *and* can connect clauses denoting actions that either overlap or occur in a sequence. In Korean, -고 denotes a simple sequence, while -어서 marks an overlapping sequence (where 'something' from the first action is used in the interpretation of the second action).

저녁 먹고 영화 봤다. *I ate dinner and saw a movie.*   [simple sequence]
나가서 저녁 먹었다. *I went out and ate dinner (outside).* [overlapping sequence]

도서관에 가고 친구 만났어. (The meeting was somewhere other than the library.)
도서관에 가서 친구 만났어. (The meeting took place in the library.)

The following paragraph helps show the contrast between -고 and -어서.

아침에 일어나서 샤워하고 밥 먹고 학교 가서 공부 좀 하다가 친구 만나서 점심 먹고 커피 한 잔 하고 저녁에 들어와서 두 시간 동안 한국어 복습하고 이메일 좀 하고 잤어.

-어서 (but not -고) can be replaced by the more colloquial -어 가지고/갖고:

아침에 일어나 갖고...학교 가 가지고...친구 만나 가지고...들어와 갖고...

- **-더니** (see *21.2.1* to compare with -었더니)

Used with second and third person only, -더니 evokes many incidental meanings such as background, cause/reason, and even contrast. The basic meaning that is shared by all uses of -더니 is sequence.

뚱뚱하더니 싹 빠졌네.
  He used to be fat, but has lost it all.

과식을 하더니 배탈이 났나 봐.
  She was overeating and it looks like she has a stomach problem.

여자친구가 생기더니 사람이 완전히 달라졌어요.
  He changed completely once he got a girlfriend.

어제는 푹푹 찌더니 오늘은 좀 낫네요.
  Yesterday was steaming hot, but today is a bit better.

- **-어다**

  The referent of the direct object in the -어다 clause is transferred from one place to another.

커피 좀 갖다 드릴까요?	*Shall I bring some coffee for you?*
오는 길에 좀 사다 줄래요?	*Would you buy it on the way and bring it for me?*
친구 좀 집에 태워다 주고 올게요.	*I'll be back after giving my friend a ride home.*

- **-자마자, -기가 무섭게** 'as soon as'

  -자마자 is neutral, but -기가 무섭게 expresses the speaker's feeling of being taken aback by just how soon something happens after an earlier event.

  대학 졸업하자마자 결혼했습니다.
  > *He got married as soon as he graduated from college.*

  수업이 끝나자마자 어디론가 사라졌다.
  > *She disappeared somewhere as soon as the class was over.*

  월급을 타기가 무섭게 다 써 버렸어요, 글쎄.
  > *The minute he received his salary, he used it up, you know.*

  장마가 끝나기가 무섭게 본격적인 무더위가 찾아왔다.
  > *Just as soon as the rainy spell is over, the scorching heat is here in full force.*

- **-는 즉시, -는 대로** 'immediately'

  전화 받는 즉시 나와야 돼, 알았지?
  > *You have to come out immediately when you get my phone call, got it?*

  음식 쓰레기는 생기는 즉시 갖다 버려라.
  > *As soon as you have food trash, take it out immediately.*

  날씨 풀리는 대로 다시 날을 잡자.
  > *Let's set the date again as soon as the weather warms up.*

  아침에 일어나는 대로 전화해.
  > *Call me as soon as you get up in the morning.*

  태국에 도착하는 대로 이메일 할게요.
  > *I'll e-mail you as soon as I arrive in Thailand.*

- **-는 순간** 'the moment when'

  너를 처음 보는 순간 가슴이 뛰었어.
  > *My heart skipped a beat the moment I saw you for the first time.*

  그 소식을 듣는 순간 눈 앞이 깜깜해졌다.
  > *I felt utter darkness the moment I heard the news.*

- **-다(가)** (shift of action, change of status)

  공부하다 말고 무슨 딴 생각이야?
  What distracting thoughts are you having in the middle of studying?

  밤새 못 자다가 이제야 잠이 들었어요.
  He couldn't sleep all night, but fell asleep only just now.

  이 길로 곧장 가다가 좌회전하면 됩니다.
  You can go straight this way and make a left turn.

  몇 번 사양을 하다가 그냥 받았어요.
  I tried to decline it several times, but then just accepted it.

  이렇게 꾸물거리다 늦겠다.
  I am afraid that we'll be late moving at this snail's pace.

  정말 알다가도 모를 일이에요.
  It's really beyond my comprehension.

- **-었다(가)** (shift after completion of the first action)

  화장실에 좀 갔다 올게.   *I'll be back after using the restroom.*

  갈비는 양념에 재었다가 구워라.   *Barbecue the galbi after keeping it marinated.*

  껐다가 한번 다시 켜 보세요.   *Try turning it off and then turning it back on.*

- **-다...-다 한다** (repeated alternation of two actions)

  하루종일 비가 오다 안 오다 하네요.
  It's been raining off and on all day.

  이랬다 저랬다 하지 말고 확실하게 해.
  Make your attitude clear without flip-flopping.

  기름값이 계속 올랐다 내렸다 하네요.
  The gas price keeps going up and down.

  정신이 왔다 갔다 한다.
  I'm feeling out of it. [My mind is going back and forth.]

21.2.4 Time: before, after, until

- **-기 (직)전** '(immediately) before'

  더 늦기 전에 정밀검사를 받아 보십시오.
  Get a complete check-up before it gets too late.

  어두워지기 전에 숙소로 돌아 왔어요.
  We came back to our lodgings before it got dark.

  건물이 폭파되기 직전에 구조되었대요.
  I heard that he got rescued just before the building exploded.

  얼마나 추웠는지 냉동되기 일보직전이었다구요.
  It was so cold that I was just a step away from freezing, you know.

- **-은 다음, -은 후, -은 뒤** 'after'

다음 is most common in speaking; 후 is formal-sounding; 뒤 is usually used in weather forecasts or recipes.

우선 발등의 불부터 끈 다음에 천천히 생각해 보자.
  Let's think about it in a leisurely way after taking care of the super-urgent thing first.

지하철에서 내린 다음에 버스로 갈아타야 되나요?
  Should I transfer to a bus after getting off the subway?

법대를 졸업한 후에 판사가 되는 게 목표입니다.
  It's my goal to become a judge after graduating from law school.

박사학위를 받은 직후에 강단에 섰다.
  She started teaching immediately after getting her Ph.D.

맑은 뒤 차차 흐려지겠습니다.
  It will become gradually cloudy after being sunny.

물이 팔팔 끓기 시작한 뒤 시금치를 넣는다.
  Put in the spinach after the water starts boiling hard.

- **-을 때까지** 'until'

자리가 날 때까지 여기서 기다리지요.
  Why don't we wait here until a seat becomes available?

전원이 다 참석할 수 있을 때까지 바베큐 파티를 연기하자.
  Let's postpone our barbecue party until everyone can attend it.

- **-기까지** 'up to'

This pattern implies that a lot of time and effort has been put into achieving some sort of success.

이 책이 나오기까지 우리는 피나는 노력을 했다.
  We've made extreme efforts to get to the point where this book came out.

우리가 결혼에 골인하기까지 정말 우여곡절이 많았어요.
  *There were a lot of complications and twists up to the point
  where we finally got married.*

21.2.5 *Cause/reason*

- **-어서, -니까**

The two forms most frequently used to express cause/reason, -어서 and -니까, are often interchangeable.

핸드폰이 있어서/있으니까 너무 편해요.
  It's so convenient to have a cell phone.

너무 많아서/많으니까 뭘 먹어야 할지 모르겠다.
  I don't know what to eat because there's so much food.

길눈이 어두워서/어두우니까 운전 못 하겠어요.
  It's hard to drive with a bad sense of direction.

운전을 안 하다 해서/하니까 겁이 난다.
  I get nervous driving because I haven't driven for a while.

However, there is a difference between the two: -니까 is appropriate for the speaker's reasoning or justification of a statement or a proposal/command, while -어서 is most natural for a straightforward and established causal relation.

이 컴퓨터는 정품이 아니니까 너무 믿지 마세요.
  Don't trust it too much because this computer is not an authorized one.

이 컴퓨터는 정품이 아니어서/아니라서 고장이 자주 나요.
  This computer is not an authorized product, so it breaks down often.

Use only -니까, not -어서

To provide reasoning or justification for the speaker's proposal or command:

가까우니까 걸어가죠.
  Why don't we walk since it's close?

오늘은 너무 늦었으니까 내일 가자.
  Let's go tomorrow since it's too late today.

주말에는 붐비니까 주중에 가는 게 어때?
  How about going there during week days since it gets crowded on weekends?

아무 때고 괜찮으니까 전화 주세요.
  Give me a call anytime because it's fine with me.

When the relation is discovered spontaneously by the speaker:

담배를 피우니까 이상하게 머리가 아픈 거 있지.
  It's strange that my head hurts when I smoke a cigarette.

닭도리탕 보니까 소주 한 잔 생각난다.
  Looking at the spicy chicken stew, I feel like having a glass of soju.

이제 이메일 주소 알았으니까 자주 연락할게.
  Now that I know your e-mail address, I'll be in touch often.

When the speaker is challenged to justify the result:

차가 막혔으니까 늦었지 (왜 늦어?).
  I was late because there was a traffic jam, of course (why else?).

표가 매진됐으니까 못 갔지.
  I couldn't go because the tickets were sold out, of course.

NOTE: -오니/사오니 is archaic-sounding, but is used in certain formal situations such as for automated messages: 지금은 부재 중이오니 (or 전화를 받을 수 없사오니) 메시지를 남겨 주시기 바랍니다 'I'm not in right now (I can't answer the phone right now), so please leave a message.'

Use only -어서, not -니까

If the causal relation is completely established or clearly expected and there is no need to explain or justify (-니까 sounds unnatural at best):

차가 막혀서 늦었습니다.	*I'm late because of the slow traffic.*
표가 매진돼서 못 갔어.	*I couldn't go because the tickets were sold out.*
출퇴근 시간이어서 붐빈다.	*It's rush hour, so it's crowded.*
선약이 있어서 못 갈 거 같아요.	*I have a previous engagement, so I don't think I can go.*

In fixed expressions:

늦어서 죄송합니다.	*I'm sorry for being late.*
못 알아봐서 미안하다.	*I'm sorry for not having recognized you.*
전화 주셔서 감사합니다.	*Thank you for the phone call.*
민망해서 혼났어요.	*I felt terrible because I was embarrassed.*

- **-기 때문에**

This is usually found in formal/written language rather than in speaking. It places a strong focus on the reason, and like -어서, it cannot be followed by a command or proposal.

대부분의 자동차 사고가 음주 후 운전하기 때문에 발생한다.
  The majority of traffic accidents occur because people drive after drinking.

해양학을 전공했기 때문에 바다에 관심이 많다.
  Because she majored in oceanography, she has a lot of interest in the ocean.

- **-기에, -길래**

-기에 is usually for written/formal language while -길래 is for spoken/ colloquial use.

너무 늦었기에 댁까지 모셔다 드렸습니다.
  I took her home because it was late.

싸길래 왕창 샀어.
  I bought tons because they were cheap.

기 죽어 있는 거 같길래 인심 좀 썼다.
  I was generous with him because he seemed to be in low spirits.

- **-어 가지고/갖고, -는 바람에**

These two forms are frequently employed, but usually for colloquial speech. 가지고 can indicate any type of reason, but 바람에 is most natural for a sudden happening.

어제 잠을 못 자 가지고 머리가 멍하다.
  My head feels numb because I couldn't sleep last night.

돈이 한 푼도 없어 가지고 하루종일 굶었어.
I starved all day because I didn't have a penny.

시간이 모자라 가지고 시험문제를 다 못 풀고 제출했어.
I submitted my exam without answering all the questions because I didn't have enough time.

급한 일이 생기는 바람에 모임에 못 나갔어.
I couldn't go out to the meeting because something urgent came up.

앞 차가 갑자기 멈추는 바람에 급정거를 할 수밖에 없었어요.
I had no choice but to make a sudden stop because the car in front of me stopped out of the blue.

수입품이 쏟아져 들어오는 바람에 국산품 판매가 저조합니다.
Sales for Korean-made products are slow because imported products are pouring in.

- **-(으)므로** [formal/written]

귀하는 타의 모범이 되었으므로 이 상장을 수여함 (on an award certificate)
You have been a role-model for others, hence this award.

아직 강의실을 모르므로 추후에 이메일을 통해 연락 드리겠습니다.
No information about the classroom is available yet, so I will notify you later via e-mail.

- **-느라(고)** 'as a result of doing something'

이삿짐을 싸느라고 그동안 정신없었어요.
I've been so busy for a while packing for my move.

늦잠을 자느라고 수업에 못 간다니 그게 말이 되니?
Does it make sense to say you can't go to your class because of sleeping in?

먼 길 오시느라 수고하셨습니다.
Thank you for coming this far.

- **-다고** (-다 changes to -라 for the verb -이다)

미룬다고 (해서) 해결될 일이 아니지.
It's not something that is going to be solved by postponing.

돈이 많다고 (해서) 반드시 행복한 것은 아니다.
We are not necessarily happy just because we have a lot of money.

천천히 먹어. 배고프다고 막 먹지 말고.
Eat slowly. Don't eat in a hurry just because you're hungry.

방학이라고 다들 신났어요.
Everybody is excited because it's school break.

- **-을까봐** 'for fear that ...should'

아침에 못 일어날까봐 자명종을 맞춰 놓았어.
I set the alarm because I was worried I may not be able to get up in the morning.

막차를 놓칠까봐 얼마나 걱정했는지 몰라요.
I worried so much because I was afraid that I might miss the last bus.

21.2.6 *Intention/purpose*

- **-(으)려고** (For spoken variants, -을려고, -을라고, see **8.3**.)

    젊어지려고 헬스 클럽에 등록했어.
    I registered for a health club in order to stay young.

    이번 학기에 한국어 수업 들으려고요.
    I'm planning to take a Korean class this semester.

    안 그래도 막 전화하려던 참이었는데. (-려던 < -려고 하던)
    I was in fact just about to call you.

    그냥 가려다가 잠깐 인사하려고 들렀어요. (-려다가 < -려고 하다가)
    I was just going to leave, but then I stopped by for a few minutes just to say hello.

- **-(으)러**

    Except in the case of 뭐 하러, this form must be followed by verbs of coming and going.

    친구 만나러 나갔다.   *He went out to meet a friend.*
    마사지 받으러 갔다 왔어.   *I was gone to get a massage.*
    요즘 골프치러 다니세요?   *Do you go to play golf these days?*
    뭐 하러 중고차를 사?   *What are you buying a used car for?*

- **-기 위하여/위해** [formal/written]

    국민들을 이해시키기 위하여 온갖 방편을 다 동원했다.
    They tried all sorts of measures in order to help the nation understand them.

    조국을 지키기 위해 숨진 전몰장병들의 추모식이 거행되겠습니다.
    There will be a memorial service shortly for the soldiers who died in war to protect the country.

- **-고자** [formal/written]

    정기 모임을 가지고자 하니 부디 참석해 주시기 바랍니다.
    We are planning to have a regular meeting; we sincerely hope that you will attend it.

    여러분의 의견을 듣고자 이렇게 회의를 소집했습니다.
    We called for a meeting in the hopes of listening to your opinions.

    하고자 하는 의욕만 있으면 무슨 일이든 할 수 있다.
    You can do anything if you just have the strong desire to do it.

- **-차** [formal/written]

    Combined with a few Sino-Korean nouns, -차 functions as a conjunctive.

    정기 공연차 전국을 순회할 예정이다.
    They are scheduled to tour the country for their regular concerts.

노대통령은 하와이 방문차 한국을 떠났다.
President Roh left Korea to visit Hawaii.

- **-을까 한다** 'I am thinking about…'

집세가 자꾸 올라서 아파트를 하나 살까 해요.
I'm thinking about buying an apartment because the rent keeps going up.

학기말 논문 자료 좀 찾을까 하고 도서관에 왔어요.
I came to the library thinking about collecting some materials for my final paper.

대학원에 진학할까 했었는데 생각을 바꿨어요.
I thought about entering graduate school, but I've changed my mind.

- **-을까 보다** 'I think I will…'

이번 주말에는 그냥 집에서 책이나 읽을까 봐.
I think I will just read some books at home this weekend.

차를 좀 큰 걸로 바꿀까 봐요.
I think I'll change my car into a little bigger one.

- **-을 겸** 'for dual purpose'

하숙비도 절약하고 친구도 사귈 겸 기숙사 생활을 해 보는 게 어때?
How about trying dorm life to save on the boarding house expense and also to make friends?

영어도 배우고 견문도 넓힐 겸 해외 어학연수를 계획 중입니다.
I'm planning on a language course abroad to learn English and also to broaden my experience.

- **-을 생각, -을 작정, -을 셈**

앞으로 어떻게 할 생각이야?   *What are you planning to do from now on?*

당분간 호텔에서 묵을 작정입니다. *I'm planning to stay at a hotel for a while.*

졸업을 한 해 미룰 셈이야.   *I'm planning to postpone my graduation by one year.*

21.2.7 Purpose/result

- **-게, -도록** 'so that, to the point'

These two forms are more or less interchangeable, but -도록 is less common and slightly formal-sounding compared to -게. (See *10.4.3* for -게.)

Purpose:

30 분만 더 자게 내버려 두자.
Let's leave him so he can sleep just 30 more minutes.

갈비 굽게 석탄 불 좀 피우자.
Let's start the charcoal fire so we can barbecue the galbi.

알아 들을 수 있게(끔) 다시 얘기해 봐.
Try and say that again, so I can understand.

화초가 죽지 않도록 정기적으로 물을 주세요.
Water the plants regularly so they won't die.

국이 식지 않도록 뚜껑을 덮어 놓으세요.
Put on the lid so the soup won't get cold.

Result (all fixed expressions):

코가 비뚤어지게 마셨어.	*I drank a lot until my nose got twisted.*
종일 눈이 빠지게 기다렸어.	*I waited all day until my eyes popped out.*
뼈 빠지게 일만 했어.	*I only worked my guts [bones] out.*
뭘 그렇게 뚫어지게 쳐다보니?	*What are you staring at, as if you could puncture a hole (in my face)?*
입에 침이 마르게 네 칭찬을 하더라.	*I heard him praising you until his saliva dried up.*
내가 귀에 못이 박히게 얘기했잖아.	*How many times have I told you [until a nail got hammered into your ear]?*
혀가 닳도록 여러 번 말을 했잖아.	*Didn't I tell you so many times that my tongue wore out?*
귀가 따갑도록 잔소리를 들었다.	*I heard him nagging till my ears were burning.*
손이 발이 되도록 빌었다.	*I begged and groveled for forgiveness [until my hands became feet].*

The two forms are not always interchangeable. In the following examples, choice of either -게 or -도록 is fixed. (See *17.1.2* for -도록 하다.)

나가세요? 어디 가시게요?	*Are you going out? To go somewhere?*
제발 조용히 좀 해라. 잠 좀 자게.	*Please keep quiet. So I can sleep.*
날씨가 기가 막히게 좋다.	*The weather is breathtakingly good.*
이 기회에 코를 납작하게 해 줘야지.	*I better crush his arrogance this time.*
손에 땀을 쥐게 한다.	*It makes my palms sweat.*
서울이 몰라 보게 달라졌어요.	*Seoul has become unrecognizable.*
밤새도록 열이 나고 아팠어요.	*I was sick with fever all night [till dawn].*
죽도록 사랑했는데...	*I loved her to death but...*

21.2.8 Condition

- **-(으)면**

  누가 보면 두 사람이 사귀는 지 알겠다.
  If anybody saw them, they would think that the two are dating.

  될 수 있으면 영양소를 고루고루 섭취하도록 하세요.
  If possible, try to take all nutrients evenly.

  한국말을 잘 하려면 한국말을 가능한 한 많이 사용해야 한다.
  You should use Korean as much as possible if you want to be good at it.

  숙제 다 했으면 이 것 좀 도와 줄래?
  Would you help me with this if you're done with your homework?

- **-(으)면...-을텐데/(으)련만**

  조금만 더 열심히 했으면 합격했을텐데.
  I would have passed (the exam) if I had worked harder.

  운동을 좀 열심히 하면 좋으련만.
  How nice it would be if he exercised diligently.

  내가 여유가 있으면 좀 도와 주련만.
  I'd help them a bit if I could afford it.

- **-었더라면, -었던들**

  좀 일찍 떠났더라면 늦지 않았을텐데...
  If we had left early, we wouldn't have been late.

  미리 연락을 해 줬더라면, 이런 불상사는 없었을 거 아니에요?
  If you had informed us in advance, there wouldn't have been a mishap like this.

  조금만 더 젊었던들 새로운 분야에 도전할 수 있을텐데...
  If I were just a bit younger, I would be able to take up the challenge of a new field.

  내가 키가 더 크고 날씬했던들 슈퍼모델 대회에 출전했을텐데...
  If I had been taller and slimmer, I would have competed in the supermodel contest.

- **-다면** (-다 changes to -라 for the verb -이다)

  내일 지구가 멸망한다면, 오늘 하루 무엇을 하겠습니까?
  What would you do today if tomorrow were the end of the world?

  만일 내가 복권에 당첨된다면, 세계일주를 하고 싶어요.
  I would like to travel around the world if I won the lottery.

  만약 그 말이 사실이라면, 내 손에 장을 지지겠다.
  If that were true, I'd be a monkey's uncle. [I'd cook stew in my hands.]

  네가 나라면 어떻게 하겠니?
  What would you do if you were me?

- **-거든** (used with a command or proposal)

조금 있다가 드라마 끝나거든 가라.   *Go in a little while after the drama is over.*

너무 비싸거든 사지 마세요.   *Don't buy it if it's too expensive.*

비 오거든 소풍가는 거 취소하자.   *Let's cancel the picnic if it rains.*

- **-어야(만)** 'only if'

두 가지 시험에 다 붙어야만 운전면허를 받을 수 있습니다.
  You can get a driver's license only if you pass two types of tests.

하늘을 봐야 별을 따지.
  You have to take necessary action to achieve an intended goal.
  [Only if you look at the sky, can you grab a star.]

지원자가 학생이어야/학생이라야 합니까?
  Do the applicants have to be students?

- **-는 한** 'as long as'

힘이 닿는 한 도와 드릴게요.
  I will help you to the best of my ability.

될 수 있는 한 자극적인 음식은 피하도록 하셔야 됩니다.
  You should avoid spicy food as much as possible.

- **-을 경우** 'in case'

제가 늦을 경우를 대비해서, 마당에 불 좀 켜 놓으세요.
  In case I'm late, please turn on the light in the yard.

만에 하나라도 내가 못 올 경우에 내 대신 회의에 참석 좀 해 줄래?
  Just in case I can't come, can you attend the meeting on my behalf?

21.2.9 Concession ('even if; even though')

- **-어도**

표백제를 써도 얼룩이 안 지워져요.
  The stain doesn't come out even if I use bleach.

그런 일은 상상만 해도 끔찍하다.
  It's scary even just to imagine such a thing.

삼일 전까지만 해도 이번 모임에 나온다고 했는데.
  Even as recently as three days ago she said she would come to this meeting.

이 돈은 무슨 일이 있어도 (or 하늘이 두 쪽 나도) 갚아야 돼.
  You must pay this money back no matter what happens (even if the sky falls).

찔러도 피 한 방울 안 나올 사람이야.
  He's really a cold-blooded person. [Even if he's stabbed, no blood will come out.]

늦어도 다음주 월요일까지는 제출하겠습니다.
  I'll submit it by next Monday at the latest.

더워도 너무 덥다.
Even though it's hot (because it's summer), it's too hot.

-(이)라도 is used instead of -(이)어도 for the verb -이다.

말이라도 고맙다.   *I'm grateful even if it's just words.*

이제부터라도 늦지 않았어요.   *It's not late even if we start from now.*

최소한 전화라도 해 줬어야지.   *You should have at least phoned me.*

아무 거라도 좋으니 빨리 주세요.   *Anything is fine, so give it to me quickly.*

- ### -더라도, -을지라도

  좀 고생이 되더라도 당분간 참아.
  Hang in there for the time being even if it's tough.

  더 일찍 왔더라도 친구가 떠나는 걸 볼 수 없었을 거예요.
  Even if you had come earlier, you wouldn't have been able to see your friend leaving.

  문제가 어려웠다치더라도 어떻게 하나도 못 맞출 수가 있어?
  Even though the questions were tough, how can you not get even one answer correct?

  아무리 친한 사이라 할지라도 공과 사는 구분해야 합니다.
  No matter how close a relationship they have, they must draw a line between public and private matters.

  몸은 비록 떨어져 있을지라도 마음은 항상 너한테 가 있어.
  Even if I'm physically away from you, my mind is always with you.

- ### -고도

  눈 감고도 찾아갈 수 있어요.   *I can find the place even with my eyes closed.*

  술을 마시고도 안 마셨대.   *He says he didn't drink even though he did.*

- ### -어서라도

  나를 봐서라도 이번 한번만 눈 감아 줘.
  Even if it's for my sake, please overlook it just this time.

  융자를 받아서라도 이 집은 꼭 사고 싶어요.
  Even if I have to get a loan, I really want to buy this house.

  휴가를 내서라도 그 친구 결혼에는 꼭 참석하려고 해요.
  Even if I have to take a vacation, I intend to be sure to attend that friend's wedding.

- ### -는데도/은데도, -음에도 (불구하고) 'in spite of'

  비가 오는데도 많은 사람들이 축구 경기를 보기 위해 모였다.
  Many people gathered to watch the soccer game in spite of the rain.

  교통이 불편한데도 불구하고 이렇게 와 주셔서 감사합니다.
  Thank you for coming in spite of the difficult traffic.

밤이 늦었음에도 불구하고 학생들의 시위는 계속되었다.
Although it was late at night, the students' demonstration continued.

늦은 시간임에도 불구하고 거리는 사람들로 붐볐다.
Although it was late at night, the street was filled with people.

- **-어야**

멀어야 얼마나 멀겠어요?	*Even if it's far, how far can it be?*
지금 가 봐야 아무도 없을 거야.	*There won't be anyone even if we go there now.*
참을래야 도저히 참을 수가 없어.	*Even if I try, I can't possibly bear it.*
밑져야 본전이지, 뭐.	*Oh well, I'm none the worse for the loss.*

- **-어 봤자** [spoken/colloquial]

지금 전화해 봤자 없을걸.	*I don't think he's home even if you call.*
얘기해 봤자 입만 아플 거다.	*It will only hurt your mouth to say it.*
차도 없는데 운전 배워봤자죠, 뭐.	*No point in learning how to drive, you know, when I don't even have a car.*
뛰어 봤자 벼룩이죠.	*He couldn't have run that far. [It's a flea even if he jumps.]*

- **-은들** (used with rhetorical questions)

비싼들 얼마나 비싸겠니?	*If it's expensive, how expensive can it be?*
후회한들 무슨 소용이 있겠어?	*What's the use of regretting?*
친엄마를 찾은들 뭐하겠어요?	*What would it achieve to find my birth mother?*

- **-기로서니**

아무리 기분이 나쁘기로서니 말을 그렇게 심하게 하면 안 되지.
No matter how upset you are, you shouldn't use such harsh language.

비싼 옷 좀 샀기로서니 그걸 갖고 뭘 그렇게 잔소리를 하니?
Even if I bought some expensive clothes, do you have to nag like that?

- **-을망정, -을지언정**

비록 가난할망정 남한테 구걸하지는 않는다.
Even though I'm poor, I don't beg from others.

고맙다고는 못 할망정 왜 화를 내?
If you can't say 'thank you,' you better not be angry at least.

굶어 죽을지언정 그런 일을 하고 싶지 않아요.
Even if I have to starve to death, I don't want to do such a thing.

포기를 할지언정 도움을 청하고 싶은 생각은 없습니다.
Even if I have to give up, I don't have any desire to ask for help.

- **-(으)나마**

작으나마 성의로 받아 주세요.
Although it's small, please accept it as a token of my appreciation.

도와주진 못하나마 방해는 하지 말아야지요.
If you can't help, you better not interfere at least.

비록 적은 돈이나마 치료비에 보태세요.
It's not much, but please use it to defray your medical expenses.

멀리서나마 생일 축하드려요.
I congratulate you on your birthday, although it's from far away.

- **-(으)면...-었지**

죽으면 죽었지, 너하고는 같이 안 갈래.
Even if I died, I wouldn't want to go with you.

같이 가기 싫으면 싫었지, 왜 소리를 지르고 그래?
Even if you don't want to go with me, why do you have to yell?

헤어지면 헤어졌지, 더 이상은 못 참겠어요.
Even if we break up, I can't stand it any longer.

- **-거늘** [literary/old-fashioned]

어린 애들도 질서를 알거늘 하물며 어른이 안 지켜서야 말이 됩니까?
Does it make sense for adults not to maintain order when even children do it?

동물도 자기 새끼는 귀한 줄 알거늘 너는 어찌 동물만도 못하냐?
Aren't you worse than animals; even they know how precious their little ones are.

21.2.10 Contrast

- **-지만**

차린 건 없지만 많이 드세요.
I didn't prepare much food, but help yourself.

피곤하시겠지만 이 서류 좀 검토해 주시겠어요?
You must be tired, but would you please go over this document for me?

운동이 중요하다지만 지나친 운동은 오히려 몸에 해롭다.
Exercise is said to be important, but excessive exercise does more harm than good for the body.

- **-(으)나** [formal/written]

의견에 따르긴 하겠으나 결과는 책임지지 않겠습니다.
I'll follow your decision, but not take responsibility for the result.

좋은 약은 입에 쓰나 몸에 이롭다.
Good medicine is bitter to the mouth but good for the body.

- **-는데/은데** (used for a mild and implicit contrast)

  공부는 잘하는데 사교성이 없어.   *She's good academically but not sociable.*

  알았었는데 생각이 안 나네요.   *I used to know but can't remember.*

  물건은 좋은데 값이 비싸다.   *It's a good product but expensive.*

- **-건만** (used for an emphatic contrast, followed by something disappointing)

  할 일은 많건만 시간이 너무 없다.
   I have so much to do, but have so little time.

  나이는 먹을 만큼 먹었건만 사람이 왜 그 모양이지?
   He's old enough, but how come he's so immature?

- **-(으)면서** 'while, at the same time'

  매일 만나면서 안 만난대요.   *They see each other every day, but they say that they don't.*

  많이 잤으면서 뭐가 피곤해?   *Why are you tired after having slept so much?*

  감이 얇으면서도 질긴 것 같다.   *It seems that the cloth is thin, yet durable.*

- **-되**

  가기는 가되 너무 일찍 가진 마.   *You can go, but don't go too early.*

  마시긴 마시되 적당히 마셔라.   *You can drink, but drink moderately.*

- **-는 게** (used to express regrets and excuses)

  일찍 온다는 게 (그만) 차가 막히는 바람에 늦었어요.
   I meant to come early but because of heavy traffic, I was late.

  한 번 찾아 뵙는다는 게 (그만) 어떻게 하다보니까…
   I meant to come and pay you a visit, but somehow…

- **-는/은 반면에** [formal/written]

  대외적으로 명성를 얻고 있는 반면에 대내적으로는 불신을 사고 있다.
   They are earning fame on the outside, but incurring distrust on the inside.

  카펫은 경제적인 반면에 위생적이지는 않다.
   A carpet is economical but not sanitary.

- **-것과는 달리, -것과는 대조적으로** [formal/written]

  예상했던 것과는 달리 상황이 그리 나쁘지 않았다.
   The situation wasn't that bad, unlike what was expected.

  뉴스에 보도되는 것과는 대조적으로 경제가 아직도 많이 침체되어 있다.
   The economy is still very down in contrast to what's reported on the news.

22 Complex sentences

This chapter concentrates on the use of quoted clauses, adnominal clauses (such as 하는 일 and 입던 옷), -지 clauses, and nominalizations involving -기 and -음.

22.1 Quoted/reported clauses

Through direct and indirect quotes, speakers report what they have said or heard and what they think, believe, intend, and so on.

22.1.1 Direct quotes

A direct quote – stating exactly what was heard or thought – is expressed with the help of -하고 for onomatopoeic sounds and either -하고 or -라고 for speech and thoughts. (Double quotation marks are used for speech, and single quotation marks for thoughts in Korean.)

"딩동댕" 하고 초인종이 울렸다.
  'Ding-dong-dang,' the door bell rang.
"내일 우리집에 올래?" 하고/라고 물었다.
  'Will you come over to my place tomorrow?,' he asked.
'아픈 거 아닌가' (하고) 걱정했어요.
  I was worried (thinking), 'Isn't she sick?'
'괜찮아 지겠지' (하고 생각)했는데 증세가 더 심해졌어.
  I thought, 'It'll get better,' but the symptoms got worse.
'좀 더 열심히 했으면 좋았을걸' 하고 후회가 돼요.
  I regret it (thinking), 'It would have been nice if I had worked harder.'
'이게 웬 떡이냐' 했어요.
  I thought to myself, 'What a windfall this is.'

Some direct quotes have become part of fixed expressions.

뭐니 뭐니해도 소주에는 삼겹살이 최고지요.
  Pork belly meat is the best for drinking soju with, no matter what they say.
이제 와서 나 몰라라 하면 어떡해?
  How can you say you don't care at this point?
이래라 저래라 말이 많아요.
  He's very bossy with his demands [saying, 'Do it this way, do it that way'].

보자 보자 하니까 못 하는 말이 없어.
Because I'm so patient with you, you don't watch what you say.

22.1.2 Indirect quotes

An indirect quote – paraphrasing and reporting what was heard or thought – is formulated in the report style, which is similar in many respects to the casual speech style, as illustrated below. The reported information is accompanied by -고 했다 in written/formal/neutral language, by (-고) 그랬다 in spoken/colloquial language, by -고 물었다 for questions, and so on.

	Casual speech style 한다/하니(하냐)/해라/하자		**Report style** 한다/하냐/하라/하자	
Statement	본다 좋다	찾는다 (책)이다	Same as to the left except: (책)이다 is changed to (책)이라.	
Question	보니/보(느)냐 좋으니/좋으냐	찾니/찾(느)냐 책이니/책이냐	보(느)냐 좋으냐	찾(느)냐 책이냐
Command	보아라	찾아라	보라	찾으라
Proposal	보자	찾자	Same as to the left	

The report style differs from the casual speech style in two major ways. First, questions allow only the -냐 ending (으냐 after a consonant for descriptive verbs), whereas the casual speech style allows either -니 or -냐. Second, the report style command ending is -(으)라, while a casual speech command calls for -어/아라. Here are some examples.

"책을 찾는다/찾았다."
→ 책을 찾는다고/찾았다고 했다.   *He said he was looking for/found the book.*

"음식 맛이 좋다/좋았다."
→ 음식 맛이 좋다고/좋았다고 한다.   *They say the food is/was delicious.*

"비 오면 연기할 거예요."
→ 비 오면 연기할 거라 그랬어요.   *They said they'd postpone it if it rains.*

"뭘 보니?"
→ 뭘 보냐고 물었다.   *She asked me what I was looking at.*

"날씨 좋으니?"
→ 날씨 좋으냐고 물었다.   *He asked me if the weather is nice.*

"이제 가 봐."
→ 이제 가 보라고 하십니다.   *He says that you can go now.*

"밥 먹어라."
→ 밥 먹으라(고) 그랬어요.   *I told her to eat.*

"같이 보자."
→ 같이 보자(고) 그랬어요.   *I suggested that we see it together.*

All other styles, including those with special endings, give way to the above one and only report style. The following table presents an overview of how sentences with various types of endings are indirectly quoted.

Original sentence	Indirect quote (followed by 했다, 그랬다, 물었다, etc.)
Statement	
"갑니다" or "가(요)"	간다고
"갔어요"	갔다고
"가겠어요"	가겠다고
"갈게요"	가겠다고 or 간다고
"갈 거예요"	갈 거라고
Question	
"합니까?" or "해(요)?"	하냐고
"했습니까?"	했냐고
"하겠습니까?"	하겠냐고
"할 거야?"	할 거냐고
"할래요?"	하겠냐고
Command	
"앉아(요)" or "앉아라"	앉으라고
Proposal	
"앉읍시다" or "앉아(요)"	앉자고

NOTE: The suffix -었 is always retained, but -겠 and -을 may be replaced as long as the intended meaning does not change.

Here are some samples that compare indirect quotes in various styles to their direct quote counterparts. (The honorific suffix -시 can be added depending on who is making the report to whom, regardless of whether it originally appeared in the speech being reported – see ch. **2**.)

할머니가 "내가 곧 가마" 그러셨어.   *Grandma said, 'I'll come soon.'*
→ 할머니가 곧 오신다(고) 그러셨어.   *Grandma said she'll come soon.*

"같이 갈게요" 그랬어.   *They said, 'We'll come together.'*
→ 같이 오겠다(고)/온다(고) 그랬어.   *They said they'll come together.*

"나하고 결혼합시다" 그러디?   *Did he say, 'Let's get married'?*
→ 자기하고 결혼하자(고) 그러디?   *Did he ask you to marry him?*

"내 생일이 언제인지 알아요?" 하고 물었다.
He asked, 'Do you know when my birthday is?'
→ 자기생일이 언제인지 아냐고 물었다.
He asked whether I know his birthday.

선생님이 "호텔 직원이 친절했어요?" 라고 물으셨다.
The teacher asked, 'Were the hotel employees kind?'
→ 선생님이 호텔직원이 친절했냐고 물으셨다.
The teacher asked whether the hotel employees were kind.

"파티에 같이 갈래?" 하고 묻더라.
'Do you want to go to the party with me?,' he asked.
→ 파티에 같이 가겠냐고 묻더라.
He asked me whether I would go to the party with him.

점원이 "학생이신가요?" 하고 묻더라구요.
The store clerk asked, 'Are you a student?'
→ 점원이 학생이냐고 묻더라구요.
The store clerk asked whether I'm a student.

나한테 "다음에 또 오세요" 라고 분명히 말했어요.
He clearly said to me, 'Please come again next time.'
→ 나한테 다음에 또 오라고 분명히 말했어요.
He clearly said to me to come again next time.

22.1.3 주다 *and indirect quotes*

The verb 주다 is quoted in a special way when it is used for commands and requests.

Original sentence ('give it to ME' or 'do it for ME')	Indirect quote (followed by 했다, 그랬다, 부탁했다, etc.)
"(해) 주십시오"	(해) 주십사고
"(해) 주세요"	(해) 주십사고 or (해) 달라고
"(해) 줘요"	(해) 달라고
"(해) 줘"	(해) 달라고
"(해) 줘라/주라"	(해) 달라고
"(해) 줄래?"	(해) 달라고 or (해) 주겠냐고
"(해) 주시겠어요?"	(해) 달라고 or (해) 주시겠냐고

주십사 (not 주시라) is used in indirect quotes when the person to whom the command/request is directed merits an honorific form.

사장님께 "꼭 전화 주십시오"하고 부탁 드렸습니다.
I asked the president, 'Please make sure to give me a call.'

→ 사장님께 꼭 전화 주십사(고) 부탁 드렸습니다.
   I asked the president to make sure to give me a call.

교수님께 "추천서 좀 써 주세요" 하고 부탁 드렸어.
   I asked the professor, 'Please write a recommendation letter for me.'

→ 교수님께 추천서 좀 써 주십사(고) 부탁 드렸어.
   I asked the professor to write a recommendation letter for me.

Elsewhere 달라 is used, including when the -시 used in the original sentence is a marker of courtesy rather than a marker of honorification.

"여기 해장국 하나 주세요." (courtesy -시 in 주세요 to a younger waitress)
   'Please give me one haejangkuk (morning soup).'

→ 내가 저 아가씨한테 해장국 하나 달라고 부탁했어.
   I asked the waitress to give us a haejangkuk.

"나 좀 도와 줘요" 그러더라.   *He was saying, 'Please do me a favor.'*

→ 자기 좀 도와 달라 그러더라.   *He was asking to do him a favor.*

These exceptional changes of the command/request forms of 주다 into 주십사 and 달라 take place only when the person making the request is also the beneficiary of the action. Notice the contrasts in the following three pairs of examples.

"나 군밤 좀 갖다 줄래?"

→ 엄마가 군밤 좀 갖다 **달라(고)** 그러셨어. (asker = beneficiary)
   ***Mom** told me to bring some roasted chestnuts to **her**. (Mom = her)*

When the beneficiary is someone other than the person making the request, the regular report style is used.

"오빠 군밤 좀 갖다 줘라"

→ 엄마가 오빠한테 군밤 좀 갖다 **주라(고)** 그러셨어. (asker ≠ beneficiary)
   ***Mom** told me to take some roasted chestnuts to my **older brother**.*

"할머니 군밤 좀 갖다 드려라"

→ 엄마가 할머니한테 군밤 좀 갖다 **드리라(고)** 그러셨어. (asker ≠ beneficiary)
   ***Mom** told me to take some roasted chestnuts to **Grandma**.*

In some cases, 달라 is used in place of 주라 in a question expressing an indirectly quoted request.

Question is understood as an indirect request:
"후추 좀 갖다 주시겠어요?"
   Would you bring me the black pepper?

→ 웨이터한테 후추 좀 갖다 달라고 했어요.
   I asked the waiter to bring me the black pepper.

Question is understood either as an inquiry or as an indirect request:

"저하고 결혼해 주시겠어요?"
  Would you marry me?

→ 자기하고 결혼해 주겠냐고 묻더라구요.
  He was asking whether I would marry him.

"저하고 결혼해 주시겠어요?"
  Would you marry me?

→ 자기하고 결혼해 달라(고) 그러더라구요.
  He was asking me to marry him.

22.1.4 *Various types of quoting verbs*

In addition to the basic quoting verbs (했다, 그랬다, 물었다), an indirect quote can also be followed by any verb of saying or thinking and even by another clause.

- Followed by saying-type verbs

누나라고 불러.	*Call me your sister.*
자기는 범인이 아니라고 우긴다.	*He insists that he didn't commit the crime.*
잘했다고 칭찬해 줬어요.	*I praised him for doing a good job.*
술을 입에 대지 않겠다고 맹세해.	*Make the pledge that you'll stop drinking.*
다시는 늦지 말라고 경고했어.	*I warned him not to be late again.*
아이들을 잘 돌봐 달라고 신신당부했어.	*I repeatedly asked her to take good care of the kids.*
차 한 대 사달라고 노래를 한다.	*He's repeatedly asking me to buy him a car.*
빨리하라고 재촉 좀 해요.	*Please push him to do it fast.*

- Followed by thinking-type verbs

반드시 성공할 거라고 확신한다.	*I strongly believe that we'll surely succeed.*
불가능하다고 결론내렸습니다.	*I concluded that it'll be impossible.*
일등할 거라곤 예측 못 했다.	*I didn't expect that we'd rank at the top.*
열심히 한 덕분이라고 봐요.	*I think it was thanks to the hard work.*

- Followed by a clause

몸이 좀 안 좋다고 보약 먹어요.
  He's taking herbal medicine because he's not feeling too well.

한 학기 휴학하겠다고 이번학기 등록을 안 했어요.
  She didn't register this semester, saying that she's taking a semester off.

너도나도 유학가겠다고 영어 배우느라 야단들이에요.
  Everybody is crazy about learning English so they can study abroad.

추천서를 써 달라고 이메일이 왔어.
An e-mail message came asking me to write a recommendation for her.

음주운전하지 말라고 수차례 주의를 받았다.
I've received several warnings not to drive drunk.

22.1.5   Reduction of indirect quotes in colloquial speech or hearsay

A shortened quotative pattern is frequently used in colloquial speech. It makes use of reduced endings (without -고 하 or -고 그러) for each of the four speech styles – 간답니다 instead of 간다(고 하)ㅂ니다, 간단다 instead of 간다(고 그러)ㄴ다, and so on. The reduced forms are often used to convey hearsay without the need to reveal the source of information.

Statements: 'I hear/I heard…'; 'They say…'

존댓말 (Formal)		반말 (Casual)	
합니다 style	*해요* style	*해* style	*한다* style
간답니다	간대요	간대	간댄다/간단다
아니랍니다	아니래요	아니래	아니랜다/아니란다
가냡니다	가내요	가내	가낸다/가냔다
가랍니다	가래요	가래	가랜다/가란다
가잡니다	가재요	가재	가잰다/가잔다

NOTE: 간다더라 is frequently used instead of 간다(고 하)더라 (see *16.1.6*).

Here are actual samples of reduced indirect quotes and of their direct quote counterparts. As with the regular report styles, -었 is always retained, but -겠 and -을 may be replaced as long as the intended meaning does not change. Thus, "안 갈래" may be quoted as 안 간대 or 안 가겠대, for example.

"오늘이 결혼기념일이야."
→ 오늘이 결혼기념일이랍니다.
I hear that today is their wedding anniversary.

"결혼한 지 오래 됐어요."
→ 결혼한 지 오래 됐다던데요.
I hear that it's been a long time since they got married.

"밤에는 영하로 내려가겠습니다."
→ 일기예보에서 그러는데, 밤에는 영하로 내려간대요 (or 내려갈 거래요).
According to the weather report, it will go below zero tonight.

"저녁에 좀 늦을 거예요."
→ 형이 저녁에 좀 늦는대요 (or 늦을 거래요).
I heard that brother will be a bit late this evening.

"금방 갈 거야."
→ 할아버지가 금방 오신댔어 (or 오실 거래).
    Grandpa said he'll come soon.

"할머니, 언제 오실 거예요?"
→ 손녀딸이 나보고 언제 올 거내.
    My grand-daughter was asking me when I'll be coming.

"중매 결혼하셨어요?"
→ 사람들이 나한테 중매결혼했내요.
    People ask whether I had an arranged marriage.

"당장 결혼합시다."
→ 그 남자가 나보고 당장 결혼하잰다.
    He's asking me to marry him right away.

"늦지 마세요."
→ 집사람이 나보고 오늘 늦지 말랬는데...
    My wife told me not to be late today.

"전화 받아라."
→ 언니, 할머니가 전화 받으라서.
    Sis, Grandma is telling you to answer the phone.

"전화 받으세요."
→ 할머니, 언니가 전화 받으시래요.
    Grandma, sister is telling you to answer the phone.

"오빠보고 나한테 전화 좀 해 달라 그래."
→ 오빠, 언니가 전화 좀 해 달래.
    Brother, sister is asking you to give her a call.

"오빠보고 나한테 전화 좀 해 달라 그래."
→ 오빠, 할머니가 전화 좀 해 달라서.
    Brother, Grandma is asking you to give her a call.

The following examples illustrate reported speech that occurs inside questions.

내일 비 온답니까?	*Did they say it will rain tomorrow?*
혼자 오래요?	*Did they ask you to come by yourself?*
같이 가재니?	*Did he ask you go with him?*
왜 오랬어요?	*Why did you tell me to come?*
저 사람 누구래요?	*Who do they say that person is?*
뭐가 그렇게 바쁘대니?	*Why does he say he's so busy?*

This reduced form is used only to quote something oneself; it cannot be used to ask someone to convey a quote to someone else. For that, a quoting verb is required – 오빠한테 전화 왔다(고) 그래 'Tell brother that there's a phone call for him,' 할아버지한테 먼저 드시라(고) 그래 'Tell Grandpa to go ahead and eat first,' and so on.

The reduced form -단다 or -(이)란다 can be employed to indicate emphasis ('I'm telling you,' 'you know') as in 어제는 너무 피곤해서 온종일 잠만 잤단다 'I slept all day yesterday, you know, because I was too tired,' 오늘이 이모부 생일이란다 'Today is your uncle's birthday.'

22.1.6 *Special patterns involving indirect quotes*

For the purposes of confirmation or clarification, the verb following a quote is sometimes omitted, leaving just -고 to end the sentence – 언제 오신다고(요)? 'When did you say you're coming?' (See *17.6.1* for more on special endings involving quotes.)

The quoted part of a sentence is often followed directly by a conjunctive suffix. For example, -다면서 or -(이)라면서 is used to request confirmation of information that the speaker heard from someone else.

하와이는 한여름에도 그렇게 덥지 않다면서요?
I hear that Hawaii is not too hot even in the middle of the summer, is that true?

약혼한 사이라면서?
I heard that you two are engaged, are you?

Here are more examples in which the quote is followed by a conjunctive suffix.

이 집이 맛있다기에 한 번 와 봤어요.
Because I hear this place is delicious, I thought I'd come and try it.

괜찮으시다면 저희 집에서 차 한잔 하시겠어요?
If it's okay with you, would you like to have a cup of tea at my place?

이게 얼마냐하면 자그마치 네 한 달 용돈 두배 값이야.
Do you know how much this is; it's twice as much as your monthly allowance.

비온다더니 해만 쨍쨍 나네요.
I heard it would rain, but it's only bright and sunny.

이 근처에 아주 잘하는 한국식당이 하나 있다는데.
I hear that there's a very good Korean restaurant around here.

22.2 Adnominal clauses

Adnominal clauses, which are formed with the help of a special set of suffixes (see *16.2.2*), provide information about the noun to their right – 청바지가 잘 어울리는 **여자** 'a girl who looks good in blue jeans' or 이해심이 많은 **남자** 'a guy who is very understanding.'

No matter how long the adnominal clause is (it can be very long in writing), it always precedes the noun it describes. The entire portion of the sentence that comes before the noun (boldfaced in the example below) is a clause that describes it.

혹독한 다이어트로 7 킬로그램을 감량, 77 사이즈의 의상을 55 사이즈로 바꿔 놓은 후 영화 '위대한 사랑'에서 섹시한 몸매를 과시한 **김선희도** 운동의 중요성을 강조했다.

Sunhee Kim, who lost 15 pounds through a strict diet, changing her dress size from 77 to 55 and showing off her sexy figure in the movie 'Great Love,' also emphasized the importance of exercise.

It's also important to remember that there can be more than one adnominal clause for the same noun:

여기가 바로 어제 책을 산, 서울에서 제일 큰 서점이다.
This is the very bookstore where I bought a book yesterday, which is the biggest in Seoul.

22.2.1 Types of adnominal clauses based on the noun described

For purposes of illustration, we divide adnominal clauses into several types, depending on the sort of noun that they occur with.

• Ordinary nouns:
  (Notice that prepositions in the English translations have no counterparts in the following Korean adnominal clauses.)

아는 여자	*the woman that I know*
춥던 날씨	*the weather that was cold*
학생들이 잘 가는 식당	*the restaurant that students frequently go* ***to***
비밀을 털어 놓을 친구	*a friend that one can tell secrets* ***to***
과일 깎는 칼	*the knife that one peels fruit* ***with***
살빠지는 약	*diet pill* [medicine ***with*** which one loses weight]
사람 보는 눈	*insight into people* [eyes ***with*** which one judges people]
키스하는 장면	*the scene* ***in*** *which they kiss*
졸업한 학교	*the school one graduated* ***from***

지진이 일어난 시간	*the time **at** which the earthquake hit*
결혼할 사람	*the person **to** whom one will get married;* or *the person who will marry*

- Nouns that indicate a general class:

거/것 is employed for a concrete thing, 일 for an abstract thing, and 데/곳 for a place. (곳 sounds formal compared to 데.)

국립 박물관에 볼 것이 많아요.	*There are a lot of things to see in the National Museum.*
가장 매웠던 건 떡볶이였어요.	*The most spicy thing was ttŏkbokki.*
어차피 알게 되실 일이에요.	*It's something you'll get to find out anyhow.*
어제 밥 먹으러 간 데가 어디지?	*Where was it that we went to eat yesterday?*
뜻이 있는 곳에 길이 있다.	*Where there's a will, there's a way.*

- Nouns that sum up and/or classify the adnominal clause:

일주일에 한 번씩 찜질방에 가는 게 **습관**이 됐다. (게 < 것이)
   It has become my habit to go to the sauna once a week.

그냥 한 번 해 본 **소리**예요.
   It's something that I just said without any particular intention.

주식값이 뛸 **확률**이 높습니다.
   There's a high probability that the stock price will jump.

사람들하고 어울리기 싫어하는 **경향**이 있어요.
   He has a tendency not to like to mingle with people.

그 선수의 장점은 왼손잡이인 **점**이다.
   That player's strength is the fact that he is left-handed.

Ambiguity in the meaning of 거 /것

내일 먹을 거예요.	*That's the thing to eat tomorrow.*	(concrete thing)
	I'll eat it tomorrow.	(fact)
보낼 거 없어요.	*There's nothing to send.*	(concrete thing)
	There's no need to send it.	(fact)

- *Nouns that indicate a result*

비오는 **소리**예요.	*It's the sound of the rain falling.*
고기 타는 **냄새**가 난다.	*I smell the odor of meat burning.*
꿰맸던 **자국**이에요.	*It's a scar from the stitches.*

- *Special nouns*

The following (mostly bound) nouns combine with adnominal clauses to create special patterns. The exact meaning of each noun is often difficult to identify.

이왕 온 **김**에 며칠 더 쉬다 갑시다.
While we're here, let's take a few more days of break before going back.

말 나온 **김**에 지금 하는 게 어떨까요?
While we're on the subject, what about doing it now?

아예 떡 본 **김**에 제사 지내지요.
Since we have what we need, why don't we go ahead and do it?
[*Since we have the rice cake, why don't we hold the memorial service?*]

일이 항상 마음 먹은 **대로** 되는 건 아냐.
Things don't always turn out the way we wish.

소식 듣는 **대로** 나한테 좀 알려 줘.
Let me know as soon as you hear any news.

멀리 피서를 가는 **대신** 근처 계곡에서 하루 놀다 왔어요.
Instead of going to a far-away summer resort, we spent a day at a nearby valley.

많은 분들이 도와 주셔서 감사할 **따름**입니다.
I can only be thankful for the help from so many people.

외동딸인 나로선 형제 많은 친구가 부러울 **따름**이다.
As an only child, I can't help envying friends with lots of siblings.

나 자신도 못 믿는 **마당**에 누구를 믿겠어?
How can I trust anyone when I can't even trust myself?

해질 **무렵**에 경치가 제일 멋있어요.
The scenery around sunset is the most beautiful.

그거야 내가 알 **바** 아니지.
That's none of my business.

들리는 **바**에 의하면, 그 친구가 해고당했대요.
From what I hear, he was laid off.

말씀 드린 **바**와 같이, 다음 주에 모임을 갖겠습니다.
As I announced before, we'll be having a meeting next week.

굶어 죽으란 **법**은 없다.
We're not going to starve to death.

여자만 일하라는 **법**이 어디 있어?
Who says only women have to work?

퇴학을 당할 **법**도 하죠.
He deserves to be expelled from school.

먹는 **족족** 살이 찐다.
Every time I eat anything, it adds to my weight.

돈이 생기는 **족족** 다 써 버렸어요.
  Every time I earned any money, I used it up.

백수된 **지** 오래됐어.
  It's been a long time since I lost my job.

전공을 바꾼 **지** 이제 일 년밖에 안 됐어요.
  It's been only a year since I changed my major.

힘들어 죽을 **지경**이에요.
  It's so tough that I'm on the verge of dying.

그렇지 않아도 전화하려던 **참**이었는데.
  In fact, I was just about to call you.

배고프던 **참**에 잘됐다. 같이 먹으러 가자.
  I was actually hungry, so it's great. Let's go eat together.

옷을 입은 **채** 그냥 바다에 들어갔어요.
  I entered the sea with my clothes on.

모르는 **척** 슬쩍 지나쳤다.
  I passed by, pretending that I didn't recognize her.

보고도 못 본 **체**하는 거 있지.
  You know, he saw me but pretended that he didn't notice me.

그 사람이 너를 괜히 미워할 **턱**이 있겠니?
  Why would he hate you for no reason?

내가 그걸 알 **턱**이 있니?
  How would I know that?

아이들이 떠드는 **통**에 책을 읽을 수가 없어요.
  I can't read the book with the children making so much noise.

22.2.2 Adnominal clauses involving quotes

Nouns such as 사실, 소문, 말, 소리, -거/것, and so on are often accompanied by a preceding quote or report followed by an adnominal suffix. These constructions are useful in situations such as the following.

- To express the nature (fact, rumor, etc.) of a quote/report

  아들이 전사했다는 **사실**을 아직 모르고 있어요.
    They still don't know the fact that their son died in the war.

  마약을 복용한다는 **소문**을 들었어요.
    I heard a rumor that she's taking drugs.

  생일인데 축하한다는 **말** 한마디도 없었어.
    There was not even a single congratulatory word, although it's my birthday.

  나한테 헤어지자는 **소리**를 수십 번도 더 했어.
    She asked me more than a dozen times to break up with her.

파티에 오라는 **얘기**도 없었는데 어떻게 불쑥 가?
  How do we barge in when there wasn't even a word inviting us to the party?

죽을 때까지 헤어지지 말자던 **약속**을 벌써 잊었니?
  Have you already forgotten our promise not to break up till death?

노래를 하나 배워 가지고 가라는 **충고**를 받았습니다.
  I received advice to learn a song before I go there.

해일이 발생했다는 **소식**은 정말 충격적이었어요.
  The news that the tsunami occurred was really shocking.

사장이 뇌물을 받았다는 **보도**가 신문에 크게 났더라.
  The report that the company president received bribes hit the newspaper headlines.

내가 법을 어겼다는 **증거**를 대 보세요.
  Present some evidence that I broke the law.

- To quote a proverb (see *12.1.4*)

  중이 제머리 못 깎는다는 **속담**이 있지요.
    The saying goes, 'One cannot scratch one's own back.'
    [A monk can't cut his own hair.]

  인생은 사십부터라는 **말**이 있잖아요.
    There is a saying that life begins at 40.

- To emphasize something

  민주주의라고 하는 **것**은...   *So-called democracy is...*

  시차가 있다는 **걸** 잊었다.   *I forgot the fact that there's a time difference.*

  그 사람 만나기 싫단 **말**야.   *I'm telling you that I don't want to meet him.*

- Fixed expressions

  이렇다 할 직업이 없다.   *He doesn't have a job to speak of.*

  하면 된다는 신념   *the belief that it will get done if you do it*

  난다 긴다 하는 사람   *extremely competent and successful person*

  내노라하는 집안   *influential family*

22.3 -지 clauses

-지 clauses are used to express questions, conjectures, things that one knows or doesn't know, and so on. They are built with the help of an adnominal suffix on the clause and -지, and are typically followed by verbs such as 알다, 모르다, and 물어보다.

어디 사는지 아세요?   *Do you know where he lives?*

집에 있는지 (없는지) 모르겠다.   *I don't know whether (or not) she is home.*

22.3.1 What's inside -지 clauses

Here are some examples of -지 clauses involving various types of verbs.

- With an action verb (오다):

언제 오는지 아니?	*Do you know when he's coming?*
언제 왔는지 몰라요.	*I don't know when he came.·*
언제 왔었는지 기억 안 나요.	*I don't remember when he came (and left).*
비가 어찌나 오던지 앞이 안 보일 정도였어요.	*It was raining so hard that I couldn't see anything.*
비가 얼마나 왔던지 차들이 다 물에 잠겼어요.	*It rained so much that all the cars were under water.*
언제 올지/올는지 몰라요.	*I don't know when he'll come.*
언제 오겠는지/올래는지 물어 봐.	*Ask when he'll be coming.*
이미 왔을지도/왔을는지도 몰라.	*He may have come already.*

- With descriptive verbs (좋다 and -이다):

날씨가 좋은지 모르겠다.	*I wonder whether the weather is good.*
날씨가 좋았는지 모르겠네.	*I wonder whether the weather was good.*
날씨가 얼마나 좋았(었)는지 몰라.	*I can't believe how good the weather was.*
날씨가 어찌나 좋(았)던지 사람들이 다 바닷가에 나왔더라.	*The weather was so good that everyone came out to the beach.*
언제가 좋을지/좋을는지 모르겠어.	*I don't know when will be a good time.*
다음주가 좋겠는지 한 번 여쭤 봐.	*Ask whether next week will be okay.*
지난주가 더 좋았을지도/ 좋았을는지도 몰라요.	*Last week might have been better.*
어떤 사람인지 궁금해요.	*I'm curious what kind of person she is.*
어떤 사람이었(었)는지 알고 싶다.	*I want to know what kind of person she was.*
어찌나 착한 사람이(었)던지 지금도 생각나요.	*She was such a nice person that I still remember her.*
나쁜 사람일지도/일는지도 몰라.	*She may be a bad person.*
누가 적합한 사람이겠는지 알아 봐.	*Find out who'll be suitable for it.*
좋은 사람이었을지도/ 이었을는지도 모르죠.	*She might have been a good person.*

NOTE: The above examples include two special patterns: 어찌나/얼마나…-지 'so…(that…)' and -지도 모른다 'might; be possible.'

22.3.2 What's outside -지 clauses

Various types of verbs other than 알다, 모르다, and 물어보다 can follow -지 clauses.

연세가 어떻게 되시는지 맞춰 봐.	*Guess how old he is.*
커피맛이 어땠는지 기억나?	*Do you remember how the coffee tasted?*
왜 그런지 조사해 보자.	*Let's investigate why that is the case.*
어떤 선물이 좋을지 생각해 봐.	*Think about what would be good for a gift.*
몇 명이나 올지 파악이 안 된다.	*I can't figure out how many are coming.*
어디를 갈지 망설이고 있어요.	*I'm hesitating on where I should go.*
어떻게 될지 뻔하다.	*It's obvious how it's going to end up.*
붙을지 떨어질지 미지수예요.	*It's still to be seen whether I'll pass or fail.*

In some cases, there is no following verb, creating a gentle question.

어제 보낸 메일은 받으셨는지요?	*I wonder whether you received the mail I sent yesterday – did you?*
요즘 어떻게 지내시는지요?	*How are you doing these days?*

-지 clauses are also often followed by particle phrases such as -에 대해(서)/ 관해(서) 'as to; with regard to.'

어떤 직장을 구할지에 대해서 고민 중입니다.
I am thinking hard as to what type of job I should find.

-지 sometimes alternates with -줄 when the verb that follows an indirect question is 알다 or 모르다.

몇 살인지/몇 살인줄 알아요?	*Do you know how old I am?*
여행간지/여행간줄 알았어요.	*I knew (or thought) you went on a trip.*
이렇게 좋은지/좋은줄 몰랐어요.	*I didn't know it's this good.*

When 알다 follows a -지 clause, it can be ambiguous between 'know' and 'think.'

여행간지 알고 있었어. 그래서 전화 안 했어.
I knew you were gone on a trip. So I didn't call.

여행간지 알았는데 집에 있었네.
I thought you were gone on a trip but hey, you were home.

22.4 Nominalization

Nominalization allows a verb or a clause to function as a noun. There are two ways to do this.

22.4.1 By attaching -음 (or ㅁ)

Except for simple nouns such as 웃음 'laughter,' 싸움 'a fight,' and so on, this type of nominalization is usually employed for an abstract proposition or a completed action. It has a formal and written flavor. (See *10.4.1* for simple nouns.)

친구의 소중함을 알게 되었다.
   I realized the importance of friends.

그 사람이 무죄임이 판명됐다.
   His being not guilty has been proved (by the verdict).

날씨가 추워짐에 따라 난방비 걱정이 늘고 있습니다.
   As the weather gets colder, concern about heating bills is increasing.

우편 분실사고에 대하여 영사관에서는 책임이 없음을 알려드립니다.
   We'd like to let you know that the consulate is not responsible for lost mail.

남자친구임에 틀림없다.
   There's no doubt about him being her boyfriend.

NOTE: Some of the -음 patterns can be replaced by an adnominal pattern involving -거/것, which tends to be more colloquial.

친구가 소중한 걸 알게 되었다.   *I realized that friends are important.*
그 사람이 무죄인 것이 판명됐다.   *It's been proved that he's not guilty.*
남자친구인 게 틀림없다.   *There's no doubt that he is her boyfriend.*

-음 is often used to mark an abbreviated sentence in brochures, public announcements, notes, and letters. It is also used when closing a letter to a superior/older person.

연령제한 없음   *No age restriction.*
가정교사 구함   *Private tutor wanted.*
개근상장을 수여함   *a certificate granted for perfect attendance*
회사로 갈게요. (오늘 수업이 없음)   *I'll go to your workplace. (No class today.)*
서하늘 올림/드림   *Respectfully, Hanul Seo* (in closing a letter)

22.4.2 By attaching -기

Except for simple nouns such as 크기 'size,' 보기 'sample,' and so on, a nominalization of this type is used to express an act or a fact. It retains its actional or stative meaning, even though it functions as a noun. This style of nominalization is more common in colloquial Korean.

Here are some examples of -기 nominalizations organized according to what they are followed by. Many of these patterns are worth learning by heart.

- Followed by a particle

이 옷은 행동하기(가) 불편하다.	*This outfit is uncomfortable to move in.*
사람 만나기를 꺼려요.	*He's reluctant about meeting people.*
나를 알기를 우습게 알아.	*She thinks little of me.*
질이 좋기는 한데 너무 비싸다.	*It's good quality, but too expensive.*
스트레스 풀기에 좋은 방법이다.	*It's a good way to release the stress.*
그 집은 요리 잘하기로 소문났어.	*The restaurant is famous for its food.*
잠자코 듣기만 해.	*Don't say anything, just listen.*
시원하기도 하고 섭섭하기도 하고 그렇죠 뭐.	*I feel relieved and sad at the same time, I guess. (It's bittersweet.)*

- Followed by a noun

지각하기 일쑤예요.	*He's frequently tardy.*
생각하기 나름이죠.	*It depends on how you think, of course.*

- Followed by -이다

정말 그러기야? 혼자 먹기야?	*Are you really going to do that? Are you going to eat without me?*
거짓말하기 없기예요.	*You're NOT going to lie, okay?*
방청권 얻기는 하늘에 별따기다.	*It's impossible to get a ticket for the show.*
옆구리 찔러 절받기다. (= 엎드려 절받기)	*It's like fishing for compliments. [Forcing someone to bow to you. (Receiving a bow while lying down)]*
땅짚고 헤엄치기야.	*It's a piece of cake. [Swimming while touching the ground with one's hands.]*

Some -기 patterns can be replaced by the adnominal pattern involving -거/것.

놀기가 일하기보다 어렵다.	*To play is harder than to work.*
노는 게 일하는 것보다 어렵다.	*Playing is harder than working.*

However, some -기 patterns cannot be replaced in this way. Notice the difference in meaning and acceptability illustrated in the following pairs.

고기가 먹기(가) 좋다.	*This meat is easy to eat.*
고기 먹는 게 좋다. (게 < 것이)	*Meat eating is good; I like to eat meat.*

여기서 수영하기(가) 좋다.   *Here is good for swimming.*
여기서 수영하는 게 좋다.   *I like to swim here.*

비오기(가) 쉬워.   *It's likely to rain.*
(no appropriate -는 것 counterpart)

(no appropriate -기 counterpart)
걸어가는 게 낫겠다.   *I think it'll be better to walk.*

English Index

Korean Index